Beginning XNA 3.0 Game Programming

From Novice to Professional

Alexandre Santos Lobão,
Bruno Evangelista,
José Antonio Leal de Farias,
and Riemer Grootjans

Beginning XNA 3.0 Game Programming: From Novice to Professional

Copyright © 2009 by Alexandre Santos Lobão, Bruno Evangelista, José Antonio Leal de Farias, Riemer Grootjans

ISBN-13 (pbk): 978-1-4302-1817-3

ISBN-13 (electronic): 978-1-4302-1818-0

Printed and bound in the United States of America 9 8 7 6 5 4 3 2 1

Distributed to the book trade worldwide by Springer-Verlag New York, Inc., 233 Spring Street, 6th Floor, New York, NY 10013. Phone 1-800-SPRINGER, fax 201-348-4505, e-mail orders-ny@springer-sbm.com, or visit http://www.springeronline.com.

For information on translations, please contact Apress directly at 2855 Telegraph Avenue, Suite 600, Berkeley, CA 94705. Phone 510-549-5930, fax 510-549-5939, e-mail info@apress.com, or visit http://www.apress.com.

Apress and friends of ED books may be purchased in bulk for academic, corporate, or promotional use. eBook versions and licenses are also available for most titles. For more information, reference our Special Bulk Sales–eBook Licensing web page at http://www.apress.com/info/bulksales.

The source code for this book is available to readers at http://www.apress.com.

Contents at a Glance

Contents

Foreword

It's hard to believe the runaway popularity XNA has achieved in the short period of time since it was released in late 2006. At that time, I got together with a couple friends to check out (with some trepidation, I must confess) whether games really could be written in managed code.

We were very excited, and everyone wanted to know if you could get the same benefits you obtain from writing games using managed code as you do when creating standard Windows programs. We knew people in the game programming community were worried about managed code's execution speed, and many people simply didn't believe a "real" game could be created using XNA. As time passed, though, more and more people began to realize the truth: there are a great number of benefits to using managed code, and the performance concerns are exaggerated.

You haven't experienced the full potential of the Xbox 360 or, indeed, Windows until you've created your own homegrown games for these innovative systems—and with the XNA Framework, the only limit is your imagination!

From an educational perspective, due to its simplicity, XNA is also a great choice for anyone who wants to learn or teach the C# programming language. That's not to mention the fact that game development offers an excellent common ground for collaboration between computer science students and their counterparts in other disciplines such music, the arts, design, and so on.

In fact, XNA has become such an important technology for Microsoft that it created a new game development category for the famous Imagine Cup (http://www.imaginecup.com), the largest student contest run by the company.

With the release of the XNA Framework 3.0, as back in 2006, I have again become excited about the future of game development. And when I see a book like this, which explains the basics of game programming and XNA in a clear and simple style, I get even more excited, and I hope you will be as well.

Whether you've never tried to write a game before or are simply looking for advice on the best way to do things in XNA, I think you'll be happy with what you find. After reading this book, you'll be able to apply your newfound knowledge to write your own XNA cross-platform games.

I'm waiting to see what the ever-growing community of XNA game developers will create next. It's exciting to think that we'll probably see games that break all the rules of the current gaming genres we see today, because with a vibrant community comes innovation, and with innovation comes truly unique ideas.

I look forward to the games of the future—I hope you'll be the person writing them!

Amintas Lopes Neto
Academic Relations Manager, Microsoft Brazil

About the Authors

ALEXANDRE SANTOS LOBÃO is a passionate man. His first passion was reading, starting with large books—Mark Twain, Érico Veríssimo, Jules Verne, Monteiro Lobato, Alexandre Dumas, and others—when he was 7 years old. When he was 12, he discovered his next two passions: playing and creating games (by that time on his first Apple computer), and writing.

Many years later, these passions flourish. Now he is a teacher of academic game development courses, has written four books on the topic, and has participated in some Brazilian game development contests, both as a contestant and as a judge. He has also written short-story books, children's books, and young adult books. In 2008, he released his first romance, *The Name of the Eagle*. And, of course, he still loves to read, from Ken Follett to Paulo Coelho.

His ultimate passions—starting in 1995 and still burning now—are his wife, Waléria, and his kids, Natália and Rafael.

Alexandre believes that lives need passion to be lived entirely, and hopes that this book helps light this passion in readers' hearts. You can find his work at http://www.AlexandreLobao.com.

BRUNO EVANGELISTA is a game developer with a passion for computer graphics. Bruno started programming when he was 10 years old—his father taught him how to write programs in BASIC—and he always dreamed of creating games instead of just playing them.

Bruno was a graphics programmer at VirsaT, which developed the Peixis game, winner of the JogosBR 2006 (the Brazilian national contest of complete games), and he was also a software engineer at Olympya. He has also worked on projects and game demos developed with C++, C#, and Java using DirectX, OpenGL, and XNA.

Besides his professional experience, Bruno has hosted courses and tutorials about shader development, XNA, and OpenGL at conferences and universities, such as the Brazilian Symposium on Computer Graphics and Image Processing (SIBGRAPI), Brazilian Symposia on Games and Digital Entertainment (SBGames), Gamefest Brazil, Federal University of Minas Gerais (UFMG), Pontifical Catholic University of Minas Gerais (PUC-MG), and Veiga Almeida University, Rio de Janeiro (UVA-RJ).

As an avid XNA developer, Bruno has taken second and third place, respectively, in the 2006 and 2007 XNA Challenge Brazil competitions.

Bruno received his Bachelor of Science degree in Computer Science from PUC-MG in 2006 and is currently a Master of Science candidate in Computer Science at UFMG. He lives in Belo Horizonte, Brazil. You can find his work at http://www.BrunoEvangelista.com.

■JOSÉ ANTONIO LEAL DE FARIAS has been a game programmer since he acquired his first computer in 1985, when he tried to draw aliens on an 80-by-25 pixel screen. After obtaining a degree in computer science, he established one of the first game companies in Brazil in 1997, called Hardcode Entertainment. He has worked on many diverse gaming projects in Europe and the United States. In 2004, he received the Most Valuable Professional (MVP) award from Microsoft for his contributions to the Brazilian coding community. In 2006, he established the Sharp Games community, devoted to studying and spreading advice about the XNA platform. You can find the portal for Sharp Games at http://www.sharpgames.net.

■RIEMER GROOTJANS received a degree in electronic engineering with a specialization in informatics at the Vrije Universiteit Brussel in Brussels, Belgium. He is currently working as a member of a research team toward a PhD degree. The goal of the team is to develop a real-time 3D depth-sensing camera, and he is responsible for (among other things) the visualization of the 3D data.

For several years, Riemer has been maintaining a web site with tutorials for DirectX. Since the launch of XNA in December 2006, he has ported all his content to XNA and is helping more than 2,000 people on their path to XNA success every day. In July 2007 and 2008, he received the Microsoft MVP Award for his contributions to the XNA community.

About the Technical Reviewer

FABIO CLAUDIO FERRACCHIATI is a senior consultant and a senior analyst/developer using Microsoft technologies. He works for Brain Force (http://www.brainforce.com) in its Italian branch (http://www.brainforce.it). He is a Microsoft Certified Solution Developer for .NET, a Microsoft Certified Application Developer for .NET, a Microsoft Certified Professional, and a prolific author and technical reviewer. Over the past ten years, he has written articles for Italian and international magazines and coauthored more than ten books on a variety of computer topics. You can read his LINQ blog at http://www.ferracchiati.com.

Acknowledgments

I would like to thank David Weller—although he could not help with this book—for being a great buddy and a source of inspiration for me and for many guys from the academic and indie game development communities. And a special thanks to Amintas Neto, from Microsoft Brazil, for his great work fostering XNA development at Brazilian universities.

Alexandre Santos Lobão

I would like to thank God for his countless blessings and for giving me the opportunity to work on this great book; my parents Kathia and Gledson, who always motivated me to do my best; my stepfather Claudio, my stepmother Celida, and my brothers for all their support; and my girlfriend Helenice for all these great years together.

Also a special thanks to Alessandro Silva, a great friend and game developer who studied with me during my university years; Carlos Augusto, who contributed some assets for the XNA TPS game; and Francisco Ardisson, who helped translate some parts of the book.

In this long journey, I had a few mentors and guides who helped me to get here and who I cannot forget to mention: Theldo Franqueira, Marcelo Nery, Fabio Policarpo, Rosilane Mota, Luiz Chaimowicz, Renato Ferreira, Esteban Clua, Fabio Tirelo, and Harlen Batagelo. Thank you for all I have learned from you!

Bruno Evangelista

First, I'd like to thank all the Sharp Games community for the encouragement and suggestions they provided me, and especially my friends Shinji and Amintas Neto for everything they've done for XNA in Brazil.

I also need to say thanks to Microsoft; to its MVP program; to Leonardo Tolomelli, my MVP lead; and to all other MVPs in Brazil who always are a source of inspiration for me.

Also a special thanks to my wife Cecir for having enormous love and patience with me when this book was being planned and written; to my four-year-old son, Leonardo, for his critical sense of what is a good game; and to my parents for continuing to love a son who read books on assembly language when the other boys read *Spiderman* comics.

José Antonio Leal de Farias

I thank my girlfriend Elisa and my family, for the love and support they've given me while I was working on this book.

I would like to express my appreciation and thankfulness to the skillful group of professionals at Apress that put a lot of work in the organization and guidance during the completion this book. Special thanks to Joohn Choe, for the many useful ideas and additions.

Furthermore, I thank the people on my forum, for their enthusiasm and contributions.

Last, but definitely not least, I would like to thank the other authors for the efforts they put in my parts of the book while I was not available.

Riemer Grootjans

Introduction

According to the point-of-sale information compiled by NPD Group (http://www.npd.com), a leading US marketing information provider, computer and video game sales totaled more than seven billion dollars in each of the past three years. The video game software industry accounts for more than six billion dollars of this total. If we include portable and console hardware, software, and accessory sales, in 2006, the video game industry generated revenue of close to twelve and a half billion dollars, exceeding the previous record of around two billion dollars. These figures alone might be reason enough to interest someone in learning XNA and becoming a game developer, trying to get a share of a market that's more profitable than the Hollywood moviemaking one.

But let's be fair and not hide the facts. Unfortunately, there are few openings in this area—about one game programming job per every thousand "real-life" programming jobs. Worse than that, on average, the game industry pays its programmers less than other industries do.

After digesting these facts, if you still think that working as a game developer might be cool and rewarding, then this book is for you! We also have some good news: now that Microsoft has opened its LIVE market to XNA games made by the community, there is a potential market of ten million people for your homemade games!

This book has the goal of introducing you to XNA, the cross-platform game programming framework from Microsoft, and also presenting you with basic concepts from the game programming industry, showing how these concepts apply to the XNA world. The samples in this book, which include some complete games, will give you the knowledge you need to create your own simple games.

That said, this book won't present you with hard-core math and physics or dig into advanced programming concepts, which are indeed needed if you really want to become a professional game developer. Instead, this book is a first step into this industry, presenting an overview of most of the things you need to know and giving you a road map for further studies in this area.

More than that, this book intends to be fun! One of the most interesting things you'll see in the game programming industry is the unmatched passion of the people who work in it. If there's one goal for this book, it's to light this passion in novices' hearts with simple explanations and, especially, with cool game examples, so this fire can keep burning in the years to come.

After all, this is a book written with a lot of passion!

What Is XNA?

XNA is a play on words. It stands for "XNA's Not an Acronym." Microsoft's world is so full of acronyms that it decided to create a name that looks like an acronym, but isn't, just for fun.

With Microsoft XNA, for the first time ever, a nonprofessional game developer can create single and multiplayer games that can run on a PC, the Xbox 360 console, and the Zune. The concept of bringing to the average Joe the power to create his own games for the Xbox 360 is a great technological innovation, which comes with many efforts from Microsoft to establish an active community for game creators, as well as to establish programs in the academic area to support institutions that wish to create courses using retail Xbox 360 consoles.

These efforts become obvious when you realize that Microsoft XNA Game Studio 3.0 can be downloaded at no charge from Microsoft's site (http://www.microsoft.com/XNA). Microsoft also offers free game content, including video tutorials, starter kits (ready-made games, which can be freely customized), samples, and other support content at the XNA Creators Club web site (http://creators.XNA.com).

The last step in making Microsoft LIVE known as the "YouTube for games" is the ability to upload the games you created and distribute (or even sell) them to anyone in the world with a LIVE connection. No wonder the nonprofessional game programmer community is so excited by XNA Game Studio and the frequent updates and new content on the XNA Creators Club site!

The greatest secret behind XNA's success is that it's easy—much easier than any console programming application programming interface (API) or Windows game programming API. That's because of the abstraction it provides for details that you need to worry about in other APIs. XNA uses the same integrated development environment (IDE)—XNA Game Studio Express—and the same framework for developing games for Windows, Xbox 360, and Zune platforms, which ensures a high degree of compatibility. However, there are differences in the lower layer: the Xbox 360 and the Zune run a compact version of the .NET Framework, so you must be careful—not all functions available in Windows will run on the Xbox 360 or Zune.

We'll address all this in detail in this book, but you can always find the latest information about XNA architecture at Microsoft's XNA site and at the XNA Creators Club site.

Who This Book Is For

This book is written for anyone who wants to start developing games for the Windows, Xbox 360, and/or Zune platforms. It can be used as a first step on a long road toward a game development career or as a guide to hobby game development. For example, perhaps you have a great idea for a simple game—the next Tetris—and have always wanted to have the basic knowledge, straight and simple, of how to create games. So, this book is for you if you want to have fun creating or modifying simple games and sharing them with friends.

How This Book Is Structured

This book is organized so you can start learning generic game programming concepts, such as common gaming terminology and math, see how these concepts are implemented in XNA, and then apply these concepts to real games. We believe that this organization improves your learning, so you'll be ready to create your own XNA games after finishing the book. Here's a quick chapter-by-chapter rundown:

Chapter 1, Game Planning and Programming Basics: This chapter presents important game planning concepts that will help you create great games, and also some general game programming concepts and how these concepts map to XNA. You'll also create your first XNA program.

Chapter 2, 2D Graphics, Audio, and Input Basics: This chapter introduces some fundamental concepts related to 2D game programming. You'll also see with some samples that demonstrate how the XNA Framework implements these concepts.

Chapter 3, Creating Your First 2D Game: This chapter is where the real fun begins! You'll find out how to put together the ideas presented in the first two chapters to create a complete game, named Rock Rain.

Chapter 4, Improving Your First 2D Game: Still in the 2D programming world, in this chapter, you'll explore other concepts such as creating menus, moving through game screens, managing players' scores, and more.

Chapter 5, Basics of Game Networking: In this chapter, you'll learn about one of the most exciting features of XNA 3.0: the ability to create network-enabled games. You'll see how to connect different machines, either directly or through LIVE.

Chapter 6, Rock Rain Live!: Getting back to your 2D game, in this chapter, you'll create a multiplayer version. This includes a new opening scene that allows players to create or join a match in other machines.

Chapter 7, Rock Rain Zune: Just to show how simple it is to make a game for the Zune, in this chapter, you'll create a Rock Rain version that runs on this device.

Chapter 8, 3D Game Programming Basics: This chapter introduces the fundamentals of 3D game programming. You'll learn how to create a 3D scene, load and manipulate 3D objects, move the camera, and everything else you need to know to start digging into virtual 3D worlds.

Chapter 9, Rendering Pipeline, Shaders, and Effects: Getting deeper into the 3D world, you'll learn more details about the XNA Content Pipeline and the use of effects and shaders in XNA, paving the way to create your first 3D game.

Chapter 10, Lights, Camera, Transformations!: In this chapter, you'll create the base objects used in any 3D game, which will help you manage lights and cameras, and apply transformations to your 3D objects.

Chapter 11, Generating a Terrain: Every 3D game that uses a landscape needs a terrain. This chapter presents the steps for creating, adjusting, and drawing the terrain, and also how to calculate object collisions with the terrain.

Chapter 12, Skeletal Animation: XNA 3.0 doesn't offer default support to read and play animations created by the modelers along with the 3D models. This chapter shows you how to create a custom model processor to read and play animation data.

Chapter 13, Creating a Third-Person Shooter Game: In this chapter, you put it all together, using the knowledge from the previous chapters to create a simple 3D third-person shooter game.

Chapter 14, Closing Words: As we said, this book is fun, and includes a lot of information about game programming, but it's only a first step. In this chapter, we present the advice we always give to our students when finishing a game programming course.

Prerequisites

Before you continue to the first chapter, be sure to download and install the latest version of XNA, which is easy to find in the Downloads section at http://www.microsoft.com/XNA. We also recommend that you download the DirectX Software Development Kit (SDK), which comes with some content and utilities you can use when learning XNA. Don't forget, also, to download and install the XNA starter kits and samples at `http://creators.XNA.com`. All these tools and samples are free to download and use.

If you don't have a copy of Microsoft Visual Studio, you should also download a free copy of Microsoft Visual C# Express, from `http://www.microsoft.com/XNA`.

Book Code and Errata

Although you can maximize your learning by typing the book code while you're reading, some-times you simply can't wait to see the code running. If you're in a hurry, look for the book name at the Apress site, `http://www.apress.com`. All the book code is available for download from this book's details page.

Although Apress and the authors make their best efforts to ensure that there are no errors in the book code or text, sometimes an error appears. You can always find the most recent code and any text or code errata at the Apress site, `http://www.apress.com`. Again, just look for the book name.

Contacting the Authors

Alexandre Lobão is available from his personal web site, at `http://www.AlexandreLobao.com`, which includes all his works as an author, comics writer, and movie script writer.

Bruno Evangelista also maintains a personal web site, with his game programming projects, including downloadable content, at `http://www.BrunoEvangelista.com`.

José Leal is the head of a top Brazilian C# programming community, Sharp Games, avail-able at `http://www.sharpgames.net`.

Riemer Grootjans can be contacted through the forum of his XNA community site at `http://www.riemers.net`.

■ ■ ■

CHAPTER 1

Game Planning and Programming Basics

In this chapter, we present some fundamental concepts of planning and programming games that you should keep in mind when creating games. You'll learn the basic ideas involved in creating a game and discover how XNA makes game development easy for you.

Planning the Game

The effort involved in creating a good game starts long before the coding phase. Somewhat undervalued by nonprofessional game programmers, planning is the most important phase of your game development project. In this phase, you define the guidelines for all the next stages.

Before thinking about which game you'll create, you need to choose your *target market*. This choice will define the direction for your entire game development effort.

Target Market

NPD Group, a market research company, divides the market into six categories (information copyrighted by NPD Group, 2008):

- Heavy gamers, who constantly play games and are responsible for most of the market sales

- Avid console gamers, who buy mainly console games and might play console games many hours a day

- Mass-market gamers, who usually buy only blockbuster games

- Prefer-portable gamers, who prefer playing games using portable devices

- Secondary gamers, who usually don't buy games and play games bought by other people

- Infrequent gamers, who play games occasionally

We won't provide an extensive study of these segments, but will highlight some significant points about the two "edge" categories.

Infrequent gamers are also called *casual players*. Games for this player category must be easy to play, without a complex storyline, and must provide challenging but brief levels to give the player a feeling of accomplishment in short matches. Games for such a market usually don't rely on highly detailed 3D graphics or extraordinary sound effects, and include card games (poker, hearts, solitaire, and so on), puzzles (Tetris, Sudoku, crosswords, and so on), board games (mah-jongg, chess, checkers, and so on), and similar. Don't be fooled by the simplicity of such games. Although they might be easier to develop, they rely on balanced levels and game play to sustain the appeal for the players, which can be hard to achieve.

Heavy gamers are also called *hard-core gamers*. These players take playing games seriously. They usually prefer difficult challenges and a good storyline that helps the players immerse themselves in the game world. Games for such players usually include extremely detailed 3D environments, engaging background music and sound effects, and a long game-play experience with many challenges.

Game Genre

Once you choose the target market, the next logical step is to define the game genre. There are many divisions of game genres, but, sticking with NPD Group's research approach, the game genre with the greatest growth in the past couple of years is family entertainment. Of all the games sold in 2007, 17.2 percent were categorized as family games—that's more than one of every six games sold. In addition, of the games sold in 2007, 56.6 percent were rated Early Childhood (EC), Everyone (E), and Everyone 10+ (E10+). The NPD Group's data indicate that only 15 percent of games sold last year were rated Mature (M). (This information is copyrighted by NPD Group, 2008).

Also, according to the Entertainment Software Association (ESA) web site (http://www.theesa.com), more women over 18 years old (around 33 percent of all game players) than boys under 18 years old are playing games. Also, 26 percent of Americans over the age of 50 played video games in 2008. This is a huge difference from the early years of video games, when most gamers were males younger that 25.

If you are planning to sell your game, or simply distribute it freely to as many people as possible, it's important to keep this kind of information in mind. Choosing the target market and the game genre for your game will help you to narrow down your choices about which game to develop. And, if you already have a game in mind, thinking about these points will help you to refine your ideas to the next step: defining the team involved in the game development project and choosing your place in such a team.

The Game Team

Another important game development concept is *the game team*. Smaller teams, or even a single multiskilled person, might create games for casual players. Creating games for hard-core players might involve a team with dozens of people skilled in different areas.

Although you might be able to develop games on your own, developing a game is always more than simply coding. You'll need nice graphics and sound effects, and you'll need to design the game levels, just to name a few different activities in the game project. In a big game development project, you'll need skills such as the following:

Project management: Someone must be in charge of controlling the time involved, the scope of your project, the resources needed, communications, coordination between team members, and so on. Even if you're developing a game with a few friends, it's crucial to define who's in charge—who will solve problems and define the project's direction.

Script writers: The script writers are responsible for writing the game's storyline, ultimately defining the challenges to face and the mysteries to solve. They usually help define the whole game background, such as the game characters, the dialogue, and the level division.

Level designers: Level designers usually create and use tools to define each of the game levels, according to the programming requirements given by the coding team and the story written by the script writers.

Artists: Artists is a broad category, encompassing concept art creators, computer art creators, the people responsible for texturing (creating textures for the 3D models), computer colorists, and so on. These folks create the splash (opening) game screen, game menus, and static images, and might also create the art for the marketing team.

Modelers: These people are responsible for creating the 3D models for the game, following the concept and computer art.

Animators: Creating a 3D model is not the same thing as animating it, so some teams include specialists in creating the model animations for the game. This team also creates the *cut-scenes* (the video sequences presented in the beginning of the game and at special points in the game, such as when a player wins a challenge, or at the beginning and end of each level).

Musicians: This is also a broad category, which ranges from the responsibility for writing (and playing) the game background and ambience music to the people who create voices and sound effects for the game.

Programmers: Programmers are in charge of writing the game code, including all math and physics calculations needed to create the desired game effects. This book is intended for people in this category.

Testers: It's not a good idea for the same person who wrote the code to be responsible for testing it. The goal for the testers is to find as many bugs as they can. They attempt to do unexpected things inside the game, so the bugs surface in the game development process, instead of during the player's game.

This list could continue. A big game team could also include people who are responsible for preparing and conducting the marketing efforts for the game; people who deal with publishing channels; and people who take care of the needed hardware and software infrastructure for the game development and, sometimes, for the game publishing (if the project includes Internet game servers, for example).

Game Planning

Choosing the game's target market and genre, and selecting the right people for the game project, aren't the only key points you need to think about when planning your game. Here are some items you simply can't afford to overlook when planning your game:

Game goal: Everything starts with a clearly defined game goal: to win the World Cup, to defeat the evil mage and avoid the world's destruction, to save as many lemmings as you can in each level, and so on. This goal ultimately guides the creation of the game storyline and defines whether it's an innovative game or just another clone of a best-selling title.

Ending criteria: Along with the game goal, it's also important to define the game-end criteria: when to end the game, which includes the player's winning criteria (usually the game goal or some goal related to it) and the game over criteria (when the number of lives reaches zero, when time is up, and so on). When defining the game over criteria, it's also important to define how the player will return to a new game. Providing a saving or autosaving feature is crucial for long games, but might diminish the challenge for a short game such as chess or solitaire.

Storyline: Closely related to the game goal, the storyline provides a background that explains and justifies the game goal and is crucial to keep the player immersed in the game. When the game has a storyline to be followed (not all games have one), everything in the game must contribute to it. The wrong music or a small out-of-place detail in a game would break the illusion as much as seeing someone using a wristwatch in a movie such as *Gladiator* or *Troy*. Creating nonlinear storylines makes the players feel like their decisions affect the game flow, which, although hard to achieve, greatly improves the gaming experience.

Playability: Playability refers to how easy and fun the game is to play. The first 15 playing minutes are vital for players to decide if they will keep playing, so the game should provide a balance of easy-to-control movements for beginners and complex (and harder to use) movements for advanced players.

Replayability: This term refers to the desire players have, after finishing a game, to play again. For simple games such as Tetris, the appeal of playing again is obvious, but for more complex games, you must plan this appeal in the form of built-in features (such as extra levels unlocked every time the player finishes the game), or as game extensions the player can download or buy.

Forgiveness: Entering in the details of game play, this concept refers to the programmer's ability to provide the correct balance between mathematical accuracy and playability. For example, in a shooter game, if the player shoots a bullet that passes close to an enemy without touching the enemy, it's better to count it as an accurate shot. On the other hand, the programmer might choose to decrement the player's energy only for enemy shots that hit the player character's torso, ignoring bullets hitting head, arms, and legs, to make the game easier.

Challenge: You might say that challenge is the opposite of forgiveness. It's the game's ability to provide difficult but not impossible challenges to beat. If the game is too easy or too hard, the player will simply exchange it for a better-balanced one. The game can provide different skill levels to choose from, and must offer levels with increasingly difficult challenges to keep the player interested.

Reward: Rewarding players when they win is as important as offering good challenges for them to beat. These rewards might be special items, money, energy, lives, unlocking new levels, and so on. They include in-level challenge prizes (such as an amount of gold and extra experience gained for every monster defeated), end-of-level awards (such as presenting a cut-scene and giving bonus points), achievements (either LIVE achievements, which are presented in your game profile at Xbox 360 LIVE, or in-game achievements, such as the achievements in the Spore game), and a big show at the game ending. Remember that nothing is more frustrating for a player than spending dozens of hours to win a game, only to see a puny "congratulations" screen at the end!

Saving and registering: How the game saves the evolution of player characters throughout the game and the means it provides to the players to register their experience are important parts of the game's playability and reward system. In long games, providing a way for players to start easily from where they left off, a way to register their high scores and compare their scores to other people's scores, and even the ability to "take pictures" from the game to present later to their friends might make the difference needed to provide the right appeal.

Game ecosystem: Nowadays, the game team must remember that a video game isn't just the individual piece of game software. It includes communities of players on the Internet, homemade extensions created by fans, and so on. These considerations must guide all game development—from planning a long-term game franchise, coding a game that allows expansions, and establishing marketing approaches to increment the participation of fans in online communities, among other initiatives.

Polishing: A great game is great only if every detail is planned and developed to contribute to player immersion. Such details should be tested to make sure they work as planned. If a game appears to offer some freedom of choice to the player, but presents a "you can't do this" message—or, even worse, an error message—every time the player tries something imaginative, it's halfway to a total failure. Remember to include test time in every game project, even the simpler ones!

Enough planning for now. In the next section, you'll create your first XNA project and explore the game programming concepts behind it.

XNA Game Programming Concepts

In this section, you'll create an empty XNA game solution, and then dig into the solution details to understand the basic concepts behind the program.

If you haven't done so already, download and install the latest version of XNA Game Studio and Visual C# Express Edition from the download section of the XNA Creators Club web site (`http://creators.xna.com`). If you already have Visual Studio 2008 Professional, XNA 3.0 will work just fine with that version. The examples in this book work in either programming environment.

■**Note** XNA 3.0 runs with Visual C# Express 2008 or Visual Studio Professional 2008. XNA 2.0 runs with the 2005 version of these tools. If you open a project created with XNA 2.0, an upgrade wizard will pop up and convert most of the project to the new version.

Once everything is in place, follow these steps:

1. Start Visual C# and choose File ➤ New Project. You'll see the New Project dialog box, as shown in Figure 1-1.

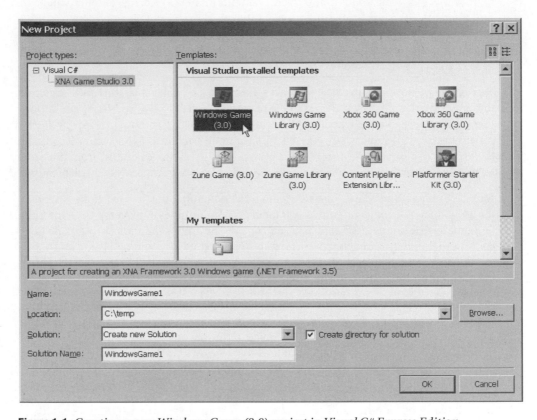

Figure 1-1. *Creating a new Windows Game (3.0) project in Visual C# Express Edition*

2. In the New Project dialog box, click the Windows Game (3.0) project type. Notice the Location field in this dialog box; it shows the location in which your project will be created. You're free to change this location to another directory of choice. Click OK to create a new game project named WindowsGame1.

3. Once the project is created, click the Start Debugging icon (the green arrowhead) in the toolbar, or press the F5 key to run the newly created game. Although it's not impressive right now—just a blue screen—as you'll see, this project has all the basics you need to start coding a game.

4. Close the game window.

Notice the files that were created for you, which appear in the Solution Explorer window, as shown in Figure 1-2.

Figure 1-2. *The Solution Explorer window for a new Windows Game project*

Along with an icon file (Game.ico) and a thumbnail file (GameThumbnail.png), your new project has two code files: Program.cs and Game1.cs. Also, it has a Content folder, which will contain the game content (sounds, images, 3D models, and so on).

To better understand what XNA provides for you, let's look at the basic game structure.

General Game Structure

The central logic for every game includes preparing the environment where the game will run, running the game in a loop until the game ending criteria is met, and cleaning up the environment.

The idea of having the main program logic running in a loop is crucial for a game, because the game needs to keep running whether or not it has user interaction. This doesn't happen with some commercial applications, which do something only in response to user input.

The following pseudocode presents a game structure, including the game loop:

```
Initialize graphics, input and sound controllers
Load resources
Start game loop.  In every step:
    Gather user input
    Perform needed calculations  (AI, movements, collision detection, etc.)
    Test for game ending criteria - if met, stop looping
    Draw (render) screen, generate sounds and game controller feedback
Finalize graphics, input, and sound
Free resources
```

This is a simplified view—for instance, you can load resources inside the game loop when beginning each game level—but it still provides a good idea about a game's internal details.

Before XNA, this game structure had to be coded from scratch, so you needed to contend with many details that weren't directly related to your game. XNA hides most of this complexity from you. When you create a new Windows Game project, the two code files created encompass creating an object of the Microsoft.Xna.Framework.Game class (Game1 object), presenting the code with the meaningful methods of this class you need to override, and calling the Run method, which starts the game loop.

The next pseudocode fragment presents Game1 methods organized as the generic game loop presented before, so you can understand the general structure of the code before entering its details.

```
Game1() - General initialization (Game1.cs)
Initialize() - Game initialization (Game1.cs)
LoadContent() - Load Graphics resources (Game1.cs)
Run() - Start game loop (Program.cs).  In every step:
   Update() - Read user input, do calculations, and test for game ending (Game1.cs)
   Draw() - Renderization code (Game1.cs)
UnloadContent() - Free graphics resources (Game1.cs)
```

Comparing the two preceding pseudocode excerpts, you can see that the Windows Game project type provides you with a ready-made basic game structure, so you can start by adding your game-specific code.

Now, let's look at the details for the Program.cs file. Open this file, and you will see that it contains only ten code lines (not counting the using statements):

```
static class Program
{
    static void Main(string[] args)
    {
        using (Game1 game = new Game1())
        {
            game.Run();
        }
    }
}
```

This code fragment includes the Program class, where you have the XNA application entry point—the Main function. This function has only two lines: one for creating the game object from the Game1 class, and another for calling the Run method of this object, which, as you already know, starts the game loop.

Note that by creating the object in a using statement, it is automatically freed when the statement ends. Another point to remember is that the args argument on the Main function receives the command-line parameters used when calling the game. If you wish to include command-line arguments in your game—such as special cheat codes for helping you test the game—this is where you need to deal with them.

The Game1 class is implemented in the Game1.cs file. A quick look at the Game1 class reveals that it's derived from the Microsoft.Xna.Framework.Game class, the base class offered by XNA that encapsulates window creation, graphics, audio and input initialization, and the basic game logic we already talked about.

■**Note** You can rename the Game1 class to better reflect your game; for example, you might name it Breakout for a Breakout game clone. If you do this, don't forget to rename the corresponding variable declaration and creation in the Program.cs file.

Now open the Game1.cs file. We'll explore its details in the next sections.

Game Initialization

The Game1 class starts by defining and creating objects that will reference the graphics device manager, most commonly referred to in the gaming world as the *device*, and a SpriteBatch object, used to draw text and 2D images. The Game1 class constructor also configures the root directory for the content manager, which is the entry point for the XNA Content Pipeline, so that the XNA Framework is informed of where to find game content (graphics, sounds, 3D models, fonts, and so on). The following code bit presents the device and content manager initialization:

```
public class Game1 : Microsoft.Xna.Framework.Game
    {
        GraphicsDeviceManager graphics;
        SpriteBatch spriteBatch;


        public Game1()
        {
            graphics = new GraphicsDeviceManager(this);
            Content.RootDirectory = "Content";
        }
```

In the next sections, you'll see some details about the device and the Content Pipeline, so you can get an overall idea of what's happening behind the scenes.

The Graphics Device Manager

The graphics device manager is your entry point to the graphics handling layer. It includes methods, properties, and events that allow you to query and change this layer. In other words, the device represents the way to manage the access to the graphics card's features.

For now, all you need to know is that by creating the graphics object of the GraphicsDeviceManager class, a game window is created for you, and you'll use the graphics object when performing any graphics operation. All the complexities of querying the features and initializing the 3D graphics layer are hidden from you.

The Content Pipeline

The Content Pipeline is one of the most interesting features XNA provides, because it simplifies how your game deals with content generated by different content generation tools.

In a non-XNA game, you need to worry about how to load game content such as audio, graphics, and 3D models. Where is the content located? How will your program read this content? Do you have the correct libraries to read the content in the format it was generated in by the commercial 3D tool you used to create it?

The Content Pipeline streamlines the processing of all game content so you can deal with it easily. It comprises a number of steps, which include importers to read the content and generate a well-known format, a processor that reads this format, a content compiler that generates the ready-to-use content, and finally the content manager. Figure 1-3 presents a high-level view of the Content Pipeline.

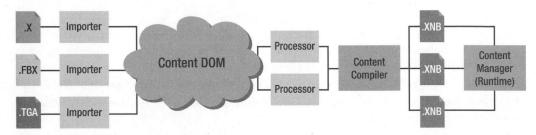

Figure 1-3. *The XNA Content Pipeline*

One interesting thing about the Content Pipeline is that it is based on content you effectively include in your C# project. That means that when the project is built, the content is transformed into a recognizable format and moved to a known directory, so the program will always know where to find the content and how to read it.

XNA 3.0 also offers content discovery and playing features that allow your game to load and play sounds without using the Content Pipeline. These features were created for Zune support, as you will see in Chapter 7.

When including content in your XNA program, you use one of the content importers provided as part of the framework. These importers normalize the content data, putting it in a format that can be easily processed later. The importers support the following file formats:

- *3D file formats*: X (used by DirectX), FBX (transport file format, originally created by Autodesk and supported by most commercial and many freeware tools)

- *Material file formats*: FX (effect files, which can be used to describe 3D model rendering details or add effects to the 3D scene)

- *2D file formats*: BMP, DDS, JPG, PNG, and TGA (the most commonly used image file formats)

- *Font description*: SPRITEFONT (XML files used by XNA, which describe how to generate a texture map from a specific font type size; the game then uses the images on the texture map to write text on the screen)

- *XML files*: XML format files copied to the game deployment directory, which can be used to store game settings, for example

- *Audio file formats*: XAP (audio project generated by the XACT tool), WAV, WMA, and MP3

After the importers process the content, when the game is running, the processors will read this content and generate an object the game can handle.

Finally, the game uses the content manager to read such objects so they can be easily used.

You can extend the content compiler to include new processors, and you can also extend the Content Pipeline with new importers, so you don't need to stick to the predefined formats.

■**Tip** You can find many examples of how to extend the Content Pipeline at the XNA Creators Club web site (`http://creators.xna.com`). For instance, the skinned mesh sample presents a Content Pipeline extension to read animation data from FBX files.

Game Initialization Methods in an XNA Game

Looking back at the game logic pseudocode, you can see that before entering the game loop, you must do the needed initialization and load the game resources. In addition to the general game initialization done in the class constructor, seen in the previous sections, such initialization is done in the `Initialize` and `LoadContent` methods. For now, all you need to know is why there are two initialization routines; later chapters will provide more details about each of these methods.

The `Initialize` method is called once when you execute the `Run` method (which starts the game loop), just before the game loop starts. This is the correct place to include any nongraphical initialization routines, such as preparing the audio content.

The `Initialize` method also includes a call to its base method, which iterates through a `GameComponents` collection and calls the `Initialize` method for each of them. That means that for more sophisticated games, you can create game components that the `Game` class will also call. But don't worry about this detail right now; we'll get back to it upcoming chapters.

The graphics are loaded in a separate method because sometimes the game needs to reload the graphics. The graphics are loaded according to the current device settings to provide maximum performance. So, when these settings change (such as when you change the game resolution or when you go from windowed to full-screen mode), you need to reload the graphics. The `LoadContent` method is called every time the game needs to load or reload the graphics.

Game Finalization

Because XNA's internal closing routines and XNA's garbage collector do most of the finalization routines for you, the finalization is simplified.

The basic game project you created includes an overload for the `UnloadContent` method. Like its peer used to load graphics, this method is called every time the game needs to free any graphics resources you have loaded.

Advanced games might include specific routines in each game class to load and unload graphic resources, which would be called by the `Game` class's load and unload methods.

Game Loop

Most of the game processing occurs inside the game loop. Here, the game checks if there is player input to process, the game characters' artificial intelligence is calculated, the game components' movements are executed, the collisions between them are considered, the game-ending criteria are checked, the controller vibration is activated, the sound is played, and the screen is drawn.

The Microsoft.Xna.Framework.Game class provides two overridable methods that are called by the game loop: Update, where you must include the game calculations, and Draw, where you draw the game components. Let's take a closer look at these methods, presented in the next code snippet, to highlight some relevant details:

```
protected override void Update(GameTime gameTime)
{
    // Allows the game to exit
    if (GamePad.GetState(PlayerIndex.One).Buttons.Back ==
        ButtonState.Pressed)
            this.Exit();
    // TODO: Add your update logic here
    base.Update(gameTime);
}

protected override void Draw(GameTime gameTime)
{
    graphics.GraphicsDevice.Clear(Color.CornflowerBlue);
    // TODO: Add your drawing code here
    base.Draw(gameTime);
}
```

The first important point to discuss is the gameTime parameter received by both methods. This parameter is crucial to all the game logic, because the game must know how much time has passed since the last step of the game loop to do the correct calculations—for example, to calculate the correct position for the game components according to their speeds in the game. Let's take a closer look at the GameTime class properties:

ElapsedGameTime: This property represents the amount of game time since the last time the game loop was called. Dealing with game time means that the game loop is called a fixed number of times per second, so the game logic can use game time as a basic unit of time to perform calculations. Creating games based on game time instead of real time is easier, because the game can define movements expressed in units per game update, simply incrementing the game components by the calculated rate in every update. When the IsFixedTimeStep property of the Game class is true, this class ensures that Update will be called the correct number of times per second, dropping frames in a game slowdown if necessary.

ElapsedRealTime: This property represents the amount of real time since the last time the game loop was called. By setting the IsFixedTimeStep property of the Game class to false, the game loop will run at maximum speed, being called as many times as possible per second. This could increase the code complexity, but also might allow for greater speed in the game.

TotalGameTime and TotalRealTime: These properties represent the total amount of time since the game started, counted in game time (fixed units per second) or real time.

IsRunningSlowly: If the Game class is calling the Update method less than defined in the Game.TargetElapsedTime property, this property is set to true, so the game has the information to do any needed adjustments.

Another detail worth mentioning about the Update method is that it comes with predefined code for ending the game when the Back button is pressed in the Xbox 360 controller:

```
if (GamePad.GetState(PlayerIndex.One).Buttons.Back == ButtonState.Pressed)
    this.Exit();
```

The GamePad class allows access to the current state of the controller and enables the game to fire the controller vibration. The class doesn't buffer user input, so the information you gather is exactly synchronized with current user interaction. As you can infer from the previous code, you can check for buttons, triggers, thumbsticks, or directional pad status. We'll talk about dealing with player input in the next chapter, including gamepad, mouse, and keyboard input.

The Draw method includes a line to clear the graphics device, filling the game window with a single color—CornflowerBlue:

```
graphics.GraphicsDevice.Clear(Color.CornflowerBlue);
```

As we stated earlier, the device (represented here by the graphics variable) is your interface to the graphics layer and will be used in every graphics operation. In this case, the code uses the GraphicsDevice property, which exposes properties and methods that allow reading and configuring many details about game rendering. We won't get into further details about this class now; you'll learn more about it in the next chapters.

Summary

This chapter covered basic game programming concepts presented in an XNA Windows Game project type. These general concepts are present in any game, so make sure you understand the idea behind the general game structure, especially the idea of the game loop:

```
Initialize graphics, input and sound controllers
Load resources
Start game loop.  In every step:
    Gather user input
    Perform needed calculations  (AI, movements, collision detection, etc.)
    Test for game ending criteria - if met, stop looping
    Draw (render) screen, generate sounds and game controller feedback
Finalize graphics, input, and sound
Free resources
```

It's also important to review the mapping of this general structure for games to the XNA Game class overridable methods:

```
Game1() - General initialization (already written for us)
Initialize() - Include nongraphics initialization here
LoadContent() - Include graphics initialization here
Run() - Start game loop.  In every step:
    Update() - Include code here to read and process user input, do calculations
               for AI, movements, and collisions, and test for game ending
    Draw() - Include the drawing (renderization) code here
UnloadContent() - Free graphics resources
```

In the next chapter, you'll write some simple examples that explore 2D game programming concepts, so you'll be ready to start creating 2D games with XNA.

■ ■ ■

CHAPTER 2

2D Graphics, Audio, and Input Basics

In this chapter, you'll create a simple program that manipulates simple 2D graphics. By doing so, you'll explore some relevant 2D game-creation concepts, such as the use of sprites and collision-detection algorithms. You'll also see how to deal with user input in XNA. Finally, you'll learn some basics of using audio in your games. By the end of this chapter, you'll be ready to start creating 2D games.

2D Graphics

In the previous chapter, you learned how to create an empty Windows Game project using XNA Game Studio. Now, you'll create a basic project that displays two simple 2D images on the screen. You'll learn how to move these images and make them collide with the window borders and against each other. But first, you need to be familiar with some of the terminology related to graphics in a game.

Common Gaming Terms

Many terms used in game programming jargon describe specific uses of graphics in a game. The following are some of the most common ones:

Sprite: A *sprite* is a 2D image that can be manipulated independently from the rest of a game scene. This term is used often to describe the image displayed or the class used by the game to display the image (which includes properties such as velocity, position, width, height, and so on). Because the computer always draws the 2D image as a rectangle, a sprite usually encompasses transparent areas so it provides the illusion of a nonrectangular drawing. The term *animated sprite* refers to a sprite whose images change at predetermined time intervals, to generate the illusion of movement (such as a walking man or a spinning wheel).

Textures: A *texture* refers to a 2D image loaded in a 3D model, which can be seen from any point of view, depending on the position of the model and the position of the camera used to render the scene. You can use textures to help create the illusion of a highly detailed model, when a detailed image is mapped over a simple 3D model.

Billboard: In the 3D world, a *billboard* is a texture that is mapped to a special plane that is always perpendicular to the camera axis. Using 3D-like images in billboarding is an effective technique for creating game components—such as a tree, a road sign, or a torch in the wall—without the need to create highly detailed models. This allows more detailed scenes with the same rendering processing power.

■**Tip**   The Billboards sample provided at the XNA Creators Club web site (`http://creators.xna.com/en-US/sample/billboard`) demonstrates how the billboarding technique can be used effectively.

Background: A 2D game scene is usually composed of a background image with many sprites displayed over it. When this background is a moving image, you have a *scrolling background*, which is the main characteristic in games called *scrollers*. It's also worth mentioning *parallax scrolling*, a special scrolling technique in which the 2D game has more than one scrolling background with different scrolling speeds, which provides the illusion of a 3D environment. For example, while the player character moves to the left, trees and bushes behind it move at the player's speed, mountains "far away" from the character move slowly, and clouds in the sky move very slowly.

■**Tip**   The Microsoft Developer Network (MSDN) site has a nice example of how to improve the Platformer Starter Kit (which comes as a new game project type when you install XNA 3.0) by including levels with parallax scrolling. You can find this example at `http://msdn.microsoft.com/en-us/library/dd254919.aspx`.

Tiles: These are small images used as tiles to compose a bigger image, usually a level background. For example, platform games typically use tiles to create different platform levels based on the same basic images. The term *tiled map* is often used to describe game levels created with tiles, and sometimes to describe files with the information needed to create such levels based on tiles. A classic example of the use of tiles is for building a terrain. Role-playing games (RPGs) usually provide a level editor application that lets you build the levels by picking different tiles from the application and joining them together.

In the next sections, you'll create a simple XNA program to demonstrate the concepts of drawing sprites, moving them on the screen, and handling sprite collisions with other sprites and with the game window border. However, before you start coding, let's take a quick look at the 2D coordinate systems and screen coordinates.

2D and Screen Coordinate Systems

While it's not our goal to cover all math concepts involved in creating 2D games, if you understand the basic ideas introduced in this chapter, you'll be able to build on this knowledge when creating your own 2D games and easily comprehend other related concepts.

You probably heard about 2D coordinate systems in geometry class. Just to remind you, Figure 2-1 represents a triangle, expressed by each of its vertices, in a 2D coordinate system. Analyze the vertices' coordinates to make sure you understand the concept.

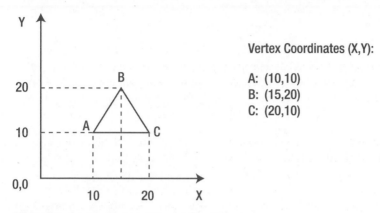

Figure 2-1. *A triangle in a 2D coordinate system*

The main difference between the coordinate system presented in Figure 2-1 and the coordinates used when creating a 2D game—called *screen coordinates*—is that the axis origin is not at the bottom left. Instead, the axis origin is located in the top-left position, as depicted in Figure 2-2. Compare Figures 2-1 and 2-2 to understand how this difference impacts the vertices' definition: the higher a vertex appears on the screen, the lower its y-axis coordinates.

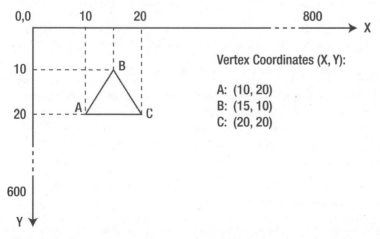

Figure 2-2. *The same triangle as in Figure 2-1, but in screen coordinates*

Another important detail is that the screen coordinates are directly related to the screen resolution. So, if you configure your monitor to an 800 × 600 resolution, that means that the x axis will have 800 pixels (each pixel is an independent point on the screen) and the y axis will have 600 pixels, as suggested in Figure 2-2.

Drawing a Sprite Using XNA

Let's now create a simple example in XNA to display a sprite in a given position on the screen.

Start by creating a new project, or by opening the empty project you created in the previous chapter.

Creating the Sprite Class

To group the sprite image and some associated properties (such as position, size, and velocity), you'll create a simple class, which will be extended as we explore new concepts in this chapter.

To create the class, right-click the project name in the Solution Explorer window and choose Add New Item. In the New Item dialog box, choose Class as the item type and name it clsSprite. Add the following code in the clsSprite.cs file:

```
using Microsoft.Xna.Framework.Graphics;   // For Texture2D
using Microsoft.Xna.Framework;  //  For Vector2
class clsSprite
{
   public Texture2D texture { get; set;}  // Sprite texture, read-only property
   public Vector2 position { get; set; }  // Sprite position on screen
   public Vector2 size { get; set; }      // Sprite size in pixels

   public clsSprite (Texture2D newTexture, Vector2 newPosition, Vector2 newSize)
   {
       texture = newTexture;
       position = newPosition;
       size = newSize;
   }
}
```

This is a simple sprite class, which includes the following properties:

texture: Stores the sprite image using XNA's Texture2D class. This class has many properties and methods to help deal with textures; you'll see some of them in Chapters 3 and 4. The texture is stored in this class as a 2D grid of *texels*. Similar to pixels, which are the smallest unit that can be drawn on the screen, texels are the smallest unit that can be stored by the graphics processing unit (GPU), and they include color and transparency values.

size: Stores the sprite's size using XNA's Vector2 class. This class has two properties, X and Y, which are used to store the image width and height.

position: Stores the position of the sprite using XNA's Vector2 class. The X and Y properties of the class store the screen coordinates for the sprite.

For now, this class stores only the sprite properties, and does not include any methods. These properties are created using the C# simplified version for defining a get/set structure.

Adding the Sprite Image

The first step in creating a sprite is to include a new image in your game, so you can use it through the Content Pipeline. Choose any image you would like to use for this example, as long as it is in one of the formats supported by XNA (listed in Chapter 1). For our example, we used a simple 64 × 64 pixel image of a blue ball with a magenta background, which we created with Windows Paint and saved as `ball.bmp`.

■**Tip** XNA allows you to create transparent sections in your sprite in two ways. You can use an advanced image editor, such as Photoshop, GIMP (`http://www.gimp.org`), or Paint.NET (`http://www.getpaint.net`) to create image files with transparent areas. Alternatively, you can simply color the areas you don't want to show with magenta. In our example, the background of the ball image will not be drawn. When creating images with magenta areas in Windows Paint, don't save them in JPG format, because this format does not preserve the original colors when saving.

To add your image to your project, right-click the project's `Content` folder in the Solution Explorer window and select Add ➤ Existing Item, as shown in Figure 2-3. By default, the Add Existing Item dialog box will list all content types supported by XNA 3.0. Choosing Texture Files in the "Files of type" list in this dialog box will make it easier to find an image file.

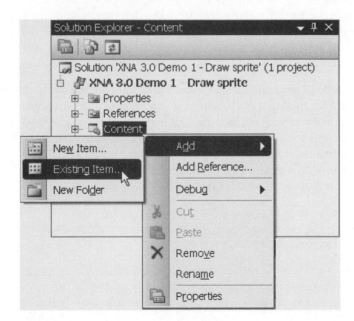

Figure 2-3. *Adding an image to the game project*

After including the image in the game solution, select the image name in the Solution Explorer window and press F4. This brings up (if it's not already visible) the Properties window for the recently included image, as shown in Figure 2-4.

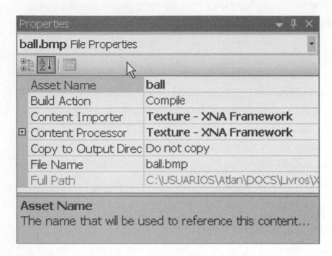

Figure 2-4. *The image properties*

The Properties window presents information such as the content importer and the content processor used for this content (also called *asset*), which were introduced in the previous chapter The Asset Name property defines how your code will refer to this content.

Drawing the Sprite on the Screen

Once you have an image, the next step is including the code for drawing it on the screen. To do this, you'll need a SpriteBatch (an XNA class that draws sprites on the screen) and the texture that will be used as the sprite image (in this case, you'll load this texture into your clsSprite class).

Usually, there is more than one way to code a particular task. In this case, you can read the texture from the clsSprite class and draw it in the Draw method of the Game1 class, or you can extend your clsSprite class to create a Draw method that will draw the sprite. Let's go with the former option, by including this new method in the clsSprite class:

```
public void Draw(SpriteBatch spriteBatch)
{
    spriteBatch.Draw(texture, position, Color.White);
}
```

The Draw method has many overloads, which allow you to draw only part of the original texture, to scale or rotate the image, and so on. Here, you are using the simplest one, which receives only three arguments: the texture to draw, the position in screen coordinates (both are already properties of clsSprite class), and a color channel modulation used to tint the image.

Using any color other than white in this last parameter draws the image with a composition of its original colors and color tone.

■Note For information about the other `Draw` method overloads, see the MSDN documentation for the XNA 3.0 `SpriteBatch.Draw` method (`http://msdn.microsoft.com/en-us/library/microsoft.xna.framework.graphics.spritebatch.draw.aspx`). For example, If you want to rotate your image, look for the overloads that expect the `rotation` parameter, or use the `SpriteEffects` parameter, if you just want to flip the sprite horizontally or vertically. Overloads with a `scale` parameter allow you to change the size of the sprite, which can be used in many ways, such as to create a zoom effect.

Now let's adjust the `Game1` class. A new Windows Game project already creates a `SpriteBatch` object for you, so you'll start by creating a `clsSprite` object in the `Game1` class. Include this definition at the beginning of the class, just after the device and `SpriteBatch` objects that were automatically created for you. You'll see something like the next code fragment:

```
public class Game1 : Microsoft.Xna.Framework.Game
{
    GraphicsDeviceManager graphics;  // The device
    SpriteBatch spriteBatch;         // The sprite renderer

    clsSprite mySprite1;             // My sprite class
```

Obviously, you need to create these objects with valid values before using them. You do so in the `LoadContent` method, which is where you include graphics initialization (as discussed in the previous chapter). Because the project already creates the `SpriteBatch` object, all you need to do is create the `clsSprite` object:

```
protected override void LoadContent()
{
    // Load a 2D texture sprite
    mySprite1 = new clsSprite(Content.Load<Texture2D>("ball"),
                        new Vector2(0f, 0f), new Vector2(64f, 64f));

    // Create a new SpriteBatch, which can be used to draw textures
    spriteBatch = new SpriteBatch(GraphicsDevice);
}
```

■Note The previous code sample uses `Vector2(0f, 0f)` to define a zeroed 2D vector, but you could use the `Vector2.Zero` static property as well. The XNA Framework offers such properties to improve the code's readability.

Even though you included a single code line (for creating the mySprite1 object), a lot of things are going on. You created your sprite class by using the content manager to load the Texture2D based on the image asset name, ball. You also defined the sprite position as (0, 0) and decided on the sprite size: 64 pixels wide and 64 pixels tall.

For the SpriteBatch's creation, you're passing the graphics device as a parameter. In the previous chapter, we mentioned that the device (represented here by the GraphicsDevice variable) is your entry point to the graphics handling layer, and through it you do any graphical operations. Here, you are informing the SpriteBatch which device it should use when drawing the sprites. In the next section, you'll see how to use the device to change the program's window size.

It's always a good programming practice to destroy everything you created when the program ends. To do this, you need to dispose of the texture of clsSprite you created in the LoadContent method. As you probably guessed, you do this in the UnloadContent method. The code for disposing of the object follows:

```
protected override void UnloadContent()
{
    // Free the previously allocated resources
    mySprite1.texture.Dispose();
}
```

■Note You could also create a Dispose method in the clsSprite class to dispose of the texture, and call it from the UnloadContent method. This would be a more object-oriented code practice. It's up to you to choose the code practice you think is best.

Finally, you need to include code to draw the sprite using the SpriteBatch object you created. You use the SpriteBatch, as its name suggests, to draw a batch of sprites, grouping one or more calls to its Draw method inside a block started by a call to the Begin method and closed by a call to the End method, as follows:

```
protected override void Draw(GameTime gameTime)
{
    graphics.GraphicsDevice.Clear(Color.CornflowerBlue);

    spriteBatch.Begin();
    mySprite1.Draw(spriteBatch);
    spriteBatch.End();

    base.Draw(gameTime);
}
```

The Begin method can also receive parameters that will be used when rendering every sprite in the block. For instance, if the texture has transparency information, you can tell the SpriteBatch to take this into account when drawing, by changing the Begin code line to the following:

```
spriteBatch.Begin(SpriteBlendMode.AlphaBlend);
```

Another very interesting parameter of the Begin method is transformMatrix, which receives a transformation matrix that will apply transformations (scale, rotation, or translation) to the entire batch of sprites being drawn. You will learn more about matrices in Chapter 8.

Running the program now results in a window with the sprite sitting in the upper-left corner—the (0, 0) position of the program window—as shown in Figure 2-5.

Figure 2-5. *The sprite rendered in the (0, 0) position of the program window*

Changing the Window Size

If you want to change the size of the window (for example, to a 500 × 300 window), you can inform the device about the new dimensions (through the graphics object) in the Game1 constructor, by including the following code lines just after the creation of the graphics object:

```
graphics.PreferredBackBufferWidth = 500;
graphics.PreferredBackBufferHeight = 300;
```

In these lines, you're changing the *backbuffer* width and height, which reflects in the window size, because you're working in windowed mode. This backbuffer is part of the technique used to draw the game scene without image flickering, called *double buffering*. In double buffering, you use two places, or *buffers*, to draw and display the game scene; while the first one is presented to the player, the second, invisible one (the backbuffer) is being drawn. After the drawing is finished, the backbuffer content is moved to the screen, so the player doesn't see only part of the scene if it takes too long to be drawn (the bad visual effect known as *flickering*).

Fortunately, you don't need to worry about such details, because XNA hides this complexity from you. But now you know why the property is called PreferredBackBufferWidth, instead of something like PreferredWindowsWidth!

Moving the Sprite on the Screen

Because you work directly with screen coordinates when creating 2D games, moving a sprite is simple. All you need to do is draw the sprite in a different position. By incrementing the x coordinate of the sprite position, the sprite moves to the right; by decrementing, you move the sprite to the left. If you want to move the sprite down on the screen, you need to increment the y coordinate. You move the sprite up by decrementing the y coordinate. Keep in mind that the (0, 0) point in screen coordinates is the upper-left corner of the window.

The XNA Framework basic game project provides a specific place to do the game calculations: the Update overridable method.

You can move the sprite by simply adding one line in the code, incrementing the X position of the sprite, according to the following line of code:

```
mySprite1.position.X += 1;
```

Because you use the sprite's position property when rendering the sprite in the Draw method, by including this line, you'll be able to see the sprite moving across the window, to the right, until it disappears from the screen.

To create a more game-like sprite, let's do something a little more sophisticated. First, create a new property in the clsSprite class, velocity, that defines the sprite velocity on both the x and y axes. Then modify the class constructor to receive and store the screen coordinates, so you can include a method that moves the sprite according to the given velocity, which doesn't let the sprite move off the screen.

To begin, delete the code line that changes the X position of the sprite. Next, modify the sprite class constructor, and change the sprite creation code in the Game1 class. In the clsSprite.cs file, make the following adjustment to the class constructor:

```
private Vector2 screenSize { get; set; } // Screen size
public clsSprite (Texture2D newTexture, Vector2 newPosition,
                  Vector2 newSize, int ScreenWidth, int ScreenHeight)
{
    texture = newTexture;
    position = newPosition;
    size = newSize;
    screenSize = new Vector2(ScreenWidth, ScreenHeight);
}
```

Change the sprite-creation code accordingly in the Game1.cs file, in the LoadContent method:

```
mySprite1 = new clsSprite(Content.Load<Texture2D>("xna_thumbnail"),
                  new Vector2(0f, 0f), new Vector2(64f, 64f),
                  graphics.PreferredBackBufferWidth,
                  graphics.PreferredBackBufferHeight);
```

Create a new property in the sprite class, velocity:

```
public Vector2 velocity { get; set; }  // Sprite velocity
```

Set this velocity to (1,1) in the LoadContent method, after the sprite-creation code, so you'll inform the sprite that it should move one pixel per update on both the x and y axes. This way, the sprite will move diagonally across the screen.

```
mySprite1.velocity = new Vector2(1, 1);
```

You have the screen bounds, and you have the speed. Now you need to create a method—let's call it Move—in the sprite class that moves the sprite according to the sprite velocity, respecting the screen boundaries. The code for this method follows:

```
public void Move()
{
    // If we'll move out of the screen, invert velocity

    // Checking right boundary
    if (position.X + size.X + velocity.X > screenSize.X)
        velocity = new Vector2(-velocity.X, velocity.Y);
    // Checking bottom boundary
    if (position.Y + size.Y + velocity.Y > screenSize.Y)
        velocity = new Vector2(velocity.X, -velocity.Y);
    // Checking left boundary
    if (position.X + velocity.X < 0)
        velocity = new Vector2(-velocity.X, velocity.Y);
    // Checking upper  boundary
    if (position.Y + velocity.Y < 0)
        velocity = new Vector2(velocity.X, -velocity.Y);
    // Since we adjusted the velocity, just add it to the current position
    position += velocity;
}
```

Because Vector2 classes represent both the sprite position and velocity, you could simply add the vectors to change the sprite position. However, because you don't want to add the velocity if it will take the sprite off the screen, you include code to invert the velocity in this situation.

Checking for left and top screen boundaries is a direct test, because the sprite position is given by its upper-left corner. However, when checking if the sprite will leave the screen on the right, you must add the sprite width to the sprite's X position to make the sprite bounce with its right corner, or it would leave the screen before bouncing back. Similarly, when checking if the sprite is leaving through the bottom of the screen, you must add the sprite height to its Y position so the sprite will bounce with its bottom.

As a final step, include the call to the sprite's Move method in the Update method of the Game1.cs class:

```
mySprite1.Move();
```

Read the code carefully to be sure you understand the tests, and then run the code. The sprite will move across the screen and bounce against the window borders!

Coding for Collision Detection

Making the sprite bounce on the window borders is already a simple collision-detection test, but in 2D games, you usually want to test for collisions between sprites.

If you do an Internet search for "collision-detection algorithm," you'll find thousands of pages describing many different algorithms for detecting collisions on 2D and 3D systems. Here, we'll present a simple example to help you understand the concept.

When testing for collisions, it's usually not reasonable to test every single pixel of a sprite against every single pixel of another sprite, so the collision-detection algorithms are based on approximating the object shape with some easily calculated formula. The most common collision-detection algorithm uses *bounding boxes*, which approximate the object shape with one or more rectangles, or "boxes." Figure 2-6 shows a plane sprite, whose form is approximated by two boxes.

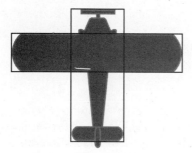

Figure 2-6. *Two boxes may be used to calculate collisions for a plane sprite.*

An easy way to implement the bounding-box test is simply to check if the x,y position of the upper-bound corner in the first box (which wraps the first sprite you want to test) is inside the second box (which wraps the second object to test). In other words, check whether the X and Y values of the box being tested are less than or equal to the corresponding X and Y values of the other box, plus the width of the other box.

In your clsSprite class, implement a method (named Collides) that will receive a sprite as a parameter, and test the received sprite against the current sprite. If there's a collision, the method will return true.

```
public bool Collides(clsSprite otherSprite)
{
    // Check if two sprites collide
    if (this.position.X + this.size.X > otherSprite.position.X &&
        this.position.X < otherSprite.position.X + otherSprite.size.X &&
        this.position.Y + this.size.Y > otherSprite.position.Y &&
        this.position.Y < otherSprite.position.Y + otherSprite.size.Y)
        return true;
    else
        return false;
}
```

Check this code against the diagram in Figure 2-7, to be sure you understand the algorithm.

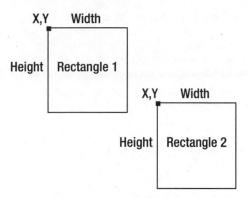

Figure 2-7. *Two nonoverlapping boxes*

According to the code sample, the two boxes will overlap only if both the x and y coordinates of rectangle 2 are within range (X to X + width, Y to Y + height) of rectangle 1. Looking at Figure 2-7, you see that the y coordinate for rectangle 2 is not greater than the y coordinate plus the height of rectangle 1. This means that your boxes might be colliding. But when checking the x coordinate of rectangle 2, you see that it's greater than the x coordinate plus the width of rectangle 1, which means that no collision is possible.

Figure 2-8 illustrates a case in which you do have a collision. In this case, you can check that both x and y positions of rectangle 2 are within the range of rectangle 1. In the code sample, you also do the opposite test, checking if the x and y coordinates of rectangle 1 are within the range of rectangle 2. Because you're checking just one point, it's possible for rectangle 2's top-left corner to be outside rectangle 1, but for the top-left corner of rectangle 1 to be inside rectangle 2.

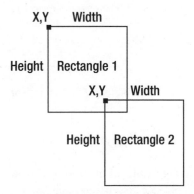

Figure 2-8. *Two overlapping boxes*

To test your method, you'll create a second, standing sprite in the middle of the window. To do this, you need to replicate the sprite-creation code and include the code for testing collisions in the Update method of the Game1 class.

First, include the sprite's variable definition at the beginning of the Game1 class, along with the previous sprite definition.

```
clsSprite mySprite2;
```

Now, in the LoadContent method, include the code for the sprite creation and set its starting velocity:

```
mySprite2 = new clsSprite(Content.Load<Texture2D>("xna_thumbnail"),
                    new Vector2(218f, 118f), new Vector2(64f, 64f),
                    graphics.PreferredBackBufferWidth,
                    graphics.PreferredBackBufferHeight);
mySprite2.velocity = new Vector2(3, -3);
```

In the UnloadContent method, include the code for disposing of the sprite:

```
mySprite2.texture.Dispose();
```

In the Update method, include the code to move the second sprite:

```
mySprite2.Move();
```

Finally, in the Draw method, include the code for drawing the new sprite. The code for drawing the two sprites follows:

```
spriteBatch.Begin(SpriteBlendMode.AlphaBlend);
mySprite1.Draw(spriteBatch);
mySprite2.Draw(spriteBatch);
spriteBatch.End();
```

If you run the program now, you'll see both sprites, but they aren't bouncing yet. You can make them bounce by including a call to the Collides method in the Update method and changing the velocity between the sprites, as follows:

```
if (mySprite1.Collides(mySprite2))
{
    Vector2 tempVelocity = mySprite1.velocity;
    mySprite1.velocity = mySprite2.velocity;
    mySprite2.velocity = tempVelocity;
}
```

In this code, you store the velocity of mySprite1 in the tempVelocity variable, set the velocity of mySprite1 to the velocity to mySprite2, and then set the velocity of mySprite2 to tempVelocity, thus changing the velocity between the sprites.

If you run the code now, you'll see the sprites moving and bouncing against each other and against the window borders, as shown in Figure 2-9.

Although the collision is detected using the bounding-box algorithm, after some tests, you will see a problem: if the boxes collide diagonally, the circles will bounce before they really "hit" each other.

When testing for collisions between circles, you can simply check if the distance between the circle centers are less than the sum of their radius. If it is, there is a collision. This provides a precise way to test for circle collisions.

Figure 2-9. *The sprites now move and collide.*

To change your clsSprite code to support collisions between two circle sprites, create two new read-only properties, center and radius, which are calculated according to the other sprite properties.

```
public Vector2 center{ get{ return position + (size/2);}  } // Sprite center
public float radius { get { return size.X / 2; } } // Sprite radius
```

Next, create a new method for testing this specific type of collision:

```
public bool CircleCollides(clsSprite otherSprite)
{    // Check if two circle sprites collided
    return (Vector2.Distance(this.center, otherSprite.center) <
        this.radius + otherSprite.radius);
}
```

Finally, change the Update method of the Game1 class to call CircleCollides instead of Collides. You'll see that the circles will now bounce only when they actually collide.

Game Input

In this section, we'll explore basic concepts of dealing with user input in XNA. You'll create an improved version of the previous example, in which you'll move the second sprite you created using the Xbox 360 gamepad.

Using the Xbox 360 Gamepad

When you create a new XNA Windows Game project type, the Update method of the Game1 class already includes code for dealing with user input:

```
// Allows the game to exit
if (GamePad.GetState(PlayerIndex.One).Buttons.Back == ButtonState.Pressed)
    this.Exit();
```

This code presents the GamePad class: the basic entry point to get user input from the Xbox 360 gamepad. If you explore the GamePad properties and methods using Visual C# Express IntelliSense, you'll easily understand how to use the GetState method to get the current state of buttons (Buttons structure), the thumbsticks (ThumbSticks structure), directional pad (DPad structure), and the controller triggers (Triggers structure). There is also a property to inform you if the gamepad is connected (IsConnected).

Another interesting detail is that you can vibrate the gamepad by calling the SetVibration method of the GamePad class.

Let's see how you can use this information to improve your example.

First, in the Game1 class, remove the code that sets the starting velocity of mySprite2 in the LoadContent method and remove the call to mSprite2.Move in the Update method. These changes will prevent mySprite2 from moving by itself. You also need to change the collision-detection code, simplifying it to merely invert the mySprite1 velocity, as follows:

```
if (mySprite1.Collides(mySprite2))
    mySprite1.velocity *= -1;
```

Now, to make the second sprite move according to gamepad input, all you need to do is include two new code lines in the Update method of the Game1 class:

```
// Change the sprite 2 position using the left thumbstick
Vector2 LeftThumb = GamePad.GetState(PlayerIndex.One).ThumbSticks.Left;
mySprite2.position += new Vector2(LeftThumb.X, -LeftThumb.Y) * 5;
```

In this code, you're adding a Vector2 to mySprite2.position. This vector is five times the value of the left thumbstick, except that you invert the Y property of the left thumbstick. If you think this is weird, recall from the earlier discussion in the "2D and Screen Coordinate Systems" section that the X position increments from left to right, and the Y position increments from the top to the bottom of the screen. The values of the X and Y properties of the thumbsticks range from –1 to 1, according to how much the thumbstick is pushed to the right or the bottom (positive values) or left and up (negative values). Therefore, you must invert the y coordinate to move the ball as expected. The multiplication by five is simply to make the ball move faster, according to the gamepad input.

To make the gamepad vibrate when mySprite1 collides with mySprite2 is also easy. Simply change the collision-detection code in the Update method of the Game1 class to reflect the next code fragment:

```
if (mySprite1.Collides(mySprite2))
{
    mySprite1.velocity *= -1;
    GamePad.SetVibration(PlayerIndex.One, 1.0f, 1.0f);
}
```

```
else
    GamePad.SetVibration(PlayerIndex.One, 0f, 0f);
```

Note that you need to set the gamepad vibration to zero when the sprites are not colliding; otherwise, it keeps on vibrating continuously.

Run the program now and move the sprite with the gamepad. When the sprites overlap, mySprite1 bounces and the gamepad vibrates.

■**Note** The second and third arguments of the SetVibration method range from 0 to 1, and define the speed for the left (low-frequency) and right (high-frequency) motors. You can include code in your program to generate different types of vibrations depending on the game conditions—for example, if the game collision is on the left or on the right of the player character.

Using the Keyboard

If, instead of the gamepad, you want to use the keyboard to control the sprite position, you can use Keyboard.GetState to get the current state of any key:

```
KeyboardState keyboardState = Keyboard.GetState();
if (keyboardState.IsKeyDown(Keys.Up))
    mySprite2.position += new Vector2(0, -5);
if (keyboardState.IsKeyDown(Keys.Down))
    mySprite2.position += new Vector2(0, 5);
if (keyboardState.IsKeyDown(Keys.Left))
    mySprite2.position += new Vector2(-5, 0);
if (keyboardState.IsKeyDown(Keys.Right))
    mySprite2.position += new Vector2(5, 0);
```

Using the Mouse

If, on the other hand, you want to use the mouse to control the sprite, you could use Mouse.GetState to get the current position of the mouse, and include code to make the sprite head to the current mouse position with the following code:

```
if (mySprite2.position.X < Mouse.GetState().X)
    mySprite2.position += new Vector2(5, 0);
if (mySprite2.position.X > Mouse.GetState().X)
    mySprite2.position += new Vector2(-5, 0);
if (mySprite2.position.Y < Mouse.GetState().Y)
    mySprite2.position += new Vector2(0, 5);
if (mySprite2.position.Y > Mouse.GetState().Y)
    mySprite2.position += new Vector2(0, -5);
```

Game Audio

In this section, you'll improve your example by including background sound and a bouncing sound effect, thus exploring basic audio concepts in XNA.

XNA deals with sound using the same structure it uses to manage graphics: the Content Pipeline. To XNA, sound is just another type of game content. But there is a difference, in fact: although you can directly add graphics content in a XNA game project, the sound content to be added must be in a specific file format, generated by the Microsoft Cross-Platform Audio Creation Tool, known as XACT.

Creating Audio Content with XACT

You use XACT to create sound banks and wave banks, compiled into an XAP file, which the game can then use through the content manager.

In this section, you'll learn the basics of how to create audio content with XACT and use it in a program, so you'll be ready to include audio content in your games. In the following chapters, you'll see how to do this when creating real games!

Follow these steps to create a new XACT project:

1. Start XACT by choosing Start ➤ Programs ➤ Microsoft XNA Game Studio 3.0 ➤ Tools ➤ Cross-Platform Audio Creation Tool (XACT).

2. In the XACT main window, choose File ➤ New Project to create a new audio project, and save it as MySounds.

3. On the left side of the window, MySounds now appears as a root node, with many types of child nodes below it. Right-click Wave Bank and select New Wave Bank in the pop-up menu, as shown in Figure 2-10.

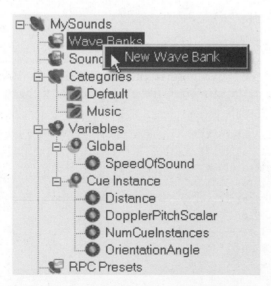

Figure 2-10. *Creating a new wave bank in XACT*

4. A new, blank window with the new wave bank appears. Right-click this window to see a pop-up menu that offers options for wave banks, as shown in Figure 2-11, and choose Insert Wave File(s).

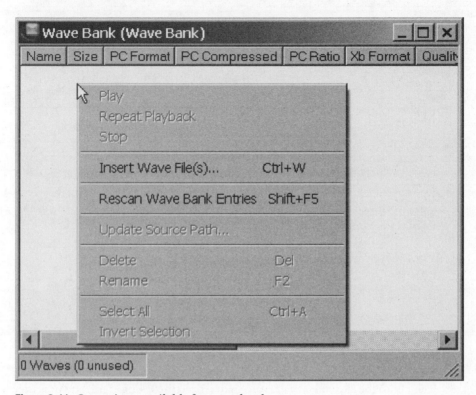

Figure 2-11. *Operations available for wave banks*

5. To stick with easily found wave files (sound files with a .wav extension), search for the chord.wav and notify.wav files on your hard disk. These files are installed by default in Windows, as system event sounds. (Alternatively, you can choose any available wave files.) The two files are inserted in your wave bank.

6. You also need to create a sound bank. Right-click the Sound Banks item on the left side of the window and choose to insert a new sound bank. A new window, with the newly created sound bank, appears on the right.

7. To better arrange your windows, select Windows ➤ Tile Horizontally. The windows are now easier to see, as shown in Figure 2-12.

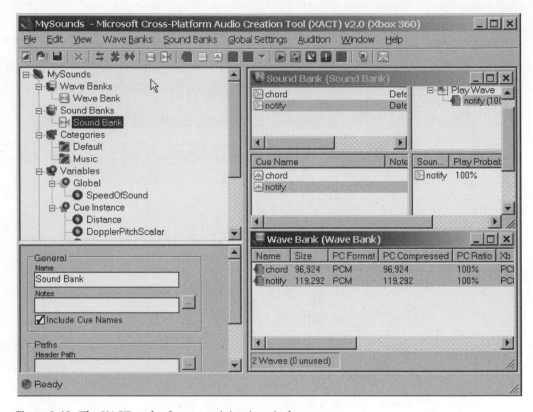

Figure 2-12. *The XACT tool, after organizing its windows*

8. Select both the file names in the wave bank (by Ctrl-clicking them) and drag them to the second panel in the left of the Sound Bank window—the panel with Cue Name and Notes columns. The file names in the wave bank turn from red to green, and the file names are added as contents in the sound list and cue list in the Sound Bank window.

9. Let's use a looping sound, so you can learn how to play, pause, and stop sound to use as background music in games. To do this, in the sound list, click the notify sound. In the properties pane that appears beneath the tree list on the right, under Looping, you'll see an Infinite check box. Mark this check box, as shown in Figure 2-13.

10. Save the project as MySounds.xap. You're ready to use the sounds in your program!

■**Note** To hear the sound samples from the sound bank or from the wave bank inside XACT by clicking the Play button on the XACT toolbar, the XACT Auditioning Utility must be running. Run it by choosing Start ➤ Programs ➤ Microsoft XNA Game Studio 3.0 ➤ Tools ➤ XACT Auditioning Utility.

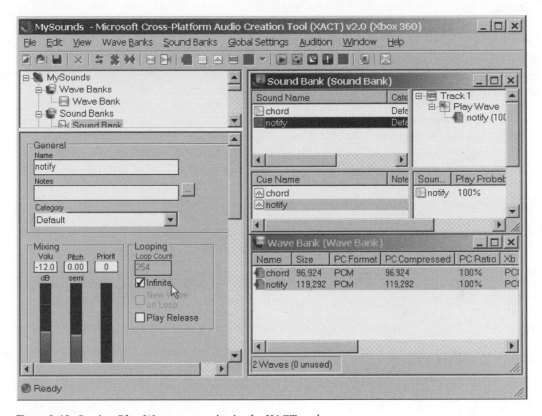

Figure 2-13. *Setting Play Wave properties in the XACT tool*

Using Audio in Games

XNA makes using audio content in games as simple as using graphics and dealing with player input.

As a first step, you need to include the audio content in the solution, so you can use it in your game. Then you define the audio-related objects, initialize these objects, and finally, use the content in the game code.

You include the audio content in the game in the same way you included graphics content earlier in this chapter: by right-clicking the Content folder in the Solution Explorer window and choosing Add Existing Item from the pop-up menu. Remember that in the Add Existing Item dialog box, all types of files are listed by default. You can choose Audio Files in the "Files of type" drop-down list to make it easier to find the MySounds.xap file you created in the previous section. You don't need to include the .wav files as content in the project, because the final wave bank will contain all sound files included in the audio project when you compile your game.

After including the MySounds.xap file in the solution, you need to create the following three objects to manage the file contents:

AudioEngine: This object is the program reference to the audio services in the computer, and is used mainly to adjust a few general settings and as a parameter to create the wave and sound banks. When creating an AudioEngine object in your program, you need to use the name of the global settings file for the XACT content as a parameter. This settings file name is generated when the XAP file is compiled, and as a default has the same name as the XAP file, with an .xgs extension.

WaveBank: This is a collection of wave files. To create this bank in your code, you need to pass as parameters the AudioEngine object (which must be previously created) and the compiled wave bank file, which is generated when you compile your project with the default name Wave Bank.xwb. Although the wave bank is not explicitly used in your program, you need to create this object, because the sound cues in the sound bank depend on the wave files in this bank.

SoundBank: This is a collection of sound cues. You can define cues as references to the wave files stored in the wave bank, along with properties that establish details on how to play these wave files and methods that let you manage their playback.

The next code sample shows how to extend the previous example by including code to create and initialize the audio components:

```
// Audio objects
AudioEngine audioEngine;
WaveBank waveBank;
SoundBank soundBank;

protected override void Initialize()
{
    audioEngine = new AudioEngine(@"Content\MySounds.xgs");
    // Assume the default names for the wave and sound banks.
    // To change these names, change properties in XACT.
    waveBank = new WaveBank(audioEngine, @"Content\Wave Bank.xwb");
    soundBank = new SoundBank(audioEngine, @"Content\Sound Bank.xsb");

    base.Initialize();
}
```

You can play a sound in two ways: with a simple playback or in a playback loop. Once you initialize the audio objects, doing a playback is a matter of calling a simple method: PlayCue. You can improve on the previous example by playing a sound cue every time the sprites collide. Find the collision detection test in the Update method of the Game1 class, and adjust it to play the chord sound sample, as follows:

```
if (mySprite1.Collides(mySprite2))
{
    mySprite1.velocity *= -1;
    GamePad.SetVibration(PlayerIndex.One,1.0f, 1.0f);
    soundBank.PlayCue("chord");
}
```

```
else
     GamePad.SetVibration(PlayerIndex.One, 0f, 0f);
```

You can also extend the sample by including the infinite looping sound you defined in the XACT project. However, to do this, you need more control over the sound than simply starting to play it from the sound bank. You need a way to start it, and then stop, pause, and resume it when needed, and some way to know the current state of the sound (playing, paused, stopped, and so on). The Cue object provides the methods and properties you need. Let's extend our example by creating a new Cue object, named MyLoopingSound, in Game1:

```
Cue myLoopingSound;
```

In the Initialize method, read the sound cue and play it by including the following code fragment:

```
myLoopingSound = soundBank.GetCue("notify");
myLoopingSound.Play();
```

In this code fragment, you use the Play method to start the playback of the notify sound. Because you set the Looping property in the XACT interface of this sound to Infinite (see Figure 2-13), the sound will continuously play when you start your program. Run the program now and hear it for yourself.

The Cue object offers a series of methods and properties that give you better control over the playback. The next code sample presents an example of how to pause and resume the cue when the B button on the Xbox 360 gamepad is pressed. If you don't have a gamepad plugged into your computer, you can change this to a keyboard key or a mouse button, using what you learned earlier in this chapter.

```
// Play or stop an infinite looping sound when pressing the B button
if (GamePad.GetState(PlayerIndex.One).Buttons.B -- ButtonState.Pressed)
{
    if (myLoopingSound.IsPaused)
        myLoopingSound.Resume();
    else
        myLoopingSound.Pause();
}
```

■**Note** The Stop method for the Cue object lets you stop the sound immediately or "as authored," which means that the audio engine will wait for the end of the current sound phase or the next transition to stop the sound gracefully. But remember that if you stop a sound, you can't play it again, unless you call the GetCue method once again.

Summary

In this chapter, you learned the basic 2D graphics vocabulary, and how to create a simple XNA program that enables you to load, display, and move images.

It's important to remember how to load a `Texture2D` from the Content Pipeline:

```
Texture2D MyTexture = Content.Load<Texture2D>("xna_thumbnail")
```

and how to display this texture using a `SpriteBatch` object:

```
spriteBatch.Begin();
spriteBatch.Draw(MyTexture, new Vector2(0f, 0f), Color.White);
spriteBatch.End();
```

You also saw that with a few lines of code, you can not only create sprites that collide in XNA, but also deal with player input and play sounds.

When reading player input, remember the basic objects: `GamePad`, `Keyboard`, and `Mouse`. These three objects provide a `GetState` method that allows you to get the player input, returning, respectively, a `GamePadState`, `KeyboardState`, and `MouseState` object, each with the information from the corresponding input device.

To add audio, remember that before using any sound in your game, you need to create a project in XACT, which generates the XAP content file that can be included in your game solution. Once the content is in place and the proper audio object's initialization is done, you can play sounds directly from the sound bank using the `Play` method, or get a `Cue` object from the sound bank and use its properties and methods to play, pause, resume, and stop playing a sound.

With this knowledge, you're now prepared to put it all together in a real game. That's exactly what you'll do in the next chapter. Get your umbrella and prepare for the Rock Rain—the complete game you'll create next!

CHAPTER 3

Creating Your First 2D Game

In this chapter, you'll create your first game and explore some of the techniques discussed in the previous chapter. Your first game will be both simple and fun. It will run on a PC or on an Xbox 360 console.

But as trivial as the game might seem, it still must be well planned. Many projects fail because of too little effort in this phase, which leads to projects without a defined end, or projects that are finished but do not achieve their goals. Planning involves discovering the questions that must be answered before starting a game project. This book intends to teach making games the right way, so let's start right.

Design for the First Game: Rock Rain

You're an intergalactic explorer, and you're stuck in an endless asteroid field! How long will you resist this rock rain? This is the main theme of your game, a frenetic challenge where you need to dodge a lot of asteroids that pass rapidly across the screen. It's like an Asteroids clone.

This is a simple and old game concept. Players need to avoid getting hit by meteors, and the longer they remain without a collision, the more points they get. Additionally, the quantity of meteors increases as time goes by, making the challenge harder and harder. To satisfy your curiosity, Figure 3-1 shows an example of a screen in your first game.

Right now, you'll clarify the game *constraints and rules* before you program anything. In the case of Rock Rain, they're simple:

- The player is able to move freely around the screen and cannot leave the screen boundaries.

- The meteors appear at the top of the screen and move down with a random angle and speed. After some time, a new meteor is added to this "rain."

- The score is determined by the number of meteors on the screen.

- If the player collides with a meteor, the player's score will be zeroed, and the game will restart with the initial quantity of meteors.

Values such as the starting quantity of meteors and how long it should take before another meteor is added to the screen were not specified, because they're game parameters, rather than rules.

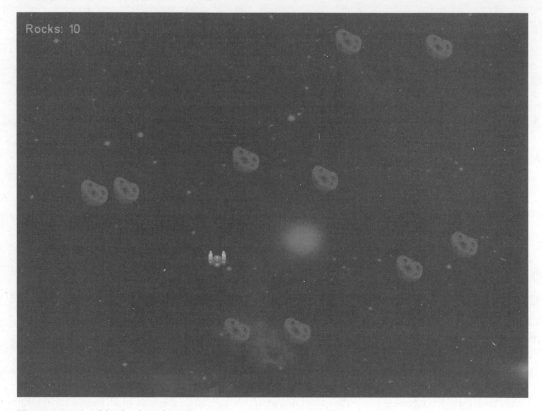

Rocks: 10

Figure 3-1. *Final look of Rock Rain*

From a game programmer's point of view, things like spaceships, meteors, and scores are *objects* in your game. You should also detail these objects before you start programming anything.

Each object in the game has its own characteristics and *behavior*: the rocks fall, the player controls the spaceship, the score grows with the meteor count, and so on. The correct definition of the behavior and the state control of the game's objects are the most challenging tasks in game programming. That's why your game should be well thought out before you start to build anything.

You also need to consider the audio portions for the game. For Rock Rain, you'll have only three sound effects: music that plays while the game is active, a sound that plays when a new meteor is added to the game, and an explosion sound that plays when the player collides with a meteor. And as another feature, when a collision occurs, you'll make the player's Xbox 360 gamepad shake, to give an impact effect.

Let's Get to It

As you might have guessed, your first game is created as an XNA Windows Game project, which you've explored in the previous chapters. So, start by opening Visual Studio and creating a new Windows Game project called RockRain. The Solution Explorer window will look like Figure 3-2.

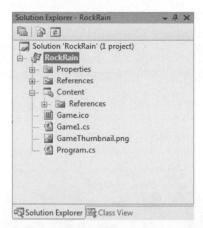

Figure 3-2. *The Solution Explorer window after creating the Rock Rain project*

As explained in Chapter 1, the Content folder is a special item in XNA projects. In this folder, you'll place all the game's assets, such as images, sounds, and so on—everything that should be loaded through the Content Pipeline.

You can download all the files used in this project from the book's details page at the Apress web site (http://www.apress.com).

Drawing the Background

Start by putting a background in your game. For a space game, nothing is better than an image of a galaxy! Add the file SpaceBackground.dds to the Content folder.

You should load this texture so that it fits the whole screen of the game. First, define the texture in your code. Add this attribute to your Game1 class:

```
// Background texture
private Texture2D backgroundTexture;
```

As you saw in the previous chapter, you'll load this texture and initialize the spriteBatch object in the LoadContent method:

```
// Create a new SpriteBatch, which can be used to draw textures.
spriteBatch = new SpriteBatch(GraphicsDevice);
// Load all textures
backgroundTexture = content.Load<Texture2D>(" SpaceBackground");
}
```

You need to load the texture using the spriteBatch object. Declare it in the Game1 class:

```
private SpriteBatch spriteBatch = null;
```

Now you can draw the background. Add the following code in the Draw method of the Game1 class:

```
// Draw background texture in a separate pass.
spriteBatch.Begin();
spriteBatch.Draw(backgroundTexture,new Rectangle(0, 0,
            graphics.GraphicsDevice.DisplayMode.Width,
            graphics.GraphicsDevice.DisplayMode.Height),
            Color.LightGray);
spriteBatch.End();
```

Run the game by pressing F5. If everything is correct, the result will look like Figure 3-3.

Figure 3-3. *Rock Rain background*

Creating the Player's Game Component

The player is represented in the game as a small spaceship that can be controlled using an Xbox 360 gamepad or a PC keyboard. The image of this spaceship is in the RockRain.png file. Add it to the project inside the Content folder. This texture contains the image of the player's spaceship and also the meteors that the player must avoid (see Figure 3-4).

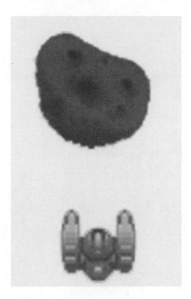

Figure 3-4. *Player and meteor texture*

As you did for the background, first declare the texture in the Game1 class:

private Texture2D meteorTexture;

Then load it in the LoadContent method immediately after loading the background texture:

meteorTexture = content.Load<Texture2D>(" RockRain");

■**Note** The graphics in this chapter and the next were built using SpriteLIB GPL, available from http://
www.flyingyogi.com/fun/spritelib.html. SpriteLib GPL is a collection of static and animated graphic
objects (also commonly known as *sprites*).

Now you'll create a class that represents the player in the game. Add a new GameComponent
to the project, name the file Ship.cs (as in Figure 3-5), and click OK. The new file added to the
project contains a class that derives from GameComponent. This game component will be visible
in the game; therefore, it must be drawn. Derive from DrawableGameComponent so that you have
a Draw method you can use to draw in the game.

This game component copies the texture region that contains the picture of the spaceship
in the specified position. To accomplish that, it needs the texture where this picture is, the
coordinates of the picture in this texture, and the coordinates on the screen where the picture
must be rendered.

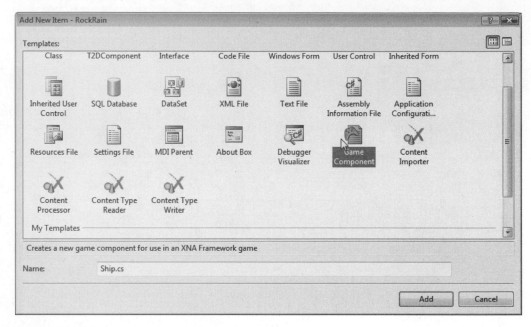

Figure 3-5. *Adding a new game component*

The component needs to move according to the Xbox 360 gamepad or PC keyboard controls. Also, it must remain within the screen boundaries; that is, the spaceship cannot disappear by leaving the defined borders of the game's window.

See that you have two steps of a DrawableGameComponent well defined:

- In the Draw method, you copy the spaceship picture to the screen.

- In the Update method, you update the screen according to the Xbox 360 gamepad or keyboard state.

This class code follows:

```
#region Using Statements
using System;
using System.Collections.Generic;
using Microsoft.Xna.Framework;
using Microsoft.Xna.Framework.Graphics;
using Microsoft.Xna.Framework.Input;
#endregion

namespace RockRain
{
    /// <summary>
    /// This is a game component that implements the player ship.
```

```csharp
        /// </summary>
        public class Ship : Microsoft.Xna.Framework.DrawableGameComponent
        {
            protected Texture2D texture;
            protected Rectangle spriteRectangle;
            protected Vector2 position;

            // Width and height of sprite in texture
            protected const int SHIPWIDTH = 30;
            protected const int SHIPHEIGHT = 30;

            // Screen area
            protected Rectangle screenBounds;

            public Ship(Game game, ref Texture2D theTexture)
                : base(game)
            {
                texture = theTexture;
                position = new Vector2();

                // Create the source rectangle.
                // This represents where the sprite picture is in the surface
                spriteRectangle = new Rectangle(31, 83, SHIPWIDTH, SHIPHEIGHT);

#if XBOX360
                // On the 360, we need to be careful about the TV's "safe" area.
                screenBounds = new Rectangle(
                        (int)(Game.Window.ClientBounds.Width * 0.03f),
                        (int)(Game.Window.ClientBounds.Height * 0.03f),
                        Game.Window.ClientBounds.Width -
                        (int)(Game.Window.ClientBounds.Width * 0.03f),
                        Game.Window.ClientBounds.Height -
                        (int)(Game.Window.ClientBounds.Height * 0.03f));#else
                screenBounds = new Rectangle(0,0,
                    Game.Window.ClientBounds.Width,
                    Game.Window.ClientBounds.Height);
#endif
            }

            /// <summary>
            /// Put the ship in your start position in the screen
            /// </summary>
            public void PutinStartPosition()
            {
                position.X = screenBounds.Width / 2;
                position.Y = screenBounds.Height - SHIPHEIGHT;
            }
```

```csharp
/// <summary>
/// Update the ship position
/// </summary>
public override void Update(GameTime gameTime)
{
    // Move the ship with the Xbox controller
    GamePadState gamepadstatus = GamePad.GetState(PlayerIndex.One);
    position.Y += (int)((gamepadstatus.ThumbSticks.Left.Y * 3) * -2);
    position.X += (int)((gamepadstatus.ThumbSticks.Left.X * 3) * 2);

    // Move the ship with the keyboard
    KeyboardState keyboard = Keyboard.GetState();
    if (keyboard.IsKeyDown(Keys.Up))
    {
        position.Y -= 3;
    }
    if (keyboard.IsKeyDown(Keys.Down))
    {
        position.Y += 3;
    }
    if (keyboard.IsKeyDown(Keys.Left))
    {
        position.X -= 3;
    }
    if (keyboard.IsKeyDown(Keys.Right))
    {
        position.X += 3;
    }

    // Keep the ship inside the screen
    if (position.X < screenBounds.Left)
    {
        position.X = screenBounds.Left;
    }
    if (position.X > screenBounds.Width - SHIPWIDTH)
    {
        position.X = screenBounds.Width - SHIPWIDTH;
    }
    if (position.Y < screenBounds.Top)
    {
        position.Y = screenBounds.Top;
    }
    if (position.Y > screenBounds.Height - SHIPHEIGHT)
    {
        position.Y = screenBounds.Height - SHIPHEIGHT;
    }
```

```
            base.Update(gameTime);
        }


        /// <summary>
        /// Draw the ship sprite
        /// </summary>
        public override void Draw(GameTime gameTime)
        {
            // Get the current sprite batch
            SpriteBatch sBatch =
                (SpriteBatch)Game.Services.GetService(typeof(SpriteBatch));

            // Draw the ship
            sBatch.Draw(texture, position, spriteRectangle, Color.White);

            base.Draw(gameTime);
        }


        /// <summary>
        /// Get the bound rectangle of ship position in screen
        /// </summary>
        public Rectangle GetBounds()
        {
            return new Rectangle((int)position.X, (int)position.Y,
                SHIPWIDTH, SHIPHEIGHT);
        }
    }
}
```

Note that the Draw method does not create a SpriteBatch, as was created when you rendered the background texture. Ideally (following the "batch" concept), you should not keep creating and destroying SpriteBatch objects, because this jeopardizes the application's performance. You could create a "global" SpriteBatch and use it in your classes. However, this would create a coupling between your game components and a global attribute of a specific game (which is not desirable in object-oriented programming). XNA has an excellent solution to supply this global object and still allow you to reuse the component's code easily: the *game service*.

You can think of a game service as a service that is available to anyone who has a reference to a Game. The idea behind it is that a component should be able to depend on certain types, or services, for its functionality. If that service isn't available, then the component can't operate correctly.

In this case, the Draw method will look for an active SpriteBatch directly in the GameServices collection and use it to draw itself on the screen. Of course, you must add this SpriteBatch to GameServices. So, add the following code directly after creating the SpriteBatch in the LoadContent method of the Game1 class:

```
// Add the SpriteBatch service
Services.AddService(typeof(SpriteBatch), spriteBatch);
```

All the GameComponent items in your game will use this SpriteBatch.

Let's talk a little about this class. The Update method checks the keyboard and Xbox 360 gamepad to update the Position attribute and change the position of the ship on the screen. In this method, you also check if the ship is inside the screen boundaries. If not, the code puts the ship inside the visible area of the screen.

The GetBound method just returns the rectangle that has the ship boundaries in the screen. You'll use this rectangle later to do collision tests with meteors. Finally, the PutinStartPosition puts the ship in its initial position, centered horizontally in the bottom area of the screen. This method is called when you need to put the ship in its starting position; for example, when a new round starts.

Now let's test this GameComponent. Create a Start method that will be used to initialize the game objects (only the player for the moment), as follows:

```
/// <summary>
/// Initialize the game round
/// </summary>
private void Start()
{
    // Create (if necessary) and put the player in start position
    if (player == null)
    {
        // Add the player component
        player = new Ship(this, ref meteorTexture);
        Components.Add(player);
    }
    player.PutinStartPosition();
}
```

Observe that the player attribute contains a reference to the player's GameComponent. You also need to add this component to the components list of the Game itself to be able to have XNA call the Draw and Update methods of this object in the game.

Finally, declare the player attribute in the Game1 class:

```
private Ship player;
```

Now let's go back to the game's logic as a whole. The game's logic is normally implemented inside the Update method of the Game class. In this case, you can start with the following code:

```
/// <summary>
/// Allows the game to run logic such as updating the world,
/// checking for collisions, gathering input, and playing audio.
/// </summary>
/// <param name="gameTime">Provides a snapshot of timing values.</param>
protected override void Update(GameTime gameTime)
{
    // Allows the game to exit
    gamepadstatus = GamePad.GetState(PlayerIndex.One);
    keyboard = Keyboard.GetState();
```

```
    if ((gamepadstatus.Buttons.Back == ButtonState.Pressed) ||
        (keyboard.IsKeyDown(Keys.Escape)))
    {
        Exit();
    }

    // Start if not started yet
    if (player == null)
    {
        Start();
    }

    // Update all other components
    base.Update(gameTime);
}
```

Initially, this code checks if the user pressed the Esc key or the Back button on the Xbox 360 gamepad, which ends the game. Then, if necessary, the code starts the game through the Start method.

One detail is still missing. The Draw method of your game draws only the background. You also need to make it draw all the other GameComponent items of the game, so add the following code immediately after the code that draws the background:

```
// Start rendering sprites
spriteBatch.Begin(SpriteBlendMode.AlphaBlend);
// Draw the game components (sprites included)
base.Draw(gameTime);
// End rendering sprites
spriteBatch.End();
```

Save and execute the code. Now you can move the spaceship around the screen with the Xbox 360 gamepad or the PC arrow keys. Observe that all the movement logic of the spaceship is being handled by its own component that you created, although XNA automatically calls its Update method through the base.Update call of the Game1 class. You'll create meteors following the same principle. The difference is that the player won't move the meteors.

Creating the Meteors

The concepts you used to create a component for the player are the same that you'll use to create the meteors. The only difference is that the meteors' initial position and movement depend on a random factor. The meteors' code follows:

```
#region Using Statements
using System;
using System.Collections.Generic;
using Microsoft.Xna.Framework;
using Microsoft.Xna.Framework.Content;
using Microsoft.Xna.Framework.Graphics;
#endregion
```

```
namespace FirstGame
{
    /// <summary>
    /// This is a game component that implements the rocks the player must avoid.
    /// </summary>
    public class Meteor : Microsoft.Xna.Framework.DrawableGameComponent
    {
        protected Texture2D texture;
        protected Rectangle spriteRectangle;
        protected Vector2 position;
        protected int Yspeed;
        protected int Xspeed;
        protected Random random;

        // Width and height of sprite in texture
        protected const int METEORWIDTH = 45;
        protected const int METEORHEIGHT = 45;

        public Meteor(Game game, ref Texture2D theTexture)
            : base(game)
        {
            texture = theTexture;
            position = new Vector2();

            // Create the source rectangle.
            // This represents where the sprite picture is in the surface
            spriteRectangle = new Rectangle(20, 16, METEORWIDTH, METEORHEIGHT);

            // Initialize the random number generator and put the meteor in
            // its start position
            random = new Random(this.GetHashCode());
            PutinStartPosition();
        }

        /// <summary>
        /// Initialize meteor position and velocity
        /// </summary>
        protected void PutinStartPosition()
        {
            position.X = random.Next(Game.Window.ClientBounds.Width - METEORWIDTH);
            position.Y = 0;
            Yspeed = 1 + random.Next(9);
            Xspeed = random.Next(3) - 1;
        }

        /// <summary>
        /// Allows the game component to draw your content in the game screen
```

```
        /// </summary>
        public override void Draw(GameTime gameTime)
        {
            // Get the current sprite batch
            SpriteBatch sBatch =
                        (SpriteBatch) Game.Services.GetService(typeof(SpriteBatch));

            // Draw the meteor
            sBatch.Draw(texture, position, spriteRectangle, Color.White);

            base.Draw(gameTime);
        }


        /// <summary>
        /// Allows the game component to update itself.
        /// </summary>
        /// <param name="gameTime">Provides a snapshot of timing values.</param>
        public override void Update(GameTime gameTime)
        {
            // Check if the meteor is still visible
            if ((position.Y >= Game.Window.ClientBounds.Height) ||
                (position.X >= Game.Window.ClientBounds.Width) || (position.X <= 0))
            {
                PutinStartPosition();
            }

            // Move meteor
            position.Y += Yspeed;
            position.X += Xspeed;

            base.Update(gameTime);
        }


        /// <summary>
        /// Check if the meteor intersects with the specified rectangle
        /// </summary>
        /// <param name="rect">test rectangle</param>
        /// <returns>true, if has a collision</returns>
        public bool CheckCollision(Rectangle rect)
        {
            Rectangle spriterect = new Rectangle((int)position.X, (int)position.Y,
                        METEORWIDTH, METEORHEIGHT);
            return spriterect.Intersects(rect);
        }
    }
}
```

The PutinStartPosition method puts the meteor in a random horizontal position at the top of the screen, and also obtains the vertical and horizontal displacement speed of the meteor, which each call of the class's Update method refreshes.

A CheckCollision method verifies if the rectangle that delimits the meteor intersects with a rectangle passed as a parameter. This will be the rectangle that delimits the position of the player's spaceship on the screen.

Now let's put the meteors on the screen. Add the following code in the Start method of the Game1 class:

```
// Add the meteors
for (int i = 0; i < STARTMETEORCOUNT; i++)
{
    Components.Add(new Meteor(this, ref meteorTexture));
}
```

The STARTMETEORCOUNT constant defines the initial number of meteors that will appear in the game. Declare it in the Game1 class as follows:

```
private const int STARTMETEORCOUNT = 10;
```

Execute the program by pressing F5. Look at the beauty of the meteor rain. Note that each instance of the Meteor component behaves in an independent way, just as the Ship component does.

Creating the Game Logic

Your game components are nearly ready. Now you need to make them work together; that is, when the player's spaceship collides with a meteor, the game will restart.

So, just as you have a Start method that initializes the game components, create a method called DoGameLogic that executes the game logic itself. Right now, this method only iterates the game component list, to check if a meteor collided with the player's spaceship. If there's a collision, the meteors should be taken out of the game so that they can be re-created in their initial position. This code follows:

```
/// <summary>
/// Run the game logic
/// </summary>
private void DoGameLogic()
{
    // Check collisions
    bool hasCollision = false;
    Rectangle shipRectangle = player.GetBounds();
    foreach (GameComponent gc in Components)
    {
        if (gc is Meteor)
        {
            hasCollision = ((Meteor)gc).CheckCollision(shipRectangle);
            if (hasCollision)
            {
```

```
                // Remove all previous meteors
                RemoveAllMeteors();
                // Let's start again
                Start();

                break;
            }
        }
    }
}
/// <summary>
/// Remove all meteors
/// </summary>
private void RemoveAllMeteors()
{
    for (int i = 0; i < Components.Count; i++)
    {
        if (Components[i] is Meteor)
        {
            Components.RemoveAt(i);
            i--;
        }
    }
}
```

You should call the DoGameLogic method inside the Update method of the Game1 class, immediately before the line that contains the base.Update(gameTime) call. This calls your game logic inside the game loop. Execute the program and see that when the spaceship collides with the meteor, the program puts all the objects in their initial position, and continues this loop until the user leaves the application.

Now let's make the player's life a little harder. In your game, a new meteor will be added after some time has passed. As the meteors behave in an independent way, you just need to add a new Meteor component to the game, and it does all the rest. This is done with the method in the following code. Call this method inside the doGameLoop method, after the foreach loop.

```
/// <summary>
/// Check if it is time for a new rock!
/// </summary>
private void CheckforNewMeteor()
{
    // Add a rock each ADDMETEORTIME
    if ((System.Environment.TickCount - lastTickCount) > ADDMETEORTIME)
    {
        lastTickCount = System.Environment.TickCount;
        Components.Add(new Meteor(this, ref meteorTexture));
        rockCount++;
    }
}
```

The ADDMETEORTIME constant represents the interval, in milliseconds, at which a new meteor should be added. Declare it in the Game1 class as follows:

```
private const int ADDMETEORTIME = 5000;
```

This 5 seconds (or 5,000 milliseconds) setting is a "magic number," and you can change it to alter the game difficulty later.

Two new attributes store the number of meteors added (rockCount) and the time to calculate the desired interval (lastTickCount). Declare them as follows:

```
private const int ADDMETEORTIME = 5000;
private int lastTickCount;
private int rockCount;
```

You should initialize these attributes in the Start method, so add the following code to this method:

```
// Initialize a counter
lastTickCount = System.Environment.TickCount;
// Reset rock count
rockCount = STARTMETEORCOUNT;
```

So, every 5 seconds, a new meteor is added to the game.

Run the game again, and see how long you can play without hitting a rock.

Adding Sounds

As you saw in Chapter 2, it is very simple to add music and sound effects to your games. For Rock Rain, you'll use two WAV files for sound effects and a MP3 file for background music Add the following files to the Content folder:

- Explosion.wav is an explosion sound that plays when the player collides with a meteor.

- Backmusic.mp3 is the game's background music.

- Newmeteor.wav plays when a new meteor is added to the game.

Before you do anything else, declare the audio objects in the Game1 class:

```
// Audio stuff
private SoundEffect explosion;
private SoundEffect newMeteor;
private Song backMusic;
```

Initialize them in the LoadContent method of the Game1 class:

```
// Load audio elements

explosion = Content.Load<SoundEffect>("explosion");
newMeteor = Content.Load<SoundEffect>("newmeteor");
backMusic = Content.Load<Song>("backmusic");
```

```
// Play the background music
MediaPlayer.Play(backMusic);
```

Also, add the following code inside the DoGameLogic method, so that the explosion sound is played before calling the Start method again:

```
explosion.Play();
```

Then add the following code inside CheckforNewMeteor, immediately after the line that contains rockCount++:

```
newMeteor.Play();
```

This plays a sound when a new meteor is added to the game.

Run the game again. You'll see how the sound effects make the game even more entertaining.

Adding a Scoreboard

The Rock Rain scoreboard will show the current number of meteors on the screen. First, you need to create the game source and draw it in the game.

Then add a new SpriteFont. Call it font and add the following code to declare an object for it:

```
private SpriteFont gameFont;
```

Initialize the object in the LoadGraphicsContent method, just as you did with the other contents, inside the if statement, as follows:

```
// Load game font
gameFont = content.Load<SpriteFont>("Content\\font");
```

The scoreboard is a typical GameComponent, but to show that you don't need to create a component for it, you'll draw this scoreboard in the Draw method of the Game1 class. You can draw it immediately after drawing the game sprites. Add the following code in the Draw method of the Game1 class:

```
// Draw score
spriteBatch.Begin();
spriteBatch.DrawString(gameFont, "Rocks: " + rockCount.ToString(),
new Vector2(15, 15), Color.YellowGreen);
spriteBatch.End();
```

Notice that you used a separate spriteBatch object to draw the scoreboard. This way, the steps to draw the background picture, the sprites, and the scoreboard are also separated in the video card, avoiding any possible "confusion" that the card might experience.

■**Caution** Be careful with the use of third-party fonts in your games. Some fonts, such as TrueType and OpenType, are not royalty-free and have legal restrictions regarding their use. This is especially true of fonts used by Windows. You can find many free fonts on web sites across the Internet.

Shake, Baby!

Your game is almost ready. Now let's add one more effect to the game: the vibration. When players collide with a meteor, in addition to the explosion sound, you'll make the Xbox 360 gamepad vibrate to simulate the impact.

As you saw in the previous chapter, you can start and finish the Xbox 360 gamepad vibration through the SetVibration method. You're going to create a nonvisual GameComponent that will help you with this effect.

Add a new GameComponent to the project with the following code:

```
#region Using Statements
using System;
using System.Collections.Generic;
using Microsoft.Xna.Framework;
using Microsoft.Xna.Framework.Input;
#endregion

namespace FirstGame
{
    /// <summary>
    /// This component helps shake your Xbox 360 gamepad
    /// </summary>
    public class SimpleRumblePad : Microsoft.Xna.Framework.GameComponent
    {
        private int time;
        private int lastTickCount;

        public SimpleRumblePad(Game game)
            : base(game)
        {
        }

        /// <summary>
        /// Allows the game component to update itself.
        /// </summary>
        /// <param name="gameTime">Provides a snapshot of timing values.</param>
        public override void Update(GameTime gameTime)
        {
            if (time > 0) {
                int elapsed = System.Environment.TickCount - lastTickCount;
                if (elapsed >= time)
                {
                    time = 0;
                    GamePad.SetVibration(PlayerIndex.One, 0, 0);
                }
            }
            base.Update(gameTime);
        }
    }
```

```
/// <summary>
/// Turn off the rumble
/// </summary>
protected override void Dispose(bool disposing)
{
    GamePad.SetVibration(PlayerIndex.One, 0, 0);

    base.Dispose(disposing);
}

/// <summary>
/// Set the vibration
/// </summary>
/// <param name="Time">Vibration time</param>
/// <param name="LeftMotor">Left Motor Intensity</param>
/// <param name="RightMotor">Right Motor Intensity</param>
public void RumblePad(int Time, float LeftMotor, float RightMotor)
{
    lastTickCount = System.Environment.TickCount;
    time = Time;
    GamePad.SetVibration(PlayerIndex.One, LeftMotor, RightMotor);
}
}
}
```

In this class, the RumblePad method receives the amount of time that the controller should vibrate and the vibration motor's intensity as parameters.

As usual, declare it in the Game1 class, as follows:

```
// Rumble effect
private SimpleRumblePad rumblePad;
```

Initialize it in the Initialize method of the Game1 class:

```
rumblePad = new SimpleRumblePad(this);
Components.Add(rumblePad);
```

Make the controller vibrate immediately after executing the explosion sound, in the DoGameLogic method:

```
// Shake!
rumblePad.RumblePad(500, 1.0f, 1.0f);
```

Congratulations—you've just finished your first game!

An Xbox 360 Version of Rock Rain

You know that XNA technology allows you to create games for the PC as well as the Xbox 360. If you wish to make a console version of Rock Rain, all you need to do is create a copy of this project for Xbox 360. Just right-click the RockRain project in the Solution Explorer window and choose

Create Copy of Project for Xbox 360, as shown in Figure 3-6. Compile the project, and it's ready to go. You immediately have a game that works on the Xbox 360.

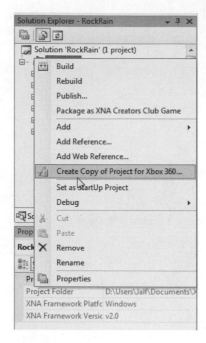

Figure 3-6. *Creating an Xbox 360 version of Rock Rain*

However, not everything is that simple. First, to deploy your game to the Xbox 360, you need an XNA Creators Club subscription, which enables your PC and the correctly registered console to communicate. (Your subscription can be renewed annually or every three months.) Additionally, to deploy the game, your console must be connected to the Xbox LIVE network.

You also need to take into account the difference between TVs (used by the console games) and monitors (used by the PC games). With an ordinary PC monitor, you have access to all areas of the screen. With a TV, you're forced to use what is called the *safe area*, which is the area visible on the TV screen. In other words, not everything that you put on the screen is visible on an ordinary TV. Older TVs can display less of the space outside the safe area than ones made more recently. Flat-panel, plasma, and liquid crystal display (LCD) screens generally can show most of the "unsafe" area.

This leads you to a problem regarding the *margin* of the screen. As the player cannot leave the margin of the screen, knowing exactly where the visible margin of the screen is can be a problem. Normally, the game industry works with a 3 to 5 percent physical margin.

So, in your Ship class, which represents the player's spaceship, add this code in the part where you calculated the size of the screen, in the class constructor:

```
#if XBOX360
      // On the 360, we need to be careful about the TV's "safe" area.
      screenBounds = new Rectangle((int)(Game.Window.ClientBounds.Width * 0.03f),
                            (int)(Game.Window.ClientBounds.Height * 0.03f),
                            Game.Window.ClientBounds.Width -
       (int)(Game.Window.ClientBounds.Width * 0.03f),
       Game.Window.ClientBounds.Height -
        (int)(Game.Window.ClientBounds.Height * 0.03f));
#else
      screenBounds = new Rectangle(0,0,Game.Window.ClientBounds.Width,
                  Game.Window.ClientBounds.Height);
#endif
```

Now, when you want to build the Xbox 360 project, compile the code that creates the rectangle that defines the screen margin with a size 3 percent smaller than the rectangle of a PC project, which takes all the monitor space. It's that simple.

Summary

In this chapter, you learned the basics of creating 2D games, and you went through a small project planning phase, focusing on the items that the game programmer and designer should have in mind before starting to write any code.

You also learned how to model your game using game components and create the game logic itself, modifying and testing the state of these components inside the game's loop. You saw that you can implement simple sprites using GameComponent objects and take advantage of all the classes that XNA already offers.

You also saw how you can add sounds and vibration effects to your game, as well as use a conditional compilation to solve the TV safe area issue of video game consoles.

■ ■ ■

CHAPTER 4

Improving Your First 2D Game

Let's face reality. Rock Rain is cool, fun, but—it's too simple, isn't it? In this chapter, you're going to add some more characteristics of a "real game" to it. We'll show you some more sophisticated techniques you can use to create a better game. Let's go.

Planning Rock Rain's New Version

A striking feature of any game is missing in Rock Rain: the presentation screen! When the player runs the game, he is immediately thrown in the meteor field without warning. The ideal would be to show a screen—the game presentation—leading to another screen with instructions, the game help, and an option to start the game itself. That's much more elegant.

Let's also change some aspects of the playability. Now the game will have animated sprites and an energy meter, and will be able to be played by two players simultaneously. That's more interesting, isn't it?

So, start by creating a new project, as you did in the previous chapter. Name the project `RockRainEnhanced`. Add a new folder called `Core`, and add to this folder the `SimpleRumblePad` component that you created in the version of Rock Rain in the previous chapter. You can download more media content for this game, including new textures and sounds, from this book's details page at the Apress web site (`http://www.apress.com`). Add those files in your project's `Content` folder.

Creating the Game Screens

All modern games have many *screens*: a screen for the opening, a screen for the instructions, a screen for the game itself, and so on. Because each screen shows a lot more than a simple image, in the game industry, it's common to call these screens *scenes*.

A scene is composed (normally) of some background image, background music, and a group of "actors" that "act" in the scene to show to the user some information about the game. For example, Figure 4-1 shows the opening screen of Rock Rain Enhanced.

Figure 4-1. *Opening screen of Rock Rain Enhanced*

In this scene, you have a nice background screen and two words that come up from the screen's margin to form the word "Rock Rain," as well as an options menu for the game, along with background music.

Note that you have some actors here in this scene. Besides the sprites that have moved to form the game's title, you have an animated menu that moves with the Xbox 360 gamepad or keyboard. This group of images, sounds, and actors forms this scene. The user can go to another scene according to the menu options. In this version of Rock Rain, you have three scenes: the *start scene*, the *help scene*, and the *action scene*. Figure 4-2 shows the flow of these game scenes.

Now, using XNA terms, each game scene is a GameComponent that has other GameComponents representing the actors of the scene. Each scene has its own unique qualities, but the scenes also have some things in common. For example, each scene contains its own collection of GameComponents that represents the actors in that scene. Also, in each scene, a method shows it or closes it according to the flow of the scenes that the user chose (when you open the action scene, you'll need to also close the start scene, for example).

You'll also be able to *pause* each scene. This is useful when you want to interrupt a game for a fast trip to the bathroom, for example. You do this by simply *not* executing the Update method of the scene's GameComponents. Remember that XNA calls the Update method to update the status of a GameComponent. If it isn't called, the GameComponent won't be updated, and it will be "stopped" in the game scene.

In this architecture, the only GameComponents that will be added to the list of the game's components are the scenes, because the other GameComponents that build the scene itself will be added to the lists of components of the proper scene.

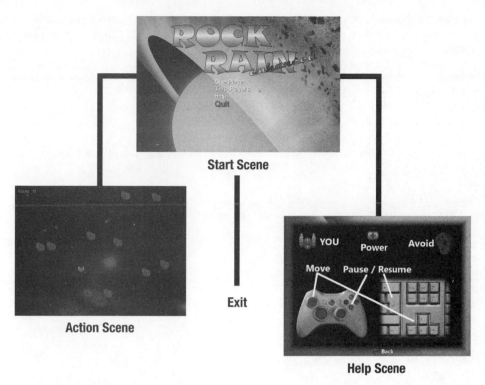

Figure 4-2. *Flow of the game scenes*

You'll initially create the class that implements the common functionality of the scenes, and then add a new GameComponent called GameScene. For project organization purposes, put it inside the Core folder.

Start with the code. First, your scene is a visual component, so derive it from DrawableGameComponent, instead of GameComponent. Next, as mentioned, each scene contains your own list of actors, meaning that it has your own list of GameComponents. Start declaring it in the class as follows:

```
/// <summary>
/// List of child GameComponents
/// </summary>
private readonly List<GameComponent> components;
```

Also add a property to expose the Components list, to be able to add to new actors to the scene from the derived classes:

```
/// <summary>
/// Components of game scene
/// </summary>
public List<GameComponent> Components
{
    get { return components; }
}
```

In the constructor of this class, you'll initialize this list and set that the component will not be visible or will have its status updated initially, using the attributes `Visible` and `Enabled` of the `DrawableGameComponent` class:

```
/// <summary>
/// Default constructor
/// </summary>
public GameScene(Game game) : base(game){
    components = new List<GameComponent>();
    Visible = false;
    Enabled = false;
}
```

Then, to show or hide the scene, change the values of these attributes. You create two methods for this:

```
/// <summary>
/// Show the scene
/// </summary>
public virtual void Show()
{
    Visible = true;
    Enabled = true;
}
/// <summary>
/// Hide the scene
/// </summary>
public virtual void Hide()
{
    Visible = false;
    Enabled = false;
}
```

Now you need to handle the actors of the scene correctly. For each call to the `Update` method of the scene, you must call the respective method for each actor in the scene, to update your status. If the object of the scene is disabled (`Enabled = false`), then XNA won't call the `Update` method, and none of the actors of the scene will be updated either, because its respective `Update` methods won't have executed:

```
/// <summary>
/// Allows the GameComponent to update itself
/// </summary>
/// <param name="gameTime">Provides a snapshot of timing values</param>
public override void Update(GameTime gameTime)
{
    // Update the child GameComponents (if Enabled)
    for (int i = 0; i < components.Count; i++)
    {
```

```
        if (components[i].Enabled)
        {
            components[i].Update(gameTime);
        }
    }
    base.Update(gameTime);
}
```

The drawing code for the actors is similar. For each Draw method executed in the scene, call the Draw method for each DrawableGameComponent that is inserted in the list of components of the scene:

```
/// <summary>
/// Allows the GameComponent to draw your content in the game screen
/// </summary>
public override void Draw(GameTime gameTime)
{
    // Draw the child GameComponents (if drawable)
    for (int i = 0; i < components.Count; i++)
    {
        GameComponent gc = components[i];
        if ((gc is DrawableGameComponent) &&
            ((DrawableGameComponent) gc).Visible)
        {
            ((DrawableGameComponent) gc).Draw(gameTime);
        }
    }
    base.Draw(gameTime);
}
```

In short, all that this GameComponent does is correctly manipulate calling the Draw and Update methods of the game class, drawing and updating the other GameComponents that compose a scene. Also, note that the Show and Hide methods show and hide a game scene, avoiding the execution of the Draw and Update methods using the Visible and Enabled properties. Simple, isn't it?

Let's create three GameComponents derived from this class: one for the start scene of the game, another for the help scene, and another for the action scene itself. The game class will show the correct scene according to the game state. That is, you start in the opening scene, and then players can go to the action scene, and return to the opening after losing all their lives. Alternatively, players can choose to go to the help scene from the start scene, and so on, until they choose the option to leave the start scene.

So, add three GameComponents called StartScene, HelpScene, and ActionScene, respectively. As you start with the help scene, declare it in the Game1 class of your game, as follows:

```
// Game scenes
protected HelpScene helpScene;
// Active game scene
protected GameScene activeScene;
```

Note that these three GameComponents will be derived from the GameScene class, seen before. However, you don't need to change them now—you'll go back to each of them shortly. The activeScene attribute contains the active scene in the game.

Creating the Help Screen

Let's start with the most simple scene in this game. In this scene, you'll show the game instructions, and the user will be able to click the A button on the Xbox 360 gamepad or the Enter key on the keyboard to go back to the initial scene.

This scene contains only the instructions for how to play the game, and you can create it just by showing a simple image with the game instructions. However, as the scene is composed of GameComponents, first you need one GameComponent to draw images.

Add a new GameComponent to the Core folder and name it ImageComponent.cs. Again, this component is a visual component, so derive it from DrawableGameComponent instead of GameComponent.

This GameComponent is able to draw a texture on the screen in centered mode or stretched mode, to fit the image on the screen. Add the following enumeration, which the constructor will use to inform the component that the image must be drawn:

```
public enum DrawMode
{
    Center = 1,
    Stretch,
};
```

You already know that you need a Texture2D object, a Rectangle object, and a SpriteBatch object to draw an image, along with the proper attribute that describes how the image will be drawn in this case. Declare these objects in the class:

```
// Texture to draw
protected readonly Texture2D texture;
// Draw mode
protected readonly DrawMode drawMode;
// SpriteBatch
protected SpriteBatch spriteBatch = null;
// Image Rectangle
protected Rectangle imageRect;
```

In the class constructor, calculate the destination rectangle of the image on the screen, which depends on how the image will be drawn, in the DrawMode enumeration value:

```
/// <summary>
/// Default constructor
/// </summary>
/// <param name="game">The game object</param>
/// <param name="texture">Texture to draw</param>
/// <param name="drawMode">Draw mode</param>
public ImageComponent(Game game, Texture2D texture, DrawMode drawMode)
    : base(game)
```

```
{
    this.texture = texture;
    this.drawMode = drawMode;
    // Get the current sprite batch
    spriteBatch = (SpriteBatch)
        Game.Services.GetService(typeof (SpriteBatch));

    // Create a rectangle with the size and position of the image
    switch (drawMode)
    {
        case DrawMode.Center:
        imageRect = new Rectangle((Game.Window.ClientBounds.Width -
            texture.Width)/2,(Game.Window.ClientBounds.Height -
            texture.Height)/2,texture.Width, texture.Height);
        break;
        case DrawMode.Stretch:
            imageRect = new Rectangle(0, 0, Game.Window.ClientBounds.Width,
                Game.Window.ClientBounds.Height);
        break;
    }
}
```

In the Draw method, you just use the SpriteBatch object to draw the image:

```
/// <summary>
/// Allows the GameComponent to draw itself
/// </summary>
/// <param name="gameTime">Provides a snapshot of timing values</param>
public override void Draw(GameTime gameTime)
{
    spriteBatch.Draw(texture, imageRect, Color.White);
    base.Draw(gameTime);
}
```

Putting an image in a scene might not be as simple as you thought it would be. If this image is shown on a TV or on an ordinary monitor with a 4:3 aspect ratio, it will be displayed correctly. However, if it is drawn on a widescreen monitor or regular TV, it can be distorted and look weird on the screen.

So, you can create two images: one for the 4:3 monitors and TVs, and another for widescreen. You can choose the image to be drawn according to the screen type, although you'll always need to create two versions of each image that you want to show. Another often used alternative is to draw *two* overlapping images. One image is in the background, distorted to take up the whole screen (both 4:3 and widescreen), and another is drawn centered on top, so it looks okay on either type of monitor. In your game, you'll use the textures in Figure 4-3.

Also note the treatment that was given to the input processing. You always compare the device's previous state with its current state to check if a user in fact pressed a button or key in the current scene.

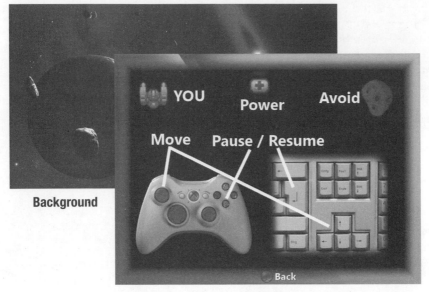

Figure 4-3. *Images that are part of the help scene*

That way, your help scene has only two GameComponents that draw images: one to draw the background image and another to draw the foreground image with the instructions. Add a new class called HelpScene and add the code from Listing 4-1.

Listing 4-1. *Help Scene GameComponent*

```
#region Using Statements

using Microsoft.Xna.Framework;
using Microsoft.Xna.Framework.Graphics;
using RockRainEnhanced.Core;

#endregion

namespace RockRainEnhanced
{
    /// <summary>
    /// This is a GameComponent that represents the help scene
    /// </summary>
```

```
public class HelpScene : GameScene
{
    public HelpScene(Game game, Texture2D textureBack, Texture2D textureFront)
        : base(game)
    {
        Components.Add(new ImageComponent(game, textureBack,
            ImageComponent.DrawMode.Stretch));
        Components.Add(new ImageComponent(game, textureFront,
            ImageComponent.DrawMode.Center));
    }
}
}
```

Also add the following code in the Game1 class and change the LoadContent method to see this component in action. You just load the associated content, create an instance of HelpScene, and execute the Show method of the HelpScene object:

```
// Textures
protected Texture2D helpBackgroundTexture, helpForegroundTexture;

/// <summary>
/// LoadContent will be called once per game and is the place to load
/// all your content
/// </summary>
protected override void LoadContent()
{
    // Create a new SpriteBatch, which can be used to draw textures
    spriteBatch = new SpriteBatch(graphics.GraphicsDevice);
    Services.AddService(typeof (SpriteBatch), spriteBatch);

    // Create the Credits / Instruction scene
    helpBackgroundTexture = Content.Load<Texture2D>("helpbackground");
    helpForegroundTexture = Content.Load<Texture2D>("helpForeground");
    helpScene = new HelpScene(this, helpBackgroundTexture,
            helpForegroundTexture);
    Components.Add(helpScene);
    helpScene.Show();
    activeScene = helpScene;
}
```

Execute the code. The result appears in Figure 4-4. See how the scene is adequately shown both in normal format (4:3) and in widescreen (16:9).

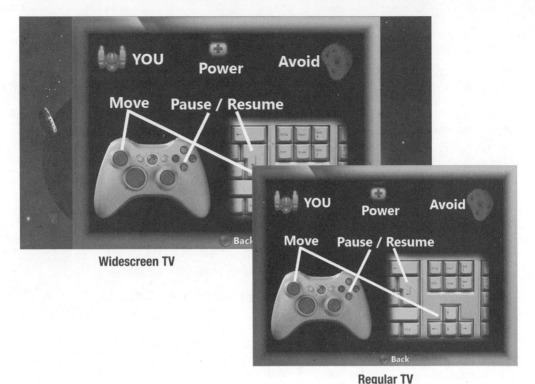

Figure 4-4. *Help scene in normal and widescreen format*

Creating the Opening Screen

The opening screen of a game always gives a "taste" of the game itself. Normally it's something striking, which must show some of the game features and give the user a navigation menu between the game itself, options, help, and so on.

For Rock Rain, you'll create a scene with the game name in large letters coming from the screen borders and an option menu right beneath (1980s arcade style), with a background with some meteor theme. You'll use the textures in Figure 4-5 to do this.

Then you'll have four actors in the opening screen. One is named "Rock," which comes into the scene from the left and goes to the center. The second one is named "Rain," and comes from the right also to the center of the screen. The third is named "enhanced," which keeps blinking right below the word "Rain."

The fourth actor shows after the preceding three, and is a menu with the game options. Because it's a little more sophisticated than just a sprite animation, you'll first create a GameComponent to handle menus.

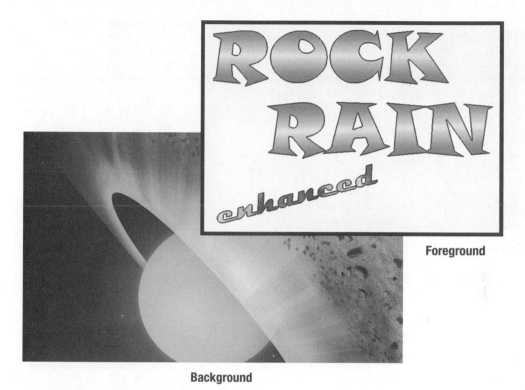

Foreground

Background

Figure 4-5. *Textures of the opening screen*

Creating an Audio Library Class

Your game is now composed of several scenes, and various sound effects will be used by these scenes. It's good practice to create a class to load and maintain a bank of audio content to facilitate the access to your music and sound effects in scenes. Create this class, and then add a new class to call audiolibrary and declare new objects with sound effects and game music to this class:

```
private SoundEffect explosion;
private SoundEffect newMeteor;
private SoundEffect menuBack;
private SoundEffect menuSelect;
private SoundEffect menuScroll;
private SoundEffect powerGet;
private SoundEffect powerShow;
private Song backMusic;
private Song startMusic;
```

You need access to these objects through properties, of course. Declare the properties as follows:

```
public SoundEffect Explosion
{
    get { return explosion; }
}
public SoundEffect NewMeteor
{
    get { return newMeteor; }
}
public SoundEffect MenuBack
{
    get { return menuBack; }
}
public SoundEffect MenuSelect
{
    get { return menuSelect; }
}
public SoundEffect MenuScroll
{
    get { return menuScroll; }
}
public SoundEffect PowerGet
{
    get { return powerGet; }
}
public SoundEffect PowerShow
{
    get { return powerShow; }
}
public Song BackMusic
{
    get { return backMusic; }
}
public Song StartMusic
{
    get { return startMusic; }
}
```

And just to make everything better encapsulated, create a method to load all this content within this class:

```
public void LoadContent(ContentManager Content)
{
    explosion = Content.Load<SoundEffect>("explosion");
    newMeteor = Content.Load<SoundEffect>("newmeteor");
```

```
    backMusic = Content.Load<Song>("backMusic");
    startMusic = Content.Load<Song>("startMusic");
    menuBack = Content.Load<SoundEffect>("menu_back");
    menuSelect = Content.Load<SoundEffect>("menu_select3");
    menuScroll = Content.Load<SoundEffect>("menu_scroll");
    powerShow = Content.Load<SoundEffect>("powershow");
    powerGet = Content.Load<SoundEffect>("powerget");
}
```

The idea is that all scenes have access to an instance of the class that will contain the entire audio content of your game, as with the instance of SpriteBatch. So let's initialize an instance of this class immediately after initialization of spriteBatch in the LoadContent method in the Game1 class:

```
// Load audio elements
audio = new AudioLibrary();
audio.LoadContent(Content);
Services.AddService(typeof(AudioLibrary), audio);
```

Now you can get the audio instance whenever you need to play some music or sound effects in your scenes, which you'll start to do next.

Creating the Menu Component

Your menu for the game will be simple and functional at the same time. It will be drawn using two different fonts, where the bigger font will highlight the selected item.

Start adding a new GameComponent called TextMenuComponent in the Core folder. Again, this component is a visual component, so derive it from DrawableGameComponent, instead of GameComponent.

In this component, you'll need two fonts to draw the text in normal and selected status, a string list with the items to be drawn, the color of the regular and selected items, the size and position of the menu, and, as always, a SpriteBatch object to draw the text in the screen. Add the following code to the class to declare these objects:

```
// SpriteBatch
protected SpriteBatch spriteBatch = null;
// Fonts
protected readonly SpriteFont regularFont, selectedFont;
// Colors
protected Color regularColor = Color.White, selectedColor = Color.Red;
// Menu position
protected Vector2 position = new Vector2();
// Items
protected int selectedIndex = 0;
private readonly List<string> menuItems;
// Size of menu in pixels
protected int width, height;
```

Also add a set of properties to handle these attributes:

```
/// <summary>
/// Set the menu options
/// </summary>
/// <param name="items"></param>
public void SetMenuItems(string[] items)
{
        menuItems.Clear();
        menuItems.AddRange(items);
        CalculateBounds();
}

/// <summary>
/// Width of menu in pixels
/// </summary>
public int Width
{
        get { return width; }
}
/// <summary>
/// Height of menu in pixels
/// </summary>
public int Height
{
        get { return height; }
}
/// <summary>
/// Selected menu item index
/// </summary>
public int SelectedIndex
{
        get { return selectedIndex; }
        set { selectedIndex = value; }
}
/// <summary>
/// Regular item color
/// </summary>
public Color RegularColor
{
        get { return regularColor; }
        set { regularColor = value; }
}
/// <summary>
/// Selected item color
/// </summary>
```

```
public Color SelectedColor
{
        get { return selectedColor; }
        set { selectedColor = value; }
}
/// <summary>
/// Position of component on screen
/// </summary>
public Vector2 Position
{
        get { return position; }
        set { position = value; }
}
```

Notice the CalculateBounds method in the SetMenuItems method. The items on the menu are drawn centered horizontally. To do this, you need to calculate the width and the height of the menu—values that might vary in accordance with the items that have been added to the component and the font size. The CalculateBounds method does this calculation using the MeasureString method of the SpriteFont class, which gets the string size in pixels using this font.

```
/// <summary>
/// Get the menu bounds
/// </summary>
protected void CalculateBounds()
{
    width = 0;
    height = 0;
    foreach (string item in menuItems)
    {
        Vector2 size = selectedFont.MeasureString(item);
        if (size.X > width)
        {
            width = (int) size.X;
        }
        height += selectedFont.LineSpacing;
    }
}
```

The Draw method that draws these elements is simple, because you need only a loop drawing each item, below each other, using the correct font for the selected and regular entries. Each item is drawn with a little overlapped shadow, created by drawing the same text twice, which gives a better look to the text. The code of this method follows:

```
/// <summary>
/// Allows the GameComponent to draw itself
/// </summary>
/// <param name="gameTime">Provides a snapshot of timing values</param>
```

```
public override void Draw(GameTime gameTime)
{
    float y = position.Y;
    for (int i = 0; i < menuItems.Count; i++)
    {
        SpriteFont font;
        Color theColor;
        if (i == SelectedIndex)
        {
            font = selectedFont;
            theColor = selectedColor;
        }
        else
        {
            font = regularFont;
            theColor = regularColor;
        }

        // Draw the text shadow
        spriteBatch.DrawString(font, menuItems[i],
            new Vector2(position.X + 1, y + 1), Color.Black);
        // Draw the text item
        spriteBatch.DrawString(font, menuItems[i],
            new Vector2(position.X, y), theColor);
        y += font.LineSpacing;
    }

    base.Draw(gameTime);
}
```

In fact, the drawn part of this class is the simplest part. This component must handle the user input as well, using the keyboard (up and down arrows) or the Xbox 360 gamepad. You want some sound effects to notify users when they change or select a menu item. In this case, add some new attributes to this class, to handle sound and user input:

```
// Used to handle input
protected KeyboardState oldKeyboardState;
protected GamePadState oldGamePadState;
// For audio effects
protected AudioLibrary audio;
```

As before, the Update method is the right place to handle the user input. You just check the keyboard and the gamepad state, as you saw in the previous chapters, to change the attribute's selectedIndex value:

```csharp
/// <summary>
/// Allows the GameComponent to update itself
/// </summary>
/// <param name="gameTime">Provides a snapshot of timing values</param>
public override void Update(GameTime gameTime)
{
    GamePadState gamepadState = GamePad.GetState(PlayerIndex.One);
    KeyboardState keyboardState = Keyboard.GetState();

    bool down, up;
    // Handle the keyboard
    down = (oldKeyboardState.IsKeyDown(Keys.Down) &&
        (keyboardState.IsKeyUp(Keys.Down)));
    up = (oldKeyboardState.IsKeyDown(Keys.Up) &&
        (keyboardState.IsKeyUp(Keys.Up)));
    // Handle the D-pad
    down |= (oldGamePadState.DPad.Down == ButtonState.Pressed) &&
            (gamepadState.DPad.Down == ButtonState.Released);
    up |= (oldGamePadState.DPad.Up == ButtonState.Pressed) &&
        (gamepadState.DPad.Up == ButtonState.Released);

    if (down || up)
    {
        audio.MenuScroll.Play();     }

    if (down)
    {
        selectedIndex++;
        if (selectedIndex == menuItems.Count)
        {
            selectedIndex = 0;
        }
    }
    if (up)
    {
        selectedIndex--;
        if (selectedIndex == -1)
        {
            selectedIndex = menuItems.Count - 1;
        }
    }

    oldKeyboardState = keyboardState;
    oldGamePadState = gamepadState;

    base.Update(gameTime);
}
```

Finally, in the class constructor, you must initialize all these things:

```
/// <summary>
/// Default constructor
/// </summary>
/// <param name="game">Main game object</param>
/// <param name="normalFont">Font for regular items</param>
/// <param name="selectedFont">Font for selected item</param>
public TextMenuComponent(Game game, SpriteFont normalFont,
    SpriteFont selectedFont) : base(game)
{
    regularFont = normalFont;
    this.selectedFont = selectedFont;
    menuItems = new List<string>();

    // Get the current sprite batch
    spriteBatch = (SpriteBatch)
        Game.Services.GetService(typeof (SpriteBatch));

    // // Get the audio library
    // audio = (AudioLibrary)
        Game.Services.GetService(typeof(AudioLibrary));

    // Used for input handling
    oldKeyboardState = Keyboard.GetState();
    oldGamePadState = GamePad.GetState(PlayerIndex.One);
}
```

Adding More to the Opening Screen

As you did with the HelpScene, add a new class called StartScene, derived from GameScene. In this scene, you have an initial animation with two sprites (the "Rock" and "Rain" words), a menu, background music, and another sprite with the word "enhanced" flashing on the screen. Start adding the following attributes to the StartScene class:

```
// Misc
protected TextMenuComponent menu;
protected readonly Texture2D elements;
// Audio
protected AudioLibrary audio;// SpriteBatch
protected SpriteBatch spriteBatch = null;
// GUI stuff
protected Rectangle rockRect = new Rectangle(0, 0, 536, 131);
protected Vector2 rockPosition;
protected Rectangle rainRect = new Rectangle(120, 165, 517, 130);
protected Vector2 rainPosition;
protected Rectangle enhancedRect = new Rectangle(8, 304, 375, 144);
protected Vector2 enhancedPosition;
```

```
protected bool showEnhanced;
protected TimeSpan elapsedTime = TimeSpan.Zero;
```

The attributes rockRect, rainRect, and enhancedRect refer to the rectangle that contains the images for the "Rock," "Rain," and "enhanced" in the texture. The attributes rockPosition, rainPosition, and enhancedPosition contain the position of these items on the screen. Draw these images in your chosen positions, but change the position of the "Rock" and "Rain" sprites to obtain a nice initial animation. When the "Rock" and "Rain" words are in the correct place, you'll flash the "enhanced" word on the screen and show the initial menu.

All this is done in the Update method, as follows. Note the calculations for the Xbox 360 version, to handle the 16:9 screen width.

```
/// <summary>
/// Allows the GameComponent to update itself
/// </summary>
/// <param name="gameTime">Provides a snapshot of timing values</param>
public override void Update(GameTime gameTime)
{
    if (!menu.Visible)
    {
        if (rainPosition.X >= (Game.Window.ClientBounds.Width - 595)/2)
        {
            rainPosition.X -= 15;
        }

        if (rockPosition.X <= (Game.Window.ClientBounds.Width - 715)/2)
        {
            rockPosition.X += 15;
        }
        else
        {
            menu.Visible = true;
            menu.Enabled = true;

            MediaPlayer.Play(audio.StartMusic);#if XBOX360
            enhancedPosition = new Vector2((rainPosition.X +
            rainRect.Width - enhancedRect.Width / 2), rainPosition.Y);
#else
            enhancedPosition =
                new Vector2((rainPosition.X + rainRect.Width -
                enhancedRect.Width/2) - 80, rainPosition.Y);
#endif
            showEnhanced = true;
        }
    }
    else
    {
        elapsedTime += gameTime.ElapsedGameTime;
```

```
        if (elapsedTime > TimeSpan.FromSeconds(1))
        {
            elapsedTime -= TimeSpan.FromSeconds(1);
            showEnhanced = !showEnhanced;
        }
    }

    base.Update(gameTime);
}
```

The Draw method draws the sprites in your actual position and draws the "enhanced" sprite if the "Rock" and "Rain" sprites are in their final position (controlled by the showEnhanced attribute):

```
/// <summary>
/// Allows the GameComponent to draw itself
/// </summary>
/// <param name="gameTime">Provides a snapshot of timing values</param>
public override void Draw(GameTime gameTime)
{
    base.Draw(gameTime);

    spriteBatch.Draw(elements, rockPosition, rockRect, Color.White);
    spriteBatch.Draw(elements, rainPosition, rainRect, Color.White);
    if (showEnhanced)
    {
        spriteBatch.Draw(elements, enhancedPosition, enhancedRect,
                        Color.White);
    }
}
```

You need to do some more work here. The Show method must put these sprites in their initial position and start the audio effects. The Hide method must stop the background music; otherwise, this music will play in another scene, won't it? The code for these methods follows:

```
/// <summary>
/// Show the start scene
/// </summary>
public override void Show()
{
    audio.NewMeteor.Play();
    rockPosition.X = -1*rockRect.Width;
    rockPosition.Y = 40;
    rainPosition.X = Game.Window.ClientBounds.Width;
    rainPosition.Y = 180;
    // Put the menu centered in screen
    menu.Position = new Vector2((Game.Window.ClientBounds.Width -
                                menu.Width)/2, 330);
```

```csharp
    // These elements will be visible when the "Rock Rain" title
    // is done
    menu.Visible = false;
    menu.Enabled = false;
    showEnhanced = false;

    base.Show();
}

/// <summary>
/// Hide the start scene
/// </summary>
public override void Hide()
{
    MediaPlayer.Stop();    base.Hide();
}
```

In the constructor, you must initialize everything, including the Menu component with the game options:

```csharp
/// <summary>
/// Default Constructor
/// </summary>
/// <param name="game">Main game object</param>
/// <param name="smallFont">Font for the menu items</param>
/// <param name="largeFont">Font for the menu selected item</param>
/// <param name="background">Texture for background image</param>
/// <param name="elements">Texture with the foreground elements</param>
public StartScene(Game game, SpriteFont smallFont, SpriteFont largeFont,
                  Texture2D background,Texture2D elements)
    : base(game)
{

    this.elements = elements;
    Components.Add(new ImageComponent(game, background,
                                     ImageComponent.DrawMode.Center));

    // Create the menu
    string[] items = {"One Player", "Two Players", "Help", "Quit"};
    menu = new TextMenuComponent(game, smallFont, largeFont);
    menu.SetMenuItems(items);
    Components.Add(menu);

    // Get the current sprite batch
    spriteBatch = (SpriteBatch) Game.Services.GetService(
                                    typeof (SpriteBatch));
    // Get the audio library
    audio = (AudioLibrary)
                            Game.Services.GetService(typeof(AudioLibrary));}
```

Now modify the code of the LoadContent method in the Game1 class to load the content needed in this scene:

```
/// <summary>
/// LoadContent will be called once per game and is the place to load
/// all your content
/// </summary>
protected override void LoadContent()
{
    // Create a new SpriteBatch, which can be used to draw textures
    spriteBatch = new SpriteBatch(graphics.GraphicsDevice);
    Services.AddService(typeof (SpriteBatch), spriteBatch);
    // Create the Credits / Instruction scene
    helpBackgroundTexture = Content.Load<Texture2D>("helpbackground");
    helpForegroundTexture = Content.Load<Texture2D>("helpForeground");
    helpScene = new HelpScene(this, helpBackgroundTexture,
            helpForegroundTexture);
    Components.Add(helpScene);

    // Create the start scene
    smallFont = Content.Load<SpriteFont>("menuSmall");
    largeFont = Content.Load<SpriteFont>("menuLarge");
    startBackgroundTexture = Content.Load<Texture2D>("startbackground");
    startElementsTexture = Content.Load<Texture2D>("startSceneElements");
    startScene = new StartScene(this, smallFont$, largeFont,
        startBackgroundTexture, startElementsTexture);
    Components.Add(startScene);

    startScene.Show();
    activeScene = startScene;
    }
}
```

Declare these objects in the Game1 class to see the scene in action:

```
protected StartScene startScene;
protected Texture2D startBackgroundTexture, startElementsTexture;
// Fonts
private SpriteFont smallFont, largeFont
```

Execute the program, and you should see something similar to Figure 4-1.

Creating the Action Scene

Up to now, you've created only the opening and help scenes of the game. The most important scene is still missing: the game scene itself! This scene will look like the first version of Rock Rain, with the addition of some game rule changes and two-player support. Still, there is an interesting change: the use of animated sprites.

Creating a Game Component to Animate Sprites

As seen in Chapter 2, animated sprites are a basic resource in any 2D game. They allow you to have actors in the scene that are more than a single moving image, giving the illusion of animation, just as in TV cartoons. In Rock Rain's case, you're using animated sprites to animate your meteors, which now spin while they move on the screen. So, create a class called Sprite and use the code in Listing 4-2 for this GameComponent. This code is just an improved version of the code shown in Chapter 2. Put it inside the project's Core folder.

Listing 4-2. *The Sprite GameComponent*

```
#region Using Statements

using System;
using System.Collections.Generic;
using Microsoft.Xna.Framework;
using Microsoft.Xna.Framework.Graphics;

#endregion

namespace RockRainEnhanced.Core
{
    /// <summary>
    /// This is a GameComponent that implements an animated sprite
    /// </summary>
    public class Sprite : DrawableGameComponent
    {
        private int activeFrame;
        private readonly Texture2D texture;
        private List<Rectangle> frames;

        protected Vector2 position;
        protected TimeSpan elapsedTime = TimeSpan.Zero;
        protected Rectangle currentFrame;
        protected long frameDelay;
        protected SpriteBatch sbBatch;

        /// <summary>
        /// Default constructor
        /// </summary>
        /// <param name="game">The game object</param>
        /// <param name="theTexture">Texture that contains the sprite frames</param>
        public Sprite(Game game, ref Texture2D theTexture)
            : base(game)
        {
            texture = theTexture;
            activeFrame = 0;
        }
```

```csharp
/// <summary>
/// List with the frames of the animation
/// </summary>
public List<Rectangle> Frames
{
    get { return frames; }
    set { frames = value; }
}


/// <summary>
/// Allows the GameComponent to perform any initialization it needs to
/// before starting to run.  This is where it can query for any required
/// services and load content.
/// </summary>
public override void Initialize()
{
    // Get the current sprite batch
    sbBatch = (SpriteBatch) Game.Services.GetService(typeof (SpriteBatch));

    base.Initialize();
}


/// <summary>
/// Allows the GameComponent to update itself
/// </summary>
/// <param name="gameTime">Provides a snapshot of timing values</param>
public override void Update(GameTime gameTime)
{
    elapsedTime += gameTime.ElapsedGameTime;

    // It's time for a next frame?
    if (elapsedTime > TimeSpan.FromMilliseconds(frameDelay))
    {
        elapsedTime -= TimeSpan.FromMilliseconds(frameDelay);
        activeFrame++;
        if (activeFrame == frames.Count)
        {
            activeFrame = 0;
        }
        // Get the current frame
        currentFrame = frames[activeFrame];
    }
```

```
            base.Update(gameTime);
        }

        /// <summary>
        /// Draw the sprite.
        /// </summary>
        /// <param name="gameTime">Provides a snapshot of timing values</param>
        public override void Draw(GameTime gameTime)
        {
            sbBatch.Draw(texture, position, currentFrame, Color.White);

            base.Draw(gameTime);
        }
    }
}
```

The Update method changes the current frame each *n* milliseconds to create the animation illusion, and the Draw method draws the current frame in the current position on the screen. Now you'll use this class to create an animated sprite of the meteors. Create a class called Meteor and use the code in Listing 4-3.

Listing 4-3. *The Meteor GameComponent*

```
using System;
using System.Collections.Generic;
using Microsoft.Xna.Framework;
using Microsoft.Xna.Framework.Graphics;
using RockRainEnhanced.Core;

namespace RockRainEnhanced
{
    /// <summary>
    /// This class is the animated sprite for a meteor
    /// </summary>
    public class Meteor : Sprite
    {
        // Vertical velocity
        protected int Yspeed;
        // Horizontal velocity
        protected int Xspeed;
        protected Random random;

        // Unique ID for this meteor
        private int index;
```

```csharp
public Meteor(Game game, ref Texture2D theTexture) :
    base(game, ref theTexture)
{
    Frames = new List<Rectangle>();
    Rectangle frame = new Rectangle();
    frame.X = 468;
    frame.Y = 0;
    frame.Width = 49;
    frame.Height = 44;
    Frames.Add(frame);

    frame.Y = 50;
    Frames.Add(frame);

    frame.Y = 98;
    frame.Height = 45;
    Frames.Add(frame);

    frame.Y = 146;
    frame.Height = 49;
    Frames.Add(frame);

    frame.Y = 200;
    frame.Height = 44;
    Frames.Add(frame);

    frame.Y = 250;
    Frames.Add(frame);

    frame.Y = 299;
    Frames.Add(frame);

    frame.Y = 350;
    frame.Height = 49;
    Frames.Add(frame);

    // Initialize the random number generator and put the meteor in your
    // start position
    random = new Random(GetHashCode());
    PutinStartPosition();
}

/// <summary>
/// Initialize meteor position and velocity
/// </summary>
```

```
public void PutinStartPosition()
{
    position.X = random.Next(Game.Window.ClientBounds.Width -
        currentFrame.Width);
    position.Y = 0;
    YSpeed = 1 + random.Next(9);
    XSpeed = random.Next(3) - 1;
}

/// <summary>
/// Update the meteor position
/// </summary>
public override void Update(GameTime gameTime)
{
    // Check if the meteor is still visible
    if ((position.Y >= Game.Window.ClientBounds.Height) ||
        (position.X >= Game.Window.ClientBounds.Width) ||
        (position.X <= 0))
    {
        PutinStartPosition();
    }

    // Move meteor
    position.Y += Yspeed;
    position.X += Xspeed;

    base.Update(gameTime);
}

/// Vertical velocity
/// </summary>
public int YSpeed
{
    get { return Yspeed; }
    set
    {
        Yspeed = value;
        frameDelay = 200 - (Yspeed * 5);
    }
}

/// <summary>
/// Horizontal velocity
/// </summary>
```

```
        public int XSpeed
        {
            get { return Xspeed; }
            set { Xspeed = value; }
        }

        /// <summary>
        /// Meteor identifier
        /// </summary>
        public int Index
        {
            get { return index; }
            set { index = value; }
        }

        /// <summary>
        /// Check if the meteor intersects with the specified rectangle
        /// </summary>
        /// <param name="rect">test rectangle</param>
        /// <returns>true, if has a collision</returns>
        public bool CheckCollision(Rectangle rect)
        {
            Rectangle spriterect =new Rectangle((int) position.X, (int) position.Y,
                currentFrame.Width, currentFrame.Height);
            return spriterect.Intersects(rect);
        }
    }
}
```

This class is similar to the first version in the previous chapter, but the code that adds the animation frames is in the constructor. All the rest follows the same previous logic. The meteors will "fall," but now with an animation where they appear to spin. Cool, isn't it?

You also added a property Index to get a unique identifier for each meteor in the game, to be able to get a specified meteor when needed (you'll use this feature in the next version of Rock Rain).

Let's create one more GameComponent to centralize all the meteor treatment. This class will be responsible for drawing and updating all the game's meteors, as well as doing the collision test and adding new meteors as time goes by. The advantage of having an object to manage other objects is that the game design becomes simpler, and, at the same time, more efficient. For example, you don't need to pass through all the GameComponents to do a collision test, as in the version in the previous chapter. Now you pass through just the GameComponents that are under control of this manager, which controls only the meteors. This way, you gain a little performance benefit.

Add a class called MeteorsManager and add the code in Listing 4-4.

Listing 4-4. *The MeteorsManager GameComponent*

```
#region Using Statements

using System;
using System.Collections.Generic;
using Microsoft.Xna.Framework;
using Microsoft.Xna.Framework.Graphics;
using RockRainEnhanced.Core;

#endregion

namespace RockRainEnhanced
{
    /// <summary>
    /// This GameComponent implements a manager for all meteors in the game
    /// </summary>
    public class MeteorsManager : DrawableGameComponent
    {
        // List of active meteors
        protected List<Meteor> meteors;
        // Constant for initial meteor count
        private const int STARTMETEORCOUNT = 10;
        // Time for a new meteor
        private const int ADDMETEORTIME = 5000;

        protected Texture2D meteorTexture;
        protected TimeSpan elapsedTime = TimeSpan.Zero;
        protected AudioLibrary audio;

        public MeteorsManager(Game game, ref Texture2D theTexture)
            : base(game)
        {
            meteorTexture = theTexture;
            meteors = new List<Meteor>();
        }

        /// <summary>
        /// Allows the GameComponent to perform any initialization it needs to
        /// before starting to run.  This is where it can query for any required
        /// services and load content.
        /// </summary>
        public override void Initialize()
        {
            // Get the audio library
            audio = (AudioLibrary)
                    Game.Services.GetService(typeof(AudioLibrary));
            meteors.Clear();
```

```csharp
    Start();

    for (int i = 0; i < meteors.Count; i++)
    {
        meteors[i].Initialize();
    }

    base.Initialize();
}

/// <summary>
/// Start the meteor rain
/// </summary>
public void Start()
{
    // Initialize a counter
    elapsedTime = TimeSpan.Zero;

    // Add the meteors
    for (int i = 0; i < STARTMETEORCOUNT; i++)
    {
        AddNewMeteor();
    }
}

/// <summary>
/// All meteors in the game
/// </summary>
public List<Meteor> AllMeteors
{
    get { return meteors; }
}

/// <summary>
/// Check if it is time for a new meteor
/// </summary>
private void CheckforNewMeteor(GameTime gameTime)
{
    // Add a rock each ADDMETEORTIME
    elapsedTime += gameTime.ElapsedGameTime;

    if (elapsedTime > TimeSpan.FromMilliseconds(ADDMETEORTIME))
    {
        elapsedTime -= TimeSpan.FromMilliseconds(ADDMETEORTIME);
```

```csharp
            AddNewMeteor();
            // Play a sound for a new meteor
            audio.NewMeteor.Play();                }
}

/// <summary>
/// Add a new meteor in the scene
/// </summary>
private void AddNewMeteor()
{
    Meteor newMeteor = new Meteor(Game, ref meteorTexture);
    newMeteor.Initialize();
    meteors.Add(newMeteor);
    // Set the meteor identifier
    newMeteor.Index = meteors.Count - 1;

}

/// <summary>
/// Allows the GameComponent to update itself
/// </summary>
/// <param name="gameTime">Provides a snapshot of timing values</param>
public override void Update(GameTime gameTime)
{
    CheckforNewMeteor(gameTime);

    // Update meteors
    for (int i = 0; i < meteors.Count; i++)
    {
        meteors[i].Update(gameTime);
    }

    base.Update(gameTime);
}

/// <summary>
/// Check if the ship collided with a meteor
/// <returns>true, if has a collision</returns>
/// </summary>
public bool CheckForCollisions(Rectangle rect)
{
    for (int i = 0; i < meteors.Count; i++)
    {
        if (meteors[i].CheckCollision(rect))
        {
            // BOOM!!
            audio.Explosion.Play();
```

```
                        // Put the meteor back to your initial position
                         meteors[i].PutinStartPosition();

                         return true;
                    }
                }
            return false;
        }


        /// <summary>
        /// Allows the GameComponent to draw your content in the game screen
        /// </summary>
        public override void Draw(GameTime gameTime)
        {
            // Draw the meteors
            for (int i = 0; i < meteors.Count; i++)
            {
                meteors[i].Draw(gameTime);
            }

            base.Draw(gameTime);
        }
    }
}
```

Observe that this class contains a great deal of the code that was previously inside the Game1 class in the previous chapter, but essentially it does the same thing. You'll use this class later to compose the action scene.

■**Note** Overall, it's a good idea to create a management class for each group of GameComponents in a game. It's normal to see classes such as EnemyManager, WizardManager, and so on, because this puts all the complexity of this type of game element in only one class. This simplifies the code and maximizes the reuse of these components in other games.

Adding the Scoreboard

Another element you need to create for the action scene is the scoreboard. This scoreboard shows the quantity of points and energy of the player's ship. This class is simple: it only draws two lincs of text on the screen. Add a class to the project called Score, and add the code in Listing 4-5.

Listing 4-5. *The Score GameComponent*

```
#region Using Statements

using Microsoft.Xna.Framework;
using Microsoft.Xna.Framework.Graphics;

#endregion

namespace RockRainEnhanced
{
    /// <summary>
    /// This is a GameComponent that implements the game score
    /// </summary>
    public class Score : DrawableGameComponent
    {
        // SpriteBatch
        protected SpriteBatch spriteBatch = null;

        // Score position
        protected Vector2 position = new Vector2();

        // Values
        protected int value;
        protected int power;

        protected readonly SpriteFont font;
        protected readonly Color fontColor;

        public Score(Game game, SpriteFont font, Color fontColor)
            : base(game)
        {
            this.font = font;
            this.fontColor = fontColor;
            // Get the current sprite batch
            spriteBatch = (SpriteBatch)
                        Game.Services.GetService(typeof (SpriteBatch));
        }

        /// <summary>
        /// Points value
        /// </summary>
```

```csharp
public int Value
{
    get { return value; }
    set { this.value = value; }
}

/// <summary>
/// Power value
/// </summary>
public int Power
{
    get { return power; }
    set { power = value; }
}

/// <summary>
/// Position of component on screen
/// </summary>
public Vector2 Position
{
    get { return position; }
    set { position = value; }
}

/// <summary>
/// Allows the GameComponent to draw itself
/// </summary>
/// <param name="gameTime">Provides a snapshot of timing values</param>
public override void Draw(GameTime gameTime)
{
    string TextToDraw = string.Format("Score: {0}", value);

    // Draw the text shadow
    spriteBatch.DrawString(font, TextToDraw, new Vector2(position.X + 1,
                        position.Y + 1), Color.Black);
    // Draw the text item
    spriteBatch.DrawString(font, TextToDraw,
                        new Vector2(position.X, position.Y),
                        fontColor);

    float height = font.MeasureString(TextToDraw).Y;
    TextToDraw = string.Format("Power: {0}", power);
    // Draw the text shadow
    spriteBatch.DrawString(font, TextToDraw,
        new Vector2(position.X + 1, position.Y + 1 + height),
        Color.Black);
```

```
            // Draw the text item
            spriteBatch.DrawString(font, TextToDraw,
                new Vector2(position.X, position.Y + 1 + height),
                fontColor);

            base.Draw(gameTime);
        }
    }
}
```

Again, this looks like the code in the previous version, only this time it is encapsulated in a class. Also, the text is now drawn with a little shadow under it, to enhance the legibility and give it a touch of style, as you did with the Menu component.

Creating the Energy Source

The change in Rock Rain's playability brings up the need for an interesting additional component. The player's ship now contains a finite energy source, which decreases over time and falls even more after a meteor collision. You must provide a means for players to recharge their ships, so they can stay in the game longer, accumulating more points.

You'll create a new GameComponent, which looks like a small barrel of energy that shows up at regular intervals and "falls" together with the meteors. If the player touches this power source game component, it will refuel the ship with more energy. The idea is that the player keeps an eye out for this new element and tries to obtain it without hitting any incoming meteors.

Add a new class called PowerSource and add the code in Listing 4-6.

Listing 4-6. *The PowerSource GameComponent*

```
#region Using Statements

using System;
using System.Collections.Generic;
using Microsoft.Xna.Framework;
using Microsoft.Xna.Framework.Graphics;
using RockRainEnhanced.Core;

#endregion

namespace RockRainEnhanced
{
    /// <summary>
    /// This is a GameComponent that implements the power source element
    /// </summary>
    public class PowerSource : Sprite
    {
        protected Texture2D texture;
        protected Random random;
```

```
public PowerSource(Game game, ref Texture2D theTexture)
    : base(game, ref theTexture)
{
    texture = theTexture;

    Frames = new List<Rectangle>();
    Rectangle frame = new Rectangle();
    frame.X = 291;
    frame.Y = 17;
    frame.Width = 14;
    frame.Height = 12;
    Frames.Add(frame);

    frame.Y = 30;
    Frames.Add(frame);

    frame.Y = 43;
    Frames.Add(frame);

    frame.Y = 57;
    Frames.Add(frame);

    frame.Y = 70;
    Frames.Add(frame);

    frame.Y = 82;
    Frames.Add(frame);

    frameDelay = 200;

    // Initialize the random number generator and put the power
    // source in your start position
    random = new Random(GetHashCode());
    PutinStartPosition();
}

/// <summary>
/// Initialize position and velocity
/// </summary>
public void PutinStartPosition()
{
    position.X = random.Next(Game.Window.ClientBounds.Width -
        currentFrame.Width);
    position.Y = -10;
    Enabled = false;
}
```

```csharp
public override void Update(GameTime gameTime)
{
    // Check if the power source is still visible
    if (position.Y >= Game.Window.ClientBounds.Height)
    {
        position.Y = 0;
        Enabled = false;
    }

    // Move
    position.Y += 1;

    base.Update(gameTime);
}

/// <summary>
/// Check if the object intersects with the specified rectangle
/// </summary>
/// <param name="rect">test rectangle</param>
/// <returns>true, if has a collision</returns>
public bool CheckCollision(Rectangle rect)
{
    Rectangle spriterect =
        new Rectangle((int) position.X, (int) position.Y,
        currentFrame.Width, currentFrame.Height);
    return spriterect.Intersects(rect);
}
    }
}
```

You did a similar thing with the Meteor class, creating an animation with the list of frames and updating its vertical position as time goes by, to give the "falling" effect.

Creating the Player's Game Component

You're almost finished creating the components for the action scene, but the main actor is still missing: the player! In this new version, the code for the player's GameComponent is mostly the same as in the previous chapter, but with the addition of multiplayer support. This support differs from the previous version mainly in the treatment of energy, keyboard, points, and the way the player is drawn. The code of the Player class is in Listing 4-7.

Listing 4-7. *The Player GameComponent*

```csharp
#region Using Statements

using System;
using Microsoft.Xna.Framework;
using Microsoft.Xna.Framework.Graphics;
using Microsoft.Xna.Framework.Input;
```

```csharp
#endregion

namespace RockRainEnhanced
{
    /// <summary>
    /// This is a GameComponent that implements the player ship
    /// </summary>
    public class Player : DrawableGameComponent
    {
        protected Texture2D texture;
        protected Rectangle spriteRectangle;
        protected Vector2 position;
        protected TimeSpan elapsedTime = TimeSpan.Zero;
        protected PlayerIndex playerIndex;

        // Screen area
        protected Rectangle screenBounds;

        // Game stuff
        protected int score;
        protected int power;
        private const int INITIALPOWER = 100;

        public Player(Game game, ref Texture2D theTexture, PlayerIndex playerID,
            Rectangle rectangle) : base(game)
        {
            texture = theTexture;
            position = new Vector2();
            playerIndex = playerID;

            // Create the source rectangle.
            // This represents where the sprite picture is in the surface
            spriteRectangle = rectangle;

#if XBOX360
    // On the 360, we need to take care about the TV "safe" area.
            screenBounds = new Rectangle((int)(Game.Window.ClientBounds.Width *
                0.03f),(int)(Game.Window.ClientBounds.Height * 0.03f),
                Game.Window.ClientBounds.Width -
                (int)(Game.Window.ClientBounds.Width * 0.03f),
                Game.Window.ClientBounds.Height -
                (int)(Game.Window.ClientBounds.Height * 0.03f));
#else
            screenBounds = new Rectangle(0, 0, Game.Window.ClientBounds.Width,
                Game.Window.ClientBounds.Height);
#endif
        }
```

```csharp
/// <summary>
/// Put the ship in your start position on screen
/// </summary>
public void Reset()
{
    if (playerIndex == PlayerIndex.One)
    {
        position.X = screenBounds.Width/3;
    }
    else
    {
        position.X = (int) (screenBounds.Width/1.5);
    }

    position.Y = screenBounds.Height - spriteRectangle.Height;
    score = 0;
    power = INITIALPOWER;
}

/// <summary>
/// Total points of the player
/// </summary>
public int Score
{
    get { return score; }
    set
    {
        if (value < 0)
        {
            score = 0;
        }
        else
        {
            score = value;
        }
    }
}

/// <summary>
/// Remaining power
/// </summary>
public int Power
{
    get { return power; }
    set { power = value; }
}
```

```csharp
/// <summary>
/// Update the ship position, points, and power
/// </summary>
public override void Update(GameTime gameTime)
{
    // Move the ship with the Xbox controller
    GamePadState gamepadstatus = GamePad.GetState(playerIndex);
    position.Y += (int) ((gamepadstatus.ThumbSticks.Left.Y*3)*-2);
    position.X += (int) ((gamepadstatus.ThumbSticks.Left.X*3)*2);

    // Move the ship with the keyboard
    if (playerIndex == PlayerIndex.One)
    {
        HandlePlayer1KeyBoard();
    }
    else
    {
        HandlePlayer2KeyBoard();
    }

    // Keep the player inside the screen
    KeepInBound();

    // Update score
    elapsedTime += gameTime.ElapsedGameTime;

    if (elapsedTime > TimeSpan.FromSeconds(1))
    {
        elapsedTime -= TimeSpan.FromSeconds(1);
        score++;
        power--;
    }

    base.Update(gameTime);
}

/// <summary>
/// Keep the ship inside the screen
/// </summary>
private void KeepInBound()
{
    if (position.X < screenBounds.Left)
    {
        position.X = screenBounds.Left;
    }
```

```csharp
        if (position.X > screenBounds.Width - spriteRectangle.Width)
        {
            position.X = screenBounds.Width - spriteRectangle.Width;
        }
        if (position.Y < screenBounds.Top)
        {
            position.Y = screenBounds.Top;
        }
        if (position.Y > screenBounds.Height - spriteRectangle.Height)
        {
            position.Y = screenBounds.Height - spriteRectangle.Height;
        }
    }


    /// <summary>
    /// Handle the keys for player 1 (arrow keys)
    /// </summary>
    private void HandlePlayer1KeyBoard()
    {
        KeyboardState keyboard = Keyboard.GetState();
        if (keyboard.IsKeyDown(Keys.Up))
        {
            position.Y -= 3;
        }
        if (keyboard.IsKeyDown(Keys.Down))
        {
            position.Y += 3;
        }
        if (keyboard.IsKeyDown(Keys.Left))
        {
            position.X -= 3;
        }
        if (keyboard.IsKeyDown(Keys.Right))
        {
            position.X += 3;
        }
    }


    /// <summary>
    /// Handle the keys for player 2 (ASDW)
    /// </summary>
    private void HandlePlayer2KeyBoard()
    {
        KeyboardState keyboard = Keyboard.GetState();
```

```csharp
            if (keyboard.IsKeyDown(Keys.W))
            {
                position.Y -= 3;
            }
            if (keyboard.IsKeyDown(Keys.S))
            {
                position.Y += 3;
            }
            if (keyboard.IsKeyDown(Keys.A))
            {
                position.X -= 3;
            }
            if (keyboard.IsKeyDown(Keys.D))
            {
                position.X += 3;
            }
        }


        /// <summary>
        /// Draw the ship sprite
        /// </summary>
        public override void Draw(GameTime gameTime)
        {
            // Get the current sprite batch
            SpriteBatch sBatch = (SpriteBatch)
                Game.Services.GetService(typeof (SpriteBatch));

            // Draw the ship
            sBatch.Draw(texture, position, spriteRectangle, Color.White);

            base.Draw(gameTime);
        }

        /// <summary>
        /// Get the bound rectangle of ship position on screen
        /// </summary>
        public Rectangle GetBounds()
        {
            return new Rectangle((int) position.X, (int) position.Y,
                spriteRectangle.Width, spriteRectangle.Height);
        }
    }
}
```

As you can see, this is practically the same class as in the previous chapter, but in the Update method, you handle the user input a little differently, testing the PlayerIndex to check for the correct gamepad or keyboard keys. In a multiplayer game, you'll instantiate two objects for this class with different PlayerIndexes and different rectangles in texture, for different ship sprites.

Bringing Everything Together

Now you have all the action scene components. The meteors, the score, and the player (or players) are ready to be put to work. Next, add a class called `ActionScene`. This scene is the most complex scene of the game. It coordinates the action of all the components, as well as controls the game state, such as pause and gameOver.

Start declaring all elements of this scene, as follows:

```
// Basics
protected Texture2D actionTexture;
protected AudioLibrary audio;
protected SpriteBatch spriteBatch = null;

// Game elements
protected Player player1;
protected Player player2;
protected MeteorsManager meteors;
protected PowerSource powerSource;
protected SimpleRumblePad rumblePad;
protected ImageComponent background;
protected Score scorePlayer1;
protected Score scorePlayer2;

// GUI stuff
protected Vector2 pausePosition;
protected Vector2 gameoverPosition;
protected Rectangle pauseRect = new Rectangle(1, 120, 200, 44);
protected Rectangle gameoverRect = new Rectangle(1, 170, 350, 48);

// GameState elements
protected bool paused;
protected bool gameOver;
protected TimeSpan elapsedTime = TimeSpan.Zero;
protected bool twoPlayers;
```

These look like the attributes from the game in the previous chapter, but you now have two `Player` instances (for a multiplayer game); two attributes for controlling the game state (paused and gameOver); the components for `Score`, `PowerSource`, and `Meteors`; and so on.

The constructor initializes all these objects, as follows:

```
/// <summary>
/// Default constructor
/// </summary>
/// <param name="game">The main game object</param>
/// <param name="theTexture">Texture with the sprite elements</param>
/// <param name="backgroundTexture">Texture for the background</param>
/// <param name="font">Font used in the score</param>
```

```
public ActionScene(Game game, Texture2D theTexture,
    Texture2D backgroundTexture, SpriteFont font) : base(game)
{
    // Get the audio library
    audio = (AudioLibrary)
        Game.Services.GetService(typeof(AudioLibrary));
    background = new ImageComponent(game, backgroundTexture,
        ImageComponent.DrawMode.Stretch);
    Components.Add(background);

    actionTexture = theTexture;

    spriteBatch = (SpriteBatch)
        Game.Services.GetService(typeof (SpriteBatch));
    meteors = new MeteorsManager(Game, ref actionTexture);
    Components.Add(meteors);

    player1 = new Player(Game, ref actionTexture, PlayerIndex.One,
        new Rectangle(323, 15, 30, 30));
    player1.Initialize();
    Components.Add(player1);

    player2 = new Player(Game, ref actionTexture, PlayerIndex.Two,
        new Rectangle(360, 17, 30, 30));
    player2.Initialize();
    Components.Add(player2);

    scorePlayer1 = new Score(game, font, Color.Blue);
    scorePlayer1.Position = new Vector2(10, 10);
    Components.Add(scorePlayer1);
    scorePlayer2 = new Score(game, font, Color.Red);
    scorePlayer2.Position = new Vector2(
        Game.Window.ClientBounds.Width - 200, 10);
    Components.Add(scorePlayer2);

    rumblePad = new SimpleRumblePad(game);
    Components.Add(rumblePad);

    powerSource = new PowerSource(game, ref actionTexture);
    powerSource.Initialize();
    Components.Add(powerSource);
}
```

Here, you create two instances for the Player class. For each player, just change the PlayerIndex and the Rectangle of the image of the ship in the texture.

You also need to control the game state and define if the game is for one or two players, or check if some of the players are already dead. Add these properties to the class:

```
/// <summary>
/// Indicate the 2-players game mode
/// </summary>
public bool TwoPlayers
{
    get { return twoPlayers; }
    set { twoPlayers = value; }
}

/// <summary>
/// True, if the game is in gameOver state
/// </summary>
public bool GameOver
{
    get { return gameOver; }
}

/// <summary>
/// Paused mode
/// </summary>
public bool Paused
{
    get { return paused; }
    set
    {
        paused = value;
        if (paused)
        {
            MediaPlayer.Pause();        }
        else
        {
            MediaPlayer.Resume();          }
    }
}
```

As with all the other scenes, you can use the Show and Hide methods to initialize and release scene components. In the Show method, you start playing the background music and setting the player2 status if you have a two-player game:

```
/// <summary>
/// Show the action scene
/// </summary>
public override void Show()
{
    MediaPlayer.Play(audio.BackMusic);
    meteors.Initialize();
    powerSource.PutinStartPosition();
```

```
    player1.Reset();
    player2.Reset();

    paused = false;
    pausePosition.X = (Game.Window.ClientBounds.Width -
        pauseRect.Width)/2;
    pausePosition.Y = (Game.Window.ClientBounds.Height -
        pauseRect.Height)/2;

    gameOver = false;
    gameoverPosition.X = (Game.Window.ClientBounds.Width -
        gameoverRect.Width)/2;
    gameoverPosition.Y = (Game.Window.ClientBounds.Height -
        gameoverRect.Height)/2;

    // Is it a two-player game?
    player2.Visible = twoPlayers;
    player2.Enabled = twoPlayers;
    scorePlayer2.Visible = twoPlayers;
    scorePlayer2.Enabled = twoPlayers;

    base.Show();
}

/// <summary>
/// Hide the scene
/// </summary>
public override void Hide()
{
    // Stop the background music
    MediaPlayer.Stop();    // Stop the rumble
    rumblePad.Stop(PlayerIndex.One);
    rumblePad.Stop(PlayerIndex.Two);

    base.Hide();
}
```

And, as always, the Update method synchronizes all these objects, checking the collisions and changing the game state for game over when some players die.

```
/// <summary>
/// Allows the GameComponent to update itself
/// </summary>
/// <param name="gameTime">Provides a snapshot of timing values</param>
public override void Update(GameTime gameTime)
{
```

```
    if ((!paused) && (!gameOver) && (!Guide.IsVisible))
    {
        // Check collisions with meteors
        HandleDamages();

        // Check if a player gets a power boost
        HandlePowerSourceSprite(gameTime);

        // Update score
        scorePlayer1.Value = player1.Score;
        scorePlayer1.Power = player1.Power;
        if (twoPlayers)
        {
            scorePlayer2.Value = player2.Score;
            scorePlayer2.Power = player2.Power;
        }

        // Check if player is dead
        gameOver = ((player1.Power <= 0) || (player2.Power <= 0));
        if (gameOver)
        {
            player1.Visible = (player1.Power > 0);
            player2.Visible = (player2.Power > 0) && twoPlayers;
            // Stop the music
            MediaPlayer.Stop();                // Stop rumble
            rumblePad.Stop(PlayerIndex.One);
            rumblePad.Stop(PlayerIndex.Two);
        }

        // Update all other GameComponents
        base.Update(gameTime);
    }

    // In gameOver state, keep the meteors' animation
    if (gameOver)
    {
        meteors.Update(gameTime);
    }
}
```

The HandleDamages and HandlePowerSourceSprite methods check the collisions with the meteors (and lose some player power), check the collision with the power source (and add some power to the player), and check if a player has zero or less power to end the game and put the player in a game over state.

The HandleDamages method is also similar to the collision test method from the previous chapter. Again, this method checks the collision with the players and meteors and one player with another player. For each collision, the player loses ten points and ten power units.

```
/// <summary>
/// Handle collisions with a meteor
/// </summary>
private void HandleDamages()
{
    // Check collision for player 1
    if (meteors.CheckForCollisions(player1.GetBounds()))
    {
        // Shake!
        rumblePad.RumblePad(PlayerIndex.One, 500, 1.0f, 1.0f);
        // Player penalty
        player1.Power -= 10;
        player1.Score -= 10;
    }

    // Check collision for player 2
    if (twoPlayers)
    {
        if (meteors.CheckForCollisions(player2.GetBounds()))
        {
            // Shake!
            rumblePad.RumblePad(PlayerIndex.Two, 500, 1.0f, 1.0f);
            // Player penalty
            player2.Power -= 10;
            player2.Score -= 10;
        }

        // Check for collision between the players
        if (player1.GetBounds().Intersects(player2.GetBounds()))
        {
            rumblePad.RumblePad(PlayerIndex.One, 500, 1.0f, 1.0f);
            player1.Power -= 10;
            player1.Score -= 10;
            rumblePad.RumblePad(PlayerIndex.Two, 500, 1.0f, 1.0f);
            player2.Power -= 10;
            player2.Score -= 10;
        }
    }
}
```

The HandlePowerSourceSprite method does the same job, but with the PowerSource sprite. If a player collides with this sprite, the player gets 50 power units. The method also checks if it's time to send a new power source in the game, using an interval of 15 seconds.

```
/// <summary>
/// Handle power-up stuff
/// </summary>
```

```
private void HandlePowerSourceSprite(GameTime gameTime)
{
    if (powerSource.CheckCollision(player1.GetBounds()))
    {
        // Player 1 gets the power source
        audio.PowerGet.Play();          elapsedTime = TimeSpan.Zero;
        powerSource.PutinStartPosition();
        player1.Power += 50;
    }

    if (twoPlayers)
    {
        // Player 2 gets the power source
        if (powerSource.CheckCollision(player2.GetBounds()))
        {
            audio.PowerGet.Play();            elapsedTime = TimeSpan.Zero;
            powerSource.PutinStartPosition();
            player2.Power += 50;
        }
    }

    // Check for sending a new power source
    elapsedTime += gameTime.ElapsedGameTime;
    if (elapsedTime > TimeSpan.FromSeconds(15))
    {
        elapsedTime -= TimeSpan.FromSeconds(15);
        powerSource.Enabled = true;
    }
}
```

And finally, the Draw method just draws some objects for a specified game state:

```
/// <summary>
/// Allows the GameComponent to draw itself
/// </summary>
/// <param name="gameTime">Provides a snapshot of timing values</param>
public override void Draw(GameTime gameTime)
{
    // Draw all GameComponents
    base.Draw(gameTime);

    if (paused)
    {
        // Draw the "pause" text
        spriteBatch.Draw(actionTexture, pausePosition, pauseRect,
            Color.White);
    }
```

```
    if (gameOver)
    {
        // Draw the "gameover" text
        spriteBatch.Draw(actionTexture, gameoverPosition, gameoverRect,
            Color.White);
    }
```

Observe that once again a great deal of the game logic that you created in the previous chapter was kept. You added only the two-player support and two more game states: one when the user pauses the game (pressing the Enter key or pressing the A button on the Xbox 360 gamepad during the game), or when one of the players runs out of energy. When this happens, the game shows a message on the screen and waits for the player to press the Enter key or the A button on the Xbox 360 gamepad.

Navigating Between the Scenes

With all the scenes created, now you only need to show them according to the user's selections. Through the menu in the opening scene, users can show the help scene, the action scene (with one or two players), or just leave the game. Here, you'll use a technique in which you concentrate all the inputs that refer to the navigation or control of the scene states in one class. In this case, you use the Game1 class, so that you have a central point where you start the scenes and control the Game1 class's state. Add the following code in the Game1 class:

```
private readonly GraphicsDeviceManager graphics;
private SpriteBatch spriteBatch;

// Textures
protected Texture2D helpBackgroundTexture, helpForegroundTexture;
protected Texture2D startBackgroundTexture, startElementsTexture;
protected Texture2D actionElementsTexture, actionBackgroundTexture;
// Game scenes
protected HelpScene helpScene;
protected StartScene startScene;
protected ActionScene actionScene;
protected GameScene activeScene;

// Audio stuff
protected AudioLibrary audio;

// Fonts
private SpriteFont smallFont, largeFont, scoreFont;

// Used to handle input
protected KeyboardState oldKeyboardState;
protected GamePadState oldGamePadState;
```

In the LoadContent method, add the code to create and load the content for the ActionScene object:

```
// Create the action scene
actionElementsTexture = Content.Load<Texture2D>("rockrainenhanced");
actionBackgroundTexture = Content.Load<Texture2D>("SpaceBackground");
scoreFont = Content.Load<SpriteFont>("score");
actionScene = new ActionScene(this, actionElementsTexture,
    actionBackgroundTexture, scoreFont);
Components.Add(actionScene);

// Start the game in the start scene
startScene.Show();
activeScene = startScene;
```

Again, in this class, you'll load all the game assets and initialize all the scenes, putting the StartScene as the scene to be opened initially.

The Update method handles all user input for each scene, and changes the active scene if necessary:

```
/// <summary>
/// Allows the game to run logic such as updating the world,
/// checking for collisions, gathering input, and playing audio.
/// </summary>
/// <param name="gameTime">Provides a snapshot of timing values</param>
protected override void Update(GameTime gameTime)
{
// Handle game inputs
    HandleScenesInput();

    base.Update(gameTime);
}
```

HandleScenesInput just calls the handler for the active scene in the game:

```
/// <summary>
/// Handle input of all game scenes
/// </summary>
private void HandleScenesInput()
{
    // Handle start scene input
    if (activeScene == startScene)
    {
        HandleStartSceneInput();
    }
    // Handle help scene input
    else if (activeScene == helpScene)
    {
        if (CheckEnterA())
        {
            ShowScene(startScene);
        }
    }
```

```
    // Handle action scene input
    else if (activeScene == actionScene)
    {
        HandleActionInput();
    }
}
```

The CheckEnterA method is a simple code to test the Enter key and the A button on an Xbox 360 gamepad:

```
/// <summary>
/// Check if the Enter Key or A button was pressed
/// </summary>
/// <returns>true, if Enter key or A button was pressed</returns>
private bool CheckEnterA()
{
    // Get the keyboard and gamePad state
    GamePadState gamepadState = GamePad.GetState(PlayerIndex.One);
    KeyboardState keyboardState = Keyboard.GetState();

    bool result = (oldKeyboardState.IsKeyDown(Keys.Enter) &&
        (keyboardState.IsKeyUp(Keys.Enter)));
    result |= (oldGamePadState.Buttons.A == ButtonState.Pressed) &&
            (gamepadState.Buttons.A == ButtonState.Released);

    oldKeyboardState = keyboardState;
    oldGamePadState = gamepadState;

    return result;
}
```

The HandleStartSceneInput shows the correct scene following the user selection in the menu. If a two-player game is selected, you just set the TwoPlayers attribute in the actionScene to true:

```
/// <summary>
/// Handle buttons and keyboard in start scene
/// </summary>
private void HandleStartSceneInput()
{
    if (CheckEnterA())
    {
        audio.MenuSelect.Play();        switch (startScene.SelectedMenuIndex)
        {
            case 0:
                actionScene.TwoPlayers = false;
                ShowScene(actionScene);
                break;
```

```
                case 1:
                    actionScene.TwoPlayers = true;
                    ShowScene(actionScene);
                    break;
                case 2:
                    ShowScene(helpScene);
                    break;
                case 3:
                    Exit();
                    break;
            }
        }
}
```

HandleActionInput handles input in the action scene to pause and cancel a game, using a keyboard or an Xbox 360 gamepad:

```
/// <summary>
/// Check if the Enter Key or A button was pressed
/// </summary>
/// <returns>true, if Enter key or A button was pressed</returns>
private void HandleActionInput()
{
    // Get the keyboard and gamePad state
    GamePadState gamepadState = GamePad.GetState(PlayerIndex.One);
    KeyboardState keyboardState = Keyboard.GetState();

    bool backKey = (oldKeyboardState.IsKeyDown(Keys.Escape) &&
        (keyboardState.IsKeyUp(Keys.Escape)));
    backKey |= (oldGamePadState.Buttons.Back == ButtonState.Pressed) &&
            (gamepadState.Buttons.Back == ButtonState.Released);

    bool enterKey = (oldKeyboardState.IsKeyDown(Keys.Enter) &&
        (keyboardState.IsKeyUp(Keys.Enter)));
    enterKey |= (oldGamePadState.Buttons.A == ButtonState.Pressed) &&
            (gamepadState.Buttons.A == ButtonState.Released);

    oldKeyboardState = keyboardState;
    oldGamePadState = gamepadState;

    if (enterKey)
    {
        if (actionScene.GameOver)
        {
            ShowScene(startScene);
        }
```

```
        else
        {
            audio.MenuBack.Play();              actionScene.Paused =
!actionScene.Paused;
        }
    }

    if (backKey)
    {
        ShowScene(startScene);
    }
}
```

The ShowScene method is just a helper to Show a new scene and Hide a previous scene, as follows:

```
/// <summary>
/// Open a new scene
/// </summary>
/// <param name="scene">Scene to be opened</param>
protected void ShowScene(GameScene scene)
{
    activeScene.Hide();
    activeScene = scene;
    scene.Show();
}
```

What about the Draw method? Well, all elements of your game are GameComponents now, so just let XNA do its job:

```
/// <summary>
/// This is called when the game should draw itself.
/// </summary>
/// <param name="gameTime">Provides a snapshot of timing values</param>
protected override void Draw(GameTime gameTime)
{
    // Begin
    spriteBatch.Begin();

    // Draw all GameComponents
    base.Draw(gameTime);

    // End
    spriteBatch.End();
}
```

That's it. Compile and execute the game to see the final result. The architecture is flexible, and it's easy to add new features to your game, as you'll see in Chapter 6. Try adding new meteor types or new ways to acquire energy, for instance. You'll start to understand how games are "assembled" from GameComponents.

Summary

In this chapter, you started from a simple game and evolved that into a more elaborate game with simple techniques that are useful to any kind of game. You saw the value of the GameComponents and their reuse capability. Feel free to improve and change this game and build your own awesome version of Rock Rain!

■ ■ ■

CHAPTER 5

Basics of Game Networking

This chapter introduces the basic concepts involved in creating games that support networking, so you'll be prepared to create a real multiplayer game in the next chapter. Before discussing the details of XNA support for networking, let's look at networked games in general and identify some of the most common problems faced when coding such games.

Introducing Multiplayer Games

Online multiplayer games, also known as *network-enabled games* or simply *networked games*, are hard to code. Period. That said, it's also important to state that, in XNA, this difficulty is not related to coding for connecting the machines (PC or Xbox 360) or making them communicate with each other. That's because XNA hides all complexities from you in this case, as it does with everything else in the framework.

Networked games are hard to code because there are many extra problems to deal with: your program will receive messages from the host or other players, send messages back to them, process the local player input, and perform the physics and artificial intelligence calculations, while not letting the screen freeze between each frame drawn (one of the worst things that might happen in a multiplayer game).

Fortunately, XNA can help developers with most of the communication problems, such as providing ways to control the message flow between players and host to guarantee that no message is lost and that all messages arrive in the same order they were sent. Nevertheless, there will still be some problems to solve.

Network Topology

The most common topologies for networked games are peer-to-peer and client/server connections. Because XNA network implementation is not tied to any type of connection, you can code any of these types, depending on the way you organize your network code.

Peer-to-Peer Networking

In peer-to-peer connections, every player is aware of every other player in the game, sending and receiving messages from, and to, all players, as illustrated in Figure 5-1.

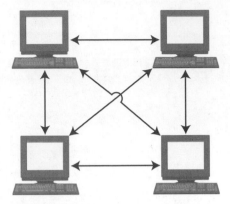

Figure 5-1. *Peer-to-peer connection*

The most obvious benefit of using this network organization is that you don't need a dedicated server to play the game, so every group of players can play it within their own local area network (LAN), or even through the Internet, as long as they know the addresses of the other members of the group.

In this type of connection, one of the players acts as a host, so all the new players connect to that player. However, once connected, the messages flow directly from one player to all others. If the player who is also the host disconnects from the game, the game might stop or simply choose another player as the new host, depending on what the game developers defined.

The main problem you face when coding peer-to-peer games is that you can't have too many players in the same game session, because the number of messages will increase exponentially with every new player who joins. For instance, in Figure 5-1 we have four players, so every time you need to update a player's status (for example, move), you send three messages, one for each player. Because you have four players, during each game turn, you exchange $4 \times 3 = 12$ messages. Making the same calculations with a five-player game increases this to $5 \times 4 = 20$ messages per turn, and in a six-player game, you'll reach $6 \times 5 = 30$ messages.

Usually, having more than ten players in the same game session is not suggested, because every message can take dozens of bytes, so you'll consume the bandwidth available in your network quickly. But it's still possible if the game development team can make the messages as small as possible; for example, passing only the players' inputs across the computers, and letting games on every player's machine calculate everything else from these inputs.

Client/Server Networking

The second most common game network topology is client/server. In this kind of network, all players connect to a host, which usually processes the messages and does the game synchronization, sending messages back to each of the players, as illustrated in Figure 5-2.

Figure 5-2. *Client/server connection*

Client/server games consume a lot less bandwidth per player, which allows you to send more data (and maybe create a more complex game). However, on the other hand, the player depends on having a host to connect to (so it usually can't be played on a home LAN).

When coding client/server games, you must decide which actions will take place on the host, and which actions will take place on the client machines. Is it better to put all the game physics and intelligence on the players' machines, using a host just as a forwarder of messages, or is it better to include all the game code on the host, leaving just the input gathering and rendering code on the players' machines?

There is no right answer to this question, because it depends largely on the game constraints and goals. When making your decision, you'll need to take into account how many players will be connected to the server, and how much it will cost the server processor to perform each activity (for all players). You also might need to verify the cost for each player's machine to do its own calculations against the bandwidth impact for doing all calculations on the server and passing the results to the players. Even when the server could do a specific operation better, you might decide to run it on the client, if passing the results of the operation will use a large amount of the available bandwidth.

Other Networking Topologies

Along with peer-to-peer and client/server, other types of network organization exist. Some are useful in game development; others are not. For example, in a ring topology, each player sends messages to one specific player, creating a ring that will eventually return to the first player in the sequence, as shown in Figure 5-3.

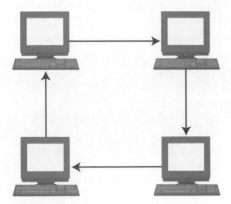

Figure 5-3. *Ring network topology*

This network organization is usually not practical for games, because the first player in the sequence would need to wait for the message to go around to every other player before it returned to that player, which can easily lead to unacceptable waiting times.

Another example of a different approach is using network groups: each player exchanges messages only with the other players in the group, and the host (which could be a dedicated server or a player) exchanges information with other groups, when needed. The group organization is designed for the number of messages passed between the groups to be as small as possible. Figure 5-4 illustrates a game network topology based on groups.

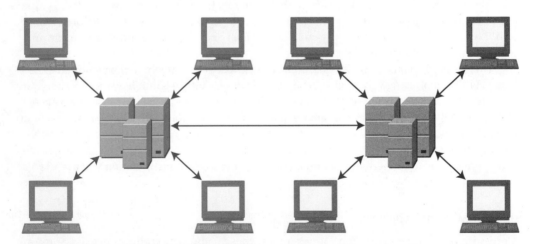

Figure 5-4. *A group-based network topology*

This approach is a mix of the client/server and peer-to-peer topologies, which aims to have the benefits of each one.

In the next section, we'll discuss some choices you must make when producing your network game project.

Turn-Based vs. Real-Time Games

Whether to design your multiplayer game as turn-based or real-time is probably one of the first decisions you'll make, and probably the one that will have the greatest impact on your game project.

The Turn-Based Approach

In turn-based games, each player will think about his move, do the proper action, and then pass the control to the next player. Although the first type of game that comes to mind is board games, such as chess or Monopoly, there are sophisticated action games based on turns, such as the old X-COM series, where you move each of your soldiers (using his energy to walk or fire), and then the enemies move, using the same rules.

Choosing this approach will save you a lot of headaches when trying to deal with the latency between your game messages, especially when running through the Internet, but might lead to a less than optimal game play, because this type of game is unusual. Never choose this approach if you have many players (say, more than three or four, depending on the game pace), because if each player needs to wait more than a couple minutes to play again, the game will rapidly become uninteresting—except, of course, if the players actually expect a delay, as in a chess match. A practical idea is letting the players communicate with one another (by voice or by typing a message), even when it is not their turn, so you can improve the interaction between players and make the waiting less boring.

The Real-Time Approach

Creating continuous action multiplayer games that support remote players, like Halo, is challenging. That's mainly because you must transfer a certain amount of data within tight time frames, which, unfortunately, depends on the response time of something beyond your control—the network. At the same time, you need to make sure that all players have synchronized information, especially in fast-paced action games where players are fighting against one another.

One possible approach is to send all the data updates to each of the players, so that you can ensure that everyone has the most recent events on their machines. However, this approach consumes the entire bandwidth available, even for just a few players.

In the other extreme, you can carefully calculate exactly which information should be sent to each player, and then send the minimum data needed. For instance, if another player is behind you or in another part of the game level, you can't see that player, so you don't need to receive information from that player. Although it saves bandwidth, this approach consumes CPUs cycles on the players' machines by calculating the data to send, leaving fewer cycles to calculate the game physics and draw the graphics.

Then again, the best approach is to find a balance according to your game requirements. There is no right answer; just minimize the data while trying not to expend too much processing time on this minimization, and keep in mind that your game may be running on slower machines or might face unpredictably bad network response times.

In the next section, we'll discuss some other points to consider when coding multiplayer games.

Some Technical Tips

In this section, we present some technical tips for creating multiplayer games. Although this is not an exhaustive list, it provides a good starting point for anyone who wants to write a networked game.

Plan the Game Carefully

Although careful planning is important for every game, it's an absolute must for multiplayer games. Because you'll have different programs, or at least different parts of the same program, interacting through the network, you must define every message that will be exchanged and every way the programs might process them.

It's crucial to the success of the game that you define where and *when* each process will occur, to guarantee that each player is synchronized. Programmers tend to forget these details, because in stand-alone programs everything occurs directly after the command is processed. However, in multiplayer games, this is not the case. For example, if you are coding a shooter game, one player can shoot another player's character and, almost at the same time, in the remote machine, the other player's character might be moving out of the firing range of the first player. If all processing occurs locally on each player's machine, the first player will see a successful shot. Although the message with the shot information did not reach the other player's machine, the remote player jumped out of the way, so the remote player will see the shot missing.

So, devising an algorithm that guarantees synchronization is as important as not using a lot of bandwidth. Considering that you might face bad response times when running across the network, this is challenging.

Code for Network Features from the Beginning

It's far better to code everything from the ground up than to try to adjust a stand-alone game to support networking. Even in a simple program, you might face situations where adjusting the program will lead to a less than optimal result, compared to writing the game with networking in mind.

If you're planning to create a game that will support networking only in a second version, prepare all your code, from the first version, to be "network-friendly." For example, isolate the routines that deal with user input from the rest of the game, so you can change these routines to receive remote input later. Also, plan how to synchronize input from all players, even if in the first version all players are local.

■Note XNA network routines allow you to create games with more than one local player. The best approach, in this case, would be to use these routines right away, to create the first version of your game. That way, it would support networking from the start, even if there is no support for remote players in the first version.

Define the Message Types and Sizes Carefully

Bandwidth is a rare and expensive thing, so use it sparingly.

After defining all messages that your programs will exchange in the project phase, you should diagram the complete flow of a typical game cycle (the game's main loop, including the calls for the Update and Draw methods of your XNA Game class), so you can check if you are forgetting anything important. You must create this flow for at least two to three players, plus the server, if any exists, because some situations will occur with three players that don't occur with two (for instance, a player can receive out-of-order messages from different players).

After being sure that you aren't forgetting anything, you must go back and recheck every message to see if you are using the minimum space possible for each message, especially those that will be exchanged most frequently. For example, a single bit can be used as a flag, so a Byte can hold up to eight flags. Also, a Byte takes 256 different values, so if your values are within this range, you can use the Byte data type instead of the Int16 one, which takes 2 bytes.

A final word on this: be sure that you know the real size of the data types you are using. For example, an Int32 takes 4 bytes, while an Int16 takes 2 bytes. Another interesting example refers to strings: they do *not* occupy the same amount of bytes as the number of characters. They have extra internal control bytes that help, for example, when defining the string's length.

■**Note** ANSI strings (1 byte per character) are the default for most Western countries, but this does not suffice for writing every character in Eastern countries, such as the kana characters in Japan and China. That's because you have only 256 possible characters in ANSI. Unicode is the default for such countries. With Unicode, every character could be one of up to 65,536 different values—enough for any language. C# adopts Unicode as its format for all strings, which means that XNA also supports Unicode.

Hide the Latency from the Player

Latency is the worst enemy of every multiplayer game programming team. And, even worse, there's no solution for this problem. It's not a bug; it's a fact of life, so you must learn—and code—to live with it.

Because you never know for sure how much time it will take to receive the next message, you can use some tricks to distract players while they wait. For example, say your game is a strategy game such as the Age of Empires series, where the player can give orders to game characters. However, the character will move only after the client machine receives confirmation from the host that the command has been received. You can make your characters say something ("Yes, master!" would suffice, although it's very innovative) just after the command is issued, so the player has the impression that the result is immediate, although it really will start (hopefully) a number of milliseconds later.

You can use this same idea with animations instead of sounds. The game character can start a little animation, such as making an "okay" sign with his hand or moving his head around as if looking for a way to start the command. This kind of trick is effective.

Another thing you can do when facing extra-long waiting times for the next message is let your program continue the action based on the last input, maybe at a lower rate. For example, if you know the speed and the direction of the other players' starships in a space battle game, you can suppose that they are still moving in the same direction, and move their spaceships a little following this supposition. However, as soon as the new message arrives, you must check and correct the other players' positions. This can be a challenge, even for experienced programmers, and can lead to problems in the game, such as a spaceship appearing to jump from one place to another. You can solve this with a smoothing trick, by adjusting the position in more than one game cycle, but this technique will add extra complexity to your game.

The important thing about latency is that while it will probably always be a problem, players didn't, don't, and won't ever accept latency in games. Few things are worse for a player than receiving a pop-up window with a message such as "waiting for the answer from the host." So, your team will need to spend some hours addressing this topic at the game project stage, if you are planning to do a serious multiplayer game.

Note XNA provides a way to simulate latency. You can easily test your program in "real conditions," with `NetworkSession.SimulatedLatency`. You can also simulate a percentage of message loss between computers, another common problem, with `NetworkSession.SimulatedPacketLoss`. You won't use these commands in this chapter, but they may be very useful for testing your own network games.

Include Single-Player Features in Your Multiplayer Game

Many players don't like, or simply don't have the money or the time, to play games with other players. Many games that are solely multiplayer have failed, so be careful if you want to follow this approach.

We'll give a simple example: Halo is a great game, and multiplayer features give a whole new experience for the players, as everyone who has played it knows. Just imagine now if Halo had no history, no computer-controlled characters, and was restricted to death-match and other player-against-player options. It would surely still be a good game given its details, but would hardly be a great game. We could say that the strongest argument against this would be Counter-Strike, which released as a modification (mod) without single-player functionality, and it's still the most downloaded Half-Life mod in history (with a few hundred thousand players left). However, the game developers did eventually release single-player functionality!

Another simple example is the Net Rumble starter kit, released with XNA 2.0 (and also works with XNA 3.0). It's a nice game, but if you play alone, all you have is a spaceship with some floating rocks to shoot, with no goal—no fun at all. Coding a computer-controlled ship might be a challenge for starters, but will surely make a real difference if you want to play alone, or even if you want to test the game while coding without partners.

Remember that having computer-controlled characters is useful even in network games, so you should spend some time thinking about this in your games.

Use Different Threads to Handle Network Messages

Here's a simple but important tip: dedicate a specific thread to message sending and receiving, and have another thread or threads deal with the game physics and artificial intelligence. This approach gives you more flexibility to hide the latency and get the most from your hardware, be it PC or Xbox.

We won't talk about multithreading in this book, but you should learn more about it when you're ready to create more advanced games.

Test, Test, Test!

Multiplayer games have extra sources of errors, and sometimes the errors are harder to find and fix, so testing from the beginning is a real must.

The first tests you should do involve message delivery and handling, to check if your code will behave properly if a network packet is lost or if it receives the packets in a different order than the order in which they were sent. For example, if a remote player makes his character crouch and then shoot, disregarding the packet arrival order in the current machine could have that character shoot before crouching, which would be undesirable.

■**Note** XNA allows you to choose if you want the framework to guarantee the reliability of the packets (so no message is ever lost), using the `SendDataOptions.Reliable` flag, and the packet order (so the messages always arrive in the same order they were sent), with `SendDataOptions.InOrder`. Although it might sound good to always have the messages arriving, and in order, setting both flags might lead to greater latency times, because the XNA Framework will do extra work and eventually resend messages. The better approach is to create a game that doesn't rely on these features.

Multiplayer game reliability is always a problem. Just imagine you have created a game that has an uptime of 99.9 percent. This means that your game can run, on the average, for 23 hours and 59 minutes without crashing. Does that sound good enough?

Well, if you have ten players in your game, using ten different machines, they will probably not crash at the same time. However, for a ten-player game, where each player has a 0.1 percent chance of crashing, the total risk of a crash for any one of the players is 0.1 percent times 10—a 1 percent risk of crash. This may sound like a low risk, but that 1 percent actually means that you'll probably have a player crashing every 100 minutes (1 hour and 40 minutes), which certainly is a bad thing. If your program is good enough, the other players can continue playing—even if it's kind of frustrating when playing in a team to see a companion freezing or disappearing from the team.

When coding your next network game, keep these figures in mind, and follow our tip: test, test, and test. And after that, test it all over again.

Introducing XNA Networking

XNA 3.0 offers a set of functions and components through the `Microsoft.Xna.Framework.GamerServices` and the `Microsoft.Xna.Framework.Net` namespaces, which enables the creation of multiplayer game hosts (that other players can connect to), handles the connections and message exchanging between players and the host, and includes many extra features, such as native support for voice communications.

XBOX LIVE COMMUNITY GAMES

The XNA network API has not changed much from XNA 2.0 to XNA 3.0. The most amazing improvement in networking features is not in the XNA API, but in the Xbox LIVE network. It now offers a Community Games area, where you can sell your games to any LIVE member!

The procedure to sell your game is simple: create the game and submit it, along with some screenshots, to LIVE Community Games for a peer review, classifying your game according to its level of violence, sex, and mature content. Microsoft has stated that it will not censure any game; however, there is still some prohibited content, such as nudity, strong sexual content, collecting gamers' personal information, and unauthorized third-party content use. According to Microsoft, this classification is "designed to help like-minded people to do like-minded things" (whatever that means).

After your submission, your game enters a pending state, where it will be reviewed by other community XNA developers. If at least three peers state that your game is not buggy and your classification is correct, it will be ready to be sold as a new LIVE Community Game! Then you can follow up your game sales in the My Business area of the XNA Creators Club web site.

For more details and updates about Xbox LIVE Community Games, visit the XNA Creators Club web site (`http://creators.xna.com/en-us/XboxLIVECommunityGames`).

In the remainder of this chapter, you'll create a simple class to illustrate the basic features needed to implement simple multiplayer games, so you'll be ready to explore these concepts further in the next chapter and later on your own.

Although coding a complete multiplayer game might be challenging, the basic steps are simple for creating a multiplayer host, where other players can connect. The game host can be a player, in a peer-to-peer game, or a server machine, if you are using the client/server approach. There are four steps to create a host:

- Sign in a gamer (with a local or remote profile).

- Create a session, establishing its properties, including available slots.

- Wait for other players to join and be ready.

- Change the session state to "game started."

Similarly, you can resume the creation of a game client in four simple steps, which are valid for both peer-to-peer and client/server games:

- Sign in a gamer (with a local or remote profile).

- Find any sessions with empty slots to join.

- Join the session.

- Change the player state to "ready."

In the next section, we'll present the `NetworkHelper` class, which you'll create to help your program use XNA's basic network features.

Starting the Gamer Services Component

In 2002, Microsoft created Xbox LIVE (officially spelled with all caps), an online service for distributing game content (such as demos, trailers, and extra content for games) and connecting Xbox players. The ability to play your console games with remote players, display your high scores online, and much more led to a widespread adoption of LIVE. By the end of 2008, there were around 15 million Gold members on Xbox LIVE. Who knows how many Silver members (free accounts) there are? This made Microsoft extend the online service for Windows Games in 2007, with the launching of Games for Windows—LIVE.

In XNA 3.0 you can connect to both Xbox and Windows LIVE services, depending on the platform on which your game is running. You can also connect up to eight Zunes on an ad hoc network, for multiplayer Zune games.

The XNA programming team packed all the complexity of manipulating LIVE profiles in the `GamerServices` namespace, making it simple for developers to use LIVE capabilities such as creating local accounts, connecting to a LIVE profile, and using many available LIVE guide user interface screens to manipulate gamer information.

The easiest way to get access to LIVE features is through the `GamerServicesComponent` that, when created in a game, runs the Gamer Services pump at regular intervals. This allows your game, for instance, to respond to user interaction such as presenting the LIVE guide when the user presses the Home key.

Let's see this in action in a simple project. Follow these steps to get started:

1. Create a new Windows Game project, and name it `XNADemo`.

2. Open the `Game1` class. Include the following code line in the class constructor, just after the line that sets the content root directory:

```
Components.Add(new GamerServicesComponent(this));
```

3. Run the game. Press the Home key on your keyboard.

4. Windows LIVE will display the opening screen shown in Figure 5-5, and let you create a new gamer profile (free of charge) if you don't have one yet, or connect to LIVE using an existing profile.

   - If you already have a local profile, or if you ever connected to a LIVE profile from your machine, a different set of screens will be presented, so you don't need to follow the next steps to create a local profile. You can log in and skip to the next section.

   - If you don't have a LIVE profile, choose Create New Profile, and you will see the screen in Figure 5-6. Proceed with the next steps to create a local profile.

Note You can sign in to LIVE from an XNA game only if you have a (paid) XNA Creators Club account. Since these accounts are not available for all countries yet, in the rest of the chapter, we will use an offline account, which will let us create multiplayer games for Windows and Zune. However, feel free to sign in and use your current profile if you already have a Creators Club account. Remember that if you want to create XNA games for Xbox 360, you will need to have a Creators Club account to submit your games.

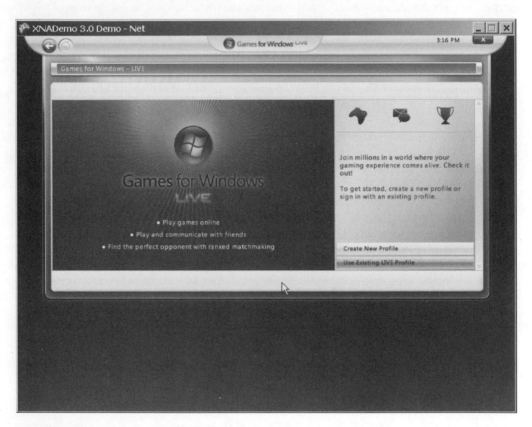

Figure 5-5. *The Games for Windows LIVE opening screen*

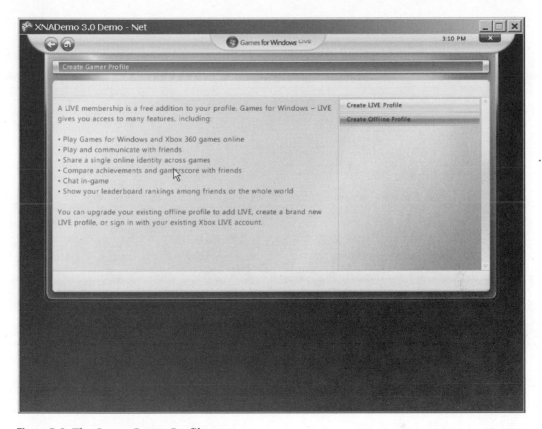

Figure 5-6. *The Create Gamer Profile screen*

5. In the Create Gamer Profile screen, choose the Create Offline Profile option. You will be prompted for a profile name, as shown in Figure 5-7. This profile name (which you can modify later) will be used to identify you when playing network games. Choose a name for your profile and click Submit.

Figure 5-7. *Entering a profile name*

6. Your local profile will be created, and the Save Game Profile screen will appear, as shown in Figure 5-8. Here, you can click Join LIVE to open Internet Explorer and navigate to the Game for Windows–LIVE site. Clicking Customize Profile enables you to configure your profile (for example, the profile image). Clicking Done takes you to a screen where you can configure details about your profile and see some functions (chat, friends, games, and so on) that will be available only if you join LIVE, as shown in Figure 5-9.

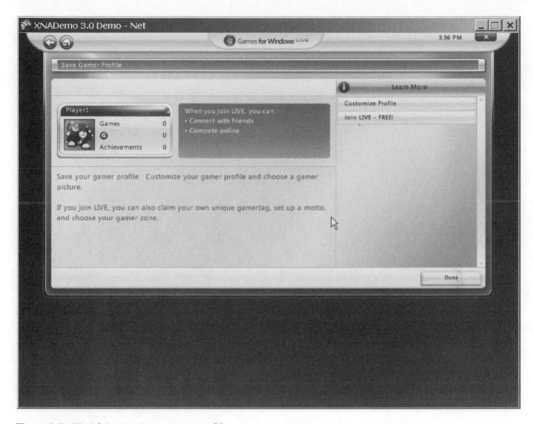

Figure 5-8. *Finishing up your new profile*

In the next section, you will continue coding the sample by creating a helper class that will demonstrate, in a simple way, the basic concepts on XNA networking.

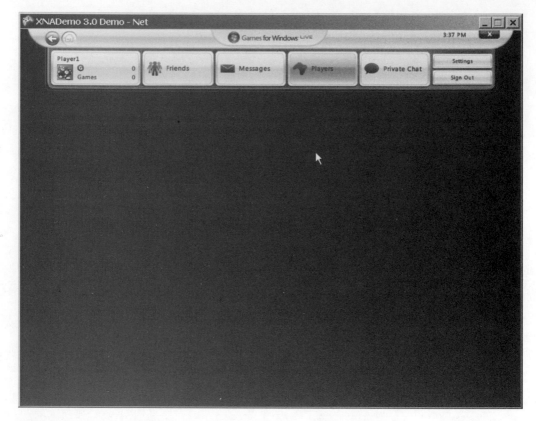

Figure 5-9. *The Games for Windows LIVE screen, for a signed-in player*

Defining the NetworkHelper Class

When creating a real project, you need to choose which approach to creating the network supporting classes is the best. For this example, which is just intended to help you understand the networking concepts, let's keep things as simple as possible. Because the client and the host programs usually have many common features, you'll create a single class, grouping all XNA network routines.

Open the XNADemo project you created in the previous section. Then right-click the project name in the Solution Explorer window and choose Add ➤ Class to create a new, empty class. Name the class NetworkHelper. Include the references to the Microsoft.Xna.Framework.Net and Microsoft.Xna.Framework.GamerServices namespaces at the beginning of the class, and you're ready to go:

```
using System;
using Microsoft.Xna.Framework.Net;
using Microsoft.Xna.Framework.GamerServices;
```

```
namespace XNADemo
{
    class clsNetWorkHelper
    {
    }
}
```

In the next sections, you'll follow the steps to create a host outlined earlier in the chapter: sign in a gamer, create a session, wait for other players to join and be ready, and then change the session state to game started. Using these steps as a guide, you will create the necessary methods and properties in your network helper class.

Signing in a Gamer

In the section "Starting the Gamer Services Component," you created a local profile with automatic sign-in (the default configuration for new profiles), so you don't need to code anything else to sign in a gamer. However, because your goal here is to learn, you'll create a method named SignInGamer, in the NetworkHelper class, which allows you to display the LIVE guide screens programmatically:

```
public void SignInGamer()
{
    if (!Guide.IsVisible)
    {
        Guide.ShowSignIn(1, false);
    }
}
```

This code fragment uses the Guide class to show the LIVE guide. This class is the entry point to any operation related to the LIVE guide. It contains methods to present the guide, show message boxes, and handle text entry and other interface elements. These methods work both in Xbox 360 and Windows.

In the code sample, first you check if the guide is visible and, if not, present it through the ShowSignIn method. This method takes two arguments: the number of panes displayed for gamers' sign-in (always 1 in Windows; 1, 2, or 4 in Xbox 360), and a flag indicating if only online profiles should be displayed. In this case, you are choosing to present one pane, and to display both online and offline profiles.

Now, if you want to display the LIVE guide—for example, when the user presses the F1 key on the keyboard—you can create a network helper object and call this method. To do this, you must define the new object in the Game1 class:

```
NetworkHelper networkHelper;
```

Then, in the Initialize method of the Game1 class, create the object:

```
networkHelper = new NetworkHelper();
```

Finally, call the method in the Update method of the Game1 class, which will look like this after your adjustment:

```
protected override void Update(GameTime gameTime)
{
    // Allows the game to exit
    if (GamePad.GetState(PlayerIndex.One).Buttons.Back ==
        ButtonState.Pressed)
        this.Exit();

    // Presents the LIVE Guide to sign in
    if (Keyboard.GetState().IsKeyDown(Keys.F1))
        networkHelper.SignInGamer();

    base.Update(gameTime);
}
```

Run the program now and press the F1 key on the keyboard. The LIVE guide pops up. Now that you have a signed-in player, the next step is to create a session.

Creating a Session

The XNA Framework NetworkSession class represents a multiplayer session and is used to create, find, join, and end sessions. It also offers a series of properties that allow you to gather information about the current session.

Note XNA 3.0 still can start only one Games for Windows—LIVE network support program per machine, so you need to run your sample on two machines to test it: one for creating the session and another to find and join the session.

To create a new session, you'll use the NetworkSession.Create method, which receives up to five parameters:

- The session type, which can be NetworkSessionType.Local (no networking, used for split-screen games; works only for Xbox 360), NetworkSessionType.SystemLink (connects two machines, Xbox 360 or PC, in the same subnet), NetworkSessionType.PlayerMatch (allows connection through the LIVE servers) and NetworkSessionType.Ranked (used for ranked commercial games that passed Xbox LIVE certification).

- The maximum number of local (in the same machine) players.

- The numbers of slots for players on this session (from 2 to a maximum of 31 players).

- The number of private slots (optional parameter), stating how many of the session slots are reserved for players who join through invitation. If this number is equal to the number of session slots, the session will accept only invited players.

- The session properties (optional parameter): a collection of custom properties that you can use to define any game-specific values, such as the game difficulty level or the time limit for the session. These properties, stored as a NetworkSessionProperties class, are also used to filter the results when searching for sessions to join.

To create the session, you'll define some private class-level variables and code a new method, CreateSession, in your NetworkHelper class:

```
private NetworkSession session = null;  // The game session
private int maximumGamers = 2;  // Only 2 will play
private int maximumLocalPlayers = 1;  // No split-screen, only remote players

public void CreateSession()
{
    if (session == null)
    {
        session = NetworkSession.Create(NetworkSessionType.SystemLink,
                                        maximumLocalPlayers,
                                        maximumGamers);
    }
}
```

Creating a multiplayer game session in XNA is simple as that: only one command, and you're good to go!

However, for this session to work, processing the network packets properly, you'll need to call its Update method on every game update cycle. To do this, include an Update method on your NetworkHelper class:

```
public void Update()
{
    if (session != null)
        session.Update();
}
```

The best way to call this method in every game loop cycle is by including the following line at the beginning of the Game1 Update method:

```
networkHelper.Update();
```

Now your session is created and ready to process network messages. You might also want to configure some details about the session behavior. For instance, you can include the following lines just after the session creation:

```
// If the host goes out, another machine will assume as a new host
session.AllowHostMigration = true;
// Allow players to join a game in progress
session.AllowJoinInProgress = true;
```

You can also configure your `NetworkHelper` class to respond to session events. To see what is going on, create a new read-only string property for your class, `Message`, and code the session event handlers to set this property properly:

```
// Message regarding the session's current state
private String message = "Waiting for user command...";
public String Message
{
    get { return message; }
}
```

Now that the message property is set up, let's include the event hooks in the `CreateSession` method, after the session creation, by incorporating the following lines:

```
session.GamerJoined +=
            new EventHandler<GamerJoinedEventArgs>(session_GamerJoined);
session.GamerLeft +=
            new EventHandler<GamerLeftEventArgs>(session_GamerLeft);
session.GameStarted +=
            new EventHandler<GameStartedEventArgs>(session_GameStarted);
session.GameEnded +=
            new EventHandler<GameEndedEventArgs>(session_GameEnded);
session.SessionEnded +=
            new EventHandler<NetworkSessionEndedEventArgs>(session_SessionEnded);
session.HostChanged +=
            new EventHandler<HostChangedEventArgs>(session_HostChanged);
```

In the previous code excerpt, you inform the session object that you'll handle every single event that it offers. However, you must keep in mind this is not necessary: you should code only the relevant events according to your game logic. For example, if you set the session property `AllowHostMigration` to `False`, the `HostChanged` event will never happen.

Getting back to our example, all you need for now is to set the `message` property you created with some explanatory messages, so you can code the game's main class to write the `message` content in the game window, and then be able to see when each event happens.

The next listing presents the code snippets for setting the `message` property on each event you created the hook for:

```
void session_GamerJoined(object sender, GamerJoinedEventArgs e)
{
    if (e.Gamer.IsHost)
        message = "The Host started the session!";
    else
        message = "Gamer " + e.Gamer.Tag + " joined the session!";
}
```

```
void session_GamerLeft(object sender, GamerLeftEventArgs e)
{
    message = "Gamer " + e.Gamer.Tag + " left the session!";
}

void session_GameStarted(object sender, GameStartedEventArgs e)
{
    message = "Game Started";
 }

void session_HostChanged(object sender, HostChangedEventArgs e)
{
    message = "Host changed from " + e.OldHost.Tag + " to " + e.NewHost.Tag;
}

 void session_SessionEnded(object sender, NetworkSessionEndedEventArgs e)
{
     message = "The session has ended";
}

void session_GameEnded(object sender, GameEndedEventArgs e)
{
    message = "Game Over";
}
```

The session events have self-explanatory names. The GamerJoined event happens every time a new gamer joins the session, so you must include the proper code for new player initialization there. The GamerLeft event occurs when a gamer leaves the session, so here you must include the code for gracefully allowing the game to continue without that player, or maybe the code to end the game, and so on.

To finish coding for session creation, you need to write only the code in the Update method of the Game1 class to start a session (let's say, when the user presses the F2 key on the keyboard):

```
// Creates a session
if (Keyboard.GetState().IsKeyDown(Keys.F2))
    networkHelper.CreateSession();
```

Your program is ready to go, but if you want to see the message with the session state, you need to code for it. Right-click your project in the Solution Explorer window and choose Add ➤ New Item. Choose to add a new SpriteFont in your project and name it Arial. Include the following line at the beginning of the Game1 class to declare the SpriteFont object:

```
SpriteFont Arial;
```

Then load the file you just included in the project by adding the following line to the LoadContent method of the Game1 class:

```
Arial = Content.Load<SpriteFont>("Arial");
```

Now, all you need is to use the SpriteBatch the XNA Framework kindly created for you to draw the message using your SpriteFont, in the Draw method of the Game1 class:

```
// Show the current session state
spriteBatch.Begin();
spriteBatch.DrawString(Arial, "Game State: " + networkHelper.Message,
                                    new Vector2(20, lineHeight), Color.Yellow);
spriteBatch.End();
```

Run your program now, and press F1 (or the Start button on your gamepad) to bring up the player sign-in screen. Sign in from this screen and close it, and then press F2 to start a new session. You can see the result—not quite impressive—in Figure 5-10.

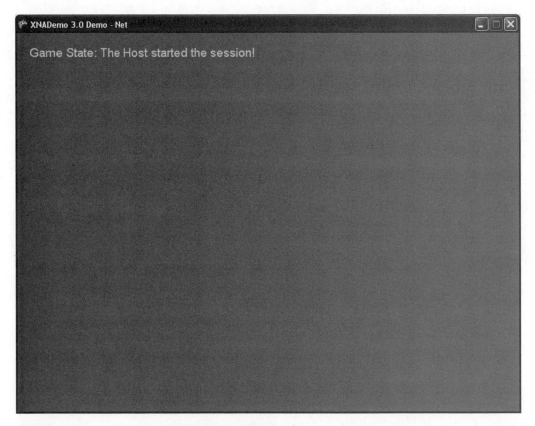

Figure 5-10. *Game screen with a "The Host started the session!" message*

■**Note** XNA Game Studio 3.0 introduces a change in the behavior of network sessions. In XNA 2.0, every time a local player signed out, the session ended. For XNA games running in Windows, this was not a problem, since you can have only one local player. However, for the Xbox 360, this was undesirable, since you can have up to four local players. With XNA 3.0, if a local player signs out, his profile is simply removed from the session, and the session will end only if there are no more local players connected to it.

In the next section, you'll code the client-side routines used to find and join sessions.

Finding and Joining a Session Synchronously

Connecting synchronously to an existing session is almost as easy as creating a session, with straightforward code. You need to search for available sessions using the Find method of the NetworkSession object, then check if a session has empty slots for you to connect, and finally join the session found.

By including the next code piece in your NetworkHelper class, you'll be able to make your sample search and join game sessions:

```
public void FindSession()
{
  // All sessions found
  AvailableNetworkSessionCollection availableSessions;
  // The session we'll join
  AvailableNetworkSession availableSession = null;

  availableSessions = NetworkSession.Find(NetworkSessionType.SystemLink,
      maximumLocalPlayers, null);

  // Get a session with available gamer slots
  foreach (AvailableNetworkSession curSession in availableSessions)
  {
      int TotalSessionSlots = curSession.OpenPublicGamerSlots +
                                    curSession.OpenPrivateGamerSlots;
      if (TotalSessionSlots > curSession.CurrentGamerCount)
          availableSession = curSession;
  }

  // If a session was found, connect to it
  if (availableSession != null)
  {
      message = "Found an available session at host " +
                        availableSession.HostGamertag;
      session = NetworkSession.Join(availableSession);
  }
  else
      message = "No sessions found!";
}
```

Let's review the code, step by step, to understand its details.

First, you define two variables that will receive objects that help you find and manage sessions: AvailableNetworkSessionCollection, which is a collection of sessions, as returned from the NetworkSession.Find method, and AvailableNetworkSession, which is an item of such a collection.

■**Note** The AvailableNetworkSession object is different from the NetworkSession object. It is only a reference to an available session, with properties that describe a session. You can use it to create a NetworkSession object through the NetworkSession.Join method.

After retrieving these objects, you use the NetworkSession.Find method to retrieve the collection of available sessions. This method receives three parameters: the network session type you are searching for (these types were discussed in the previous session); the maximum number of players; and a collection of NetworkSessionProperties custom properties, which must match the properties used in the session creation. In this example, because you created a session with no custom properties, you can simply pass null as this last argument.

After retrieving the available sessions, the previous code loops through these sessions and checks if any of them have empty slots for you to sign in, comparing the sum of the available session properties OpenPublicGamerSlots and OpenPrivateGamerSlots with the total gamers already signed in to the session, given by the CurrentGamerCount property.

Finally, you set the message NetworkHelper property with the corresponding message (stating if you did or didn't find a session to join). If you find a session with empty slots, you join the session using the NetworkSession.Join method, passing the available session found as a parameter.

To finish coding for session finding, you need to adjust the Update method of the Game1 class to call your Find method. You can fire the session to find when the user presses the F3 key on the keyboard through the following code:

```
// Looks for a session
if (Keyboard.GetState().IsKeyDown(Keys.F3))
    networkHelper.FindSession();
```

To test your program, you'll need two machines. Run the program on both machines, and follow the steps presented earlier in the section "Creating a Session" on the first computer.

On the second computer, run the program. Press the F1 key to be sure that there's a signed-in player (otherwise the session finding will fail), and then press F3 to find a session. If both computers are in the same subnet, XNA will be able to find the session, and the screen will present the message "Found an available session at host *XXX*," where *XXX* is the gamer tag signed in to the host machine, as shown in Figure 5-11.

■**Tip** The AvailableNetworkSession object has a property, QualityOfService, which is a class filled with information about the quality of the connection after the XNA Framework gathers this data (check the isAvailable property of this class to check if data is already gathered). This class has four properties, which present the minimum and average round-trip time for the network packets, and the available bandwidth from the host to the local machine and from the local machine to the host. You can find more detailed information about the AvailableNetworkSession properties and methods at http://msdn.microsoft.com/en-us/library/microsoft.xna.framework.net.availablenetworksession.aspx.

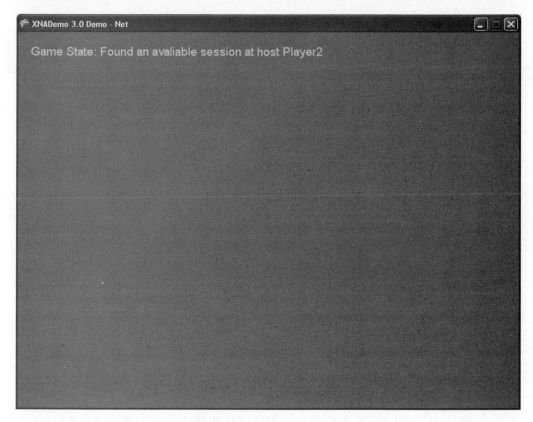

Figure 5-11. *Game screen with a "Found an available session" message*

In the next section, you'll see how to find sessions asynchronously.

Finding and Joining a Session Asynchronously

Coding for asynchronous session searching is an approach commonly used in games because you usually don't want to freeze the game and the player options when searching for available sessions. The basic idea for session finding and joining is the same as you saw in the previous section. However, here, you'll use the BeginFind and EndFind NetworkSession methods, which start a session search, indicating the function to be called when the searching is ended, and get the results from the search, respectively.

The next code sample, to be included in your NetworkHelper class, defines a new variable used to store and track the status of the asynchronous operation, and a method that will call BeginFind to start the session searching:

```
IAsyncResult AsyncSessionFind = null;
public void AsyncFindSession()
{
    message = "Asynchronous search started!";
```

```
    if (AsyncSessionFind == null)
    {
        AsyncSessionFind = NetworkSession.BeginFind(
            NetworkSessionType.SystemLink,  maximumLocalPlayers, null,
            new AsyncCallback(session_SessionFound), null);
    }
}
```

BeginFind receives the same parameters from the Find method discussed in the previous section (session type, maximum number of players, and custom session properties), plus the address of the callback function (which is called when the search results are ready). BeginFind also receives an object used to store the state of the asynchronous operation (let's not bother about this last one right now; it's fine just to pass a null value).

In the previous code sample, you passed session_SessionFound as the callback function for BeginFind. The next code excerpt presents the code for the callback function that, as you'll see, is very similar to your previously coded FindSession method:

```
public void session_SessionFound(IAsyncResult result)
{
  // All sessions found
  AvailableNetworkSessionCollection availableSessions;
  // The session we will join
  AvailableNetworkSession availableSession = null;

  if (AsyncSessionFind.IsCompleted)
  {
      availableSessions = NetworkSession.EndFind(result);

      // Look for a session with available gamer slots
      foreach (AvailableNetworkSession curSession in
               availableSessions)
      {
          int TotalSessionSlots = curSession.OpenPublicGamerSlots +
                                  curSession.OpenPrivateGamerSlots;
          if (TotalSessionSlots > curSession.CurrentGamerCount)
              availableSession = curSession;
      }

      // If a session was found, connect to it
      if (availableSession != null)
      {
          message = "Found an available session at host" +
                        availableSession.HostGamertag;
          session = NetworkSession.Join(availableSession);
      }
      else
          message = "No sessions found!";
```

```
        // Reset the session finding result
        AsyncSessionFind = null;
    }
}
```

This code excerpt is almost identical to your FindSession synchronous method; in fact, only three lines are different:

- The test to check the AsyncSessionFind.IsCompleted property to see if the results are already available

- Using NetworkSession.EndFind (instead of NetworkSession.Find) to retrieve the available sessions collection

- The last line of the listing, where you simply reset the AsyncSessionFind result variable

So, if you understand the synchronous session searching concepts, you have just a few new things to learn when dealing with asynchronous ones.

All you need to do now is to revise the Update method of the Game1 class to call the new asynchronous session-finding method, by including the following lines:

```
// Find a session asynchronously
if (Keyboard.GetState().IsKeyDown(Keys.F4))
    networkHelper.AsyncFindSession();
```

You can test the new code by again executing the steps you used in the previous section to join a session synchronously, except that you press the F4 key instead of F3. On the client machine, you'll see the message "Asynchronous search started!" followed, a few seconds later, by the message that states the result of the session searching.

Now you have two machines with signed-in gamers. The first one creates a session and acts as a host, and the second one joins the session created. So, it's time to inform XNA that you are ready to go and start the game!

Starting the Game

In XNA, A game session has three possible states, informed by its SessionState property:

- NetworkSessionState.Lobby: A session in this state means that the local machine has joined a session and is ready to start, but is waiting for other players to join and the host to start the game. The host knows when all players are ready by checking the IsEveryoneReady property of the session object. It can check the number of signed-in gamers by consulting Gamer.SignedInGamers.Count.

- NetworkSessionState.Playing: When the host starts the game, by calling the StartGame method of the session object, the GameStarted session event is fired for all players, and the session state changes from Lobby to Playing.

- NetworkSessionState.Ended: Similarly, the host calls the EndGame method of the session object to finish a game, firing the GameEnded session event for all players and changing the session state from Playing to Ended.

So, once you have all players connected in the same session, you need every player to report that she is ready and to include the code in the host to start and end the game.

Signaling that all local players (maximum of one in Windows; up to four in Xbox 360) are ready is easy through the session object, which has a collection with references to all local gamers' profiles. The next code sample shows a new method for your NetworkHelper class that does this job:

```
public void SetPlayerReady ()
{
    foreach (LocalNetworkGamer gamer in session.LocalGamers)
        gamer.IsReady = true;
}
```

Although you can use this method in a real game, in this sample, you have only two players, so you don't need to wait for other players to join. As soon as the second machine joins a session, the host can start the game. To do this, you can include an extra line on the gamerJoined event to start the game as soon as the host detects that another player joined the game, as presented in the following code snippet:

```
void session_GamerJoined(object sender, GamerJoinedEventArgs e)
{
    if (e.Gamer.IsHost)
    {
        message = "The Host started the session!";
    }
    else
    {
        message = "Gamer " + e.Gamer.Tag + " joined the session!";
        // Other played joined, start the game!
        session.StartGame();
    }
}
```

If you run your program now on your two test machines, pressing F2 on the host machine and pressing F3 or F4 to find the session on the second machine, the host machine will automatically start the game and present the game started message (which you coded in the GameStarted event of the session object in the earlier section "Creating a Session").

At this point, you have two machines connected in the same game. Following the general guidelines presented in this section, you can easily extend the sample by writing the code to end the game by calling the session.EndGame method.

All you need to know now is how to send data from one machine to another, and you'll have all the basic knowledge needed to include network support in your games.

Handling Messages

Sending and receiving messages is simply a matter of calling the SendData and ReceiveData methods of the LocalNetworkGamer class, which represents a local player.

Both methods can handle arrays of bytes or a packet writer, which is a binary data streamer. A packet writer receives basic data types and transforms them into an array of bytes in an efficient way. Because dealing with packet writers is easier, let's work with them. Start by creating a new class-level variable in your NetworkHelper class, named packetWriter:

```
PacketWriter packetWriter = new PacketWriter();
```

You can now use this packet writer to stream your messages to one or all the other remote players by looping through your session's LocalGamers collection and calling the SendData method, as follows:

```
public void SendMessage(string key)
{
    foreach (LocalNetworkGamer localPlayer in session.LocalGamers)
    {
        packetWriter.Write(key);
        localPlayer.SendData(packetWriter, SendDataOptions.None);
        message = "Sending message: " + key;
    }
}
```

The SendData method can define the reliability and the order reinforcement for the message in its SendDataOptions parameter, which can be set to the follows:

- None: Packet sent with no guarantees.

- InOrder: Packet sent in order, but a packet loss might happen.

- Reliable: Packet always reaches its destination, but might arrive out of order.

- ReliableInOrder: No packet loss, and all packets are delivered in the same order they were sent.

- Chat: Mark the message as chat data (new to XNA 3.0).

■**Note** The Chat option can be combined with the other members of the enumeration, such as InOrder or Reliable, and will cause the data inside the network packet to be sent without encryption. This was included to allow XNA network packets to comply with international regulations regarding encrypted chat. Keep in mind that to maintain security, other game data should not use this flag, although it's okay to mix chat data with other data (in other words, to mix encrypted and nonencrypted data) in the same packet.

Remember what we said in the beginning of this chapter: decide which option is best for your game.

Additionally, the SendData method has overloads that receive an extra NetworkGamer parameter, which allows your game to send messages to a specific player. If this parameter is not reported, the message is delivered to all signed-in players.

In the SendMessage method, you are packing only one string, but you could pack a number of variables, depending on your game logic. For example, if you want to send the left thumb-stick and both triggers' state to all other players, you can write your packet as shown in the next code fragment:

```
GamePadState GamePad1 = GamePad.GetState(PlayerIndex.One);
packetWriter.Write(GamePad1.Triggers.Left);
packetWriter.Write(GamePad1.Triggers.Right);
packetWriter.Write(GamePad1.ThumbSticks.Left);
```

The method to receive messages is just as simple: you'll loop through the local gamers' collection and check if there is any available message. If so, you need to call the ReceiveData method of the LocalNetworkGamer object until you consume all available data. ReceiveData returns arrays of bytes or a packetReader (the counterpart of packetWriter, used to write the packet), and also a NetworkGamer object with data from the remote player, which you can use to test if you want to process the message or not, depending on the game logic.

The next code excerpt presents a simple implementation of a routine that consumes messages from other players:

```
PacketReader packetReader = new PacketReader();
public void ReceiveMessage()
{
    NetworkGamer remotePlayer;  // The sender of the message

    foreach (LocalNetworkGamer localPlayer in session.LocalGamers)
    {
        // While there is data available for us, keep reading
        while (localPlayer.IsDataAvailable)
        {
            localPlayer.ReceiveData(packetReader, out remotePlayer);
            // Ignore input from local players
            if (!remotePlayer.IsLocal)
                message = "Received message: " +
                            packetReader.ReadString();
        }
    }
}
```

The send and receive routines of your game must write and read the same data structures, in the same order.

And if you want to read the left thumbstick and both triggers' data, you need to write your code for reading packets as follows:

```
remoteThumbstick = packetReader.ReadVector2();
remoteLeftTrigger = packetReader.ReadSingle();
remoteRightTrigger = packetReader.ReadSingle();
```

■Note You must use the same order for the data types when writing and reading the packets, since all data will be converted to bytes in a byte stream. If you read the information in a different order, you may not get any application errors, but you could end up with invalid data, which may be a hard problem to debug.

Now that your sending and writing routines are in place, you need to call them from the Update method of the Game1 class, to test them. Because you want to send and receive messages only when the game is running, create a new property for the NetworkHelper class that returns the current session state:

```
public NetworkSessionState SessionState
{
    get
    {
        if (session == null)
            return NetworkSessionState.Ended;
        else
            return session.SessionState;
    }
}
```

Now, let's include the calls for sending and receiving messages in the Update method, when the session is in "playing" state:

```
if (networkHelper.SessionState == NetworkSessionState.Playing)
{
    // Send any key pressed to the remote player
    foreach (Keys key in Keyboard.GetState().GetPressedKeys())
        networkHelper.SendMessage(key.ToString());

    // Receive the keys from the remote player
    networkHelper.ReceiveMessage();
}
```

To test your program, run the test from the previous section, until you have two machines connected and the game started. At this point, press any key, and you'll see the message "Sending message:" followed by the key pressed on the first machine, and the message "Received message:" followed by the key pressed on the remote machine in the second one.

Adding a Final Touch

While we presented the various concepts through this chapter, you programmed a lot of keys to have a special meaning. To help you when testing your program, what about updating the Draw method of the Game1 class to present some helper messages stating the meaning of each key? Just update this method to reflect the next code example:

```
protected override void Draw(GameTime gameTime)
{
    graphics.GraphicsDevice.Clear(Color.CornflowerBlue);

    // Show the current session state
    spriteBatch.Begin();
    spriteBatch.DrawString(Arial, "Game State: " +
                networkHelper.Message,
                new Vector2(20, 20), Color.Yellow);
    spriteBatch.DrawString(Arial, "Press:", new Vector2(20, 100),
                Color.Snow);
    spriteBatch.DrawString(Arial, " - F1 to sign in",
                new Vector2(20, 120), Color.Snow);
    spriteBatch.DrawString(Arial, " - F2 to create a session",
                new Vector2(20, 140), Color.Snow);
    spriteBatch.DrawString(Arial, " - F3 to find a session",
                new Vector2(20, 160), Color.Snow);
    spriteBatch.DrawString(Arial, " - F4 to asynchronously find a
session",
                new Vector2(20, 180), Color.Snow);

    spriteBatch.DrawString(Arial, "After the game starts, press other
keys to send messages",
                new Vector2(20, 220), Color.Snow);
    spriteBatch.End();

    base.Draw(gameTime);
}
```

Now, when you start the game, you have a quick reference for all keys that have some special meaning, as presented in Figure 5-12.

Remember that when testing this application, you need to execute the commands in order: sign in a gamer, create a session, join a session (only on the other machine), set the players as "ready," and start sending and receiving messages. For example, make sure that you never try to create or find a session if there are no signed-in players.

And that completes this chapter's example.

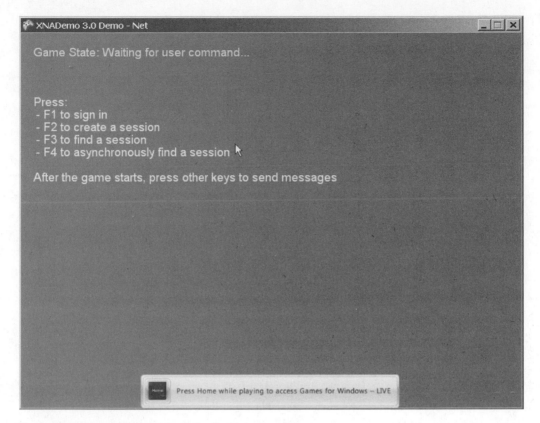

Figure 5-12. *Game screen with the key helper messages*

Summary

This chapter started by presenting some generic concepts involved in creating networked games. Planning carefully and testing the networked games thoroughly are probably the most important points, because networked games have many more potential error sources than local, single-player games.

As for XNA network features, everything is pretty simple:

- When you include the Gamer Services component in your game, you automatically have access to all LIVE guide features.

- To host a session, all you need to do is call the `NetworkSession.Create` method.

- Joining a session on a remote computer is as simple as calling the `NetworkSession.Find` method (to look for a session) and the `NetworkSession.Join` method (to join a session).

- Starting and ending a game is also simple: when the host calls the StartGame method of the session object, all players enter the game playing state and receive a GameStarted event. The GameEnd method generates opposite results, firing a GameEnded event and setting the session to a game ended state.

- Sending messages is as easy as using the PacketWriter and PacketReader classes and the SendData and ReceiveData methods of the LocalNetworkGamer class.

In the next chapter, you'll apply the XNA networking concepts you learned here to create a network-enabled version of the Rock Rain game.

■■■

CHAPTER 6

Rock Rain Live!

The game in Chapter 4 mainly showed a playability change, allowing a match between two players on the same PC or on the same Xbox 360 console. This is nice, but how about being able to play with your friend on the other side of the world? And what about matches with one player running on a PC and another one on an Xbox 360? Wouldn't that be cool?

In this chapter, you'll use the concepts in the previous chapter and add a networked multiplayer feature to Rock Rain, called multiplayer online. This new version is named Rock Rain *Live*.

Planning Rock Rain Live

Rock Rain Enhanced already implements many of the features that you need for a new multiplayer online version of Rock Rain. For the new version, you'll add a new item to the game's starting screen menu that leads to another scene with the options of network games (create a game, join a game's session, and so on). With this new scene, the start scene will look like Figure 6-1.

Still, you need to consider how your game will work in a network. You saw in the previous chapter that XNA offers all the support for data transport between the players through a network, whether it a local network or through Xbox LIVE. It's simple to send and receive data in a synchronized and safe way, but the main question is this: *what* should you send or receive between the two players to create a network match?

Remember that Rock Rain is a game in which you must dodge the meteors (and the other player) and try to get the energy source to remain as long as possible in the game. So, the two players must be synchronized so that they see the same meteors, the other player's score, the energy source, and so on; that is, they must share the same *state* of the game.

In Chapter 2, we talked a little about game state. Controlling this state is one of the most important tasks in any game. In Rock Rain Live's case, along with controlling this state, you also need to think about how to *synchronize* this state between the two players who will be playing a match through a local network or through the LIVE network from Microsoft.

In this game, you'll use a client/server architecture, described in the previous chapter, where one of the players is the game's server, offering the synchrony services of the game state itself. You'll call that player the *local player*. The other player is the game's client, consuming the data from the server to show the correct status of the game to the other player. You'll call that player the *remote player*.

Figure 6-1. *The new start scene*

It seems obvious then that the remote player will always consume information from the local player to obtain the game state. The remote player will always ask the state of the game, obtaining from the local player the score of the game, the meteors' positions, and so on. This means that the local player will always have "control" of the game state, and it's up to that player to change this state (add a new meteor, for instance).

However, the remote player controls a new game state: its own position on the screen. You'll also need to inform the local player of the remote player's position, so that the game state stays synchronized between the two players.

This information exchange involves a lot of code, but it's not complicated. You'll create all the communication protocols to send the game state information between the players in a simple but powerful way, which can be changed or extended to other games.

Adding the Support for Network Games

Thanks to the excellent XNA network support, adding these new features to Rock Rain Enhanced is simple. Actually, you can copy all the game project code from Chapter 4 and change its name to Rock Rain Live. Also, change the classes' namespace name to RockRainLive (using Visual Studio's refactoring tool if you wish). Then add the following line in the Game1 class constructor:

```
// Add Live support
Components.Add(new GamerServicesComponent(this));
```

Also add the namespace reference:

```
using Microsoft.Xna.Framework.GamerServices;
```

Execute the game. It's the same old version of Rock Rain. Press the Home key on the keyboard or the Guide button on the Xbox 360 gamepad, and you'll see a host of new features.

Now you can start to implement your new version of Rock Rain.

Changing the Opening Screen

Since the screen flow is now different, you must change the opening screen to reflect the new Network Game option, which initially involves a menu change. So, locate the StartScene class constructor and change the line where you created the menu, as follows:

```
// Create the menu
string[] items = {"One Player", "Two Players", "Network Game",
                  "Help", "Quit"};
```

Because you added a new item, you need to change the HandleStartSceneInput method of the Game1 class so that you update the indices of the menu options that open the help screen and of the option that quits the game:

```
/// <summary>
/// Handle buttons and keyboard in StartScene
/// </summary>
private void HandleStartSceneInput()
{
    if (CheckEnterA())
    {
        audio.MenuSelect.Play();
        switch (startScene.SelectedMenuIndex)
        {
            case 0:
                actionScene.TwoPlayers = false;
                ShowScene(actionScene);
                break;
            case 1:
                actionScene.TwoPlayers = true;
                ShowScene(actionScene);
                break;
            case 3:
                ShowScene(helpScene);
                break;
```

```
            case 4:
                Exit();
                break;
        }
    }
}
```

Also, in the HandleScenesInput method of the Game1 class (which manipulates the input of all scenes), add the manipulation support for this new scene:

```
/// <summary>
/// Handle input of all game scenes
/// </summary>
private void HandleScenesInput()
{
    // Handle start scene input
    if (activeScene == startScene)
    {
        HandleStartSceneInput();
    }
    // Handle help scene input
    else if (activeScene == helpScene)
    {
        if (CheckEnterA())
        {
            ShowScene(startScene);
        }
    }
    // Handle action scene input
    else if (activeScene == actionScene)
    {
        HandleActionInput();
    }
    else
    {
        // Handle network scene input
        HandleNetworkSceneInput();
    }
}
```

Let's create the method that will manipulate the network's scene input.

```
/// <summary>
/// Handle network scene menu
/// </summary>
private void HandleNetworkSceneInput()
{
}
```

The guide that you saw in the previous chapter adds a series of services to your game, and, when it's opened, your game should not capture the user's inputs, because this could confuse the player. Therefore, also change the Update method of the Game1 class, as follows, so you don't capture the user's inputs when the guide is opened:

```
/// <summary>
/// Allows the game to run logic such as updating the world,
/// checking for collisions, gathering input, and playing audio.
/// </summary>
/// <param name="gameTime">Provides a snapshot of timing values.</param>
protected override void Update(GameTime gameTime)
{
    // Handle Game Inputs
    if (!Guide.IsVisible)
    {
        HandleScenesInput();
    }

    base.Update(gameTime);
}
```

Execute the game and everything should work normally, except the Network Game option does nothing. You'll make this option open the multiplayer game scene later.

Creating the Network Game Scene

Now you'll create the scene that allows players to create a session or join a session of a network game. Similar to what you did in Chapter 4, add a new public class called NetworkScene and derive it from GameScene (in the RockRain.Core namespace) so that you have a new scene class. First, add the namespace reference for the network support:

```
using Microsoft.Xna.Framework.GamerServices;
```

In this scene, you have only a background image, a menu, and a text line to show the messages related to the connection with the other player and background music. In it, you can choose, through the menu, to start a new network game (creating a server), join a game that's already started, or log in to the network and return to the previous scene. Each option opens a new menu, in such a way that you need to track this scene's state so that you can show the correct menu. The following enumeration creates the possible state of this scene:

```
// Scene state
public enum NetworkGameState
{
    idle = 1,
    joining = 2,
    creating = 3
}
```

As already mentioned, in this scene you have a menu, a background texture, and a blinking message. Declare the objects necessary to compose this scene:

```
// Misc
protected TextMenuComponent menu;
private readonly SpriteFont messageFont;
private Vector2 messagePosition,messageShadowPosition;
private string message;
protected TimeSpan elapsedTime = TimeSpan.Zero;

// SpriteBatch
protected SpriteBatch spriteBatch = null;

// Scene state
private NetworkGameState state;
// Used for message blink
private bool showMessage = true;
```

In the constructor, initialize these objects, as you did with all the scenes throughout Chapter 4:

```
/// <summary>
/// Default constructor
/// </summary>
/// <param name="game">Main game object</param>
/// <param name="smallFont">Font for the menu items</param>
/// <param name="largeFont">Font for the menu selected item</param>
/// <param name="background">Texture for background image</param>
public NetworkScene(Game game, SpriteFont smallFont, SpriteFont largeFont,
                    Texture2D background) : base(game)
{
    messageFont = largeFont;
    Components.Add(new ImageComponent(game, background,
                                      ImageComponent.DrawMode.Stretch));

    // Create the menu component
    menu = new TextMenuComponent(game, smallFont, largeFont);
    Components.Add(menu);

    // Get the current sprite batch
    spriteBatch = (SpriteBatch)Game.Services.GetService(
                                      typeof(SpriteBatch));
}
```

The scene state must also be the same when the user opens it:

```
/// <summary>
/// Show scene
/// </summary>
public override void Show()
{
    state = NetworkGameState.idle;

    base.Show();
}
```

The menu components largely perform the drawing of the scene itself, for images that were already added to the scene. You need to draw only the message text that keeps blinking, just as you did in the scene of the game's beginning, in Chapter 4. Note that the message is also drawn twice to give a shadow effect:

```
/// <summary>
/// Allows the game component to draw your content in game screen
/// </summary>
public override void Draw(GameTime gameTime)
{
    base.Draw(gameTime);

    if (!string.IsNullOrEmpty(message) && showMessage)
    {
        DrawMessage();
    }
}
```

```
/// <summary>
/// Helper draws notification messages before calling blocking
/// network methods.
/// </summary>
void DrawMessage()
{
    // Draw the shadow
    spriteBatch.DrawString(messageFont, message, messageShadowPosition,
        Color.Black);

    // Draw the message
    spriteBatch.DrawString(messageFont, message, messagePosition,
        Color.DarkOrange);
}
```

You should expose the message attribute of the class so that the program is able to tell the scene in which the message will be showed. You use this message to show text such as "connecting . . ." or "connection terminated":

```
/// <summary>
/// Text of the message line
/// </summary>
public string Message
{
    get { return message; }
    set
    {
        message = value;
        // Calculate the message position
        messagePosition = new Vector2();
        messagePosition.X = (Game.Window.ClientBounds.Width -
            messageFont.MeasureString(message).X)/2;
        messagePosition.Y = 130;

        // Calculate the message shadow position
        messageShadowPosition = messagePosition;
        messageShadowPosition.Y++;
        messageShadowPosition.X--;

    }
}
```

The Update method is responsible only for controlling the time to create the blink effect of the message on the screen and updating the menu to reflect the scene's current status:

```
/// <summary>
/// Allows the game component to update itself
/// </summary>
/// <param name="gameTime">Provides a snapshot of timing values</param>
public override void Update(GameTime gameTime)
{
    elapsedTime += gameTime.ElapsedGameTime;

    if (elapsedTime > TimeSpan.FromSeconds(1))
    {
        elapsedTime -= TimeSpan.FromSeconds(1);
        showMessage = !showMessage;
    }

    // Set the menu for the current state
    UpdateMenus();

    base.Update(gameTime);
}
```

The UpdateMenus method creates the menu for the current status. In particular, you create a menu when there is no user logged into the network, so that the user can log in before creating or joining a game:

```
/// <summary>
/// Build a menu for each scene state and network status
/// </summary>
private void UpdateMenus()
{
    if (Gamer.SignedInGamers.Count == 0)
    {
        string[] items = {"Sign in", "Back"};
        menu.SetMenuItems(items);
    }
    else
    {
        if (state == NetworkGameState.idle)
        {
            string[] items = {"Join a System Link Game",
                "Create a System Link Game", "Sign out", "Back"};
            menu.SetMenuItems(items);
        }
        if (state == NetworkGameState.creating)
        {
            string[] items = { "Cancel"};
            menu.SetMenuItems(items);
        }
    ]

    // Put the menu centered in screen
    menu.Position = new Vector2((Game.Window.ClientBounds.Width -
                              menu.Width) / 2, 330);
}
```

And as you've always done, expose the menu option selected so that the Game1 class is able to execute the options the user selects. Also, expose the scene state so that the Game1 class is also able to change it when needed. Then add the following code to the NetworkScene class:

```
/// <summary>
/// Gets the selected menu option
/// </summary>
public int SelectedMenuIndex
{
    get { return menu.SelectedIndex; }
}
```

```
/// <summary>
/// Scene state
/// </summary>
public NetworkGameState State
{
    get { return state; }
    set
    {
        state = value;
        menu.SelectedIndex = 0;
    }
}
```

Now you can use this scene in your game. Start by adding the declaration to a NetworkScene object in the Game1 class:

```
protected NetworkScene networkScene;
```

Then add the background texture of this new scene:

```
protected Texture2D networkBackgroundTexture;
```

The background images for this project are available with the rest of the downloadable code for this book (from the book's details page at http://www.apress.com). Add these images to the Content folder. Then change the LoadContent method, adding the following lines to load the background texture and create the network scene object:

```
// Create the network scene
networkBackgroundTexture = Content.Load<Texture2D>("NetworkBackground");
networkScene = new NetworkScene(this,smallFont,largeFont,
                       networkBackgroundTexture);
Components.Add(networkScene);
```

You need to show this scene only when the user selects it from the initial scene menu. So, add the following code to the switch found in the HandleStartSceneInput method in the Game1 class:

```
case 2:
    ShowScene(networkScene);
    break;
```

Execute the program. Select the Network Game option, and you will see something like Figure 6-2.

Next, return to the HandleNetworkSceneInput method and implement the methods that create and join a session of a network game.

Figure 6-2. *The network game scene*

Controlling the Input to the Scene

The HandleNetworkSceneInput method deals with all input originating from the menu for this scene:

```
/// <summary>
/// Handle Network Scene menu
/// </summary>
private void HandleNetworkSceneInput()
{
    if (CheckEnterA())
    {
        audio.MenuSelect.Play();
        if (Gamer.SignedInGamers.Count == 0)
        {
            HandleNotSigned();
        }
```

```
        else
        {
            HandleSigned();
        }
    }
}
```

This code separates the menu treatment for two distinct situations: when the user is connected and when the user is not connected to the network. The HandleNotSigned method contains all the code for the menu when it's showing the options for a not-connected player, and the HandleSigned method contains the options for a connected user.

All that an unconnected user can do is connect to the network or go back to the initial scene. So, the HandleNotSigned method is simple:

```
/// <summary>
/// Handle network scene menu for an unconnected user
/// </summary>
private void HandleNotSigned()
{
    switch (networkScene.SelectedMenuIndex)
    {
        case 0:
            if (!Guide.IsVisible)
            {
                Guide.ShowSignIn(1, false);
                break;
            }
            break;
        case 1:
            ShowScene(startScene);
            break;
    }
}
```

On the other hand, a user who is connected to the network can create a new game, join an already created session, change the authenticated user, or go back to the initial scene.

If this connected user is creating a game, the user can also cancel the wait for the other player. You implement these situations in the HandleSigned method, as follows:

```
/// <summary>
/// Handle network scene menu for a connected user
/// </summary>
private void HandleSigned()
{
    switch (networkScene.State)
    {
        case NetworkScene.NetworkGameState.idle:
            switch (networkScene.SelectedMenuIndex)
            {
```

```
            case 0:
                // Join a network game
                JoinSession();
                break;
            case 1:
                // Create a network game
                CreateSession();
                break;
            case 2:
                // Show the guide to change user
                if (!Guide.IsVisible)
                {
                    Guide.ShowSignIn(1, false);
                    break;
                }
                break;
            case 3:
                // Back to start scene
                ShowScene(startScene);
                break;
        }
        break;
    case NetworkScene.NetworkGameState.creating:
        // Close the session created
        CloseSession();
        // Wait for a new command
        networkScene.State = NetworkScene.NetworkGameState.idle;
        networkScene.Message = "";
        break;
    }
}
```

The CreateSession, JoinSession, and CloseSession methods are common to all network games. They start and end all the communication between the players. You'll implement them soon, but let's first create a class to help you with the network services necessary for Rock Rain Live.

Creating the NetworkHelper Class

You saw in the previous chapter that all the network services in your XNA game are centralized in the NetworkSession class. With it, you use objects from the PacketWriter and PacketReader classes to write and read network data. For organizational purposes, you'll create a class that encapsulates all the necessary data transport functionality, using these classes, so that you have only one object you can use to send and read data from the server and the client, and to the server and the client. This class is simple—just add a new class called NetworkHelper to the project, and add the following code:

```csharp
using Microsoft.Xna.Framework.Net;

namespace RockRainLive
{
    /// <summary>
    /// Helper for network services
    /// </summary>
    class NetworkHelper
    {
        // Network stuff
        private NetworkSession networkSession;
        private readonly PacketWriter serverPacketWriter = new PacketWriter();
        private readonly PacketReader serverPacketReader = new PacketReader();
        private readonly PacketWriter clientPacketWriter = new PacketWriter();
        private readonly PacketReader clientPacketReader = new PacketReader();

        /// <summary>
        /// The active network session
        /// </summary>
        public NetworkSession NetworkGameSession
        {
            get { return networkSession; }
            set { networkSession = value; }
        }

        /// <summary>
        /// Writer for the server data
        /// </summary>
        public PacketWriter ServerPacketWriter
        {
            get { return serverPacketWriter; }
        }

        /// <summary>
        /// Writer for the client data
        /// </summary>
        public PacketWriter ClientPacketWriter
        {
            get { return clientPacketWriter; }
        }
```

```csharp
/// <summary>
/// Reader for the client data
/// </summary>
public PacketReader ClientPacketReader
{
    get { return clientPacketReader; }
}

/// <summary>
/// Reader for the server data
/// </summary>
public PacketReader ServerPacketReader
{
    get { return serverPacketReader; }
}

/// <summary>
/// Send all server data
/// </summary>
public void SendServerData()
{
    if (ServerPacketWriter.Length > 0)
    {
        // Send the combined data to everyone in the session.
        LocalNetworkGamer server = (LocalNetworkGamer) networkSession.Host;

        server.SendData(ServerPacketWriter, SendDataOptions.InOrder);
    }
}

/// <summary>
/// Read server data
/// </summary>
public NetworkGamer ReadServerData(LocalNetworkGamer gamer)
{
    NetworkGamer sender;

    // Read a single packet from the network.
    gamer.ReceiveData(ServerPacketReader, out sender);
    return sender;
}
```

```
/// <summary>
/// Send all client data
/// </summary>
public void SendClientData()
{
    if (ClientPacketWriter.Length > 0)
    {
        // The first player is always running in the server...
        networkSession.LocalGamers[0].SendData(clientPacketWriter,
                                    SendDataOptions.InOrder,
                                    networkSession.Host);
    }
}

/// <summary>
/// Read the client data
/// </summary>
public NetworkGamer ReadClientData(LocalNetworkGamer gamer)
{
    NetworkGamer sender;

    // Read a single packet from the network.
    gamer.ReceiveData(ClientPacketReader, out sender);
    return sender;
}
    }
}
```

This class contains your NetworkSession object, as well as methods to send and read the data packages through the PacketWriter and PacketReader objects, both for the client and for the server. You'll use this class to implement your communication protocol in the next section. For now, you'll initialize the NetworkSession object of this class, as you did in the previous chapter, to create a game session, join an existing session, or terminate a session; that is, you'll implement the CreateSession, JoinSession, and CloseSession methods that we mentioned earlier in the chapter.

Creating the Game Sessions

Now you'll start adding the network support to your game. You'll initially create all the network session support for your new game so that later you can send and receive data between the client and the server. Then you'll declare an object for the NetworkHelper class that you created, as well as the constants for the maximum number of local players and for the game session. Add the attributes to the Game1 class:

```
// Network stuff
private readonly NetworkHelper networkHelper;
private const int maxLocalPlayers = 1;
private const int maxSessionPlayers = 2;
```

Then add a reference to the network's support classes:

```
using Microsoft.Xna.Framework.Net;
```

Next, initialize the networkHelper object in the class constructor. Also add it to the game services, because the various classes of your game will use it later on:

```
networkHelper = new NetworkHelper();
Services.AddService(typeof(NetworkHelper), networkHelper);
```

You can use this class now. First, create the method that creates the network game session. This method is called when the user selects the corresponding option in the network scene:

```
/// <summary>
/// Create a session for a game server
/// </summary>
private void CreateSession()
{
    networkHelper.NetworkGameSession = NetworkSession.Create(
                                NetworkSessionType.SystemLink,
                                maxLocalPlayers, maxSessionPlayers);
    HookSessionEvents();
    networkScene.State = NetworkScene.NetworkGameState.creating;
    networkScene.Message = "Waiting for another player...";
}
```

■**Note** This Rock Rain version can create games for local network usage, called SystemLink in XNA. The procedures for the game creation using the Xbox LIVE network are exactly the same, but require that both players have the Creators Club signature (even on the PC). This makes its professional use difficult, so we won't cover this kind of connection in this book.

You created a session using the Create method of the NetworkSession class, according to what you learned in the previous chapter. You also initialized the network scene object to reflect the action that you just took, setting its state to creating and showing a message that you were waiting for the other player to join the session.

The HookSessionEvents method initializes some event handlers to handle events for the session control, also according to what you saw in the previous chapter. In this Rock Rain version, you handle the events that happen when the player joins a game and when the player terminates the session:

```
/// <summary>
/// After creating or joining a network session, we must subscribe to
/// some events so we will be notified when the session changes state.
/// </summary>
void HookSessionEvents()
{
    networkHelper.NetworkGameSession.GamerJoined +=
        GamerJoinedEventHandler;
    networkHelper.NetworkGameSession.SessionEnded +=
        SessionEndedEventHandler;
}
```

When the session is terminated, the preceding code calls the SessionEndedEventHandler
method to display the game's network scene again, showing an error message that
was sent as the reason for the session to end (using the EndReason attribute of the
NetworkSessionEndedEventArgs class that is passed as a method parameter), as follows:

```
// <summary>
/// Event handler notifies us when the network session has ended.
/// </summary>
void SessionEndedEventHandler(object sender, NetworkSessionEndedEventArgs e)
{
    networkScene.Message = e.EndReason.ToString();
    networkScene.State = NetworkScene.NetworkGameState.idle;

    CloseSession();

    if (activeScene != networkScene)
    {
        ShowScene(networkScene);
    }
}
```

In the GamerJoinedEventHandler method, which is called when the player (local or remote)
joins a game session, you check if all (two) players have already joined the session to start the
game itself. This activates the action scene for both players and associates the player with the
corresponding Player object, which you'll subsequently use to differentiate the local player
from the remote player:

```
/// <summary>
/// This event handler will be called whenever a new gamer joins the
/// session.
/// </summary>
void GamerJoinedEventHandler(object sender, GamerJoinedEventArgs e)
{
    // Associate the ship with the joined player
    if (actionScene.Player1.Gamer == null)
    {
        actionScene.Player1.Gamer = e.Gamer;
    }
```

```
    else
    {
        actionScene.Player2.Gamer = e.Gamer;
    }

    if (networkHelper.NetworkGameSession.AllGamers.Count ==
        maxSessionPlayers)
    {
        actionScene.TwoPlayers = true;
        ShowScene(actionScene);
    }
}
```

The method to terminate the session just releases the NetworkSession object, as it did in the previous chapter:

```
/// <summary>
/// Quit the game session
/// </summary>
private void CloseSession()
{
    networkHelper.NetworkGameSession.Dispose();
    networkHelper.NetworkGameSession = null;
}
```

Finally, you have the method to join a game session:

```
/// <summary>
/// Joins an existing network session
/// </summary>
void JoinSession()
{
    networkScene.Message = "Joining a game...";
    networkScene.State = NetworkScene.NetworkGameState.joining;

    try
    {
        // Search for sessions
        using (AvailableNetworkSessionCollection availableSessions =
                    NetworkSession.Find(NetworkSessionType.SystemLink,
                                        maxLocalPlayers, null))
        {
            if (availableSessions.Count == 0)
            {
                networkScene.Message = "No network sessions found.";
                networkScene.State = NetworkScene.NetworkGameState.idle;
                return;
            }
```

```
            // Join the first session we found.
            networkHelper.NetworkGameSession = NetworkSession.Join(
                                                availableSessions[0]);

            HookSessionEvents();
        }
    }
    catch (Exception e)
    {
        networkScene.Message = e.Message;
        networkScene.State = NetworkScene.NetworkGameState.idle;
    }
}
```

This code is practically the same as in the previous chapter. You just add some messages to the network scene based on the success or failure of joining the game:

Now that you can create, terminate, and join a session in progress for a network game, you already have all the necessary structure to be able to send and receive data. You should now start to think about what your communication protocol will be. We'll cover that in the following section.

Let's Talk

A communication protocol is a "language" spoken between the client and the server. It defines the way the messages are sent and received so that with this message exchange you can keep your game state in sync.

You saw in the previous chapter that these messages are sent and received through PacketWriter and PacketReader class objects, respectively. You can send or receive any kind of data with these classes, but you need to define a protocol so that this communication is done efficiently.

Suppose that you're playing a network game with a friend on the other side of the world and you suddenly pause the game. You need to tell the other player somehow that you paused, and therefore his game must also pause, so that he doesn't obtain any advantage while you're on the toilet. How do you let the other player know that you paused, and how do you let him know when you return to the game?

In the case of Rock Rain, your protocol is simple. Each message that you send to the other player is composed of a header with a character that explains which message is being sent, followed by the message itself.

In the case of pausing the game, the header is 'P' and the message is true or false, depending on the pause status. So, when the player pauses, the header is 'P' and the message is true. When the player resumes after the pause, the header is 'P' and the message is false.

So, when you detect that the user wants to pause or stop the pause, you should send this data to the PacketWriter object corresponding to the client or to the server, depending on which one wants to change the pause state. To do this, change the HandleActionInput method of the Game1 class and add the following lines:

```
if (enterKey)
{
    if (actionScene.GameOver)
    {
        ShowScene(startScene);
    }
    else
    {
        audio.MenuBack.Play();
        actionScene.Paused = !actionScene.Paused;
        // Send the pause command to the other player
        if (networkHelper.NetworkGameSession != null)
        {
            // If we are the server, send using the server packets
            if (networkHelper.NetworkGameSession.IsHost)
            {
                networkHelper.ServerPacketWriter.Write('P');
                networkHelper.ServerPacketWriter.Write(
                                            actionScene.Paused);
            }
            else
            {
                networkHelper.ClientPacketWriter.Write('P');
                networkHelper.ClientPacketWriter.Write(
                                            actionScene.Paused);
            }
        }

    }
    if (backKey)
    {
        if (networkHelper.NetworkGameSession != null)
        {
            CloseSession();
            networkScene.State = NetworkScene.NetworkGameState.idle;
            networkScene.Message = "";
            ShowScene(networkScene);
        }
        else
        {
            ShowScene(startScene);
        }
    }
}
```

■Note Be careful when defining the format of your messages. The network traffic has a lot of influence on the performance of an online game. Overall, strive for the least amount of traffic possible, so that the server doesn't keep processing messages for too long. Besides the client/server model, XNA offers the peer-to-peer (P2P) model, which might be more adequate for games with excessive message exchange or with large states, such as the massive multiplayer online (MMO) type of games.

Notice that you put the message header first ('P') in the `ClientPacketWriter` or in the `ServerPacketWriter`, then include the message itself (`actionScene.Paused`) so that the message is now formatted and ready to be sent.

You also added new code in the treatment of the Back key. If it's activated during a network game, it makes the game terminate the connection and return to the network scene, instead of simply returning to the initial scene.

Now you need to read this message, interpret it, and change the game state (paused or not) according to the message content. It's good design to keep the method that deals with the messages close to the class that contains the game state itself. In Rock Rain's case, it's the class that represents the action scene.

Before you do anything else, you need your `NetworkHelper` object. So, declare it in the `ActionScene` class:

```
// Network stuff
private readonly NetworkHelper networkHelper;
```

Initialize it in the class constructor:

```
// Get the current server state for a networked multiplayer game
networkHelper = (NetworkHelper)
    Game.Services.GetService(typeof (NetworkHelper));
```

Now you'll create two methods in the `ActionScene` class: one to interpret the messages that come from the client, and another one for the server messages. Add the following method in the `ActionScene` class:

```
/// <summary>
///  Handle all data incoming from the client
/// </summary>
public void HandleClientData()
{
    while (networkHelper.ClientPacketReader.PeekChar() != -1)
    {
        char header = networkHelper.ClientPacketReader.ReadChar();
        switch (header)
        {
            case 'P':
                Paused = networkHelper.ClientPacketReader.ReadBoolean();
                break;
        }
    }
}
```

This method will be called when you need to interpret any message originating from the remote player (client). The while condition loops through all PacketReaders of the client to read all messages, as demonstrated in the previous chapter, and interprets them accordingly. The PeekChar method checks the first character in the message to get the message header, which contains the message type information.

In the case of a 'P' message, for a pause, all you do is assign the value of the message to the Paused attribute for the scene, which pauses the game or not.

For the pause message that comes from the server, the code is practically the same:

```
/// <summary>
///  Handle all data incoming from the server
/// </summary>
public void HandleServerData()
{
    while (networkHelper.ServerPacketReader.PeekChar() != -1)
    {
        char header = networkHelper.ServerPacketReader.ReadChar();
        switch (header)
        {
            case 'P':
                Paused = networkHelper.ServerPacketReader.ReadBoolean();
                break;
        }
    }
}
```

The difference is that you now use the server's PacketReader. Note that because the server maintains the game state, many new messages are created and interpreted here, while on the client, only this pause message and another message with the position of the remote player are sent. We'll go back to these methods later.

Now you need to call these methods; that is, you need to put all the sending and receiving of the network data in the game's loop. As you did in the previous chapter, add this in the Update method of the Game1 class, and use the methods of the NetworkHelper class that send and receive data. Put the following code in the Update method of the Game1 class:

```
// Handle the network session
if (networkHelper.NetworkGameSession != null)
{
    // Only send if we are not the server. There is no point sending
    // packets to ourselves, because we already know what they will
    // contain!
    if (!networkHelper.NetworkGameSession.IsHost)
    {
        networkHelper.SendClientData();
    }
```

```
        else
        {
            // If we are the server, transmit the game state
            networkHelper.SendServerData();
        }

        // Pump the data
        networkHelper.NetworkGameSession.Update();

        // Read any incoming network packets
        foreach (LocalNetworkGamer gamer in
                networkHelper.NetworkGameSession.LocalGamers)
        {
            // Keep reading as long as incoming packets are available
            while (gamer.IsDataAvailable)
            {
                NetworkGamer sender;
                if (gamer.IsHost)
                {
                    sender = networkHelper.ReadClientData(gamer);
                    if (!sender.IsLocal)
                    {
                        actionScene.HandleClientData();
                    }
                }
                else
                {
                    sender = networkHelper.ReadServerData(gamer);
                    if (!sender.IsLocal)
                    {
                        actionScene.HandleServerData();
                    }
                }
            }
        }
    }
}
```

So, for each game loop, you're always reading and sending the necessary data packages.
You also need to expose the Player objects to associate the network Gamer class for each
player who joins the game session. Add the following code:

```
public Player Player1
{
    get { return player1; }
}
```

```
public Player Player2
{
    get { return player2; }
}
```

Now let's add new messages to the other game states.

Synchronizing the Players

What defines a player's state? It's not only the player's position on the screen, but also that user's score and energy level. You need to inform the other player of an opponent's status so that the game stays synchronized. Create the status message for this. The header for this message is 'S', as the message is Position, Score, Energy. The 'S' message sends all the necessary information for a player, and both players (the local player, player1, and remote player, player2) must send their status through the network.

For the remote player, add the following code in the HandleClientData method of the ActionScene class:

```
case 'S':
    player2.Position =
        networkHelper.ClientPacketReader.ReadVector2();
    player2.Power =
        networkHelper.ClientPacketReader.ReadInt32();
    player2.Score =
        networkHelper.ClientPacketReader.ReadInt32();
    break;
```

If it's the 'S' message, it will be followed by the player's position (a Vector2 object) and the player's score and energy level (Int32 objects). You need to update the player2 object's attributes with only these values.

Similarly, add the following code to deal with the player's movement on the server side—in this case, in the HandleServerData method:

```
case 'S':
    player1.Position =
        networkHelper.ServerPacketReader.ReadVector2();
    player1.Power =
        networkHelper.ServerPacketReader.ReadInt32();
    player1.Score =
        networkHelper.ServerPacketReader.ReadInt32();
    break;
```

You must alter the Player class (which represents the player1 and player2 objects) to send the player's position through the network. In fact, the class must change to stop any alterations of its state by the remote player. If alterations are allowed (such as changing the position), a message must send this change to the server.

Adding Network Support to the Player Class

If you're adding network support, you also need your instance of the `NetworkHelper` class. Declare it in the `Player` class:

```
// Network stuff
private readonly NetworkHelper networkHelper;
```

Then initialize it in the class constructor:

```
// Get the current server state for a networked multiplayer game
networkHelper = (NetworkHelper)
    Game.Services.GetService(typeof (NetworkHelper));
```

Now let's change the `Update` method of this class so that it sends the `'S'` message, with the ship's status. Change the code of the method as follows:

```
if (networkHelper.NetworkGameSession != null)
{
    if (gamer.IsLocal)
    {
        // Local gamers always use the main gamepad and keyboard keys
        HandleInput(PlayerIndex.One);
        UpdateShip(gameTime);
        UpdateNetworkData();
    }
}
else
{
    HandleInput(playerIndex);
    UpdateShip(gameTime);
}
```

Note that the messages are sent only to the local player. You don't need to send the remote player's changes to that player. Also, in the case of a multiplayer game via a network, the two players don't need to divide the keyboard or use two gamepads, so they always use the same gamepad or keyboard keys.

The following `UpdateNetworkData` method creates the messages that will be sent:

```
/// <summary>
/// Update server data with the ship info
/// </summary>
private void UpdateNetworkData()
{
    if (networkHelper.NetworkGameSession.IsHost)
    {
        networkHelper.ServerPacketWriter.Write('S');
        networkHelper.ServerPacketWriter.Write(position);
        networkHelper.ServerPacketWriter.Write(power);
        networkHelper.ServerPacketWriter.Write(score);
    }
```

```
else
{
    networkHelper.ClientPacketWriter.Write('S');
    networkHelper.ClientPacketWriter.Write(position);
    networkHelper.ClientPacketWriter.Write(power);
    networkHelper.ClientPacketWriter.Write(score);

}
}
```

This adds the message data in the corresponding PacketWriter, as you did earlier. The code you added to the Update method of the Game1 class also sends this data, and the HandleClientData and HandleServerData methods of the ActionScene class handle it, the same way they handle the pause message. In this way, you'll add the network support to all the other objects that contain some game state.

Adding Network Support to the PowerSource Class

The PowerSource class, which represents the item that gives energy to the player, also contains an important state in the game: its position. Through this position and the other players' positions, you'll be able to know if any player managed to get any energy during a match.

Create a message to tell the position of this item. This message has the header 'L' and the message Position. This state is kept only on the server. Then add the following code to the HandleServerData method of the ActionScene class:

```
case 'L':
    powerSource.Position =
        networkHelper.ServerPacketReader.ReadVector2();
    break;
```

Think it's repetitive? Great!

Next, add an attribute of the NetworkHelper type and initialize it in the PowerSource class constructor, the same way as did with the Player class, and change the Update method as follows:

```
/// <summary>
/// Allows the game component to update itself
/// </summary>
/// <param name="gameTime">Provides a snapshot of timing values</param>
public override void Update(GameTime gameTime)
{
    if ((networkHelper.NetworkGameSession == null) ||
        (networkHelper.NetworkGameSession.IsHost))
    {
        // Check if the meteor is still visible
        if (position.Y >= Game.Window.ClientBounds.Height)
        {
            PutinStartPosition();
        }
```

```
        // Move
        position.Y += 1;

        networkHelper.ServerPacketWriter.Write('L');
        networkHelper.ServerPacketWriter.Write(position);
    }

    base.Update(gameTime);
}
```

The Update method updates the position of only the object that is running on the server side. The HandleServerData method sets the position of the object on the client side with the data sent by the instance that runs on the server, so that both stay synchronized.

You already synchronized the players, the energy source, and the game pause. Only the meteors are left.

Adding Network Support for the Meteors

The game's meteors are represented by two distinct classes: the Meteor class, which represents the sprite of the meteor itself, and the MeteorsManager class, which represents the entire meteor field in the game. Each class changes the game state in its own way, and you'll alter its code to add the network game support separately.

In the Meteor class, only the PutinStartPosition and Update methods change the attributes of an instance. So, you'll change these methods. But which message will be sent to represent a meteor state?

In Rock Rain, each meteor updates only its position on the screen, so you can send a message with an 'R' header and the message Index, Position. Each meteor on the screen sends this message, to inform the client of its position in the game. Because the value of the Index property can identify each meteor, let's send them together so that the client knows about which meteor position it's being informed. As explained in Chapter 5, the server keeps the entire state of the game—in this case, the meteors' positions.

First, add and initialize an instance of the NetworkHelper class, as you've done before. Change the PutinStartPosition method:

```
/// <summary>
/// Initialize meteor position and velocity
/// </summary>
public void PutinStartPosition()
{
    // Only the server can set the meteor attributes
    if ((networkHelper.NetworkGameSession == null) ||
        (networkHelper.NetworkGameSession.IsHost))
    {
        position.X = random.Next(Game.Window.ClientBounds.Width -
                                 currentFrame.Width);
        position.Y = 0;
        YSpeed = 1 + random.Next(9);
        XSpeed = random.Next(3) - 1;
    }
}
```

Following is the code for the Update method:

```
/// <summary>
/// Update the meteor position
/// </summary>
public override void Update(GameTime gameTime)
{
    // Check if the meteor is still visible
    if ((position.Y >= Game.Window.ClientBounds.Height) ||
        (position.X >= Game.Window.ClientBounds.Width) ||
        (position.X <= 0))
    {
        PutinStartPosition();
    }

    // Move meteor
    position.Y += Yspeed;
    position.X += Xspeed;

    // Send the meteor info to the client
    if ((networkHelper.NetworkGameSession != null) &&
        (networkHelper.NetworkGameSession.IsHost))
    {
        networkHelper.ServerPacketWriter.Write('R');
        networkHelper.ServerPacketWriter.Write(index);
        networkHelper.ServerPacketWriter.Write(position);
    }

    base.Update(gameTime);
}
```

This is another message that is sent only by the server, so you handle it in the HandleServerData method of the ActionScene class, as you did with the other messages:

```
case 'R':
    int meteorId = networkHelper.ServerPacketReader.ReadInt32();
    meteors.AllMeteors[meteorId].Position =
        networkHelper.ServerPacketReader.ReadVector2();
    break;
```

In the preceding code, you just set the position of the specified meteor with the position value sent in the message. Because you're doing this for each meteor, you'll then synchronize the position of all of them during the game.

Another state change situation occurs when a new meteor is added to the scene. The MeteorsManager class performs this operation. The client must be notified about a new object added by the server, so that the client can see a new meteor with the same characteristics.

Add and initialize an instance of the NetworkHelper object and change the Start method of the MeteorsManager class:

```
/// <summary>
/// Start the meteors' rain
/// </summary>
public void Start()
{
    if ((networkHelper.NetworkGameSession == null) ||
        (networkHelper.NetworkGameSession.IsHost))
    {
        // Initialize a counter
        elapsedTime = TimeSpan.Zero;

        // Add the meteors
        for (int i = 0; i < STARTMETEORCOUNT; i++)
        {
            AddNewMeteor();
        }
    }
}
```

This way, only the server is able to add new meteors, and when a new meteor is added you must send a message to inform the client. This message contains the attributes of a meteor. It has the header 'M' and the message Index, Position, Horizontal Speed, Vertical Speed.

Then change the AddNewMeteor method to send a message with the other attributes of the new meteor:

```
/// <summary>
/// Add a new meteor in the scene
/// </summary>
/// <returns>the new meteor</returns>
private Meteor AddNewMeteor()
{
    Meteor newMeteor = new Meteor(Game, ref meteorTexture);
    newMeteor.Initialize();
    meteors.Add(newMeteor);
    newMeteor.Index = meteors.Count-1;

    // Send the new meteor info to the client
    if ((networkHelper.NetworkGameSession != null) &&
        (networkHelper.NetworkGameSession.IsHost))
    {
        networkHelper.ServerPacketWriter.Write('M');
        networkHelper.ServerPacketWriter.Write(newMeteor.Index);
        networkHelper.ServerPacketWriter.Write(newMeteor.Position);
        networkHelper.ServerPacketWriter.Write(newMeteor.XSpeed);
        networkHelper.ServerPacketWriter.Write(newMeteor.YSpeed);
    }b

    return newMeteor;
}
```

And again handle this message in the HandleServerData event of the ActionScene class so that a new meteor is added to the client's meteor list:

```
case 'M':
    int index = networkHelper.ServerPacketReader.ReadInt32();
    Vector2 position =
        networkHelper.ServerPacketReader.ReadVector2();
    int xspeed = networkHelper.ServerPacketReader.ReadInt32();
    int yspeed = networkHelper.ServerPacketReader.ReadInt32();
    meteors.AddNewMeteor(index,position,xspeed,yspeed);
    break;
```

Now, the motion as well as the addition of new meteors are synchronized with the client.

There's still a third point where the game state is changed: when the Update method checks if it's necessary to add a new meteor. Only the server can execute this operation, so change the method as follows:

```
// Only the server can add new meteors
if ((networkHelper.NetworkGameSession == null) ||
    (networkHelper.NetworkGameSession.IsHost))
{
    CheckforNewMeteor(gameTime);
}
```

That's it! All the objects are now synchronized. The server will control all the game state and send it to the client so it keeps the game synchronized. The client will receive all the messages and change the status of its objects according to the content of these messages, to maintain an online match, just as if you were beside your opponent. Figure 6-3 illustrates the message traffic between the players. Now call that friend of yours who lives in Japan for a Rock Rain match!

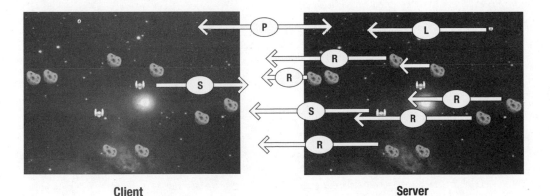

Client   **Server**

Figure 6-3. *The chat between server and client*

Summary

This chapter covered the basic principles of how to plan and create an online multiplayer game. Correct definitions for the protocol and sending messages are essential for keeping the game state synchronized between the various players. XNA offers powerful classes so that this work becomes simple, and you don't need to worry about the details of sending and receiving data through the network.

How about adding a new feature to send messages between the players? How about adding support for three or four players? If you try, you'll see that it's not that hard to make Rock Rain a massive multiplayer online game.

CHAPTER 7

■ ■ ■

Rock Rain Zune

The XNA 3.0 release added several interesting new features, but none as exciting as the provision for one more platform: the Zune! Now you can create games for this device using the same resources and facilities available to create games for the Windows and Xbox 360 platforms.

All the Zune devices have a fair amount in common. They have 16MB available for the game to run in; a 240 × 320 display, with varying dots per inch, depending on the device size; and some type of mass-storage capability, ranging from 4GB of flash to 80GB of hard drive. All the devices have built-in wireless networking as well, which is available to game developers through the XNA Framework network APIs.

Games on the Zune appear in their own category in the Zune user interface, and look and feel like other media on the device. The icon and description you provide in XNA Game Studio are copied to the device. This means browsing to games is as rich an experience as browsing to other media. When you "play" the game, it loads and runs just like other media. Once you deploy games to the Zune, you no longer need a PC connection to run them—they work just like any other media on the device.

To show how simple it is to make a game for the Zune, you will create a Rock Rain version for it, using code quite similar to that in the Windows/Xbox 360 version in Chapter 4. You'll just make some changes to accommodate the minor differences that exist between these platforms. In particular, you'll modify the game to work within the device's small display area.

Planning Rock Rain Zune

First, we want to emphasize two important points. One is that the game you'll create in this chapter has virtually the same code as you used earlier. This means you can take all the work you have done in the Rain Rock version of Chapter 4 and reuse it to create this new version of the game. XNA makes all the effort to create versions of multiplatform games simpler and cheaper. In fact, in this chapter, your work will involve mostly removing code, rather than adding code.

The second point is that the game will run on a mobile device. This may seem too obvious to you to mention, but it is very important for the design of the game itself, since the player will not play the game sitting on a couch with a joystick and a big screen. Keep in mind that people will probably play this version of Rock Rain standing up on a bus, while in a doctor's waiting room, and so on.

The usability issues related to games for mobile devices must be taken into account. Specifically, this version of Rock Rain will be designed to be played in a simple way, with only one hand, on any Zune device. The *programming* of the game is almost the same; however, the *conception* and *design* are somewhat different.

So, for the conceptual design of the Zune game, we can highlight three main differences:

Lack of multiplayer support: There's no way for two players to play at the same time on one Zune.

Lower screen resolution: With a smaller screen, some functions that depend on the size of the screen, such as the size of images, should be modified. The textures and sprites should also be changed to look better on the small screen of the Zune, which has a resolution of only 240 × 320 pixels.

Lack of full controller support: Some older versions of Zune did not have a touchpad; that is, they did not have any type of analog input, though they did have digital buttons. In the new generation of Zunes, the Zune pad simulates the analog thumbstick (actually, it looks like a mouse), but you must also add digital thumbstick support so that users of old Zune models can play your game. And there is no support for vibration, so your GamePadRumble class will not be used.

The input APIs for the device behave like an Xbox 360 controller with some pieces missing. The Zune 1.0 device control pad works like the directional pad on the Xbox 360 controller, with the Play/Pause button mapped to the B button on the controller, and the Back button on the device mapped to the Back button on the controller.

With that in mind, we can identify the classes of the game that do not need to be modified, since they do not work with anything related to user input, assembly of scenes, or the game play itself. They are GameScene, ImageComponent, Sprite, AudioLibrary, and Score.

Organizing the Game

Begin by creating a new Zune Game project, naming it RockRainZune, as shown in Figure 7-1. Then copy the following classes from Chapter 4's version of the game: GameScene, ImageComponent, Sprite, AudioLibrary, and Score. Remember to rename the namespace of the classes for the namespace of your new project: RockRainZune.

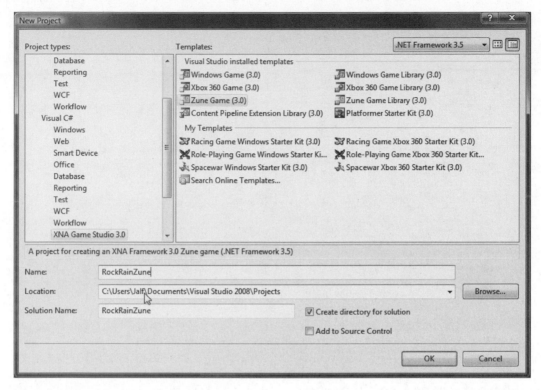

Figure 7-1. *Creating a Zune Game project*

You also need new textures. These are practically the same as used for the game in Chapter 4, but resized to fit on Zune screen. Remember the Zune display is a screen with 240 × 320 pixels, and your PC/Xbox 360 can run this game on an 1280 × 720 pixel screen, so the sprites must be scaled to a smaller screen.

The audio is the same, so add the audio files and the sprite fonts setting files in the same way as you did in Chapter 4. Figure 7-2 shows the RockRainZune project in the Solution Explorer window.

■**Note** Be aware of the space requirements for audio content in your game. Uncompressed WAV files can be used, but they need a lot of storage space on the device. If possible, use MP3 or WMA files for your sound bank to save some space.

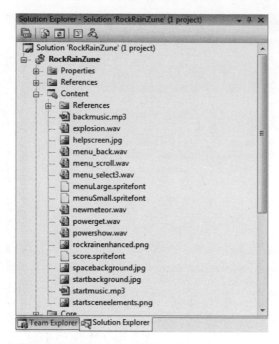

Figure 7-2. *The Content folder for the Rock Rain Zune game*

Modifying the Classes

You will now proceed with the necessary class modifications, starting with the simple adjustments and moving to the slightly harder ones.

Help Scene Changes

First, let's modify the HelpScene class, which implements the help screen of the game. It displays only a picture with the description of the controls and rules of the game. However, as in the Windows/Xbox 360 version, there is additional support for widescreen, which puts a background image behind the help image for better display on this type of screen. Obviously, the Zune does not need this feature, so you will simplify the class to display only a single image.

Copy the code from Chapter 4 (remembering to rename the namespace). Then remove the second parameter of the constructor method, for the background texture that is no longer necessary. Also remove the instantiation of the second ImageComponent, which would draw the texture. Your code should look as follows:

```
/// <summary>
/// This is a game component thats represents the Instructions scene
/// </summary>
public class HelpScene : GameScene
{
```

```
public HelpScene(Game game, Texture2D textureBack)
        : base(game)
{
    Components.Add(new ImageComponent(game, textureBack,
        ImageComponent.DrawMode.Stretch));
}
}
```

Notice that you just removed some code so the class can draw the help screen on the Zune correctly. In essence, it is exactly the same as your Windows/Xbox 360 code! Simple, huh?

Menu Changes

Some of your changes are required because of the lack of a keyboard on the Zune. First, the keyboard support component TextMenuComponent should be removed. Add the Chapter 4 version of the class to your project (do not forget the namespace change!) and remove any lines of code that refer to the oldKeyboardState attribute (including the declaration of the attribute), since you do not need any keyboard support.

In the Update method, which is used to change the menu item, you do not need further testing of whether the user has pressed a key on the keyboard, since you can use only the Zune pad. Your first part should look like this:

```
GamePadState gamepadState = GamePad.GetState(PlayerIndex.One);

// Handle the D-Pad
bool down = (oldGamePadState.DPad.Down == ButtonState.Pressed) &&
    (gamepadState.DPad.Down == ButtonState.Released);
bool up = (oldGamePadState.DPad.Up == ButtonState.Pressed) &&

    (gamepadState.DPad.Up == ButtonState.Released);
```

Did you notice that you removed the keyboard support, but otherwise the handling of the Zune pad is exactly the same? This happens because the XNA maps the Zune pad to the same classes as those used for the Windows/Xbox 360 gamepad, facilitating your work.

Furthermore, the entire code for the Draw method, properties, and so on is exactly the same! You removed the code lines that do not make sense in the Zune, but ultimately, the class is the same, thanks to .NET and your managed code, which give game developers a complete abstraction of device implementation details.

Let's now discuss changes to your code that are due to the size of the Zune screen and the new positioning of the sprites in the new textures.

Power Source Changes

The PowerSource class has the same logic in the Zune version as it did in the previous version, but the frames of the sprites are different, because the sprites' texture is smaller. In this case, you must modify the constructor of the class to reflect these changes, as follows:

```
public PowerSource(Game game, ref Texture2D theTexture)
        : base(game, ref theTexture)

{
        texture = theTexture;

        Frames = new List<Rectangle>();
        Rectangle frame = new Rectangle();
        frame.X = 55;
        frame.Y = 15;
        frame.Width = 14;
        frame.Height = 12;
        Frames.Add(frame);

        frame.Y = 29;
        Frames.Add(frame);

        frame.Y = 42;
        Frames.Add(frame);

        frame.Y = 56;
        Frames.Add(frame);

        frame.Y = 69;
        Frames.Add(frame);

        frame.Y = 81;
        Frames.Add(frame);

        frameDelay = 200;

        // Initialize the random number generator and put the power source in your
        // start position
        random = new Random(GetHashCode());
        PutinStartPosition();
}
```

Note that except for the new attributes of the frames, the code is exactly the same.

Meteor Changes

The Meteor class also needs to have its constructor changed to reflect changes in the position of frames in the new texture. In fact, every aspect of the 2D graphics is exactly the same as for the Windows/Xbox 360 version, except for the safe area. On a Zune, you don't need to worry about the TV safe area, because the Zune screen is "flat," like an LCD or a plasma TV or PC monitor. Easier, right?

The modified Meteor class is as follows:

```
public Meteor(Game game, ref Texture2D theTexture) :
    base(game, ref theTexture)
{
    Frames = new List<Rectangle>();
    Rectangle frame = new Rectangle();
    frame.X = 15;
    frame.Y = 10;
    frame.Width = 23;
    frame.Height = 24;
    Frames.Add(frame);

    frame.Y = 37;
    Frames.Add(frame);

    frame.Y = 63;
    frame.Height = 24;
    Frames.Add(frame);

    frame.Y = 89;
    frame.Height = 27;
    Frames.Add(frame);

    frame.Y = 119;
    frame.Height = 24;
    Frames.Add(frame);

    frame.Y = 145;
    Frames.Add(frame);

    frame.Y = 171;
    Frames.Add(frame);

    frame.Y = 199;
    frame.Height = 26;
    Frames.Add(frame);

    // Initialize the random number generator and
    // put the meteor in your start position
    random = new Random(GetHashCode());
    PutinStartPosition();
}
```

Another aspect to consider is that the small size of the screen changes the game play a bit. You have little room to escape from meteors, and this can make the game too difficult. In this case, it is better to reduce the speed of the meteors, so it will be easier for the player to avoid them. Therefore, in the `PutinStartPosition` method in the `Meteor` class, modify the code that calculates the vertical velocity as follows:

```
YSpeed = 1 + random.Next(3);
```

By reducing the maximum speed from 10 to 4 pixels, you are a facilitating the player's game play.

Also reduce the delay between frames in the `YSpeed` property:

```
frameDelay = 200 - (Yspeed * 2);
```

■Note You may wonder how we got these numbers. The answer is simple: through *experience*. You must experience the game play of your game and adjust it to make it fun on your target device—whether it is an Xbox 360, a PC, or a Zune. Through such tests, game designers adjust the difficulty of their game so that it is not so hard that the player does not want to play it anymore, but not so easy that the player loses interest in it. Remember that how you react to your game and your experience determine what type of game developer you are.

Player Changes

You will now work in the `Player` class, which implements the ship controlled by the player. For the Zune version, remove the multiplayer support and keyboard support. Then remove the `HandlePlayer1KeyBoard` and `HandlePlayer2KeyBoard` methods and their references. Also remove the `playerIndex` attribute, which indicates which player is associated with the object instance. Remember that since you now have only one player playing the game at a time, keeping track of which player is which is no longer necessary.

After that, you also need to update some methods that control the class behavior. The `HandleInput` method no longer needs to receive `PlayerIndex` as a parameter (because you have only one player) and no longer needs to call the methods for dealing with keyboard input. Because the `HandleInput` method happens to be where gamepad directions are set up, you will add the ability to move the ship with only the directional pad for the older versions of the Zune. You also need new movement values because of the screen size. After some tests, we discovered 3 is good enough. Your method should look as follows:

```
/// <summary>
/// Get the ship position
/// </summary>
protected void HandleInput()
{
    // Move the ship with Xbox controller
    GamePadState gamepadstatus = GamePad.GetState(PlayerIndex.One);
    if (gamepadstatus.DPad.Left == ButtonState.Pressed)
    {
        position.X -= 3;
    }
```

```
    if (gamepadstatus.DPad.Right == ButtonState.Pressed)
    {
        position.X += 3;
    }
    if (gamepadstatus.DPad.Down == ButtonState.Pressed)
    {
        position.Y += 3;
    }
    if (gamepadstatus.DPad.Up == ButtonState.Pressed)
    {
        position.Y -= 3;
    }
    // Check the thumbstick also
    position.Y += (int)((gamepadstatus.ThumbSticks.Left.Y * 3) * -2);
    position.X += (int)((gamepadstatus.ThumbSticks.Left.X * 3) * 2);
}
```

Similarly, the Update method no longer needs to inform the PlayerIndex (again, remember that you have only one player in this game), so it should be as follows:

```
/// <summary>
/// Update the ship position, points and power
/// </summary>
public override void Update(GameTime gameTime)
{
    HandleInput();
    UpdateShip(gameTime);

    base.Update(gameTime);
}
```

Again, you must change the class constructor to update the frames according to the new texture and remove the widescreen support used for the Xbox 360 version:

```
public Player(Game game, ref Texture2D theTexture) : base(game)
{
    texture = theTexture;
    position = new Vector2();

    // Create the source rectangle.
    // This represents where the sprite picture is in surface
    spriteRectangle = new Rectangle(86,11,24,22);

    screenBounds = new Rectangle(0, 0,
        Game.Window.ClientBounds.Width,
        Game.Window.ClientBounds.Height);
}
```

Core Game Changes

You are nearly finished. Your last changes to the game's code address the classes that represent the "soul" of the game: ActionScene, StartScene, MeteorsManager, and Game1. These classes run the core game code, such as the action scene (ActionScene), the opening scene (StartScene), and, of course, the main class, Game1, which contain all the game scene flow.

Start with the MeteorsManager class. This class does not handle sprites or the keyboard, but it has an important role in control of the game play: it sets the initial number of meteors and the time to add a new meteor to the game. Based on our tests of game play, we suggest you replace the values of the STARTMETEORCOUNT and ADDMETEORTIME properties as follows:

```
// Constant for initial meteor count
private const int STARTMETEORCOUNT = 5;
// Time for a new meteor
private const int ADDMETEORTIME = 6000;
```

This should make the game a little easier to be played on a small screen. You will experience a smaller number of meteors when the game starts, and a longer time between the appearance of new meteors.

For the class of the original scene, StartScene, you will have noticed that you must change the frames of the sprites that form the text "Rock Rain Enhanced" as well as their positions in the opening animation. First, change the frames of the sprites, as follows:

```
protected Rectangle rockRect = new Rectangle(3, 2, 197, 49);
protected Rectangle rainRect = new Rectangle(47, 63, 189, 48);
protected Rectangle enhancedRect = new Rectangle(7, 110, 122, 46);
```

In the Show method, modify the initial positions of these elements, as follows:

```
rockPosition.Y = 10;
rainPosition.Y = 60;
menu.Position = new Vector2((Game.Window.ClientBounds.Width -
    menu.Width)/2, 140);
```

The menu items will also be different, because you do not have multiplayer support. This is simple. Just change the menu items array, which is initialized in the constructor, for the items you have in this Zune version, and the drawing methods you've already coded in the previous version will take care of the rest:

```
// Create the menu
string[] items = {"Play!", "Help", "Quit"};
```

In the Update method, you need to update the position of the sprites to have them in the correct position during the animation, and you need to remove the widescreen support that you have for the Xbox 360:

```
/// <summary>
/// Allows the game component to update itself.
/// </summary>
/// <param name="gameTime">Provides a snapshot of timing values.</param>
public override void Update(GameTime gameTime)
```

```
{
    if (!menu.Visible)
    {
        if (rainPosition.X >= (Game.Window.ClientBounds.Width - rainRect.Width)/2)
        {
            rainPosition.X -= 5;
        }

        if (rockPosition.X <= (Game.Window.ClientBounds.Width - rockRect.Width)/2)
        {
            rockPosition.X += 5;
        }
        else
        {
            menu.Visible = true;
            menu.Enabled = true;

            MediaPlayer.Play(audio.StartMusic);

            enhancedPosition =
                new Vector2((rainPosition.X + rainRect.Width -
                enhancedRect.Width/2) - 40, rainPosition.Y+20);
            showEnhanced = true;
        }
    }
    else
    {
        elapsedTime += gameTime.ElapsedGameTime;

        if (elapsedTime > TimeSpan.FromSeconds(1))
        {
            elapsedTime -= TimeSpan.FromSeconds(1);
            showEnhanced = !showEnhanced;
        }
    }

    base.Update(gameTime);
}
```

Next, let's deal with the Game1 class. This class is responsible for overall control of the game. Here, you are concerned with only the keyboard treatment and the instantiation of the HelpScene class, which had its constructor changed a bit.

Start by removing all references to oldKeyboardState attribute (including its statement), which are used to manipulate keyboard entries. Also remove references to the helpForegroundTexture attribute, because as you saw earlier, it is no longer necessary since the HelpScene class needs only one texture for the Zune version of the game. After all these changes, the class constructor should look as follows:

```
public Game1()
{
    graphics = new GraphicsDeviceManager(this);
    Content.RootDirectory = "Content";

    // Used for input handling
    oldGamePadState = GamePad.GetState(PlayerIndex.One);
}
```

The CheckEnterA method checks if the Enter key or the A button of the Xbox 360 gamepad was pressed. Rename this method to CheckActionButton, which makes more sense in the Zune, and check only the gamepad status:

```
/// <summary>
/// Check if the Action button was pressed
/// </summary>
/// <returns>true, if button was pressed</returns>
private bool CheckActionButton()
{
    // Get the keyboard and gamepad state
    GamePadState gamepadState = GamePad.GetState(PlayerIndex.One);

    bool result = (oldGamePadState.Buttons.A == ButtonState.Pressed)
            && (gamepadState.Buttons.A == ButtonState.Released);

    oldGamePadState = gamepadState;

    return result;
}
```

As the menu items are different, you also need to update the HandleStartSceneInput method to show the correct scenes of the game:

```
/// <summary>
/// Handle buttons and keyboard in StartScene
/// </summary>
private void HandleStartSceneInput()
{
    if (CheckActionButton())
    {
        audio.MenuSelect.Play();
        switch (startScene.SelectedMenuIndex)
        {
            case 0:
                ShowScene(actionScene);
                break;
            case 1:
                ShowScene(helpScene);
                break;
```

```
        case 2:
            Exit();
            break;
    }
  }
}
```

Notice that the TwoPlayers attribute, from the ActionScene class, which indicates if the two-player mode is active, is not used anymore, because the game does not support this feature.

Your last changes are to the ActionScene class, which is actually the place where the game happens. Your work here will be just to remove the instances of objects that are not needed and adjust the frames of the sprites in accordance with the new textures. Let's go!

First, remove the declaration and references to the rumblePad, player2, scorePlayer2, and twoPlayers attributes. They are no longer needed, since you have only one player and do not have vibration support for the Zune. Also, remove the TwoPlayers property, which is no longer necessary.

Then, using the refactoring tool in Visual Studio, rename the player1 attribute to player and scorePlayer1 attribute to score, so that the code will be more readable.

Next, change the frames of the sprites to fit to the new texture, as follows:

```
protected Rectangle pauseRect = new Rectangle(84, 65, 99, 30);
protected Rectangle gameoverRect = new Rectangle(53, 108, 186, 30);
```

■**Note** Don't worry about the coordinates changes here. You can see these coordinates using you preferred graphical tool. We like to use Windows Paint.

After that, the class constructor should look like this:

```
/// <summary>
/// Default constructor
/// </summary>
/// <param name="game">The main game object</param>
/// <param name="theTexture">Texture with the sprite elements</param>
/// <param name="backgroundTexture">Texture for the background</param>
/// <param name="font">Font used in the score</param>
public ActionScene(Game game, Texture2D theTexture,
    Texture2D backgroundTexture, SpriteFont font)
    : base(game)
{
    // Get the current audio component and play the background music
    audio = (AudioLibrary)Game.Services.GetService(typeof(AudioLibrary));

    background = new ImageComponent(game, backgroundTexture,
        ImageComponent.DrawMode.Stretch);
    Components.Add(background);
```

```
        actionTexture = theTexture;

        spriteBatch = (SpriteBatch)
            Game.Services.GetService(typeof (SpriteBatch));
        meteors = new MeteorsManager(Game, ref actionTexture);
        Components.Add(meteors);

        player = new Player(Game, ref actionTexture);
        player.Initialize();
        Components.Add(player);

        score = new Score(game, font, Color.LightGray);
        score.Position = new Vector2(1, 1);
        Components.Add(score);

        powerSource = new PowerSource(game, ref actionTexture);
        powerSource.Initialize();
        Components.Add(powerSource);
    }
```

Without the two-player support, the code is much simpler. For example, here is the HandleDamages method:

```
/// <summary>
/// Handle collisions with a meteor
/// </summary>
private void HandleDamages()
{
    // Check collision for player 1
    if (meteors.CheckForCollisions(player.GetBounds()))
    {
        // Player penalty
        player.Power -= 10;
    }
}
```

And you're finished! You created a version of your game for a completely different platform in a short time, and now you have reached the best part: playing it.

Deploying the Game on the Zune

Just as you added your Xbox 360 in the XNA Game Studio Device Center, you should also add the Zune so you can send your game to it. Unlike the Xbox 360, your Zune does not need a LIVE connection to do this. The transfer will be made by the USB cable attached to the Zune.

After you've connected the Zune to your PC, in Visual Studio, select Tools ➤ Launch ➤ XNA Game Studio Device Center, and then click Add Device. It will automatically find the Zune connected to your computer, as shown in Figure 7-3, and will deploy XNA in the device. After that, the Zune will have a new option in the main menu called Games. Cool, right?

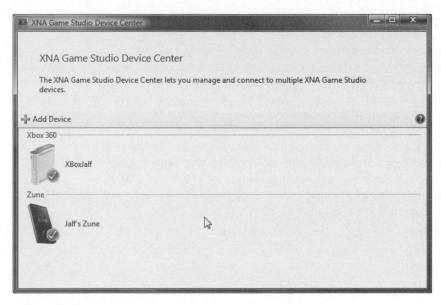

Figure 7-3. *The XNA Game Studio Device Center with the Zune added*

Now you can execute the game to check the result. Figure 7-4 shows some of the game screens on the Zune. Test and debug the game exactly as you would on your PC and the Xbox 360. Then have fun!

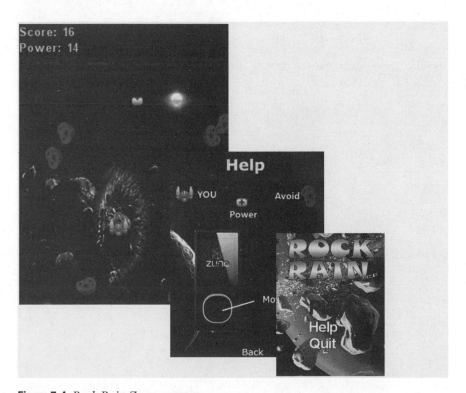

Figure 7-4. *Rock Rain Zune screens*

Summary

From this chapter's example, you saw that it's easy to create games for the Zune using XNA, as long as you limit the games to 2D (using SpriteBatch), since the Zune does not have hardware 3D acceleration. However, you have other important resources to use that we haven't touched on in this chapter. For instance, it's quite simple to use music stored on the Zune as the background music of your game. Also, since every Zune has built-in wireless support, which provides the exact same network APIs as those for Windows and Xbox 360, you can write multiplayer games for the Zune that use the equivalent of SystemLink. Then you can discover other games running nearby, create lobbies, add/remove players, and build a peer-to-peer or client/server multiplayer game as easily as you can build one for Windows or Xbox 360. For more information about developing XNA games for the Zune, see *Zune Game Development Using XNA 3.0* by Dan Waters (Apress, 2009).

CHAPTER 8

∎ ∎ ∎

3D Game Programming Basics

In Chapter 2, we talked about 2D coordinate systems, including a special case of such systems: the screen coordinate system. When dealing with 3D coordinate systems, however, a lot more is involved with defining a 3D virtual object and transforming such an object into a 2D representation on the screen.

This chapter covers the basics of creating 3D games. First, you'll learn the fundamental concepts, and then you'll see how to apply them in a simple XNA project. This will prepare you for creating a complete 3D game in the next chapters.

∎**Note** XNA 3.0 currently does not support creating 3D games for Zunes.

3D Coordinate Systems and Projections

When dealing with three Cartesian dimensions, two types of coordinate systems are used: left-handed and right-handed. These names refer to the z axis's position relative to the x and y axes. To determine this position, point the fingers of one hand to the x axis's positive direction and move them in a counterclockwise direction to the y axis's positive position. The z axis's direction is the direction your thumb points to. Figure 8-1 illustrates this concept.

To put it a different way, in the left-handed coordinate system, the z value gets bigger (the positive direction) when you go from the screen to a point away from you (considering that the x axis and the y axis are on the computer screen). The right-handed 3D system is the opposite: the z values increase toward you from the screen.

The XNA Framework works, by default, in a right-handed coordinate system (which, it's worth noting, is different from DirectX's default). This means that negative values for the z axis are visible, and the more negative they are for a given object, the farther the object is from the screen. Positive values are not shown, unless you change your camera position, as you'll see later in this chapter.

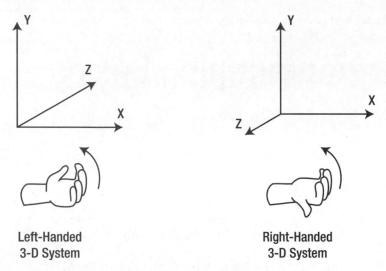

Figure 8-1. *The Cartesian 3D coordinate systems*

Now that you understand 3D coordinate systems, the next step to explore is how you can map 3D objects from this system to your computer (or Xbox 360) 2D screen.

Fortunately, XNA does all the hard mathematical work for this mapping, but you still need to understand the concept of *projections* and how they apply to XNA to issue the basic instructions for how to present the objects on the screen.

Similarly to other gaming libraries, XNA supports two different types of projections:

Perspective projection: The most common type of projection, perspective projection takes the z distance into account and adjusts the objects accordingly. This projection makes objects appear smaller when far from the screen. Depending on the position, the objects also appear deformed, as in the real world. For example, the sides of a cube that are closer to the screen seem bigger than the farther ones. Figure 8-2 shows a graphical representation of the perspective projection.

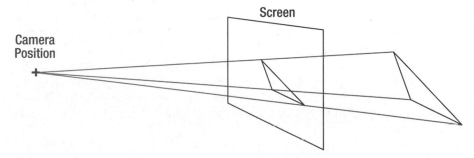

Figure 8-2. *Perspective projection*

Orthogonal projection: In this type of projection, the z component is just ignored, and the objects don't get bigger when closer to the screen or smaller when they are farther away. This projection is mostly used for 2D games (which may use "fake" 3D, just to put some sprites over others), to create head-up displays (HUDs, which are 2D interface elements such as life indicators, windows, and so on) or simpler 3D games. Figure 8-3 illustrates orthogonal projection.

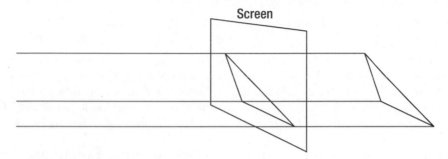

Figure 8-3. *Orthogonal projection*

You'll see later in this chapter how to use each projection type in XNA. However, before you start coding, you need to understand how 3D objects are represented in a game, which is the topic of the next section.

Vertices and Primitives

The most basic part of a 3D object is a *vertex*. Mathematically, vertices are represented solely by their 3D coordinates (which are mapped to the Vector3 data type in XNA), but in XNA, they include extra information—such as color, texture, and normal vector information—depending on the vertex format used. Table 8-1 presents the default vertex definitions provided by the XNA Framework, which can be extended by the game developer if desired.

Table 8-1. *Vertex Format Structure Definition in XNA*

Vertex Format	Description
VertexPositionColor	Defines a vertex with position and rendering color
VertexPositionTexture	Defines a vertex with position and texture coordinates, which specify how to map a given texture over this vertex, with (0, 0) being the upper-left coordinate of the texture, and (1, 1) the bottom-right limit of the texture
VertexPositionColorTexture	Defines a vertex with position, color, and texture coordinates
VertexPositionNormalTexture	Defines a vertex with position and the normal vector

Along with the vertices' position and additional data, when creating 3D objects, you also need to specify how XNA will connect these vertices, according to different drawing primitives.

■**Note** *Drawing primitives* are one of the three basic geometric primitives (points, lines, and triangles) used by XNA to render a collection of vertices. Depending on the primitive type chosen, the same set of vertices (known as the *vertex buffer* or *vertex stream*) will be rendered differently.

The triangle is used as a base to create any other 2D or 3D objects. This is because a primitive defined with only three points is guaranteed to be in a single plane and to be convex. (A line connecting any two points inside a triangle is always fully inside the triangle, which doesn't happen in some figures with four vertices.) These characteristics are the key to performing the fastest rendering possible by the graphics cards, which always use triangles as the base rendering primitives.

So, for example, if you want to draw a square on the screen, you'll use two triangles. If you want to create a cube, you'll use 12 triangles (2 for each facet), as shown in Figure 8-4.

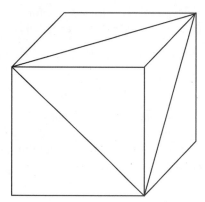

Figure 8-4. *A cube made with triangles*

In XNA, the graphics device object has a method named `DrawPrimitives` that is used to draw a vertex buffer according to a specific primitive type, defined by the `PrimitiveType` enumeration:

- PointList: Each vertex is rendered isolated from the others, so you can see a list of floating points. Figure 8-5 presents a set of vertices rendered as a point list.

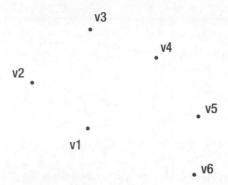

Figure 8-5. *Vertices rendered as a point list*

- LineList: The vertices are rendered in pairs, with lines connecting each pair. This call fails if you do not pass a vertex buffer with an even number of vertices. Figure 8-6 illustrates the use of a line list primitive type.

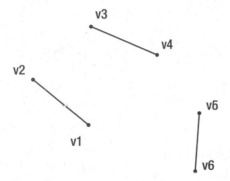

Figure 8-6. *The same vertices rendered as a line list*

- LineStrip: All the vertices in the buffer are rendered as a single, connected line. This can be useful when debugging, because this primitive type allows you to see a wireframe image of your objects, regardless of the number of vertices. Figure 8-7 presents a line strip primitive type sample.

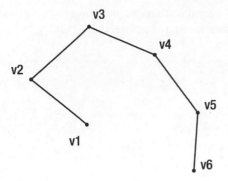

Figure 8-7. *The same vertices rendered as a line strip*

- `TriangleList`: The vertices are rendered in groups of three, as isolated triangles. This provides you with the greatest flexibility when rendering complex scenes, but there's the drawback of having duplicated vertices if you want to draw connected triangles. Figure 8-8 shows the use of the triangle list primitive type to render vertices.

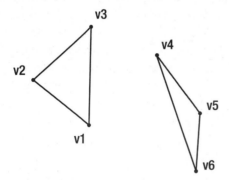

Figure 8-8. *The same vertices rendered as a triangle list*

- `TriangleStrip`: You use this primitive type when drawing connected triangles. It's more efficient for rendering scenes, because you don't need to repeat the duplicated vertices. Every new vertex (after the first two) added to the buffer creates a new triangle, using the last two vertices. Figure 8-9 presents a triangle strip primitive type example.

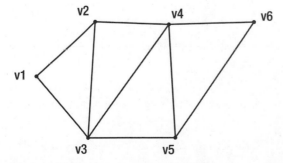

Figure 8-9. *The same vertices rendered as a triangle strip*

- TriangleFan: In this primitive, all the triangles share a common vertex—the first one in the buffer—and each new vertex added creates a new triangle, using the first vertex and the last one defined. Figure 8-10 illustrates the triangle fan type.

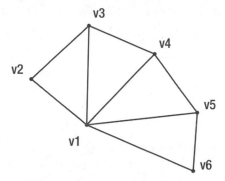

Figure 8-10. *The same vertices rendered as a triangle fan*

■**Note** When drawing triangles, you need to take special care with the triangle vertex ordering if you want XNA to know which triangles are facing the camera and which ones are not. This is important when drawing complex objects such as a donut, for example, to prevent back polygons from showing. To determine the "front" side of a triangle, follow its vertices, from the first to the last one according to their definition order, with the fingers of your right hand. Your thumb will point to the front side of the triangle, just as you saw with the right-handed coordinate system (see Figure 8-1). Drawing only the triangle front faces is XNA's default behavior. You can change this behavior by setting the GraphicsDevice.RenderState.CullMode property.

Vectors, Matrices, and 3D Transformations

Before you're ready to create your first 3D program, you need to understand a few more concepts. 3D vectors and matrices are possibly the most important concepts in 3D game creation.

Vectors

Along with storing the positional values, vectors provide many helper methods that will come in handy when creating your games. Vector3 is the most commonly used vector in 3D games, and some of its most important methods are as follows:

- Vector3.Distance: Given two points, returns a float representing the distance between them.

- Vector3.Add and Vector3.Subtract: Add and subtract two vectors. You can also use the common plus (+) and minus (-) signs to perform addition and subtraction operations on Vector3.

- Vector3.Multiply and Vector3.Divide: Multiply and divide two vectors, or a vector by a float value.

- `Vector3.Clamp`: Constrains the vector components into a given range—useful when defining lights or matrices' values that support only values within a given range.

- `Vector3.Lerp`: Calculates the linear interpolation between two vectors.

- `Vector3.SmoothStep`: Interpolates two vectors according to a `float` given as a weight value.

Additionally, `Vector3` offers a series of shortcuts for special vectors, such as `Vector.Zero` for an empty vector, `Vector3.Up` for the (0, 1, 0) vector, `Vector3.Right` for the (1, 0, 0) vector, and others. `Vector2` and `Vector4` provide similar methods and shortcuts. Many of these methods and shortcuts are used when defining matrices and executing 3D operations.

Matrices

Matrices are the basis for defining rotation, scaling, and translation of an object in the 3D world. Because matrices are used to define any 3D transformations, they are also used to define the operations needed to simulate the projections (discussed earlier in the chapter) and to transform the 3D scene according to the camera position and facing direction.

You'll see examples of each of these uses when creating your sample program. For now, let's see the use of transformation matrices to do a simple translation, and then extrapolate the idea for more complex operations. This will help you understand the importance of the use of matrices in 3D programs.

Suppose you want to move a triangle up the y axis, as shown in Figure 8-11.

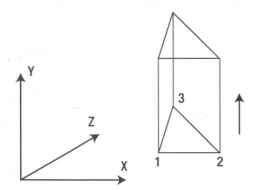

Figure 8-11. *Moving a triangle on the y axis*

Let's assume that the coordinates of the triangle vertices are as follows:

Vertex	X	Y	Z
1	50	10	0
2	70	10	0
3	55	25	0

To translate 40 units over the y axis's positive direction, all you need to do is to add 40 to each y position, and you have the new coordinates for the vertices, shown here:

Vertex	X	Y	Z
1	50	50	0
2	70	50	0
3	55	65	0

You can achieve the same results by representing each vertex as a matrix with one row and four columns, with the vertex coordinates as the first three columns and 1 as the value in the last one. You then multiply this matrix to a special matrix, constructed to produce the translation transformation to the vertex matrix.

Figure 8-12 presents the same operation applied to the first vertex.

$$\begin{matrix} x & y & z \\ [50 & 10 & 0 & 1] \end{matrix} \times \begin{bmatrix} 1 & 0 & 0 & 0 \\ 0 & 1 & 0 & 0 \\ 0 & 0 & 1 & 0 \\ 0 & 40 & 0 & 1 \end{bmatrix} = \begin{matrix} x' & y' & z' \\ [50 & 50 & 0 & 1] \end{matrix}$$

Figure 8-12. *Applying a matrix multiplication to a 3D vertex*

A little explanation about multiplication for matrices is in order. To calculate the resulting matrix, you must take each value in the row of the first matrix, multiply it by each of the values in the corresponding column in the second matrix, and then sum all of the results. So, in the previous sample, the calculations are as follows:

$x' = (50 \times 1) + (10 \times 0) + (0 \times 0) + (1 \times 0) = 50$

$y' = (50 \times 0) + (10 \times 1) + (0 \times 0) + (1 \times 40) = 50$

$z' = (50 \times 0) + (10 \times 0) + (0 \times 1) + (1 \times 0) = 0$

Put simply, you can perform translations by putting the desired values for translation over the x, y, and z positions in the last row of the transformation matrix. You can perform scaling by replacing the 1s on the diagonal with fractional values (to shrink) or values bigger than 1 (to expand), and perform rotation around any axis using a combination of sine and cosine values in specific positions in the matrix.

So, what's the big deal about using matrices? One of the biggest benefits is that you can perform complex operations by multiplying their corresponding transformation matrices. You can then apply the resulting matrix over each vertex on the 3D model, so you can perform all operations on the model by multiplying its vertices for only one matrix, instead of calculating each transformation for each vertex. For example, usually you will need to rotate, scale, and translate an object to position it in your 3D scene, and then perform new operations according to the object's movement around the scene. In this situation, instead of calculating all operations for each vertex, you multiply the transformation matrices and calculate only one operation per vertex: multiplying it by this resulting matrix.

Even better, all graphics cards have built-in algorithms to multiply matrices, so this multiplication consumes little processing power. Considering that complex 3D objects may have thousands of vertices, doing the transformations with as low a processing cost as possible is a must, and matrices allow this.

Fortunately, you don't need to understand all these mathematical details to use matrices and execute 3D transformations in your program. All game programming libraries (from OpenGL to DirectX) offer ready-to-use matrix manipulation functions, and XNA is no exception. Through the `Matrix` class, many matrix operations are available, such as the following:

- `Matrix.CreateRotationX`, `Matrix.CreateRotationY`, and `Matrix.CreateRotationZ`: Each of these creates a rotation matrix for each of the axes.

- `Matrix.Translation`: Creates a translation matrix (one or more axes).

- `Matrix.Scale`: Creates a scale matrix (one or more axes).

- `Matrix.CreateLookAt`: Creates a view matrix used to position the camera, by setting the 3D position of the camera, the 3D position it is facing, and which direction is "up" for the camera.

- `Matrix.CreatePerspectiveFieldOfView`: Creates a projection matrix that uses a perspective view, by setting the angle of viewing (*field of view*), the aspect ratio (the ratio used to map the 3D projection to screen coordinates, usually the width of the screen divided by the height of the screen), and the near and far planes, which limit which part of the 3D scene is drawn. See Figure 8-13 to better understand these concepts. Similarly, you have two extra methods, `CreatePerspectiveOffCenter` and `CreatePerspective`, which create matrices for perspective projection using different parameters.

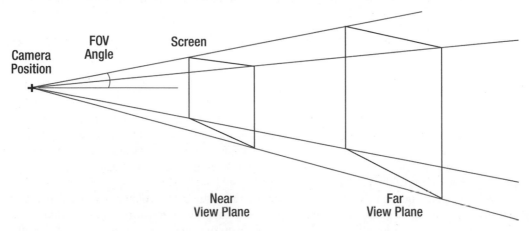

Figure 8-13. *A perspective projection definition*

■**Note** When creating projection matrices, XNA methods also expect you to pass the aspect ratio as a parameter. This ratio is needed because the pixels are not squared (normally they are more tall than wide), so a sphere can appear like an egg if the aspect ratio is not correctly defined. A concept closely related to the aspect ratio is the *viewport*, which is the portion of the 3D scene that will be drawn when rendering the scene. Because the viewport is a property of the device, in XNA, the aspect ratio is usually defined as `device.Viewport.Width / device.Viewport.Height`.

- `Matrix.CreateOrthographic`: Creates a matrix used in orthogonal, or *orthographic*, projection. This method receives the width, height, and near and far planes that define the orthographic projection, and has a similar method named `CreateOrthographicOffCenter`, which creates the orthogonal projection matrix where the center of the 3D scene does not map to the center of the screen.

You'll see the use of some of these functions in this chapter's sample code, and others in the next chapters, where you'll create a complete 3D game.

Lights, Camera . . . Effects!

If you thought that defining and playing around with a camera and lights were activities reserved for complex games, think again. XNA makes it simple to deal with a camera, lights, and special effects, but you do need to know the basics about these to create even a simple 3D game. After all, without a camera and lights, how can you see what was constructed in your 3D scene? This section will provide a high-level view of these features.

XNA's `BasicEffect` class fulfills all your needs for not only basic games, but also for some complex games. This class offers properties and methods that let you define the final details to render your 3D scene. The following are some of the most important properties of this class:

- `View`: The view matrix, which defines the camera position and direction. Usually created using `Matrix.CreateLookAt`.

- `Projection`: The projection matrix that's used to map the 3D scene coordinates to screen coordinates. Usually created through `Matrix.CreatePerspective`, `Matrix.CreateOrthographic`, or a similar method.

- `World`: The *world matrix*, which is used to apply transformations to all objects in the 3D scene.

- `LightingEnabled`: If `False`, the scene is rendered using a base light that illuminates all sides of all objects equally. If `True`, the light properties of `BasicEffect` will be used to light the scene.

- `AmbientLightColor`: Defines the color of the *ambient light*, which illuminates all sides of all objects equally. It's used only when rendering if `LightingEnabled` is set to `True`.

- DirectionalLight0, DirectionalLight1, and DirectionalLight2: Define up to three directional lights used by the effect when rendering. Each directional light is defined by its specular color (color of the light that will have a perfect, mirror-like reflection), its diffuse color (color of the light that will be reflected diffusely), and the light direction. These properties are used only if LightingEnabled is set to True.

- FogColor, FogStart, and FogEnd: Let you define "fog" for the scene, so objects in the fog range appear to be seen through a dense smoke. You can specify the fog color, along with the distance in which the fog begins and ends.

Along with these properties, one important method of BasicEffect is EnableDefaultLighting, which turns on a single, white directional light without requiring any extra light configuration.

The following code fragment presents a blueprint for what your program needs to do to render the scene properly, assuming that effect is a BasicEffect object that was properly initialized:

```
effect.Begin();
foreach(EffectPass CurrentPass in effect.CurrentTechnique.Passes)
{
   CurrentPass.Begin();
   // Include here the code for drawing the scene using this effect
   CurrentPass.End();
}
effect.End();
```

In this code, you tell the effect to Begin its processing, then loop through a collection of all EffectPass objects of the current technique used (there's also a collection of effect techniques). You also need to start and end each of the passes of the technique. Finally, you need to tell the effect to End the processing.

At first glance, the previous code might seem a bit too much for a simple rendering effect. However, you need to remember that BasicEffect is a special case of the Effect class, which is powerful and flexible, and gives programmers all the control they need to manipulate advanced effect techniques, such as the use of custom-made shaders (discussed in the next chapter).

Because BasicEffect is simpler, but is still an Effect, you must use the previous code in every program you create. However, you don't need to worry about which types of techniques a program can use, or which passes can compose each of these techniques. You'll just use this code as a blueprint, because for now, the important point is the convenience BasicEffect can provide programmers through its properties.

When creating the sample 3D game in the next chapter, you will learn more about effects. Chapter 9 explains shaders, techniques, and passes in detail.

Drawing the 3D Axis in XNA

To demonstrate the concepts discussed so far in this chapter, in this section, you'll create code to draw a line over each of the 3D axes, and the letters *X*, *Y*, and *Z* near these lines, so you can see for yourself the results of creating and manipulating a 3D scene.

The steps for creating and rendering 3D objects in XNA can be summarized as follows:

1. Define the vertex type you'll use (position plus color, texture, and so on).

2. Create an array of vertices and fill it with the vertices' data.

3. Create a vertex buffer and fill it with the vertices previously created.

4. Define the effect to be used, with projection and view matrices and the light sources, if any.

5. Inform the device which vertices you'll use.

6. Using the effect, draw the vertex buffer using a specific primitive type.

If something is not quite clear in the following code listings, browse back through the discussions in the previous pages before entering the code.

To better organize your code, create a new class named cls3Daxis. This class has some methods with the same names of the by now well-known Game1.cs class, provided for you when you create a new XNA Windows Game project: LoadContent, UnloadContent, and Draw, so you can call these methods from the main game class ones.

Create the new class and include code for three private properties: device, vertexBuffer, and effect, also creating the class constructor with code to receive and store the graphics device. You'll need the graphics device for the rendering operations, and you must also create the vertex buffer and the effect at the class level, so you can create them in the LoadContent method and release them in UnloadContent. The initial code for the class is as follows:

```
class cls3DAxis
{
    private GraphicsDevice device;
    private VertexBuffer vertexBuffer;
    private BasicEffect effect;

    public cls3DAxis(GraphicsDevice graphicsDevice)
    {
        device = graphicsDevice;
    }
}
```

Coding the Vertices and the Vertex Buffer

You'll now code a private helper method for this class, named Create3Daxis, which creates the 3D axis and fills the vertex buffer. This enables you to fulfill the first three steps of the process for creating and rendering 3D objects, as outlined at the beginning of this section.

The next code sample presents a first version of the method, which simply creates three lines representing each of the 3D axes, going from an axisLength negative position to an axisLength positive position in each axis. For example, if axisLength is 1, for the x axis, you'll draw a line from (–1, 0, 0) to (1, 0, 0).

```
private void Create3DAxis()
{
    // Size of 3D axis
    float axisLength = 1f;
    // Number of vertices we'll use
    int vertexCount = 6;

    VertexPositionColor[] vertices = new VertexPositionColor[vertexCount];
    // X axis
    vertices[0] = new VertexPositionColor(new Vector3(-axisLength, 0.0f, 0.0f),
        Color.White);
    vertices[1] = new VertexPositionColor(new Vector3(axisLength, 0.0f, 0.0f),
        Color.White);
    // Y axis
    vertices[2] = new VertexPositionColor(new Vector3(0.0f, -axisLength, 0.0f),
        Color.White);
    vertices[3] = new VertexPositionColor(new Vector3(0.0f, axisLength, 0.0f),
        Color.White);
    // Z axis
    vertices[4] = new VertexPositionColor(new Vector3(0.0f, 0.0f, -axisLength),
        Color.White);
    vertices[5] = new VertexPositionColor(new Vector3(0.0f, 0.0f, axisLength),
        Color.White);

    // Fill the vertex buffer with the vertices
    vertexBuffer = new VertexBuffer(device,
                              vertexCount * VertexPositionColor.SizeInBytes,
                              BufferUsage.WriteOnly);
    vertexBuffer.SetData<VertexPositionColor>(vertices);
}
```

For this example, you used a vertex defined by its position and color, and defined all vertex colors as white. When drawing these vertices, you'll use the line list primitive type, so every pair of vertices, in the order they were defined, will become a line.

In the last part of the previous code, you created the vertex buffer, passing the graphics device, the size of the vertex buffer (calculated by multiplying the number of vertices by the size of each vertex, given by VertexPositionColor.SizeInBytes), and the behavior of your buffer. (BufferUsage.WriteOnly means that you'll just write the vertices and use them later, without performing any updates directly on the contents of the vertex buffer.)

After creating the buffer, in the last code line, you set the vertices' data by calling the SetData method of the vertex buffer, which receives the array of vertices you created and the vertices' format (also called *custom vertex format* or *flexible vertex format*, since developers can define their own formats as needed).

To add the letters over the positive edge of each of the axes, you need to create new line segments that will form each letter. In such cases, the best you can do is to draw a little sketch so you can calculate the vertices' position for every line, in every letter. Look at the distances presented in Figure 8-14, and compare them with the next code sample, which presents the complete Create3Daxis function. Make sure you understand how the *X*, *Y*, and *Z* letters are drawn.

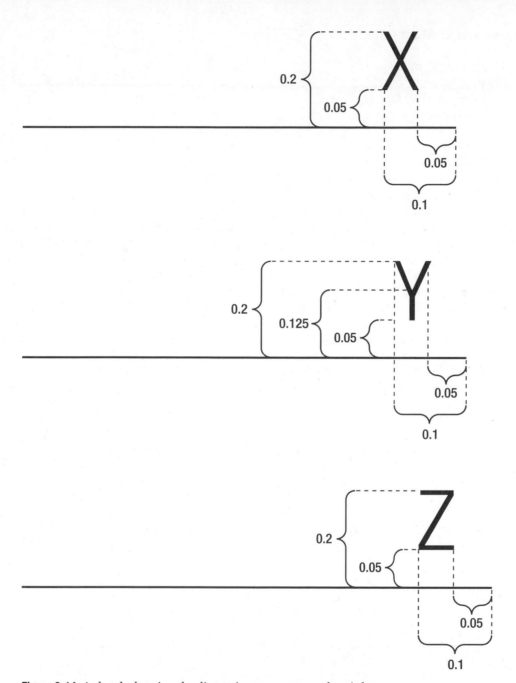

Figure 8-14. *A sketch showing the dimensions to create each axis letter*

In case you're wondering how we came up with the values presented in Figure 8-14, the answer is easy: trial and error! If you don't like the way the characters look, just adjust the values until you find the desired effect.

```
private void Create3DAxis()
{
    // Size of 3D axis
    float axisLength = 1f;
    // Number of vertices we'll use
    int vertexCount = 22;

    VertexPositionColor[] vertices = new VertexPositionColor[vertexCount];
    // X axis
    vertices[0] = new VertexPositionColor(
                new Vector3(-axisLength, 0.0f, 0.0f), Color.White);
    vertices[1] = new VertexPositionColor(
                new Vector3(axisLength, 0.0f, 0.0f), Color.White);
    // Y axis
    vertices[2] = new VertexPositionColor(
                new Vector3(0.0f, -axisLength, 0.0f), Color.White);
    vertices[3] = new VertexPositionColor(
                new Vector3(0.0f, axisLength, 0.0f), Color.White);
    // Z axis
    vertices[4] = new VertexPositionColor(
                new Vector3(0.0f, 0.0f, -axisLength), Color.White);
    vertices[5] = new VertexPositionColor(
                new Vector3(0.0f, 0.0f, axisLength), Color.White);

    // "X" letter near X axis
    vertices[6] = new VertexPositionColor(
                new Vector3(axisLength - 0.1f, 0.05f, 0.0f), Color.White);
    vertices[7] = new VertexPositionColor(
                new Vector3(axisLength - 0.05f, 0.2f, 0.0f), Color.White);
    vertices[8] = new VertexPositionColor(
                new Vector3(axisLength - 0.05f, 0.05f, 0.0f), Color.White);
    vertices[9] = new VertexPositionColor(
                new Vector3(axisLength - 0.1f, 0.2f, 0.0f), Color.White);

    // "Y" letter near Y axis
    vertices[10] = new VertexPositionColor(
                new Vector3(0.075f, axisLength - 0.125f, 0.0f), Color.White);
    vertices[11] = new VertexPositionColor(
                new Vector3(0.075f, axisLength - 0.2f, 0.0f), Color.White);
    vertices[12] = new VertexPositionColor(
                new Vector3(0.075f, axisLength - 0.125f, 0.0f), Color.Whitc);
    vertices[13] = new VertexPositionColor(
                new Vector3(0.1f, axisLength - 0.05f, 0.0f), Color.White);
    vertices[14] = new VertexPositionColor(
                new Vector3(0.075f, axisLength - 0.125f, 0.0f), Color.White);
    vertices[15] = new VertexPositionColor(
                new Vector3(0.05f, axisLength - 0.05f, 0.0f), Color.White);
```

```
        // "Z" letter near Z axis
        vertices[16] = new VertexPositionColor(
                    new Vector3(0.0f, 0.05f, axisLength - 0.1f), Color.White);
        vertices[17] = new VertexPositionColor(
                    new Vector3(0.0f, 0.05f, axisLength - 0.05f), Color.White);
        vertices[18] = new VertexPositionColor(
                    new Vector3(0.0f, 0.05f, axisLength - 0.1f), Color.White);
        vertices[19] = new VertexPositionColor(
                    new Vector3(0.0f, 0.2f, axisLength - 0.05f), Color.White);
        vertices[20] = new VertexPositionColor(
                    new Vector3(0.0f, 0.2f, axisLength - 0.1f), Color.White);
        vertices[21] = new VertexPositionColor(
                    new Vector3(0.0f, 0.2f, axisLength - 0.05f), Color.White);

        // Fill the vertex buffer with the vertices
        vertexBuffer = new VertexBuffer(device,
                    vertexCount * VertexPositionColor.SizeInBytes,
                    ResourceUsage.WriteOnly,
                    ResourceManagementMode.Automatic);
        vertexBuffer.SetData<VertexPositionColor>(vertices);
}
```

You also need to create code in the LoadContent method to call the Create3Daxis, and to free the vertex buffer property in the cls3Daxis class, within the UnloadContent method, as shown in the next code sample.

```
public void LoadContent()
{
    // Create the 3D axis
    Create3DAxis();
}
public void UnloadContent()
{
    if (vertexBuffer != null)
    {
        vertexBuffer.Dispose();
        vertexBuffer = null;
    }
}
```

This concludes the code for creating and freeing up (disposing of) the memory resources used for drawing the 3D axis's vertices. However, you can't run the program yet. You still need to code the basic effect that defines how the rendering is done, and to include calls for the cls3Daxis class in the program's main class, Game1.

In the next section, you'll finish the cls3Daxis class, setting the effect properties you need to display the axis.

Coding a Basic Effect and Rendering the 3D Scene

You learned earlier in this chapter that BasicEffect is a class XNA provides to help you create effects for rendering 3D scenes. BasicEffect includes many properties that let you define the camera position, the projection to be used, and the light sources used, for example.

The next code sample shows the complete code for the LoadContent method, including creation and configuration for a simple basic effect, which will suffice for the examples in this chapter. All of the functions and properties used in this code were explained earlier in this chapter; so this might be a good time for you to refer back to the discussions of the projection types and the view and projection matrices.

```
public void LoadContent()
{
    // Create the effect that will be used to draw the axis
    effect = new BasicEffect(device, null);

    // Calculate the effect aspect ratio, projection, and view matrix
    float aspectRatio = (float)device.Viewport.Width / device.Viewport.Height;
    effect.View = Matrix.CreateLookAt(new Vector3(0.0f, 2.0f, 2.0f), Vector3.Zero,
                        Vector3.Up);
    effect.Projection = Matrix.CreatePerspectiveFieldOfView(
                    MathHelper.ToRadians(45.0f),
                    aspectRatio, 1.0f, 10.0f);
    effect.LightingEnabled = false;

    // Create the 3D axis
    Create3DAxis();
}
```

In the CreateLookAt method, you're creating the camera two units up (y axis) from the (0, 0, 0) position, and two units outside the screen boundaries (z-axis negative values are on the screen—visible values—and positive values are outside the screen boundaries); "looking at" the Zero vector (0, 0, 0), and setting the y axis as "up" with Vector3.Up.

You then create a perspective projection matrix, "looking" in a 45-degree angle as the field of view. The rendering happens for objects from 1 to 10 units from the screen (z values from –1 to –10).

Finally, you disable lighting, so the whole scene is rendered with a simple and omnidirectional default light, which does not generate any gradients or shades.

The UnloadContent method also needs to be completed to include the disposal of the effect object, as follows:

```
public void UnloadContent()
{
    if (vertexBuffer != null)
    {
        vertexBuffer.Dispose();
        vertexBuffer = null;
    }
```

```
if (effect != null)
{
    effect.Dispose();
    effect = null;
}
}
```

Now that you've set up the vertex buffer and the effect, you need to code the Draw method of the cls3Daxis class, which will use the effect to draw the scene, following the blueprint code presented earlier, in the "Lights, Camera . . . Effects!" section.

In the next code fragment, you configure the device to use the vertex format you are using (vertices defined by their position and color). Then, you send the device vertex stream to your vertex buffer, defining the starting point in this stream (start reading from the first vertex) and the size of each vertex element. Once the device is configured, you enter the drawing loop, and call device.DrawPrimitives for every pass of the current effect technique (as explained earlier in this chapter), stating that you are drawing 11 lines (made of 22 vertices).

```
public void Draw()
{
    // Create a vertex declaration to be used when drawing the vertices
    device.VertexDeclaration = new VertexDeclaration(device,
                              VertexPositionColor.VertexElements);
    // Set the vertex source
    device.Vertices[0].SetSource(vertexBuffer, 0, VertexPositionColor.SizeInBytes);

    // Draw the 3D axis
    effect.Begin();
    foreach(EffectPass CurrentPass in effect.CurrentTechnique.Passes)
    {
        CurrentPass.Begin();
        // We are drawing 22 vertices, grouped in 11 lines
        device.DrawPrimitives(PrimitiveType.LineList, 0, 11);
        CurrentPass.End();
    }
    effect.End();
}
```

This code concludes the cls3Daxis class. All you need to do now is call this class's methods from within the Game1 main class, and you'll be able to see the 3D axis.

Coding the Main Program Calls

In the previous section, you created the cls3Daxis class, which provides methods with the same names of the main class of XNA programs: LoadContent, UnloadContent, and Draw.

To use this class, let's now create a new, empty XNA Windows Game project. As you know, the Game1 class is generated for you automatically. You need to define an object of the cls3Daxis class, initialize it, and call the corresponding methods on the Game1 class. The code for the updated methods is as follows:

```
GraphicsDeviceManager graphics;

// 3D objects
cls3DAxis my3DAxis;

protected override void Initialize()
{
    my3DAxis = new cls3DAxis(graphics.GraphicsDevice);
    base.Initialize();
}

protected override void LoadContent()
{
    // Create the 3D axis
    my3DAxis.LoadGraphicsContent();
}

protected override void UnloadContent()
{
    // Free the resources allocated for 3D drawing
    my3DAxis.UnloadContent();
}

protected override void Draw(GameTime gameTime)
{
    graphics.GraphicsDevice.Clear(Color.CornflowerBlue);
    // Draw the 3D axis
    my3DAxis.Draw();
    base.Draw(gameTime);
}
```

The result of running this code, shown in Figure 8-15, might not look as you expected. You see only the x and y axes, and this certainly doesn't seem too much like 3D. This is because the camera position is aligned with the z axis, so this axis is hidden behind the y axis, and the letter Z is not drawn, because it's behind the camera.

You could simply adjust the camera position in the cls3Daxis class, but let's do a little better, while exploring a new concept: the world matrix.

The world matrix, as explained when we talked about effects, is a property of the Effect class that contains transformations that are applied to all scene objects when rendering.

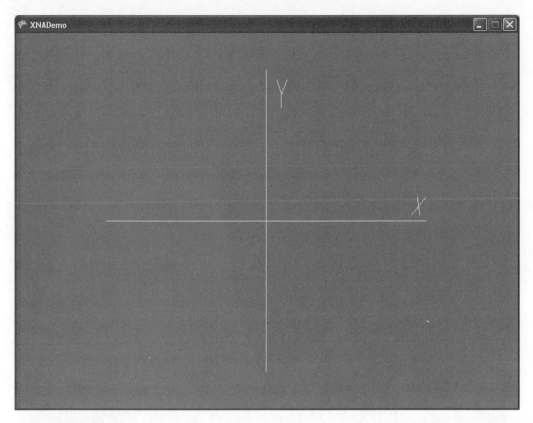

Figure 8-15. *The 3D axis*

Let's use the world matrix to make this 3D axis drawing spin, so you can see the result of rotating a 3D scene. You can do this in three easy steps:

1. Create a new property in the cls3Daxis class to store the current world matrix, defaulting to an *identity matrix* (a matrix that doesn't perform any transformation):

    ```
    public Matrix worldMatrix = Matrix.Identity;
    ```

2. Include a new line in the Draw method of this class to update the effect's World property to this matrix, so the effect receives the updated matrix and is able to use it to transform the axis drawing:

    ```
    effect.World = worldMatrix;
    ```

3. Include a new line in the Update method of the Game1 class to update the cls3Daxis worldMatrix property, incrementing the world rotation angle in every update:

```
my3DAxis.worldMatrix *= Matrix.CreateRotationY(0.01f) *

                                    Matrix.CreateRotationX(0.01f);
```

If you run your program now, you will see the nice result of spinning the 3D axis, as shown in Figure 8-16.

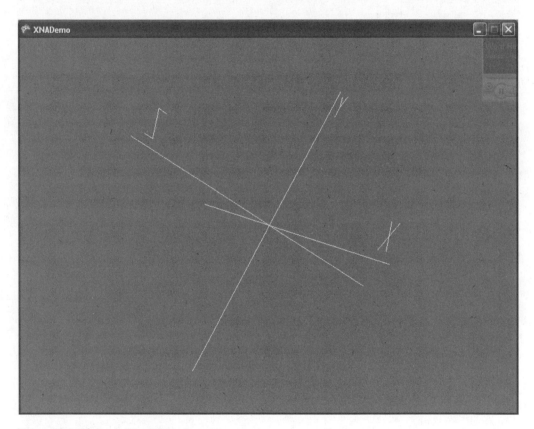

Figure 8-16. *The spinning 3D axis*

Models and Meshes

Playing around with vertices and drawing primitives is somewhat cool, and it's important to help you understand what's happening behind the scenes when you draw a 3D model. But if you want to create a game with complex 3D objects, this approach would hardly be the best choice.

In Chapter 1, you learned that XNA's Content Pipeline supports many file formats, including 3D object definition X and FBX files. These files store the definition of 3D objects, known as a *3D model* or simply a *model*.

As a simple definition, you can say a model is a hierarchy of meshes, which can be rendered independently. A *mesh* is a collection of interconnected vertices, along with some rendering information.

XNA provides special classes to manipulate models and meshes: Model and ModelMesh. Using these classes will let you load and manipulate 3D models created in tools like Maya and 3ds Max in your game. This way, you can use much more sophisticated 3D models than you could possibly create inside your program working vertex by vertex. These models can store extra information such as colors, textures, and even animations that can be used by XNA.

To create a program that manipulates models, you must first load a model as new content into your sample program.

To do this, right-click the project in the Content folder in the Solution Explorer window, choose Add ➤ Existing Content, and select an X or FBX file. In this section's example, you'll use the Cube.X file, a simple file with a cube definition that comes with the DirectX Software Development Kit (SDK), which can be downloaded from the Microsoft site (http://www.microsoft.com/directx).

■Tip You can use other models with the same code, but you may need to adjust the view and projection matrices depending on the model; or perform some transformation over the model in order to see it entirely on the game screen. After finishing this chapter's example, try loading and performing the necessary adjustments to use other models, so you'll better understand the view, projection, and transformations matrices before playing around with a full game.

Once the content is in your project, you must declare a model variable to hold the reference to this content, at the Game1 class level:

```
Model myModel;
```

In the LoadContent method, you need to include a single line that loads the model:

```
myModel = Content.Load<Model>("Cube");
```

Finally, you must include a loop in the Draw method to run through all meshes in the model and draw each one. Although there is only one mesh in this simple model, using this approach makes the code ready to draw complex models:

```
// Loop through each mesh of the model
foreach (ModelMesh mesh in myModel.Meshes)
{
    // Draw the current mesh
    mesh.Draw();
}
```

If you run your program now, you will see the mesh already loaded, along with the spinning 3D axis created in the previous section, as shown in Figure 8-17.

The image in Figure 8-17 is not very exciting, because two details prevent the image from appearing like a cube. The camera is upright on one of the cube faces, so all you see is a square. Also, there's no lighting enabled, so every face is illuminated exactly the same way. There's no shading to help you see the difference between one face and another. To work around these problems, you need to rotate the model to a better position (and maybe do some scaling, so it doesn't hide the axis), and apply lights to the model rendering.

Figure 8-17. *The first view of a 3D model (cube)*

Remember the BasicEffect class you used in the previous section? With BasicEffect, you can apply transformations to the object (through the World property), set the Projection and the View matrices (which are a must for every effect), and turn on a default light source with little effort, as you saw when we talked about effects earlier in this chapter. You can use the same projection and camera view matrices you used for cls3Daxis. A rotation of 45 degrees in both the x and y axes will turn the cube so you can see three of its faces.

Remember that a model is composed of many meshes. To use the effect to render the 3D object, you must loop through all the meshes to apply the effect to all of them.

Additionally, a mesh has a collection of effects, so it can render different parts of the mesh with different effects—a useful thing for complex meshes. Because you might have many effects for a single mesh, you need to have a second loop, running through all effects of each mesh, to be certain you'll apply the same effect in all mesh parts.

In a simple model such as your cube, you have only one mesh and only one effect on this mesh. Nonetheless, you'll create generic code that allows you to use the same program for more complex models.

The final code with the effect creation and use follows. Place it in the LoadContent method:

```
// Calculate the aspect ratio for the model
float aspectRatio = (float)graphics.GraphicsDevice.Viewport.Width /
                         graphics.GraphicsDevice.Viewport.Height;

// Configure basic lighting and do a simple rotation for the model
// (so it can be seen onscreen)
foreach (ModelMesh mesh in myModel.Meshes)
    foreach (BasicEffect effect in mesh.Effects)
    {
        // Rotate and make the model a little smaller (50%)
        effect.World = Matrix.CreateScale(0.5f) *
            Matrix.CreateRotationX(MathHelper.ToRadians(45.0f)) *
            Matrix.CreateRotationY(MathHelper.ToRadians(45.0f));
        // Set the projection matrix for the model
        effect.Projection = Matrix.CreatePerspectiveFieldOfView(
                    MathHelper.ToRadians(45.0f),
                    aspectRatio, 1.0f, 10.0f);
        effect.View = Matrix.CreateLookAt(new Vector3(0.0f, 0.0f, 3.0f),
                Vector3.Zero, Vector3.Up);
        effect.EnableDefaultLighting();
    }
```

Figure 8-18 presents the result of running the program with the newly created effect.

Note You don't need to bother to load textures if your model uses them. Model files already include information about the textures they use. Because this information includes the path where the texture files should be located, you just need to know this path and then copy the texture files to the corresponding path. You can find out the texture paths by examining the model files (in a text editor, for example) or by including the model in the project and compiling it. XNA Game Studio presents the Content Pipeline path errors stating where the model looked for the textures.

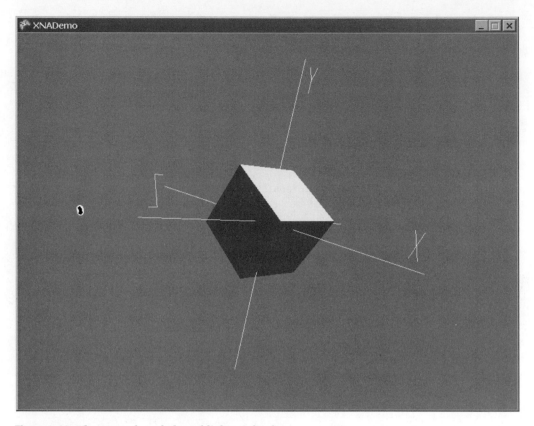

Figure 8-18. *The rotated, scaled, and lightened cube*

Summary

In this chapter, you learned the basics of 3D graphics programming. Although XNA provides you with many built-in classes and methods that reduce the program's complexity, there are still a lot of concepts to understand.

Be sure you understand the following concepts before you go on to the next chapter:

- What vertices are and what type of information can be used when defining them

- What a vertex buffer is and how to use it

- Why matrices are important, and how to use them to perform transformations in 3D objects

- What the projection matrix is, which types of projections XNA supports, and how to use them

- What the view matrix is and how you create it in XNA

- What the world matrix is, and how to use it to perform operations in all 3D scenes

- What models and meshes are, and how to load and render them in XNA

In the next chapters, you'll create a complete 3D game, so you'll be able to better exercise and explore these concepts.

CHAPTER 9

Rendering Pipeline, Shaders, and Effects

In this chapter, you'll learn some of the concepts related to the rendering pipeline, shaders, and effects. The rendering pipeline is responsible for rendering a 3D scene into a 2D image, which can then be drawn on the screen. You can use shaders to program some stages of the rendering pipeline, and use effects to describe a combination of shaders and configurations for the fixed stages of the rendering pipeline. This flexibility allows you to create custom visual effects, improving the visual aspect of the final image.

Rendering Pipeline

To visualize a 3D scene on the screen, the scene must be transformed into a 2D image. The process that transforms a 3D scene into an image is called *rendering*. Figure 9-1 shows a high-level diagram of the rendering pipeline used by XNA.

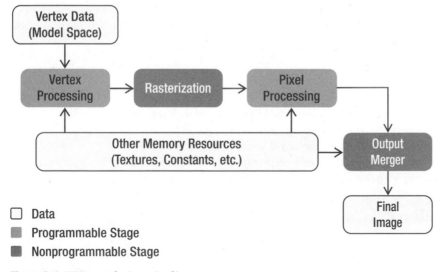

Figure 9-1. *XNA rendering pipeline*

An object in a 3D scene is described through its *mesh*, which is the collection of its vertices (and indices, if applicable). The vertices in a mesh can have many different attributes, such as position, color, normal, and texture coordinate, as explained in Chapter 8.

As illustrated in Figure 9-1, at the beginning of the rendering process, the vertices of the object's mesh are sent to the rendering pipeline, where they go through the stages of vertex processing, rasterization, and pixel processing. At the end of this process, many pixels are generated, ready to be stored in the scene's final image. Since many triangles of one object can compete for the same pixels on the screen, the last stage in the rendering pipeline—the output merger—decides which pixels are closest to the camera. The output merger stores those pixels in the final image and decides which pixels are to be discarded. This decision is based on the distance between the camera and the object, so only the closest objects are displayed, but this decision can also be influenced by transparency information.

In the old versions of the DirectX and OpenGL application programming interfaces (APIs), all the stages of the rendering pipeline were fixed (preprogrammed). This meant that a fixed set of effects was available to game programmers. This forced all games to use the same rendering processes, allowing them to change only a few predefined parameters. The result was the release of many game titles with similar graphics.

From DirectX 8.1 onward, it became possible to program some of the stages of the rendering pipeline through the creation of small programs called *shaders*. Shaders allow you to define which data is input and output from each programmable stage of the graphics processing unit (GPU), and, more important, the processing that is happening within each stage. Using shaders, you can create many new effects for games that weren't possible using the fixed pipeline.

In XNA, you use shaders to render any object to the screen. To ease game development without needing to program your own shaders, XNA provides some helper classes that contain a basic set of shaders and effects. For example, you can use the `SpriteBatch` class to draw 2D sprites, and the `BasicEffect` class to draw 3D models. These two classes use shaders in a way that's transparent to you. As their names imply, these classes support only basic rendering. The `SpriteBatch` class will render your images just as they've been saved on disk, but don't ask it to add any spotlights, reflective objects, or effects like rippling in your images. The `BasicEffect` class can render your 3D world using only basic lighting. If you want to program some fancier effects, you can create your own shaders.

Shaders

Shaders are small programs that execute inside the GPU and define how the data received from your XNA program is processed in the programmable stages of the rendering pipeline. Shaders are most commonly written in the High Level Shading Language (HLSL).

Two shaders are generally applied: a vertex shader and a pixel shader. The rasterization stage is executed between the vertex shader and the pixel shader.

Vertex Shader

The shader used in the vertex processing stage, shown in Figure 9-1, is called the *vertex shader*. The basic task of the vertex shader is to read the original coordinates of the vertices from your XNA program, transform them to 2D screen coordinates, and present them to the next stage. Additionally, along with manipulating coordinates, you can also choose to process other attributes of each vertex, such as its color, normal, and so on.

Vertex shaders allow you to execute many tasks, such as solids deforming, skeletal animation, and particle motion.

Rasterization

In the rasterization stage, your GPU determines which screen pixels each triangle occupies. All of these pixels are sent to the pixel shader (discussed next), allowing you to do one final phase of processing.

Figure 9-2 illustrates a rasterized triangle, which generates many pixels. Note especially that the vertex attributes are linearly interpolated between all the generated pixels.

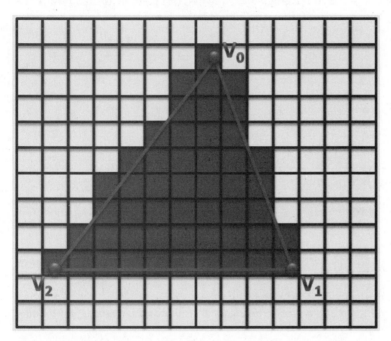

Figure 9-2. *Triangle rasterization. The gray quads represent the pixels generated.*

Pixel Shader

The main task of the pixel shader is to receive a pixel as input, calculate the final color of the pixel, and pass it on to the output merger. Each pixel can provide the pixel shader with a wide variety of data, generated by your vertex shader and linearly interpolated by the rasterizer. This allows your pixel shader to adjust the color of the pixel according to the lighting conditions, add reflections, perform bump mapping, and more. You can also use a pixel shader to apply postprocessing effects over an entire rendered scene, such as brightness, contrast and color enhancements, saturation, and blur.

Additionally, the pixel shader can change the *depth* of the pixel. This depth is used by the output merger to decide which pixels are drawn and which are not drawn. By default, this depth indicates how far the originating triangle is from the camera. However, if you want to influence the decision of the output merger, you can specify this value yourself.

High-Level Shading Language

XNA natively supports shader programming through Microsoft's HLSL. HLSL has a few built-in functions, which include math operations, texture access, and flow control. The types of data that HLSL supports are similar to those used in the C language, with the exception of vectors, matrices, and samplers.

HLSL Data Types

HLSL supports many different data types, including scalars, vectors, and matrices. Table 9-1 shows the scalar data types present in the language. Note that it is possible to create vectors and matrices for all the scalar types present in the language, such as float2, float4, bool3x3, double2x2, and so on.

Table 9-1. *HLSL Scalar Types*

Type	Value
bool	true or false
int	32-bit signed integer
half	16-bit floating point
float	32-bit floating point
double	64-bit floating point

Another data type present in HLSL is the sampler type, which is used to sample data from textures. Different sampler types, such as sampler1D, sampler2D, and sampler3D, are used to sample 1D, 2D, and 3D textures, respectively. Associated with the sampler type are a few states, which specify the texture to be sampled, the type of filtering used, and how the texture is addressed (wrapped).

Samplers should be defined at the top of your HLSL code file. Here is an example of a sampler for a 2D texture:

```
// Declares the input texture
texture skyTexture;

// Declares the sampler used to sample the skyTexture
sampler2D skySampler = sampler_state
{
    Texture = skyTexture;

    MinFilter = Linear;
    MagFilter = Linear;
    MipFilter = Linear;
```

```
    AddressU = Wrap;
    AddressV = Wrap;
    AddressW = Wrap;
}
```

The `texture` state represents the texture to be sampled, which can be read only through the use of a sampler. `MinFilter`, `MagFilter`, and `MipFilter` are the filtering states, and `AddressU`, `AddressV`, and `AddressW` are the addressing states.

■**Note** The documentation for the DirectX SDK includes a complete reference for HLSL. You can access this reference at `http://msdn2.microsoft.com/en-us/library/bb509638.aspx`.

Uniform and Varying Inputs

HLSL has two types of input data types:

Uniform input data: This is the data that is constant for all vertices/pixels in a shader during the processing of its entire input data. For example, during the rendering of a tree, its texture, the world matrix, and lighting conditions are constant. The uniform input data in a shader is set from within your XNA application.

Varying input data: This is the data that is changed in each execution of a shader. For example, during the rendering of a tree, the vertex shader needs to process all vertices of the tree. This means that the information carried inside the vertex is changed for each cycle of the vertex shader. Unlike with the uniform input data, you declare the varying input data using semantics, as discussed in the next section.

Semantics

Semantics are predefined words that HLSL uses to map input and output data to variable names. For example, each vertex of your 3D objects might contain one `float4` containing the 3D position, and another `float4` containing two texture coordinates. How is your vertex shader supposed to know which of them to use as the position?

The solution is to add the `POSITION0` semantic in the vertices' processing stage to map the position attribute of each vertex to a varying variable, as follows:

```
float4 vertexPosition : POSITION0;
```

The semantics are required in all varying input data (received from the application or passed between the rendering stages). For example, all the data output from the vertex shader that will be used in the pixel shader must be associated with a semantic. You will see some examples of using semantics in the "Creating a Simple Shader" section later in this chapter.

Semantics are not case-sensitive and are specified after the variables' names using a colon (`:`). Tables 9-2 and 9-3 show some vertex shader semantics.

Table 9-2. *Input Vertex Shader Semantics*

Input	Description	Type
POSITION[n]	Vertex position in object space	float4
COLOR[n]	Diffuse and specular color	float4
NORMAL[n]	Normal vector	float4
TEXCOORD[n]	Texture coordinate	float4
TANGENT[n]	Tangent vector	float4
BINORMAL[n]	Binormal vector	float4
BLENDINDICES[n]	Bones blend indices	int4
BLENDWEIGHT[n]	Bones blend weight	float4

Table 9-3. *Output Vertex Shader Semantics*

Output	Description	Type
POSITION[n]	Position of a vertex in homogenous space	float4(X, Y, Z, W)
COLOR[n]	Diffuse or specular color	float4
TEXCOORD[n]	Texture coordinates	float4
FOG	Vertex fog	float

You use the input vertex shader semantics for varying data received by the vertex shader. Some commonly used semantics are POSITION, COLOR, NORMAL, and TEXTURE. You use the TANGENT and BINORMAL semantics if the vertex has tangent or *binormal* vectors, which you'll need when you want to do some bump mapping in your effect. You use the BLENDINDICES and BLENDWEIGHT semantics when the vertices are linked to bones. Bones are used to deform the vertices of a mesh (as explained in Chapter 12).

The POSITION semantic is the only required output of the vertex shader. If you want to pass other data from the vertex shader to the pixel shader, TEXCOORD[n] should be used.

The [n] is an optional integer that defines the number of the resource to be used. For example, if a model has three textures, the [n] of its TEXCOORD semantic can be 0, 1, or 2; so, TEXCOORD0, TEXCOORD1, and TEXCOORD2 are valid input semantics for the vertex shader. Table 9-4 shows some pixel shader semantics.

Table 9-4. *Pixel Shader Semantics*

Input	Description	Type
COLOR[n]	Diffuse or specular color	float4
TEXCOORD[n]	Texture coordinates	float4
COLOR[n]	Output color	float4
DEPTH[n]	Output depth	float

Because the pixel shader is executed after the rasterization stage, the available input semantics are the pixel color and some texture coordinates. The texture coordinates address the texture positions that are mapped into the current pixel, and these coordinates can be used to transfer data from your vertex shader to your pixel shader.

The final data output from the pixel shader is the pixel color and depth, where the output of the pixel color is obligatory, and the output of the pixel depth is optional.

Functions

HLSL allows the creation of functions with syntax like the C language, where each function has a declaration and a body. The function declaration contains the function name and return type, and might have a list of parameters. Also, the return type of a function may have a semantic associated with it.

The following is a function used as the entry point for the pixel shader:

```
float4 simplePS(float4 inputColor : COLOR0) : COLOR0
{
    return inputColor * 0.5f;
}
```

Because the `simplePS` function is used as the entry point to the pixel shader, its parameters must have a semantic associated. In this case, the `simplePS` function scales the received color parameter by a factor of 0.5 and returns it as the final pixel color. Note that the parameters of the function can have other modifiers, such as `in`, `out`, and `inout`, which are used to define `input`, `output`, and `input/output` parameters.

We'll demonstrate how to define the functions that will be used as the entry point for the vertex and pixel shaders in the "Techniques, Passes, and Effects" section later in this chapter.

A small set of intrinsic functions are built into HLSL. These include math operations, texture access, and flow control. These functions don't necessarily map directly to the GPU assembly instructions. In fact, many of these functions are mapped to a combination of GPU assembly instructions, and they're likely to provide the best implementation for their task. Table 9-5 lists commonly used HLSL functions.

Table 9-5. *Commonly Used HLSL Functions*

Function	Description
dot	Returns the dot product of two vectors
cross	Returns the cross product of two floating-point, 3D vectors
lerp	Performs a linear interpolation between two values
mul	Performs matrix multiplication between X and Y
normalize	Normalizes the specified floating-point vector
pow	Returns X to the power of Y
reflect	Returns the reflection vector, given the entering ray direction and the surface normal
refract	Returns a refraction vector using an entering ray direction, a surface normal, and a refraction index

Table 9-5. *Commonly Used HLSL Functions (Continued)*

Function	Description
saturate	Clamps the specified value within the range of 0 to 1
tex2d	Performs a 2D texture lookup
tex3d	Performs a 3D volume texture lookup

Creating a Simple Shader

In this section, you'll put together what you've learned, and create your first shader using HLSL. As a good habit, you should start by declaring the uniform and varying variables:

```
// Matrix received from the application - Uniform
// (World * View * Projection)
float4x4 matWVP : WorldViewProjection;

// Struct used for the input vertex - Varying
struct vertexInput
{
    float4 position : POSITION0;
};

// Struct used to pass the VS output to the PS input - Varying
struct vertexOutput
{
    float4 hposition : POSITION;
    float3 color : COLOR0;
};
```

Your shader will expect the matWVP matrix to be set by your XNA application. This world-view-projection matrix is created by the camera, and it should be set by your XNA program. It is needed when your vertex shader transforms 3D positions to 2D screen coordinates.

You use the vertexInput struct to define the information that the vertex shader can expect. As you can see, this vertex shader will be capable of processing all vertices that contain position data.

You use the vertexOutput struct to define the kind of data that is passed from the vertex shader to the rasterizer, and after linear interpolation, to the pixel shader. Your vertex shader will generate the mandatory position, as well as a color.

An important note here is that the vertex position output by the vertex shader is not accessible by the pixel shader. This 2D screen position is required by the rasterizer, so a good way to remember that you cannot access it from your pixel shader is to keep in mind that it is "consumed" by the rasterizer. If you need this 2D screen position in your pixel shader, you should pass it as an additional TEXCOORDINATE[n] semantic.

Next, declare the vertex shader itself:

```
// Vertex shader code
pixelInput SimpleVS(vertexInput IN)
{
    pixelInput OUT;

    // Transform the vertex position
    OUT.hposition = mul(IN.position, matWVP);
    OUT.color = float3(1.0f, 1.0f, 0.0f);
    return OUT;
}
```

The vertex shader is called on each vertex rendered by your XNA application. This vertex is accepted by your shader as a `vertexInput` object and processed into a `pixelInput` object. In the `SimpleVS` function, you calculate the output 2D screen position by transforming (multiplying) it by the `matWVP` matrix. The output vertex color is set to yellow, RGB (1, 1, 0).

Next, you define the pixel shader:

```
// Pixel shader code
float4 SimplePS(pixelInput IN) : COLOR0
{
    return float4(IN.color.rgb, 1.0f);
}
```

This pixel shader simply returns the color received from the vertex processing stage. This color will be used as the final pixel color.

Great! Now you have defined a vertex shader and a pixel shader. In your XNA application, however, you don't specify separately which vertex shader and pixel shader should be used to render your triangles to the screen. Instead, you specify which *technique* to use.

Techniques, Passes, and Effects

In its most basic form, a *technique* is nothing more than the combination of a vertex shader and a pixel shader. The following is a technique that uses the vertex shader and pixel shader you just defined:

```
technique basicTechnique
{
    pass p0
    {
        VertexShader = compile vs_2_0 SimpleVS();
        PixelShader = compile ps_2_0 SimplePS();
    }
}
```

A technique also defines for which shader model the shader should compile. In this case, you're using the shader model 2.0 for both shaders. Higher models allow more complex shaders and more functionality, but require that the GPU support them.

As you can see, both shaders are encapsulated in what is called a *pass*. One pass reads in all vertices that should be drawn with the technique, processes them, processes the resulting pixels, and renders these pixels to the backbuffer, where they are waiting to be presented to the screen after all of the pixels have been processed. For some techniques, you may want to do this process twice during the same frame for all vertices. Therefore, such techniques will have two passes, each with a vertex shader and pixel shader.

For some more advanced effects, you'll want to use multiple techniques. You'll use a first technique to transform your scene into an intermediate image, which can be used by another technique as input.

The combination of all shaders and techniques used is called an *effect*. A simple effect will contain a vertex shader, a pixel shader, and a technique. A more advanced effect (such as shadow mapping or deferred rendering) will contain several of each.

The differentiation between effect, techniques, and shaders facilitates the shaders' programming, making it possible to reuse shader code in different techniques, and also to create different techniques targeting low-end and high-end GPUs.

Since you will usually keep all shaders and techniques corresponding to the same effect in one file, XNA calls each HLSL code file an *effect*. This allows XNA to treat effects as game assets, just like models and textures. All the effects are processed through the XNA Content Pipeline, generating manageable objects that the content manager can load at runtime.

Effect Class

At this point, you have created and coded your first complete effect in an `.fx` file. This means you can close the `.fx` file and move to your XNA project. The next step is to load this effect into your XNA program, so you can use it to render something to the screen. In your XNA program, the effect should be loaded into an object of the `Effect` class (just as an image would be loaded into an object of the `Texture2D` class). This `Effect` class allows you to configure the effect's uniform parameters, select the current effect technique, and use the effect for rendering. The following code illustrates how to load and configure an effect with XNA:

```
// XNA Effect object
Effect effect;

// Load the effect
effect = content.Load<Effect>("/effects/simpleEffect");

// Set the technique
effect.CurrentTechnique = lightEffect.Techniques["basicTechnique"];

// Configure uniform effect parameters
effect.Parameters["matWVP "].SetValue(worldViewProjectionMatrix);
```

This code initially loads the `simpleEffect` effect from the HLSL code file using the content manager's `content.Load` method. Then it defines which technique of the effect will be used; in this case, the `basicTechnique` technique you defined earlier. Finally, it sets the only uniform effect parameter defined in the HLSL code file: `matWVP`.

The following code shows how to draw an object using the loaded effect:

```
// First begin the effect
effect.Begin();

// Remember that the effect can have many passes
foreach (EffectPass pass in effect.CurrentTechnique.Passes)
{
    pass.Begin();
    // PUT YOUR DRAWING CODE HERE
    pass.End();
}

// Finally, end the effect
effect.End();
```

To draw a 3D object, you first need to begin the effect you want to use to render it, and then go through all the passes of the selected technique. For each pass, you need to begin the pass, draw the object, and end the pass. Finally, you need to end the effect. The effect pass is represented by XNA's EffectPass class, while its techniques are accessed through the CurrentTechnique property of the Effect class. If you want to change an effect parameter after the beginning of a pass, you need to call the CommitChanges method of the Effect class to update the changes.

The steps previously shown are necessary only if you're going to draw a model by yourself. When you load a 3D model from disk, the model comes with its effects stored inside its ModelMesh objects.

Effect Helper Classes

When an effect is loaded through the content manager, you don't know what parameters or techniques it has. Also, to modify an effect parameter, you must first query this parameter inside the effect, and then modify it. So, you might configure an effect parameter called lightPosition like this:

```
effect.Parameters["lightPosition"].SetValue(new Vector3(0.0f, 40.0f, 0.0f));
```

In this code, when you alter the value of the lightPosition parameter, a query is made inside the effect for the lightPosition parameter. This presents two problems: the computational overhead required to query for this parameter and the possibility of a query for an invalid parameter. Using helper classes, you can avoid these problems.

To ease the management of custom-created effects, you can create a unique helper class for each effect. Each effect helper class will store a reference for all the effect parameters, avoiding the overhead of constant querying for the parameters. The following code shows how to store a reference for the effect parameter and change its value:

```
EffectParameter param1 = effect.Parameters["lightPosition"];

// Render loop
{
    param1.SetValue(new Vector3(0.0f, 40.0f, 0.0f));
    // Draw model
    ... ...
}
```

Materials

Materials are classes that you should create to store the parameters used to configure an effect. For example, you can render two surfaces using an effect that applies a texture to each of them. In this case, the material of each surface is its texture, which you use to configure the effect used to render the surfaces. So, if the two surfaces share the same material, you could set the desired effect and the desired material, and render both surfaces in sequence by avoiding changing the effect that is currently set or its parameters.

The following are the two basic material classes that you'll create:

- `LightMaterial`: This class will store the surface properties used for lighting (diffuse color, specular color, and specular power).

- `TextureMaterial`: This class will stores a texture map and tile used to apply a texture to a surface.

You could use these two basic material classes to create more complex types of materials, such as a multitexturing material.

Here is the complete code for the `LightMaterial` class:

```
public class LightMaterial
{
    // Material properties - diffuse and specular color
    Vector3 diffuseColor;
    Vector3 specularColor;
    // Specular power (Shininess)
    float specularPower;

    // Properties
    public Vector3 DiffuseColor
    {
        get { return diffuseColor; }
        set { diffuseColor = value; }
    }
    public Vector3 SpecularColor
    {
        get { return specularColor; }
        set { specularColor = value; }
    }

    public float SpecularPower
    {
        get { return specularPower; }
        set { specularPower = value; }
    }
```

```
    public LightMaterial (Vector3 diffuseColor, Vector3 specularColor,
        float specularPower)
    {
        this.diffuseColor = diffuseColor;
        this.specularColor = specularColor;
        this.specularPower = specularPower;
    }
}
```

You store the light's diffuse and specular colors as an XNA Vector3 in the diffuseColor and specularColor attributes of the LightMaterial class, respectively. You store the light's specular power (or shininess) as a float value, in the specularPower attribute of the class. Note that the (X, Y, Z) components of the color vector represent a color in the RGB format. You also need to create properties to set and retrieve the light's diffuse color, specular color, and specular power.

Here is the complete code for the TextureMaterial class:

```
public class TextureMaterial
{
    // Texture
    Texture2D texture;
    // Texture UV tile
    Vector2 uvTile;

    // Properties
    public Texture2D Texture
    {
        get { return texture; }
        set { texture = value; }
    }
    public Vector2 UVTile
    {
        get { return uvTile; }
        set { uvTile = value; }
    }

    public TextureMaterial(Texture2D texture, Vector2 uvTile)
    {
        this.texture = texture;
        this.uvTile = uvTile;
    }
}
```

You store the texture as an XNA Texture2D in the texture attribute of the TextureMaterial class. The texture UV tile, which is used for bump mapping, is stored as an XNA Vector2 in the uvTile attribute of the class. As in the LightMaterial class, you need to create properties to set and retrieve the texture and its UV tile.

Shader Authoring Tools

During shader development, you constantly need to modify your shader, adjust its parameters, and test it using different assets (models, textures, and so on). This process can be slow and tiring if you need to recompile and execute your game every time you change something in one of its shaders. To help you during shader development, you can use a shader authoring tool.

One of the best tools available for shader authoring is NVIDIA's FX Composer, available from the NVIDIA developer web site (http://developer.nvidia.com). FX Composer, is a cross-platform integrated development environment (IDE) for shader authoring. It supports a few shader languages, including HLSL, and many types of asset formats, such as COLLADA, FBX, X, 3DS, and OBJ. Using FX Composer, you can watch the results of your shader in real time while you're developing and modifying it. Other features of FX Composer include scene management and shader performance analysis.

Summary

In this chapter, you learned about the rendering pipeline, its stages, and how to use them to process the description of a 3D scene and output a 2D image.

You also learned how to create shaders to program the programmable stages of the GPU, and the relationship between shaders, techniques, and effects.

Finally, you learned how to load, configure, and use effects with XNA. After the Content Pipeline processes the effects, you can easily load and use them to render your 3D objects.

Now that you've reviewed some basic concepts of shaders and effects, you can start drawing some 3D models. In the following chapters, you'll create more complex effects to render 3D models. For each effect, you'll also create a new helper effect class that will use the created material classes.

■ ■ ■

CHAPTER 10

Lights, Camera, Transformations!

A 3D scene may include many cameras, lights, and objects. Creating some classes to represent these objects will make your game a lot easier to manage.

In this chapter, you will create a basic framework to manage cameras, lights, and object transformations. You'll see how your game structure benefits from these classes in Chapters 11, 12, and 13, where the framework is used to create a complete 3D game.

One of the most essential components of a 3D game is the camera. Therefore, this chapter will start by showing how you can manage your camera system.

Cameras

Depending on the genre of game that you're creating, you might want to use a different type of camera, such as a fixed-position camera, a first-person camera, a third-person camera, a real-time strategy (RTS) camera, and so on. With so many different types of cameras, it is helpful to create a basic camera that can be extended to create more specific types of cameras.

A Base Camera Class

In this section, you're going to create a generic base class for cameras, called BaseCamera. This class will handle the camera view and projection matrices, defining its viewing volume, its *frustum* (truncated pyramid). Only the objects that are inside this frustum are in sight of the camera.

The camera's frustum is defined by the camera's view and projection matrices, as explained in this section. These matrices are required when your graphics card transforms your 3D scene to a 2D image. The frustum can also be used to detect whether objects are within the sight of the camera, which can help you decide whether an object should be drawn.

Camera Perspective Projection

The projection matrix created in this section defines the boundaries (the shape, if you will) of the camera frustum, which is the viewing volume that defines what is in sight of the camera. The camera frustum is specified by the viewing angle of the camera and the near and far clipping planes. You'll create the projection matrix in the SetPerspectiveFov method (given this name because the camera's field of view partly defines the viewing volume). You'll also define the Projection property, which allows your program to get the projection matrix.

The BaseCamera class supports only perspective projection, which is the most common type used in games. You can use the following code to create and update the camera perspective projection matrix:

```
// Perspective projection parameters
float fovy;
float aspectRatio;
float nearPlane;
float farPlane;

// Matrices and flags
protected bool needUpdateProjection;
protected bool needUpdateFrustum;
protected Matrix projectionMatrix;

// Get the camera projection matrix
public Matrix Projection
{
    get
    {
        if (needUpdateProjection)  UpdateProjection();
        return projectionMatrix;
    }
}

// Set the camera perspective projection
public void SetPerspectiveFov(float fovy, float aspectRatio, float nearPlane,
    float farPlane)
{
    this.fovy = fovy;
    this.aspectRatio = aspectRatio;
    this.nearPlane = nearPlane;
    this.farPlane = farPlane;
    needUpdateProjection = true;
}

// Update the camera perspective projection matrix
protected virtual void UpdateProjection()
{
    // Create a perspective field of view matrix
    projectionMatrix = Matrix.CreatePerspectiveFieldOfView(
        MathHelper.ToRadians(fovy), aspectRatio, nearPlane, farPlane);
    needUpdateProjection = false;
    needUpdateFrustum = true;
}
```

The SetPerspectiveFov method stores the new perspective projection parameters, but it does not generate the new projection matrix. Instead, it sets the needUpdateProjection variable as true, indicating that the projection matrix needs to be updated before it can be used. When the perspective projection is retrieved through the Projection property, it will update the projection matrix if needed. Finally, inside the UpdateProjection method, you generate the new perspective projection matrix using the CreatePerspectiveFieldOfView method of XNA's Matrix class.

Notice that the camera's frustum needs to be updated whenever the projection matrix is updated, as it depends on all four of the arguments that define the projection matrix.

Camera View (Position and Orientation)

A camera is not defined solely by its frustum. You also need to specify where to position your camera in your 3D world, as well as how to orient it. The camera's position and orientation in the world are defined by the view matrix created in this section. You'll create the SetLookAt method to set the camera view matrix, and the View property to retrieve it. By allowing your game to retrieve both the view and projection matrix, you make it possible for XNA to transform all 3D objects to your 2D screen.

In order to create a view matrix using the Matrix.CreateLookAt method, you need to know three camera vectors (or directions): the heading (forward) vector, the strafe (right) vector, and the up vector. These vectors uniquely define the orientation of any object in 3D space. The SetLookAt method calculates these three vectors, starting from the camera's position, its target, and its up vector.

You can find the heading vector as you would calculate any vector between two points: by subtracting its starting position from its ending position. To find the strafe vector, you're looking for the vector that is perpendicular to both the heading vector and the up vector, which is exactly what the Vector3.Cross method does. You can find more information about this operation in the next section.

You can use the following code to modify and update the camera's view matrix:

```
// Position and target
Vector3 position;
Vector3 target;

// Orientation vectors
Vector3 headingVec;
Vector3 strafeVec;
Vector3 upVec;

// Matrices and flags
protected bool needUpdateView;
protected bool needUpdateFrustum;
protected Matrix viewMatrix;
```

```
// Get the camera view matrix
public Matrix View
{
    get
    {
        if (needUpdateView)  UpdateView();
        return viewMatrix;
    }
}

// Set the camera view
public void SetLookAt(Vector3 cameraPos, Vector3 cameraTarget, Vector3 cameraUp)
{
    this.position = cameraPos;
    this.target = cameraTarget;
    this.upVec = cameraUp;

    // Calculate the camera axes (heading, upVector, and strafeVector)
    headingVec = cameraTarget - cameraPos;
    headingVec.Normalize();
    upVec = cameraUp;
    strafeVec = Vector3.Cross(headingVec, upVec);
    needUpdateView = true;
}

// Update the camera view
protected virtual void UpdateView()
{
    viewMatrix = Matrix.CreateLookAt(position, target, upVec);
    needUpdateView = false;
    needUpdateFrustum = true;
}
```

Like the SetPerspectiveFov method, the SetLookAt method stores the new view parameters of the camera but does not generate the new view matrix. Instead, it only activates the needUpdateView flag. This way, whenever your program requests the view matrix through the View property, it will be updated only when necessary.

Finally, inside the UpdateView method, you generate the new view matrix using the CreateLookAt method of XNA's Matrix class. Notice that the camera's frustum needs to be updated whenever the view matrix is updated.

Camera Coordinate System

Every time you change the camera's configuration through the SetLookAt method, you need to calculate the three camera coordinate system vectors: its heading (z axis), strafe (x axis), and up (y axis). Figure 10-1 illustrates the camera's coordinate system placed in the world coordinate system. Notice that because these vectors compose the camera's coordinate system, they must be *unitary* (their length must be exactly 1) and perpendicular to each other. You can use unitary vectors to represent directions, because the size of the vector doesn't matter in this case. For more information about coordinate systems, refer to Chapter 8.

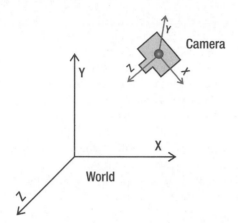

Figure 10-1. *Camera's coordinate system placed in the world coordinate system. The camera's x, y, and z axes are represented by the strafe, up, and heading vectors, respectively.*

You can calculate the camera vectors as follows:

Heading: The heading vector is the direction from the camera's position to its target position. It describes the direction the camera is facing. You can calculate this direction by subtracting the camera's position from its target position.

Up: The up vector defines the camera's up direction and is used to orient the camera. For example, you can use the vector (0, 1, 0) to orient the camera up vector as the world y axis.

Strafe: The strafe vector is the vector that is perpendicular to the heading and up vectors. This can be found by using the vector cross-product operation, which calculates a vector that is perpendicular to two other vectors at the same time. The Cross method of XNA's Vector3 class performs a cross-production operation. Note that the vectors used in the cross-product operation must be unitary vectors (or you must normalize the resulting vector after the operation), and the order in which they are passed to the Cross method changes the direction of the resulting vector.

These three vectors form the camera's coordinate system, and are used whenever you need to transform the camera based on its axes; for example, whenever you need to move the camera toward the direction it is facing.

As we mentioned, the three vectors must be perpendicular to each other, which is not fully guaranteed by the code shown earlier. For example, suppose that the camera is facing mainly forward, but also slightly upward. If you called the SetLookAt method and used the regular up vector (0, 1, 0) as a third argument, you would run into trouble, because this up vector is not completely perpendicular to the camera's heading vector. (The strafe vector will be completely perpendicular to the heading and up vectors, because it was obtained through the cross product of both vectors.) If you want to make sure that the up vector is perpendicular to the heading vector, after calculating the strafe vector, you must calculate a new up vector using a second cross-product operation between the heading and strafe vectors, as follows:

```
upVec = Vector3.Cross(strafeVec, headingVec);
```

This will give you three vectors that you can be sure are perpendicular to each other.

Camera Frustum

You'll represent the camera's frustum using XNA's BoundingFrustum class. XNA has some classes to represent volume, each of which has collision test methods. This allows you to quickly check for intersection between two objects of these classes. Specific to the camera frustum, these collision checks allow you to check whether an object is in sight of the camera.

The bounding volumes available in the XNA Framework are the BoundingBox (an axis-aligned box), BoundingSphere, and BoundingFrustum classes. To make sure the collision tests are as accurate as possible, you should use the class that most closely resembles the actual 3D object it represents. For the camera's frustum, use the BoundingFrustum class. To represent an entire person, use a BoundingBox. Use a BoundingSphere only if you want to detect collisions on a person's hand or head. So, using the XNA BoundingFrustum class, you already have methods to check whether objects are inside the frustum, which will tell you whether they are inside or outside the sight of the camera.

You'll create the UpdateFrustum method to generate the camera's frustum, and the Frustum property to retrieve it. Here, you'll generate the camera's frustum by combining the camera's view and projection matrices and using it to construct a new XNA BoundingFrustum.

As described earlier, the camera is defined by the view matrix (position and orientation) and the projection matrix (shape of the camera frustum), which is why both matrices are needed when you create the BoundingFrustum. You can use the following code to build the camera's frustum:

```
public BoundingFrustum Frustum
{
    get
    {
        if (needUpdateProjection)
            UpdateProjection();
        if (needUpdateView)
            UpdateView();
        if (needUpdateFrustum)
            UpdateFrustum();

        return frustum;
    }
}

protected virtual void UpdateFrustum()
{
    frustum = new BoundingFrustum(viewMatrix * projectionMatrix);

    needUpdateFrustum = false;
}
```

Finally, the BaseCamera class must have the abstract method Update, which defines how the camera should be updated. As Update is an abstract method, each camera class you're going to add later that inherits from the BaseCamera class must implement this method. The Update method's signature is as follows:

```
public abstract void Update(GameTime time);
```

A Third-Person Camera

In this section, you'll extend the BaseCamera class from the previous section to create a more specific type of camera: a third-person camera. For this type of camera, you'll create a class named ThirdPersonCamera, which inherits from the BaseCamera class. The third-person camera's goal is to follow an object while it moves, and the distance at which the camera follows an object must be variable. Otherwise, it would appear that the object is bound to the camera, resulting in jerky camera movement.

To make the camera follow an object—for example, the player-controlled character—you need to define some parameters, such as the following:

- The chase position, which is the position of the target object the camera must follow

- The chase direction, which is the direction the camera should move to in order to reach the target object

- The chase speed

- The chase distance, which is the distance between the camera and the chase position

Here, we will characterize the chase distance by means of three variables: minimum, desired, and maximum distances between the camera and the object. Figure 10-2 illustrates some of the parameters that need to be configured.

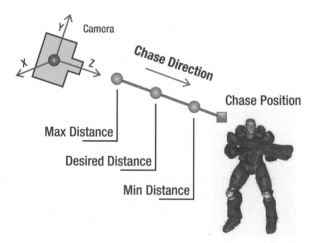

Figure 10-2. *For the third-person camera, the square is the camera's chase position and the dots are the camera's maximum, desired, and minimum allowed positions.*

Setting Chase Parameters

In the ThirdPersonCamera class, you create the SetChaseParameters method to set the camera's chase parameters that are not updated each frame: the chase distances and speed. You can configure the chase position and direction parameters, which are more frequently updated, through getter and setter methods:

```
// Chase parameters
float desiredChaseDistance;
float minChaseDistance;
float maxChaseDistance;
float chaseSpeed;

Vector3 chasePosition;
public Vector3 ChasePosition
{
    get { return chasePosition; }
    set { chasePosition = value; }
}

Vector3 chaseDirection;
public Vector3 ChaseDirection
{
    get { return chaseDirection; }
    set { chaseDirection = value; }
}

public void SetChaseParameters(float chaseSpeed,
    float desiredChaseDistance, float minChaseDistance, float maxChaseDistance){
    this.chaseSpeed = chaseSpeed;
    this.desiredChaseDistance = desiredChaseDistance;
    this.minChaseDistance = minChaseDistance;
    this.maxChaseDistance = maxChaseDistance;
}
```

Updating the Camera's Position

Every time the camera is updated, its position needs to be recalculated. The ideal, new camera position is equal to the camera's chase position, minus the chase direction, multiplied by the chase distance, as shown in Figure 10-2. The desired new camera position would be the camera's final position if it were placed at a fixed distance from the chase position. However, to allow the camera to move smoothly, the distance between the camera and the chase position may vary between a minimum and maximum range (defined in the attributes minChaseDistance and maxChaseDistance).

```
Vector3 targetPosition = chasePosition;
Vector3 desiredCameraPosition = chasePosition -
    chaseDirection * desiredChaseDistance;

float interpolatedSpeed = MathHelper.Clamp(chaseSpeed *
    elapsedTimeSeconds, 0.0f, 1.0f);
desiredCameraPosition = Vector3.Lerp(position, desiredCameraPosition,
    interpolatedSpeed);
```

This way, the new camera position is calculated through a linear interpolation between its current position and its desired position. A *linear interpolation* is an interpolation between two values that varies linearly according to a defined weight, where the weight is usually a floating-point number defined between 0 and 1. For example, a linear interpolation between the numbers 10 and 20 using the weight value 0.50 is the same as saying, "Give me 50 percent between 10 and 20," which results in the value 15. Linear interpolations using the weights 0, 0.25, and 1 result in the values 10, 12.5, and 20, respectively, as these values are 0, 25, and 100 percent between 10 and 20. Also, a linear interpolation between two 3D vectors interpolates the value of each component of the vectors (x, y, and z) linearly.

The weight used to interpolate the camera's position is calculated based on the time elapsed since the last update and the camera speed. However, because the interpolation weight must be between 0 and 1, you need to clamp its value, limiting its range between 0 and 1. You use the XNA Vector3 class's Lerp method to help you interpolate vectors. As a result, smaller values for chaseSpeed will result in a slowly reacting camera, and a longer time for the camera to start moving after the object does. Higher values for chaseSpeed will result in a quickly reacting camera and shorter time between the movement of the camera in relation to the movement of the object. (This camera reaction time is often referred to as the *lag*.)

Create the UpdateFollowPosition method to update the camera's position. Following is the code for the UpdateFollowPosition method. Note that to keep things tidy, you want all of your directions to have a length of exactly 1. This can be done by calling their Normalize method, or manually by dividing them by their length, as done for the targetVector in the following code.

```
private void UpdateFollowPosition(float elapsedTimeSeconds,
    bool interpolate)
{
    Vector3 targetPosition = chasePosition;
    Vector3 desiredCameraPosition = chasePosition- chaseDirection *
        desiredChaseDistance;

    if (interpolate)
    {
        float interpolatedSpeed = MathHelper.Clamp(
            chaseSpeed * elapsedTimeSeconds, 0.0f, 1.0f);
        desiredCameraPosition = Vector3.Lerp(position,
            desiredCameraPosition, interpolatedSpeed);
```

```
            // Clamp the min and max follow distances
            Vector3 targetVector = desiredCameraPosition - targetPosition;
            float targetLength = targetVector.Length();
            targetVector /= targetLength;
            if (targetLength < minChaseDistance)
            {
                desiredCameraPosition = targetPosition +
                    targetVector * minChaseDistance;
            }
            else if (targetLength > maxChaseDistance)
            {
                desiredCameraPosition = targetPosition +
                    targetVector * maxChaseDistance;
            }
        }

        // Needed to recalculate heading, strafe, and up vectors
        SetLookAt(desiredCameraPosition, targetPosition, upVec);
}
```

The UpdateFollowPosition method has the interpolate parameter, which defines whether the camera will be placed at its desired position (if the interpolate value is false), or will be smoothly interpolated to the desired position. When the camera chases an object for the first time, you must set the interpolate value as false, because there will be no target or movement to take into account, and initialize the camera to its starting position. You use the Boolean variable interpolate to determine whether the camera should be initialized to its starting position.

When the final camera position is calculated by interpolating its current position with its desired position, you need to check if the distance from the camera to the chase position is between the minimum and maximum chase distances defined, as shown in Figure 10-2. If the distance is smaller than the minimum, you set it to the minimum allowed distance. Otherwise, if the camera distance is greater than the maximum distance, you set it to the maximum allowed distance. These tests are important, as they ensure that the camera can chase objects that have a greater speed than the camera.

Rotating the Camera Around the Target

Another feature you'll add to the camera is the ability to rotate around its target. For that feature, you'll want a way to define the maximum rotation speed of the camera and the current rotation of the camera. Also, because you want your camera's rotation to start and stop smoothly, you'll need to keep track of the current rotational speed. Add these three properties to your ThirdPersonCamera class:

```
// Maximum allowed rotation
public static float MAX_ROTATE = 30.0f;

// Current rotation angles over the camera axes (heading, up, and strafe)
Vector3 eyeRotate;
```

```
// Rotation velocity over the camera axes
Vector3 eyeRotateVelocity;
public Vector3 EyeRotateVelocity
{
    get { return eyeRotateVelocity; }
    set { eyeRotateVelocity = value; }
}
```

The allowed camera rotation range is defined between the -MAX_ROTATE and MAX_ROTATE values. If the camera rotation is outside this range, you'll set it so that it is clamped to the borders of this range. The eyeRotate vector will store the current camera rotation, where the X, Y, and Z components of this vector represent the angle of the rotation around the camera's strafe, up, and heading axes. Finally, the eyeRotateVelocity vector will store the velocity at which the camera rotation angle is updated.

To calculate the camera view matrix taking into account the camera rotation, you'll need to overwrite the UpdateView method of the BaseCamera class. Remember that the UpdateView method is called when the camera view matrix is retrieved through the View property, and the needUpdateView flag was set to true. Following is the code for the UpdateView method of the ThirdPersonCamera class:

```
protected override void UpdateView()
{
    Vector3 newPosition = Position - Target;

    // Calculate the new camera position, rotating it around its axes
    newPosition = Vector3.Transform(newPosition,
        Matrix.CreateFromAxisAngle(UpVector,
            MathHelper.ToRadians(eyeRotate.Y)) *
        Matrix.CreateFromAxisAngle(StrafeVector,
            MathHelper.ToRadians(eyeRotate.X)) *
        Matrix.CreateFromAxisAngle(HeadingVector,
            MathHelper.ToRadians(eyeRotate.Z))
        );

    viewMatrix = Matrix.CreateLookAt(newPosition + Target,
        Target, UpVector);

    needUpdateView = false;
    needUpdateFrustum = true;
}
```

In the overwritten UpdateView method, you need to calculate the camera's position considering its rotation. The camera rotation is stored in the eyeRotation attribute and is relative to its axes. To rotate the camera around its own axes you'll first need to create a rotation matrix that rotates around an arbitrary axis. You can create this matrix using the CreateFromAxisAngle method of XNA's Matrix class. Then you can calculate the final matrix used to rotate the camera by combining the matrices that rotate the camera around its y, x, and z axes in order. You use this combined matrix to transform the position defined in world 3D coordinates into the corresponding position defined in camera coordinates (see Figure 10-1).

Updating the Camera

You must implement a final method in the ThirdPersonCamera class: the Update method, as it was defined as an abstract method in the BaseCamera class earlier in this chapter. This Update method is called every time the camera needs to be updated. Inside the Update method, you need to update the camera's attributes, as well as call the methods used to update the camera. The UpdateView and UpdateProjection methods use the camera's attributes to update the camera's view and projection matrix. These methods are called only when the view and projection matrices are retrieved through properties and need to be updated. Following is the code for the Update method of the ThirdPersonCamera class:

```
public override void Update(GameTime time)
{
    float elapsedTimeSeconds =
        (float)time.ElapsedGameTime.TotalSeconds;

    // Update the follow position
    UpdateFollowPosition(elapsedTimeSeconds, !isFirstTimeChase);
    if (isFirstTimeChase)
    {
        eyeRotate = Vector3.Zero;
        isFirstTimeChase = false;
    }

    // Calculate the new rotation based on the rotation speed
    if (eyeRotateVelocity != Vector3.Zero)
    {
        eyeRotate += eyeRotateVelocity * elapsedTimeSeconds;
        eyeRotate.X = MathHelper.Clamp(eyeRotate.X,
            -MAX_ROTATE, MAX_ROTATE);
        eyeRotate.Y = MathHelper.Clamp(eyeRotate.Y,
            -MAX_ROTATE, MAX_ROTATE);
        eyeRotate.Z = MathHelper.Clamp(eyeRotate.Z,
            -MAX_ROTATE, MAX_ROTATE);
        needUpdateView = true;
    }
}
```

In the Update method, you first update the camera's position using the UpdateFollowPosition method. Then, assuming that the camera's rotational velocity is not zero, you calculate the camera's current rotation based on its rotation velocity and the elapsed time since the last update. This ensures the camera behaves exactly the same way on PCs with different processor speeds.

Lights

Along with a working camera system, your game needs to contain lights. Lights make a big contribution to the realism of a game, especially a 3D game. A game scene can have various light sources scattered around it, which can be, for example, activated or deactivated dynamically depending on the player's position. The main drawback of placing many lights in a scene is that the higher the number of light sources, the more processing needed to render the scene. Some types of light sources used in games are directional light (for example, sunlight), spotlight (as the name says), and point light (a point that emits light in all directions).

In this section, you'll create some helper classes for the lights in your scene. Dealing with lights in this way will keep them structured, allowing your light system to be easily managed and integrated into your game engine, as demonstrated in Chapter 13.

Base Light

In this section, you'll create a base class for all the lights, named BaseLight. The BaseLight class doesn't have any methods other than its constructor. Because the different light types don't have that many resources in common, you will store only the light source color inside this base class. Each specific light will inherit from this base class and add its specific properties:

```
// Light diffuse and specular color
Vector3 color;
public Vector3 Color
{
    get { return color; }
    set { color = value; }
}
```

The color attribute of the BaseLight class is used as the color of the diffuse and specular components of the light. The diffuse color's intensity depends on the angle between the incoming light and the surface of the object, and the specular color is visible only when the light is mirrored on the object straight into the camera. An alternative would be to store the colors of the diffuse and specular components separately. Note that the (X, Y, Z) components of the color vector are used to represent a color in the RGB format.

Also, note that the lights don't have an ambient component. The ambient component is the amount and color of light that is always present in any part of the scene, and as such, it does not depend on the location of the camera or a light. It is the same for all lights in the scene.

Point Light/Omnidirectional Light

In this section, you'll create a class that inherits from the BaseLight class to define a more specific type of light: a point light (or omnidirectional light). For this type of light, you'll create a class named PointLight, which extends the BaseLight class.

Point lights are easy to define and keep track of, as you need to store only the light position inside the PointLight class:

```
public class PointLight : BaseLight
{
    // Omnidirectional light position: inherits from base class
    Vector3 position;
    public Vector3 Position
    {
        get { return position;  }
        set { position = value;  }
    }
}
```

Along with their position, you could also store the range of the point lights, which you could use to calculate the light's attenuation. However, to simplify the illumination calculus, only the light position is stored in this example.

Camera and Light Managers

To ease the camera and light management for the game, you'll create two different managers: one for cameras and another for lights.

Camera Manager

In this section, you'll create a class to manage the cameras, named CameraManager. The camera manager allows many cameras to be placed in the scene, managing which camera is active at a determined time. The active camera is the camera from which the scene is observed. Following is the complete code for the CameraManager class:

```
public class CameraManager
{
    // Active camera index and reference
    int activeCameraIndex;
    BaseCamera activeCamera;
    // Sorted list containing all cameras
    SortedList<string, BaseCamera> cameras;

    #region Properties
    public int ActiveCameraIndex
    {
        get { return activeCameraIndex; }
    }
    public BaseCamera ActiveCamera
    {
        get { return activeCamera;  }
    }
    public BaseCamera this[int index]
    {
        get { return cameras.Values[index];  }
    }
```

```csharp
public BaseCamera this[string id]
{
    get { return cameras[id]; }
}
public int Count
{
    get { return cameras.Count;  }
}
#endregion

public CameraManager()
{
    cameras = new SortedList<string, BaseCamera>(4);
    activeCameraIndex = -1;
}

public void SetActiveCamera(int cameraIndex)
{
    activeCameraIndex = cameraIndex;
    activeCamera = cameras[cameras.Keys[cameraIndex]];
}

public void SetActiveCamera(string id)
{
    activeCameraIndex = cameras.IndexOfKey(id);
    activeCamera = cameras[id];
}

public void Clear()
{
    cameras.Clear();
    activeCamera = null;
    activeCameraIndex = -1;
}

public void Add(string id, BaseCamera camera)
{
    cameras.Add(id, camera);
    if (activeCamera == null)
    {
        activeCamera = camera;
        activeCameraIndex = -1;
    }
}
```

```
    public void Remove(string id)
    {
        cameras.Remove(id);
    }
}
```

In the `CameraManager` class, the cameras are stored in a `SortedList`, which stores cameras as values with a string containing the camera name as their keys. With that, the cameras can be accessed through an integer's index or by its name. Note that the index used to access the cameras doesn't represent the order in which they were added to the camera manager, as they are sorted by name. The `CameraManager` class provides methods for the addition and removal of cameras, as well as methods to define the active camera.

Light Manager

In this section, you'll create a class to manage the lights, named `LightManager`. Similar to the camera manager, the light manager allows you to add various lights to a scene. Unlike with the camera manager, all the lights added to the light manager are considered to be active; thus, you will not need to define active light classes, as with cameras. Since the amount of ambient lighting is related to a scene, this is the place to store it. Following is the complete code for the `LightManager` class:

```
public class LightManager
{
    // Global ambient component of the scene
    Vector3 ambientLightColor;
    // Sorted list containing all lights
    SortedList<string, BaseLight> lights;

    #region Properties
    public Vector3 AmbientLightColor
    {
        get { return ambientLightColor; }
        set { ambientLightColor = value; }
    }
    public BaseLight this[int index]
    {
        get { return lights.Values[index]; }
    }
    public BaseLight this[string id]
    {
        get { return lights[id]; }
    }
    public int Count
    {
        get { return lights.Count; }
    }
    #endregion
```

```
public LightManager()
{
    lights = new SortedList<string, BaseLight>();
}

public void Clear()
{
    lights.Clear();
}

public void Add(string id, BaseLight light)
{
    lights.Add(id, light);
}

public void Remove(string id)
{
    lights.Remove(id);
}
}
```

In the LightManager class, the lights are stored in a SortedList, similar to the CameraManager class. In this way, the lights can be accessed through an integer's index or by its name. The LightManager class provides methods for adding and removing lights.

Object Transformation

Transformations are very important in 3D games. Any transformation is the combination of a translation, rotation, and scaling. As such, transformations are used to store the position and orientation of any object in your 3D world.

A transformation is stored in a matrix (which is a 4 × 4 matrix of floats). The transformation that stores the position and orientation of an object in your game is called the World matrix, as it defines where and how the object is positioned in your world. Other than World matrices, you also need the camera's View and Projection matrices to transform 3D positions to 2D screen coordinates.

To help with handling the transformation of the objects, you'll create a class named Transformation. This class stores the objects' translation, rotation, and scale, and creates a matrix that holds the combination of all these transformations, as shown in the following code:

```
// Translate
Vector3 translate;
// Rotate around the (X, Y, Z) world axes
Vector3 rotate;
// Scale the X, Y, Z axes
Vector3 scale;
bool needUpdate;
// Store the combination of the transformations
Matrix matrix;
```

```
public Vector3 Translate
{
    get { return translate; }
    set { translate = value; needUpdate = true; }
}
public Vector3 Rotate
{
    get { return rotate; }
    set { rotate = value; needUpdate = true; }
}
public Vector3 Scale
{
    get { return scale; }
    set { scale = value; needUpdate = true; }
}

public Matrix Matrix
{
    get
    {
        if (needUpdate)
        {
            // Compute the final matrix (Scale * Rotate * Translate)
            matrix = Matrix.CreateScale(scale) *
                Matrix.CreateRotationY(MathHelper.ToRadians(rotate.Y)) *
                Matrix.CreateRotationX(MathHelper.ToRadians(rotate.X)) *
                Matrix.CreateRotationZ(MathHelper.ToRadians(rotate.Z)) *
                Matrix.CreateTranslation(translate);
            needUpdate = false;
        }

        return matrix;
    }
}
```

In the Transformation class, the translation, rotation, and scale transformations are stored as XNA Vector3 objects, in the translate, rotate, and scale attributes, respectively, and you can set and retrieve them through properties. For the translation, a Vector3 object stores the X, Y, and Z components of the translation/position. For the rotation, another Vector3 object stores the amount of rotation over the three axes. The matrix attribute stores the combination of the translation, rotation, and scale transformation as an XNA Matrix. The combination of these three transformations is called the *world transformation*, as it uniquely defines where and how an object is positioned in the 3D world. You can set and retrieve this matrix attribute through the Matrix property, and it is recalculated whenever the translate, rotate, or scale transformation is updated.

You can use the CreateTranslate, CreateRotation, and CreateScale methods of XNA's Matrix class to generate the matrices used to translate, rotate, and scale an object.

Notice that the object's world transformation matrix is calculated by multiplying the scale, rotation, and translation transformations of the object, in this order. Because the matrix product is not commutative, the order in which you combine the transformations is very important.

Summary

In this chapter, you created a basic framework to handle cameras, lights, and transformations, which are common objects used in a game. You learned how to structure the camera and light classes hierarchically by having a base class that stores the common attributes and methods of the classes and that could be extended to create specific types of the base class. Using this concept, you extended the base camera class to create a third-person camera, and extended the base light class to create a point light. Finally, you created some managers to handle the cameras and lights in a scene.

CHAPTER 11

■■■

Generating a Terrain

In this chapter, you'll learn how to create a 3D terrain for your game. Terrains are an excellent way to represent outdoor environments. They can be generated at random or stored in and loaded from a 2D grayscale image, called a *height map*.

The chapter explains how you can create a terrain based on a height map. In each grid point or vertex of your terrain, you will also provide extra information such as the normal and tangent. This information will be needed by your effect, where you implement correct lighting on your terrain and enhance its appearance.

To give a photorealistic look to the terrain, you're also going to implement multitexturing in your HLSL effect (HLSL effects were introduced in Chapter 9). To top off your HLSL effect, you'll apply the more advanced normal mapping technique to it, which increases the visual detail of the terrain without adding extra triangles.

At the end of the chapter, you'll create some auxiliary methods for the terrain: one used to query the height of a position over the terrain, and another to check the collision between a ray and the terrain. Both will be very useful for creating a terrain-based game, as you'll do in Chapter 13.

Height Maps

Height maps are 2D maps used to store the height of a terrain. They're usually stored in grayscale images, where each point of the image stores the terrain's height at that position as a grayscale value. The more white a pixel is, the higher the corresponding point in the terrain should be. Figure 11-1 shows a sample height map.

To construct a terrain from a height map, you first need to build a vertex grid with the same dimensions as the height map, and then use the height value of each point (pixel) on the height map as the height (y coordinate) of a vertex on the vertex grid.

Besides its position, each vertex on the grid should contain other attributes needed in your effects, such as the normal of that point and the texture coordinates. Figure 11-2 illustrates a vertex grid with 6 × 6 vertices created over the world plane x,z, where the y height axis appears to be protruding from the page.

Figure 11-1. *An example of a height map*

How Height Maps Work

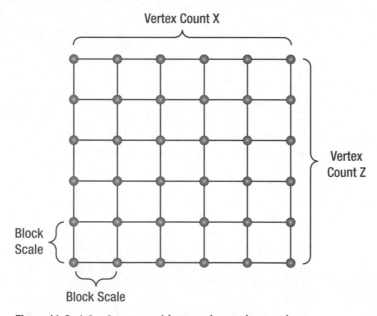

Figure 11-2. *A 6 × 6 vertex grid created over the x,z plane*

In a vertex grid, the distance between all vertically and horizontally neighboring vertices should be the same. This distance is represented by the *block scale*, as shown in Figure 11-2. A small distance between the vertices allows smooth transitions between the vertices' heights over the vertex grid, but you'll need a lot of vertices for a large terrain. A big distance between the vertices allows for larger terrains, but can yield sharp transitions between the vertices' heights. For a height map containing 256 × 256 pixels, if the distance between each pair of vertices (vertically and horizontally) is 1 meter, the total size of the generated terrain will be 255 × 255 meters.

As the terrain's height map is usually stored in 8-bit images, its height values vary between 0 and 255, where 0 (black color) represents the lowest possible height for a vertex and 255 (white color) represents the highest possible height. You can lower or raise this interval using a scale factor, which you use to multiply the height values stored in the height map by, adjusting its range. Figure 11-3 shows a 3D terrain built from the height map of Figure 11-1, rendered in wireframe (top) and solid (bottom).

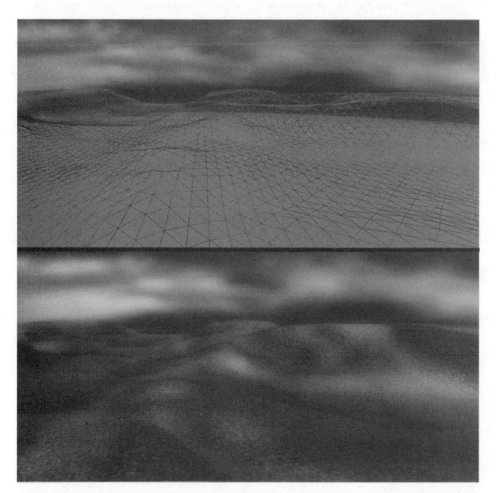

Figure 11-3. *Terrain generated from the height map in Figure 11-1 in wireframe (top) and solid rendering (bottom)*

Note that the rendered terrain in Figure 11-3 is shown correctly illuminated and textured. To achieve this effect, you need to store the normal and the texture coordinate for each vertex, as explained in this chapter.

Generating a Height Map

You can build or obtain height maps in different ways. You can find many different kinds of height maps on the Internet, including height maps of real places (such as cities or even landscapes from other planets). Because height maps are grayscale images, you can use any image editor tool to build or edit your own height maps. However, one of the simplest and fastest ways to build height maps is through the use of procedural-generation tools.

■**Note** All image formats supported by the XNA Content Pipeline are valid formats for height maps. This means that you can use almost any image you find as height map, and edit it using the program of your choice.

One such procedural-generation tool is Terragen (http://www.planetside.co.uk/terragen/). Terragen allows the generation of a height map from various user-defined parameters, such as terrain size, realism, smoothing, glaciation, and canyonism. Terragen is free to use for noncommercial applications. An artist could refine the height map generated by Terragen at a later time.

Another tool you can use to create height maps is EarthSculptor (http://www.earthsculptor.com/). EarthSculptor has some internal tools for 3D modeling of terrains, and it allows you to save the terrain model as a height map image, ready to be imported into your XNA project.

Creating the Terrain Class

In this section, you'll create the class to handle the terrain, named Terrain, where you'll initially create methods to load a height map, generate the corresponding 3D mesh, and draw it.

Loading the Terrain Height Map

You start by creating the Load method of your Terrain class, which should load a height map from disk and create the corresponding VertexBuffer and IndexBuffer. As the height map is stored as an image file, you can import it into XNA as you would import any other image: using the Content Pipeline.

```
.Texture2D heightMapTexture = Content.Load<Texture2D>(heightMapFileName);
int heightMapSize = heightMapTexture.Width*heightMapTexture.Height;
heightMap = new Color[heightMapSize];
heightMapTexture.GetData<Color>(heightMap);

this.vertexCountX = heightMapTexture.Width;
this.vertexCountZ = heightMapTexture.Height;
```

In this code, you load the image into a Texture2D object, the same way you would load any other image into your XNA project. Next, you find how many pixels the image contains, which you need to create an array capable of storing that many Color objects in the next line. Finally, you transfer all data from the image into your heightMap array, which you can easily access when you define the coordinates for your vertex grid.

You also store the size of the image, as you'll use this information to define the size of your vertex grid. vertexCountX defines the number of vertices per row (over the x axis) of the vertex grid, and vertexCountZ defines the number of vertices per column (over the z axis).

You store the height map colors in the heightMap variable, which is an attribute of your Terrain class. Note that you'll also need the height map data to be able to query the height of a position over the terrain, which you'll do at the end of this chapter.

Now that you have the height map data ready, you can generate the terrain's mesh. You create the GenerateTerrainMesh method, as described in the next section, to generate the terrain's mesh, which is composed of indices and vertices. The GenerateTerrainMesh method must be called after the height map has been loaded.

```
// Generate terrain mesh
GenerateTerrainMesh();
```

You can also store the transformations that are currently set on the terrain (translate, rotate, and scale) inside the Terrain class, using the Transformation class you created in Chapter 10. To do that, add a new attribute of type Transformation to the Terrain class, and name it transformation. Then, when the terrain's height map is loaded, you must instantiate a new Transformation:

```
transformation = new Transformation();
```

Next, you should load a custom effect for the terrain and encapsulate it in a TerrainEffect object. As described in Chapter 9, you should create a helper class for each effect that you create, to make it easier to manage and modify the effect parameters. The TerrainMaterial class is another class you create to configure the terrain effect:

```
// Load effect
effect = new TerrainEffect(
    Game.Content.Load<Effect>(TerrainEffect.EFFECT_FILENAME));
terrainMaterial = new TerrainMaterial();
```

The custom effect that we'll show you for the terrain provides a more realistic rendering using multitexturing and normal mapping, as discussed later in this chapter.

Finally, the VertexDeclaration needs to be declared once at startup, so that you're ready to tell your graphics card what kind of data is contained in your vertices:

```
// Load vertex declaration once
this.vertexDeclaration = new VertexDeclaration(GraphicsDevice,
    VertexPositionNormalTangentBinormalTexture.VertexElements);
```

Following is the complete code for the Load method of the Terrain class:

```
public void Load(ContentManager Content, string heightMapFileName,
                float blockScale, float heightScale)
{
    if (!isInitialized)
        Initialize();
```

```
    // Load heightMap file
    Texture2D heightMapTexture = Content.Load<Texture2D>(heightMapFileName);
    int heightMapSize = heightMapTexture.Width*heightMapTexture.Height;
    heightMap = new Color[heightMapSize];
    heightMapTexture.GetData<Color>(heightMap);

    this.vertexCountX = heightMapTexture.Width;
    this.vertexCountZ = heightMapTexture.Height;
    this.blockScale = blockScale;
    this.heightScale = heightScale;

    // Generate terrain mesh
    GenerateTerrainMesh();
    transformation = new Transformation();

    // Load effect
    effect = new TerrainEffect(
        Game.Content.Load<Effect>(TerrainEffect.EFFECT_FILENAME));
    terrainMaterial = new TerrainMaterial();

    // Load vertex declaration once
    this.vertexDeclaration = new VertexDeclaration(GraphicsDevice,
      VertexPositionNormalTangentBinormalTexture.VertexElements);
}
```

The Load method receives as parameters the height map's file name; the block scale, which represents the distance between the vertices; and a height scale value, used later to scale the height of the terrain. The last two parameters are stored in the Terrain class, in the attributes blockScale and heightScale, respectively.

Generating the Terrain's Mesh

The Load method shown in the previous section calls the GenerateTerrainMesh method, which still needs to be defined. To generate the terrain's mesh, you need to generate its vertices and indices. Each vertex of the grid contains a 3D coordinate and stores some attributes needed for rendering, such as the normal and the texture coordinate. The indices define the order in which the vertices should be combined to generate triangles. You should generate the mesh's indices prior to its vertices, because you can calculate some of the vertex attributes, such as the vertex normal, only if you know which vertices are used by which triangles.

Creating a Custom Vertex Format

XNA comes with a few predefined vertex structures (such as VertexPositionColor and VertexPositionColorTexture), but even the most complex vertex structure (VertexPositionNormalTexture) can store only a 3D position, a normal, and a texture coordinate. For your terrain, each vertex will need to store more information: a 3D position, normal, tangent, and texture coordinate (see the "An Overview of Terrain Techniques" section later in the chapter for an explanation of why you need all of these). This means that you need to define a custom vertex structure, capable of storing all this data for each vertex as it's transferred to your graphics card. The code for this custom vertex structure follows:

```
public struct VertexPositionNormalTangentBinormalTexture
{
    public Vector3 Position;
    public Vector3 Normal;
    public Vector2 TextureCoordinate;
    public Vector3 Tangent;
    public Vector3 Binormal;

    public static readonly VertexElement[] VertexElements = new VertexElement[]
    {
        new VertexElement(0, 0, VertexElementFormat.Vector3,
         VertexElementMethod.Default, VertexElementUsage.Position, 0),
        new VertexElement(0, 12, VertexElementFormat.Vector3,
          VertexElementMethod.Default, VertexElementUsage.Normal, 0),
        new VertexElement(0, 24, VertexElementFormat.Vector2,
          VertexElementMethod.Default,VertexElementUsage.TextureCoordinate, 0),
        new VertexElement(0, 32, VertexElementFormat.Vector3,
          VertexElementMethod.Default, VertexElementUsage.Tangent, 0),
        new VertexElement(0, 44, VertexElementFormat.Vector3,
          VertexElementMethod.Default, VertexElementUsage.Binormal, 0)
    };
    public static readonly int SizeInBytes = sizeof(float) * (3 + 3 + 2 + 3 + 3);
}
```

The VertexPositionNormalTangentBinormalTexture structure has all the attributes that you need for a vertex of your terrain: position, texture coordinate, normal, tangent, and binormal. This structure also declares a VertexElement array that contains the format of the vertex data, which has the type, size, and location of each element in the vertex stream. This is required, so the GPU on your graphics card knows where to find each attribute in the data stream.

Creating the GenerateTerrainMesh Method

You'll create two separate methods to generate the mesh's indices and vertices, respectively named GenerateTerrainIndices and GenerateTerrainVertices. You'll call these methods from the GenerateTerrainMesh method (which you will create now) to generate the mesh's vertices and indices. Then you'll create a vertex buffer (VertexBuffer) to store the mesh's vertices and an index buffer (IndexBuffer) to store the mesh's indices. Use the following code for the GenerateTerrain method:

```
private void GenerateTerrainMesh()
{
    numVertices = vertexCountX * vertexCountZ;
    numTriangles = (vertexCountX - 1) * (vertexCountZ - 1) * 2;
```

```
    // You must generate the terrain indices first
    int[] indices = GenerateTerrainIndices();

    // Then generate terrain vertices
    VertexPositionNormalTangentBinormal[] vertices =
        GenerateTerrainVertices(indices);

    // Create a vertex buffer to hold all the vertices
    vb = new VertexBuffer(GraphicsDevice, numVertices *
        VertexPositionNormalTangentBinormal.SizeInBytes, BufferUsage.WriteOnly);
    vb.SetData<VertexPositionNormalTangentBinormal>(vertices);

    // Create an index buffer to hold all the indices
    ib = new IndexBuffer(GraphicsDevice, numTriangles * 3 * sizeof(int),
        BufferUsage.WriteOnly, IndexElementSize.ThirtyTwoBits);
    ib.SetData<int>(indices);
}
```

Generating the Mesh's Indices

In this section, you'll create the GenerateTerrainIndices method to generate the indices of the terrain's mesh. The mesh's indices define in which order the vertices should be combined to generate triangles. Figure 11-4 shows the indices of the vertices in a grid and how they are combined to form triangles.

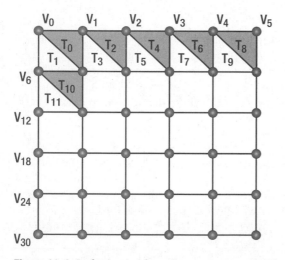

Figure 11-4. *Indexing grid vertices to create triangles*

Each quad in the terrain has two triangles: a gray triangle and a white triangle. In the first quad of the grid, the gray triangle is constructed from vertices 0, 1, and 7, while the white triangle uses vertices 0, 7, and 6.

Note that the order of the triangle's vertices is important. It should be clockwise relative to the viewer/camera, because the XNA rendering pipeline assumes that counterclockwise rendered triangles are facing backward, and culls them (removes them from the 2D screen output) by default.

Notice that there is a mathematical pattern between the indices used to create the triangles. The indices of the first and second triangles of every quadrant follow the same order, as shown in this equation:

$$T_{bottom} = V_{[Index]}, V_{[Index+1]}, V_{[Index+VertexCountX+1]}$$
$$T_{top} = V_{[Index]}, V_{[Index+VertexCountX+1]}, V_{[Index+VertexCountX]}$$

In the equation, the VertexCountX variable is equal to the number of vertices per row in the vertex grid. Using this equation, you can loop through all the quads of the vertex grid, generating the indices of its triangles.

You'll generate the mesh's indices as an array of integers that have three values for each triangle, indicating the vertices used for constructing that triangle. Following is the code for the GenerateTerrainIndices method. Notice that it corresponds to the preceding equation.

```
private int[] GenerateTerrainIndices()
{
    int numIndices = numTriangles * 3;
    int[] indices = new int[numIndices];

    int indicesCount = 0;
    for (int i = 0; i < (vertexCountZ - 1); i++)
    {
        for (int j = 0; j < (vertexCountX - 1); j++)
        {
            int index = j + i * vertexCountZ;

            // First triangle
            indices[indicesCount++] = index;
            indices[indicesCount++] = index + 1;
            indices[indicesCount++] = index + vertexCountX + 1;
            // Second triangle
            indices[indicesCount++] = index + vertexCountX + 1;
            indices[indicesCount++] = index + vertexCountX;
            indices[indicesCount++] = index;
        }
    }
    return indices;
}
```

Generating the Position and Texture Coordinate of the Vertices

Now your indices are defined, but you still need to create your vertices. Remember that each vertex of your terrain grid should store its 3D position, a texture coordinate, a normal, and a tangent.

In this section, you'll create the GenerateTerrainVertices method to generate the mesh's vertices. You'll place the terrain vertices over the world's x,z plane, centering the terrain at the world position (0, 0). To do that, you first need to calculate half the terrain size along the x and z axes, and then set the terrain's start position at minus its half size along the x and z axes (-halfTerrainWidth, -halfTerrainDepth).

You can calculate the terrain size through the terrain attributes: vertexCountX, which stores the number of vertices of the terrain along the x axis; vertexCountZ, which stores the number of vertices of the terrain along the z axis; and blockScale, which stores the distance between the vertices in the x and z axes. After calculating the terrain size, you just need to divide it by two, as shown next:

```
float terrainWidth = (vertexCountX - 1) * blockScale;
float terrainDepth = (vertexCountZ - 1) * blockScale;
float halfTerrainWidth = terrainWidth * 0.5f;
float halfTerrainDepth = terrainDepth * 0.5f;
```

You can generate the terrain's vertex grid beginning at the terrain's start position and going over each row of the vertex grid, placing the vertices (going from –x to +x), where each row is placed in a different grid column (going from –z to +z). In this way, the grid's vertices have their position coordinates incremented along the x and z axes according to the block scale that you defined (see Figure 11-2, earlier in the chapter). While placing the vertices, you'll use the previously stored height map data to set the vertex height along the y axis. Remember that you've stored colors inside your mapHeight array, which means you need to reshape each color into a single height value. For now, you'll simply take the red color component of each color as height for a vertex. You'll also scale the height of the terrain by multiplying the height of each vertex by a scale factor: the heightScale attribute of the Terrain class. You can use the following code to correctly position the vertices over the terrain's vertex grid:

```
for (float i = -halfTerrainDepth; i <= halfTerrainDepth; i += blockScale)
    for (float j = -halfTerrainWidth; j <= halfTerrainWidth; j += blockScale)
        vertices[vertexCount].Position = new Vector3(j,
                heightMap[vertexCount].R * heightScale, i);
```

Each vertex also has a U and V texture coordinate that should vary between (0, 0) and (1, 1), where (0, 0) corresponds to the top left, (1, 0) to the top right and (1, 1) to the bottom right of the texture. Figure 11-5 shows the texture coordinates of some vertices in a grid.

To calculate the correct texture coordinate for each vertex in the terrain, you first need to calculate the increment of the texture coordinate in the UV axis. You do so by dividing the maximum texture coordinate value (1.0) by the number of vertices minus 1, in each axis:

```
float tu = 0; float tv = 0;
float tuDerivative = 1.0f / (vertexCountX - 1);
float tvDerivative = 1.0f / (vertexCountZ - 1);
```

Then you scroll through all vertices, setting each vertex's texture coordinate and incrementing it.

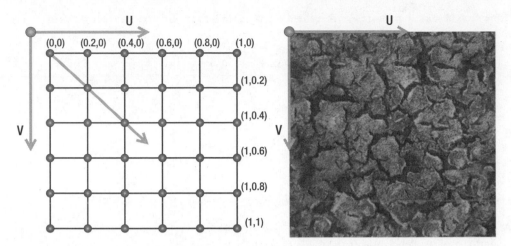

Figure 11-5. *The texture coordinates for a grid of vertices (left) and the UV axes over a texture map (right)*

In addition to the position and texture coordinate, you still need to calculate the normal, tangent, and binormal for each vertex. To do that, you will create the GenerateTerrainNormals and GenerateTerrainTangentBinormal methods, which you call at the end of the GenerateTerrainVertices method. First, here is the complete code for the GenerateTerrainVertices method:

```
private VertexPositionNormalTangentBinormalTexture[] GenerateTerrainVertices(
                                       int[] terrainIndices)
{
    float halfTerrainWidth = (vertexCountX - 1) * blockScale * 0.5f;
    float halfTerrainDepth = (vertexCountZ - 1) * blockScale * 0.5f;

    // Texture coordinates
    float tu = 0;
    float tv = 0;
    float tuDerivative = 1.0f / (vertexCountX - 1);
    float tvDerivative = 1.0f / (vertexCountZ - 1);

    int vertexCount = 0;
    VertexPositionNormalTangentBinormalTexture[] vertices =
    new VertexPositionNormalTangentBinormalTexture[vertexCountX * vertexCountZ];

    // Set vertices position and texture coordinate
    for (float i = -halfTerrainDepth; i <= halfTerrainDepth; i += blockScale)
    {
        tu = 0.0f;
```

```
            for (float j = -halfTerrainWidth; j <= halfTerrainWidth; j += blockScale)
            {
                vertices[vertexCount].Position =
                new Vector3(j, heightMap[vertexCount].R * heightScale, i);
                vertices[vertexCount].TextureCoordinate = new Vector2(tu, tv);

                tu += tuDerivative;
                vertexCount++;
            }

            tv += tvDerivative;
        }

        // Generate vertice's normal, tangent and binormal
        GenerateTerrainNormals(vertices, terrainIndices);
        GenerateTerrainTangentBinormal(vertices, terrainIndices);

        return vertices;
    }
```

Generating the Normal Vectors of the Vertices

In your HLSL effect that will render the terrain, you'll want to make sure your terrain is correctly lit. In order to perform lighting calculations, you'll need to know the normal vector in each vertex.

The normal vector of each vertex in a triangle is equal to the normal vector of the triangle, which is the vector perpendicular to the triangle. So, to calculate the normal of the vertices in a triangle, you need to calculate the normal of the triangle. You could calculate the triangle normal by taking a cross product between two vectors formed by its vertices, such as (v1-v0) and (v2-v0), because the cross product returns a vector perpendicular to these two vectors.

In a vertex grid, most vertices are shared among up to six triangles. Because of this, the normal in each shared vertex is the mean of the normals of the triangles that use the vertex. Thus, you need to sum the normal vectors of each triangle adjacent to the triangle you're working with. Then you must normalize this normal of each vertex, making the normals a unitary length but keeping the direction. Normal vectors are used in lighting calculations, and they must be of unitary length to yield correct lighting. You use the following code for the GenerateTerrainNormals method to generate the normals of the terrain's vertices:

```
private void GenerateTerrainNormals(VertexPositionNormalTangentBinormal[] vertices,
    int[] indices)
{
    for (int i = 0; i < indices.Length; i += 3)
    {
        // Get the vertex position (v1, v2, and v3)
        Vector3 v1 = vertices[indices[i]].Position;
        Vector3 v2 = vertices[indices[i + 1]].Position;
        Vector3 v3 = vertices[indices[i + 2]].Position;
```

```
    // Calculate vectors v1->v3 and v1->v2 and the normal as a cross product
    Vector3 vu = v3 - v1;
    Vector3 vt = v2 - v1;
    Vector3 normal = Vector3.Cross(vu, vt);
    normal.Normalize();

    // Sum this normal with the current vertex normal of the three vertices
    vertices[indices[i]].Normal += normal;
    vertices[indices[i + 1]].Normal += normal;
    vertices[indices[i + 2]].Normal += normal;
}

// After calculating all the normals, normalize them
for (int i = 0; i < vertices.Length; i++)
    vertices[i].Normal.Normalize();
}
```

Generating the Tangent and Binormal Vectors of the Vertices

The custom effect you'll create for the terrain uses a technique named *normal mapping*, which increases the visual details of the terrain, without adding extra triangles. Before you can start coding the normal mapping technique, every mesh's vertex must have tangent, binormal, and normal vectors. While the normal vector of a vertex is perpendicular to the terrain in that vertex, the tangent and binormal vectors touch (but not intersect!) the terrain in that vertex. The tangent, binormal, and normal vectors are also perpendicular to each other, and they form what is called *the tangent base*. Figure 11-6 illustrates the tangent, binormal, and normal vectors for different points of two different surfaces.

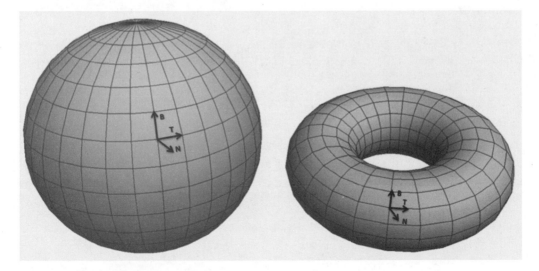

Figure 11-6. *Tangent, binormal, and normal vectors*

You can calculate the tangent vector of each vertex in the vertex grid: it's the vector that starts at one vertex and ends in the next vertex of the grid. This way, the tangent vector is oriented with the grid's x axis. Note that the tangent vector of the last vertex in a line on the grid is calculated as a vector that starts in the penultimate vertex of the line and ends in the last vertex.

Since all three vectors need to be perpendicular to each other, you can obtain the binormal vector using a cross product between the vertices' tangent and normal. Figure 11-7 shows the tangent, binormal, and normal vectors of a flat grid of vertices.

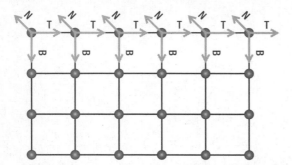

Figure 11-7. *Tangent, binormal, and normal vectors of some vertices in a flat grid*

Use the following code for the GenerateTerrainTangentBinormal method to calculate the vertices' tangent and binormal vectors:

```
public void GenerateTerrainTangentBinormal(
    VertexPositionNormalTangentBinormal[] vertices, int[] indices)
{
    for (int i = 0; i < vertexCountZ; i++)
    {
        for (int j = 0; j < vertexCountX; j++)
        {
            int vertexIndex = j + i * vertexCountX;
            Vector3 v1 = vertices[vertexIndex].Position;

            // Calculate the tangent vector
            if (j < vertexCountX - 1)
            {
                Vector3 v2 = vertices[vertexIndex + 1].Position;
                vertices[vertexIndex].Tangent = (v2 - v1);
            }
            // Special case: last vertex of the plane in the X axis
```

```
        else
        {
            Vector3 v2 = vertices[vertexIndex - 1].Position;
            vertices[vertexIndex].Tangent = (v1 - v2);
        }

        // Calculate binormal as a cross product (Tangent x Normal)
        vertices[vertexIndex].Tangent.Normalize();
        vertices[vertexIndex].Binormal = Vector3.Cross(
            vertices[vertexIndex].Tangent, vertices[vertexIndex].Normal);
    }
  }
}
```

An Overview of Terrain Techniques

At this point, you have all the code you need to read in a height map from an image file on disk, create the corresponding vertices and indices, and load them into a vertex buffer and an index buffer. To render these triangles to the screen, you could use XNA's BasicEffect class, and since you've provided valid normals, the BasicEffect class would add the correct lighting to your terrain. However, there is no way to instruct the BasicEffect class to use multiple textures on your terrain or perform other custom enhancements.

In the remainder of this chapter, we'll show you how to code your own HLSL effect that adds multitexturing and normal mapping to your terrain. For the terrain rendering, you'll create a custom effect that uses multitexturing and normal mapping. Before you get to coding, let's take a look at how these two techniques work.

The Multitexturing Technique

Using multitexturing, you can apply different layers of textures over the terrain, such as sand, grass, rocks, snow, and so on. Then you can generate the terrain's texture by blending the textures together, allowing for smooth transitions from one texture to another. For example, some parts of the terrain could have grass, others rocks, and some parts sand and grass, or snow and rocks, and so on. Figure 11-8 shows how some textures are combined to form a new texture.

In the terrain effect you're going to create, you'll combine the terrain textures based on a separate texture, called the *alpha map* (or *transparency map*), which defines the intensity of each texture over the terrain. It is called alpha map because, for each pixel, it contains four values, indicating how much of each of the four base textures needs to be blended to obtain the final color in that pixel. The alpha map is a regular RGBA color texture, with 8 bits per channel, and you're using each of the four color channels to store the intensity of the four different texture layers. This means that this technique uses five textures: four regular textures and one alpha map. For each pixel, the red value of the alpha map tells you how much you need of the first texture, the green value indicates how much you need of the second texture, and so on.

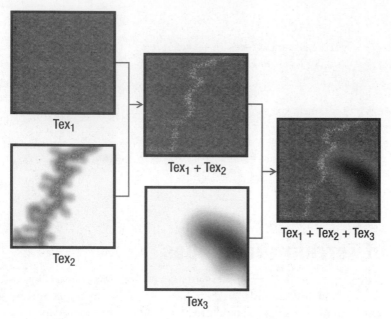

Figure 11-8. *Multitexturing—combining three different textures to create a new one*

The Normal Mapping Technique

Using the normal mapping technique, you can add the illusion of small-scale details to the terrain's mesh, without needing to increase the complexity of its mesh. You create this illusion by slightly manipulating the lighting in each pixel of your terrain. Variations in lighting are created by the deviated normals. Remember that the amount of lighting falling onto a triangle is determined by the normals of its vertices. Differing the illumination based on deviated normals creates the illusion of a 3D contour, as shown on the right side of Figure 11-9.

For example, consider the case of a stone wall. The default normals would all be pointing outward, perpendicular to the wall. With normal mapping, you adjust the normals in the pixels near the edges of the stones. The closer the pixel to the edge of the stone, the more deviated the normal should be. This example is shown in Figure 11-9.

Obviously, you need to know how much to deviate each normal beforehand. Therefore, the required normal deviations are stored in a *normal map,* which accompanies a texture. This is why you needed to calculate the tangent, binormal, and normal vectors for each vertex. In such a normal map, each pixel stores the x, y, and z components of the new surface normal inside its R, G, and B color channels.

Notice that the normal x, y, and z axes aren't on the world coordinates. Instead, they're placed in the tangent base coordinates. This way, the normal map is independent of the surface and can be applied to any type of object.

One of the weaknesses of the normal mapping technique is that when the surface is visualized from grazing angles (the angle between the surface normal and a viewer close to 90 degrees), the illusion of normal mapping disappears, and the surface will seem flat.

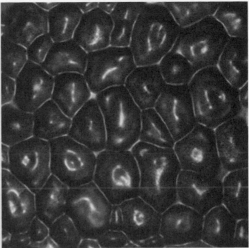

Figure 11-9. *Texturing only (left) and texturing plus normal mapping (right)*

The terrain effect you'll create for terrain rendering in the next section will support two omnidirectional light sources and multitexturing with four diffuse textures, as this is not so difficult to implement and already provides a nice final result. Later in the chapter, you will expand the effect by adding normal mapping.

Creating the Terrain Effect

To begin creating the terrain effect that uses multitexturing, open a new file and name it Terrain.fx. As good practice, you should start by defining the uniform variables. Remember from the discussion in Chapter 9 that these uniform variables should be set by XNA before the rendering operation starts and remain constant during the rendering of one frame. Also remember that they are globally accessible by your shaders.

Add the following to the top of your Terrain.fx file:

```
// -------------------------------------------------
// Matrices
// -------------------------------------------------
float4x4 matW   : World;
float4x4 matVI  : ViewInverse;
float4x4 matWVP : WorldViewProjection;

// Materials
// -------------------------------------------------
float3 diffuseColor;
float3 specularColor;
float specularPower;
```

```
// Lights
// ---------------------------------------------------
float3 ambientLightColor;
float3 light1Position;
float3 light1Color;
float3 light2Position;
float3 light2Color;

// UV tiles: 0-4 diffuse textures
float2 uv1Tile;
float2 uv2Tile;
float2 uv3Tile;
float2 uv4Tile;
float2 uvNormalTile;
```

These are the uniform variables needed for the entire effect, including both multitexturing and normal mapping. The world matrix is needed to take into account all transformations set on the terrain, such as a relocation, scaling, and rotation of the entire terrain. The ViewInverse matrix is required, as it contains the position of the camera in the 3D world. The WorldViewProjection matrix is needed to transform all 3D coordinates to 2D screen coordinates.

For the terrain material, you need to know the color and shininess of each of your two lights. You also need to know the position and color for each light, as well as how much ambient light there is present in the scene. Finally, the tiling variables allow you to stretch and shrink the textures over the terrain from within XNA.

After the uniform variables, you should define the textures that your effect needs. In total, the terrain effect will use six textures: four regular textures for the diffuse color, an alpha map, and a normal map. As explained in the previous section, the alpha map defines how the diffuse textures will be combined to form the final terrain color. Add the textures to your Terrain.fx file, as follows:

```
// Textures
// -------------------------------------------------
texture diffuseTexture1;
texture diffuseTexture2;
texture diffuseTexture3;
texture diffuseTexture4;
texture alphaTexture;
texture normalTexture;
```

This concludes the list of all variables that can be set from within your XNA application. For each texture, you also need a texture sampler, so add these samplers to your Terrain.fx file:

```
sampler2D diffuseSampler1 = sampler_state {
    Texture - <diffuseTexture1>;
    MagFilter = Linear;
    MinFilter = Linear;
    MipFilter = Linear;
    AddressU = Wrap;
    AddressV = Wrap;
};
```

```
sampler2D diffuseSampler2 = sampler_state {
    Texture = <diffuseTexture2>;
    MagFilter = Linear;
    MinFilter = Linear;
    MipFilter = Linear;
    AddressU = Wrap;
    AddressV = Wrap;
};

sampler2D diffuseSampler3 = sampler_state {
    Texture = <diffuseTexture3>;
    MagFilter = Linear;
    MinFilter = Linear;
    MipFilter = Linear;
    AddressU = Wrap;
    AddressV = Wrap;
};

sampler2D diffuseSampler4 = sampler_state {
    Texture = <diffuseTexture4>;
    MagFilter = Linear;
    MinFilter = Linear;
    MipFilter = Linear;
    AddressU = Wrap;
    AddressV = Wrap;
};

sampler2D alphaSampler = sampler_state {
    Texture = <alphaTexture>;
    MinFilter = Linear;
    MagFilter = Linear;
    MipFilter = Linear;
    AddressU = Wrap;
    AddressV = Wrap;
};

sampler2D normalSampler = sampler_state {
    Texture = <normalTexture>;
    MinFilter = linear;
    MagFilter = linear;
    MipFilter = linear;
    AddressU = Wrap;
    AddressV = Wrap;
};
```

Creating the Vertex Input and Output Structures for the Terrain Effect

Before you start work on your vertex shader, you should define which information is contained inside each vertex sent by XNA, so the vertex shader knows which information to expect. All vertices that XNA sends to your vertex shader contain the vertex position, texture coordinate, and tangent base (tangent, binormal, and normal vectors), so put this struct at the top of your Terrain.fx file.

```
struct a2v
{
    float4 position    : POSITION;
    float2 uv0         : TEXCOORD0;
    float3 tangent     : TANGENT;
    float3 binormal    : BINORMAL;
    float3 normal      : NORMAL;
};
```

Next, define which information the vertex shader should generate for each vertex. This is defined by what your pixel shader will need. The final pixel shader will need the coordinates of the six textures used, which would require six float2 objects. However, since the GPU does all the processing in tuples of four, you can gain better performance by storing two float2 objects together in a float4 object, resulting in three float4 objects.

Your pixel shader will need the view vector, the two lighting vectors (all the vectors are in the tangent space), and the normal to perform correct lighting calculations. The rasterizer stage between your vertex shader and pixel shader needs the 2D position of the vertex (as explained in Chapter 9):

```
struct v2f
{
    float4 hposition        : POSITION;
    float4 uv1_2            : TEXCOORD0;
    float4 uv3_4            : TEXCOORD1;
    float4 uv5_6            : TEXCOORD2;
    float3 eyeVec           : TEXCOORD4;
    float3 lightVec1        : TEXCOORD5;
    float3 lightVec2        : TEXCOORD6;
    float3 normal           : TEXCOORD7;
};
```

Creating the Vertex Shader for the Terrain Effect

The most basic and only required task of a vertex shader is to calculate the final 2D screen coordinate of every vertex. Whenever you're rendering a 3D scene, this calculation is done by transforming the 3D coordinate of the vertex by combining the world, view, and projection matrices:

```
OUT.hposition = mul(IN.position, matWVP);  // Vertex position in screen space
```

Now you should calculate the view vector and the two lighting vectors and transform their coordinate to the tangent space (using the tangentSpace matrix). A vector from point A to point B is found by subtracting A from B. The view vector is the vector between the current vertex and the camera (found in the inverse view matrix). A light vector is the vector between the current vertex and the light position:

```
float3 worldPosition = mul(IN.position, matW).xyz;
OUT.eyeVec = matVI[3].xyz - worldPosition;
OUT.lightVec1 = light1Position - worldPosition;
OUT.lightVec2 = light2Position - worldPosition;
```

Finally, calculate all the texture coordinates using the default texture coordinate of the surface and some tile factors. Each float4 object stores two texture coordinates, except for the last, which stores a texture coordinate and two zeros.

```
OUT.uv1_2 = float4(IN.uv0 * uv1Tile, IN.uv0 * uv2Tile);
OUT.uv3_4 = float4(IN.uv0 * uv3Tile, IN.uv0 * uv4Tile);
OUT.uv5_6 = float4(IN.uv0, 0, 0);
```

The complete vertex processing code follows:

```
v2f TerrainVS(a2v IN)
{
    v2f OUT;

    OUT.hposition = mul(IN.position, matWVP);
    OUT.normal = IN.normal;

    // Light vectors
    float3 worldPosition = mul(IN.position, matW).xyz;
    OUT.eyeVec = matVI[3].xyz - worldPosition;
    OUT.lightVec1 = light1Position - worldPosition;
    OUT.lightVec2 = light2Position - worldPosition;

    // Multitexturing
    OUT.uv1_2 = float4(IN.uv0 * uv1Tile, IN.uv0 * uv2Tile);
    OUT.uv3_4 = float4(IN.uv0 * uv3Tile, IN.uv0 * uv4Tile);
    OUT.uv5_6 = float4(IN.uv0, 0, 0);

    return OUT;
}
```

Pixel Processing for the Terrain Effect

All values generated by the vertex shader are interpolated by the rasterizer, a process that can change the length of the vectors passed from the vertex shader to the pixel shader. Therefore, the first thing you need to do in the pixel shader is normalize all the vectors, making sure their length becomes exactly 1.0 again. Remember that this needs to be done to yield correct lighting.

```
float3 eyeVec = normalize(IN.eyeVec);
float3 lightVec1 = normalize(IN.lightVec1);
float3 lightVec2 = normalize(IN.lightVec2);
float3 halfwayVec1 = normalize(lightVec1 + eyeVec);
float3 halfwayVec2 = normalize(lightVec2 + eyeVec);
float3 normal = normalize(IN.normal);
```

At this point, you have all the vectors necessary for the lighting calculation. You'll do the lighting calculation using the Phong equation, which is implemented in the phongShading method. This method takes into account the light color, the halfway vector, and the angle between the normal and the light direction. As a result, it returns how much the object should be lit in the diffuseColor output and how much more shiny the object should be in the specularColor output. Put this method immediately after your vertex shader:

```
void phongShading(in float3 normal, in float3 lightVec, in float3 halfwayVec,
                  in float3 lightColor, out float3 diffuseColor,
                  out float3 specularColor)
{
    float diffuseInt = saturate(dot(normal, lightVec));
    diffuseColor = diffuseInt * lightColor;
    float specularInt = saturate(dot(normal, halfwayVec));
    specularInt = pow(specularInt, specularPower);
    specularColor = specularInt * lightColor;
}
```

Use the method in your pixel shader to calculate the diffuse and specular lighting contributions of both lights in your scene:

```
// Calculate diffuse and specular color for each light
float3 diffuseColor1, diffuseColor2;
float3 specularColor1, specularColor2;
phongShading(normal, lightVec1, halfwayVec1, light1Color,
             diffuseColor1, specularColor1);
             phongShading(normal, lightVec2, halfwayVec2, light2Color
, diffuseColor2, specularColor2);
```

Now you know how much the pixel should be lit, but you still need to know the color of the pixel. You calculate this color by sampling and combining the four diffuse textures that are applied to the terrain according to the values in the alpha map texture. Each component of the alpha map stores a value used to linearly interpolate between the colors of the diffuse textures:

```
float3 color1 = tex2D(diffuseSampler1, IN.uv1_2.xy);
float3 color2 = tex2D(diffuseSampler2, IN.uv1_2.zw);
float3 color3 = tex2D(diffuseSampler3, IN.uv3_4.xy);
float3 color4 = tex2D(diffuseSampler4, IN.uv3_4.zw);
float4 alpha = tex2D(alphaSampler, IN.uv5_6.zw);

// Combine using the alpha map
float3 combinedColor = lerp(color1, color2, alpha.x);
combinedColor = lerp(combinedColor , color3, alpha.y);
combinedColor = lerp(combinedColor , color4, alpha.z);
```

Finally, you combine the lighting conditions with the base color of the pixel by multiplying them:

```
float4 finalColor;
finalColor.a = 1.0f;
finalColor.rgb = combinedColor * ( (diffuseColor1 + diffuseColor2) *
    materialDiffuseColor + ambientLightColor) + (specularColor1 +
    specularColor2) * materialSpecularColor;
```

The complete pixel shader code follows:

```
float4 TerrainPS(v2f IN) : COLOR0
{
    float3 eyeVec = normalize(IN.eyeVec);
    float3 lightVec1 = normalize(IN.lightVec1);
    float3 lightVec2 = normalize(IN.lightVec2);
    float3 halfwayVec1 = normalize(lightVec1 + eyeVec);
    float3 halfwayVec2 = normalize(lightVec2 + eyeVec);
    float3 normal = normalize(IN.normal);

    float3 color1 = tex2D(diffuseSampler1, IN.uv1_2.xy);
    float3 color2 = tex2D(diffuseSampler2, IN.uv1_2.zw);
    float3 color3 = tex2D(diffuseSampler3, IN.uv3_4.xy);
    float3 color4 = tex2D(diffuseSampler4, IN.uv3_4.zw);
    float4 alpha = tex2D(alphaSampler, IN.uv5_6.xy);

    float3 combinedColor = lerp(color1, color2, alpha.x);
    combinedColor = lerp(combinedColor , color3, alpha.y);
    combincdColor - lcrp(combinedColor , color4, alpha.z);

    // Calculate diffuse and specular color for each light
    float3 diffuseColor1, diffuseColor2;
    float3 specularColor1, specularColor2;
    phongShading(normal, lightVec1, halfwayVec1, light1Color,
                diffuseColor1, specularColor1);
    phongShading(normal, lightVec2, halfwayVec2, light2Color,
                diffuseColor2, specularColor2);

    // Phong lighting result
    float4 finalColor;
    finalColor.a = 1.0f;
    finalColor.rgb = combinedColor * ( (diffuseColor1 + diffuseColor2)
                * diffuseColor + ambientLightColor)
                + (specularColor1 + specularColor2) * specularColor;

    return finalColor;
}
```

Defining the Technique for the Terrain Effect

To finish your effect, you need to define a technique that combines the vertex shader and pixel shader you just defined. Use this code to finalize your Terrain.fx file:

```
technique TerrainMultiTextured
{
    pass p0
    {
        VertexShader = compile vs_2_0 TerrainVS();
        PixelShader = compile ps_2_0 TerrainPS();
    }
}
```

In the technique definition, you indicate the technique is rendered in a single pass, which vertex and pixel shader to use, and that both your vertex and pixel shaders can be compiled for shader version 2.0.

Setting the Effect Material

So far, so good, for your HLSL code. To manage the terrain effect in your XNA application, you'll create the TerrainEffect class, which will query and store all of the parameters for the effect. The helper classes help you modify and manage the effect parameters, as explained in Chapter 9. TerrainEffect will be fairly complex, so you'll also create the TerrainMaterial class, to help you configure the terrain effect. (For brevity, we won't show the code for the TerrainEffect class here, but it is available with the rest of the downloadable code for this book.)

The TerrainMaterial class stores the surface material as an attribute of type LightMaterial and the surface textures as attributes of type TextureMaterial. Following is the code for the TerrainMaterial class:

```
public class TerrainMaterial
{
    // Surface material
    LightMaterial lightMaterial;

    // Diffuse textures
    TextureMaterial diffuseTexture1;
    TextureMaterial diffuseTexture2;
    TextureMaterial diffuseTexture3;
    TextureMaterial diffuseTexture4;

    // Alpha map
    TextureMaterial alphaMapTexture;

    // Normal map
    TextureMaterial normalMapTexture;
```

```
    // Properties
    public LightMaterial LightMaterial
    {
        get { return lightMaterial; }
        set { lightMaterial = value; }
    }

    public TextureMaterial DiffuseTexture1
    {
        get { return diffuseTexture1; }
        set { diffuseTexture1 = value; }
    }

    public TextureMaterial DiffuseTexture2
    {
        get { return diffuseTexture2; }
        set { diffuseTexture2 = value; }
    }

    public TextureMaterial DiffuseTexture3
    {
        get { return diffuseTexture3; }
        set { diffuseTexture3 = value; }
    }

    public TextureMaterial DiffuseTexture4
    {
        get { return diffuseTexture4; }
        set { diffuseTexture4 = value; }
    }

    public TextureMaterial AlphaMapTexture
    {
        get { return alphaMapTexture; }
        set { alphaMapTexture = value; }
    }

    public TextureMaterial NormalMapTexture
    {
        get { return normalMapTexture; }
        set { normalMapTexture = value; }
    }

    public TerrainMaterial()
    {
    }
}
```

To configure the terrain effect, inside the Terrain class, you'll create the SetEffectMaterial method. You'll use this method to configure all the effect parameters, through the TerrainEffect helper class, before the terrain rendering.

In your scene, you'll manage the cameras and lights using the CameraManager and LightManager classes you created in Chapter 10. You can add these classes to the service container of the Game class.

■**Tip** Your main Game object has a Services property, which stores your active game services. A good habit is to make a service out of each main component of your game, such as the camera, light manager, and terrain. This way, during runtime, all components of your game can query the services container for the active camera, the active light manager, and so on. The benefit is that you can do things like suddenly change the active camera from a first-person camera to a third-person camera, without needing to inform the other components in your game. They will simply ask the main Game object for the currently active camera; they don't need to know about any behind-the-scenes changes.

Using the service container, you can get the light manager (LightManager) and obtain the scene lights, which are used by the effect:

```
// Get the light manager
LightManager lightManager = Game.Services.GetService(
    typeof(LightManager)) as LightManager;

// Get the first two lights from the light manager
PointLight light0 = lightManager[0] as PointLight;
PointLight light1 = lightManager[1] as PointLight;

// Lights
effect.AmbientLightColor = lightManager.AmbientLightColor;
effect.Light1Position = light0.Position;
effect.Light1Color = light0.Color;
effect.Light2Position = light1.Position;
effect.Light2Color = light1.Color;
```

Also, by using the service container, you can get the camera manager (CameraManager) and obtain the active camera from it, and you can read the terrain transformation from its transformation attribute of type Transformation:

```
// Get the camera manager
cameraManager = Game.Services.GetService(
    typeof(CameraManager)) as CameraManager;

// Set the camera view and projection
effect.View = cameraManager.ActiveCamera.View;
effect.Projection = cameraManager.ActiveCamera.Projection;
```

```
// Set the terrain transformation
effect.World = transformation.Matrix;
```

Finally, you configure the terrain material and the textures through the LightMaterial and TextureMaterial attributes of the TerrainMaterial classes. Following is the code for the SetEffectMaterial method:

```
private void SetEffectMaterial()
{
    // Get the light manager
    LightManager lightManager = Game.Services.GetService(
        typeof(LightManager)) as LightManager;

    // Get the first two lights from the light manager
    PointLight light0 = lightManager[0] as PointLight;
    PointLight light1 = lightManager[1] as PointLight;
    // Lights
    effect.AmbientLightColor = lightManager.AmbientLightColor;
    effect.Light1Position = light0.Position;
    effect.Light1Color = light0.Color;
    effect.Light2Position = light1.Position;
    effect.Light2Color = light1.Color;

    // Get the camera manager
    cameraManager = Game.Services.GetService(
        typeof(CameraManager)) as CameraManager;

    // Set the camera view and projection
    effect.View = cameraManager.ActiveCamera.View;
    effect.Projection = cameraManager.ActiveCamera.Projection;

    // Set the terrain transformation
    effect.World = transformation.Matrix;

    // Material
    effect.DiffuseColor = terrainMaterial.LightMaterial.DiffuseColor;
    effect.SpecularColor = terrainMaterial.LightMaterial.SpecularColor;
    effect.SpecularPower = terrainMaterial.LightMaterial.SpecularPower;
    // Textures
    effect.DiffuseTexture1 = terrainMaterial.DiffuseTexture1.Texture;
    effect.DiffuseTexture2 = terrainMaterial.DiffuseTexture2.Texture;
    effect.DiffuseTexture3 = terrainMaterial.DiffuseTexture3.Texture;
    effect.DiffuseTexture4 = terrainMaterial.DiffuseTexture4.Texture;
    effect.NormalMapTexture = terrainMaterial.NormalMapTexture.Texture;
    effect.AlphaMapTexture = terrainMaterial.AlphaMapTexture.Texture;
```

```
    // Texture UVs
    effect.TextureUV1Tile = terrainMaterial.DiffuseTexture1.UVTile;
    effect.TextureUV2Tile = terrainMaterial.DiffuseTexture2.UVTile;
    effect.TextureUV3Tile = terrainMaterial.DiffuseTexture3.UVTile;
    effect.TextureUV4Tile = terrainMaterial.DiffuseTexture4.UVTile;
    effect.TextureUVNormalTile = material.NormalMapTexture.UVTile;
}
```

Drawing the Terrain

At this point, you have stored the vertices that define the position, normal, texture coordinate, and so on. You have defined the indices that connect your vertices to form triangles, which make up the grid of your terrain. And you've created a custom effect that will be used to render the triangles to the screen, sampling their colors from four textures at the same time. Now you're ready to instruct XNA to actually render the terrain.

To draw the terrain, you initially need to call the SetEffectMaterial method, which configures the terrain effect. Then you set the terrain's vertex buffer, the index buffers, and the vertex declaration on the graphics device. You use the vertex declaration to inform the graphics device about the vertex format you're using, so that it can correctly process the vertices:

```
// Set mesh vertex and index buffer
GraphicsDevice.Vertices[0].SetSource(vb, 0,
    VertexPositionNormalTangentBinormal.SizeInBytes);
GraphicsDevice.Indices = ib;

// Set the vertex declaration
GraphicsDevice.VertexDeclaration = this.vertexDeclaration;
```

The next step is to begin the effects and go over all the effects' passes, drawing the terrain for each pass. Although your effect has only one pass, it is good practice to loop through all available passes as shown in the following code, so you can easily enhance your effect later. To draw the terrain's mesh, you use the DrawIndexedPrimitives method of XNA's GraphicsDevice. You use this method because you're drawing primitives defined by indices. Following is the complete code for the Draw method from the Terrain class:

```
public override void Draw(GameTime time)
{
    // Configure TerrainEffect
    SetEffectMaterial();
```

```
// Set mesh vertex and index buffer
GraphicsDevice.Vertices[0].SetSource(vb, 0,
    VertexPositionNormalTangentBinormal.SizeInBytes);
GraphicsDevice.Indices = ib;

// Set the vertex declaration
GraphicsDevice.VertexDeclaration = this.vertexDeclaration;

effect.Begin();
// Loop through all effect passes
foreach (EffectPass pass in effect.CurrentTechniquePasses)
{
    pass.Begin();
    // Draw the mesh
    GraphicsDevice.DrawIndexedPrimitives(PrimitiveType.TriangleList,
        0, 0, numVertices, 0, numTriangles);
    pass.End();
}
effect.End();
}
```

Running this application should render your terrain, complete with multitexturing and correct lighting.

Extending the Terrain Effect with Normal Mapping

After adding your terrain effect, you should see a beautifully colored terrain on your screen. To improve this result, you'll extend your effect with normal mapping. At the end of this section, you'll have a normal-mapped, multitextured terrain. As with most effects, this will not change the shape of the terrain, as you will enhance only the visual quality of the image.

■**Note** Here, we briefly cover the changes required to enable your effect with normal mapping. The book *Real-Time Rendering, Second Edition*, by Tomas Akenine-Möller and Eric Haines (AK Peters, Ltd., 2002) is a good reference for more information about the Phong algorithm and the normal mapping technique.

In the normal mapping technique, you adjust the normal in each pixel, as defined in a predefined normal map. The deviated normals stored in the normal map are specified in tangent space, which means you first need to find the x, y, and z axes of this tangent space. As explained earlier, these are defined by the normal, tangent, and binormal. Because these are different for each vertex, each vertex has a different tangent space, so this space should be calculated for each vertex in the vertex shader.

Vertex Processing for Normal Mapping

Add this code to your vertex shader to calculate the matrix that allows you to transform positions and vectors from world space to tangent space:

```
float3x3 tangentSpace = float3x3(IN.tangent, IN.binormal, IN.normal);
tangentSpace = mul(tangentSpace, matW);
tangentSpace = transpose(tangentSpace);
```

Remember that when you perform operations on two vectors, both vectors need to be defined in the same space. Because your normal is defined in tangent space, you'll want to transform all vectors needed for the lighting calculations into tangent space. Replace the corresponding part of your vertex shader with this code:

```
// Light vectors
float3 worldPosition = mul(IN.position, matW).xyz;
OUT.eyeVec = mul(matVI[3].xyz - worldPosition, tangentSpace);
OUT.lightVec1 = mul(light1Position - worldPosition, tangentSpace);
OUT.lightVec2 = mul(light2Position - worldPosition, tangentSpace);
```

Finally, you need to pass the texture coordinate for sampling in the normal map. This should be placed in the uv5_6 output, which still has two empty spaces:

```
OUT.uv5_6 = float4(IN.uv0, IN.uv0 * uvNormalTile);
```

Pixel Processing for Normal Mapping

In your pixel shader, you need to find the adjusted normal vector. This is done by sampling the RGB color values from the normal map. Color values are constrained to the [0,1] interval; therefore, you need to scale them into the [-1,1] interval for the x, y, and z coordinates:

```
float3 normal = tex2D(normalSampler, IN.uv5_6.zw);
normal.xy = normal.xy * 2.0 - 1.0;
```

Finally, the z component of the adjusted normal needs to be found so that the total length of the new normal is exactly 1.0:

```
normal.z = sqrt(1.0 - dot(normal.xy, normal.xy));
```

Figure 11-10 shows the final result of the terrain rendering. Notice that the terrain surface is flat. However, the normal map adds the detail of a stone pattern over the entire surface.

Figure 11-10. *Final result of the terrain rendering*

Querying the Terrain's Height

To guarantee that all scene objects remain exactly on the terrain, you should be able to query the terrain's height at any position. For example, you would query the terrain's height if you wanted to make sure the feet of a character appeared on the ground properly. You can calculate the height of any position over the terrain starting from the terrain's vertices, whose heights you stored in the height map.

To query the height of the terrain at an arbitrary world position, you first need to calculate this position relative to the terrain's vertex grid. You can do this by subtracting the queried world position from the terrain's origin position, making sure to take the terrain's world translation and rotation into account. Then you need to know in which quad of the terrain grid the position you are querying is located, which you can do by dividing the calculated position (relative to the terrain) by the terrain's block scale. Figure 11-11 shows an object in the world position (52, 48), where its position in the terrain grid is (1, 1).

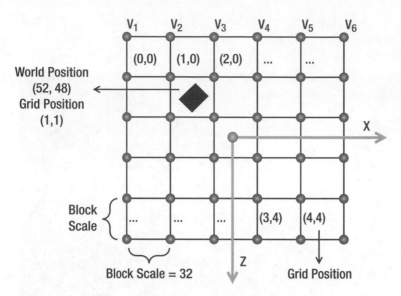

Figure 11-11. *Object position relative to the terrain grid*

The code to calculate the x,z position of an object over the terrain grid follows:

```
// Get the position relative to the terrain grid
Vector2 positionInGrid = new Vector2(
    positionX - (StartPosition.X + Transformation.Translate.X),
    positionZ - (StartPosition.Y + Transformation.Translate.Z));

// Calculate the grid position
Vector2 blockPosition = new Vector2(
    (int)(positionInGrid.X / blockScale),
    (int)(positionInGrid.Y / blockScale));
```

After you calculate in which quad of the grid the position is located, you need to find out in which of the two triangles of this quad it is located. You can do this by calculating the position of the object inside the quad and verifying if its position in the x axis is higher than its position in the z axis. When the object's x position is higher than the z position, the object will be found on the top triangle; otherwise, if the value is smaller, the object will be found on the bottom triangle, as shown in Figure 11-12.

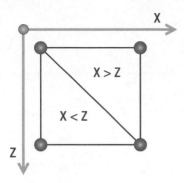

Figure 11-12. *A block in the terrain grid. If the x position inside the block is bigger than the z position, the object is in the top triangle. Otherwise, the object is in the bottom triangle.*

After finding in which triangle the object is positioned, you can obtain the height of a position inside this triangle through a bilinear interpolation of the height of the triangle's vertices. Use the following code for the GetHeight method to calculate the height of a terrain's position:

```
private float GetHeight(float positionX, float positionZ)
{
    float height = -999999.0f;
    if (heightmap == null) return height;

    // Get the position relative to the terrain grid
    Vector2 positionInGrid = new Vector2(
        positionX - (StartPosition.X + Transformation.Translate.X),
        positionZ - (StartPosition.Y + Transformation.Translate.Z));

    // Calculate the grid position
    Vector2 blockPosition = new Vector2(
        (int)(positionInGrid.X / blockScale),
        (int)(positionInGrid.Y / blockScale));

    // Check if the object is inside the grid
    if (blockPosition.X >= 0 && blockPosition.X < (vertexCountX - 1) &&
        blockPosition.Y >= 0 && blockPosition.Y < (vertexCountZ - 1))
    {
        Vector2 blockOffset = new Vector2(
            blockPosition.X - (int)blockPosition.X,
            blockPosition.Y - (int)blockPosition.Y);
```

```
        // Get the height of the four vertices of the grid block
        int vertexIndex = (int)blockPosition.X +
            (int)blockPosition.Y * vertexCountX;
        float height1 = heightmap[vertexIndex + 1];
        float height2 = heightmap[vertexIndex];
        float height3 = heightmap[vertexIndex + vertexCountX + 1];
        float height4 = heightmap[vertexIndex + vertexCountX];

        // Top triangle
        float heightIncX, heightIncY;
        if (blockOffset.X > blockOffset.Y)
        {
            heightIncX = height1 - height2;
            heightIncY = height3 - height1;
        }
        // Bottom triangle
        else
        {
            heightIncX = height3 - height4;
            heightIncY = height4 - height2;
        }

        // Linear interpolation to find the height inside the triangle
        float lerpHeight = height2 + heightIncX * blockOffset.X +
            heightIncY * blockOffset.Y;
        height = lerpHeight * heightScale;
    }
    return height;
}
```

Notice that you use this method only to ensure that all scene objects are positioned over the terrain. To produce a realistic interaction between the objects and the terrain (such as bouncing), you would need to implement a physics system.

Ray and Terrain Collision

To detect when an object in the scene intersects a part of the terrain, you need to create some collision test methods. One useful collision test is between a ray and the terrain. For example, if an object is moving in the scene, you can trace a ray in the direction in which this object is moving and get the distance between it and the terrain.

To check the ray and terrain collision, you'll do a collision test between the ray and the terrain's height map, instead of testing the ray against the terrain's mesh (many triangles). The collision test will be divided in two parts. In the first part, you'll do a linear search on the ray until you find a point outside (above) and another inside (below) the terrain. Then you'll perform a binary search between these two points to find the exact collision point with the terrain. Figure 11-13 illustrates the linear search processes, where the nearest points outside and inside the terrain are found.

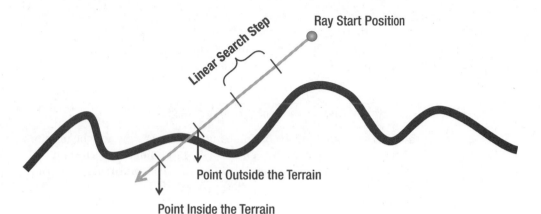

Figure 11-13. *Linear search used to find one point inside and another outside the terrain*

You can use the following code to perform the linear search on the terrain:

```
// A good ray step is half of the blockScale
Vector3 rayStep = ray.Direction * blockScale * 0.5f;
Vector3 rayStartPosition = ray.Position;

// Linear search - Loop until you find a point inside and outside the terrain
Vector3 lastRayPosition = ray.Position;
ray.Position += rayStep;
float height = GetHeight(ray.Position);
while (ray.Position.Y > height && height >= 0)
{
    lastRayPosition = ray.Position;
    ray.Position += rayStep;
    height = GetHeight(ray.Position);
}
```

After the linear search, the lastRayPosition variable stores the position outside the terrain, and the ray variable stores the position inside the terrain. You then need to perform a binary search between these two points to find the closest point to the terrain. You make this search with a fixed number of steps; 32 steps are usually enough for a good level of precision. The code for the binary search follows:

```
Vector3 startPosition = lastRayPosition;
Vector3 endPosition = ray.Position;

// Binary search with 32 steps. Try to find the exact collision point
for (int i = 0; i < 32; i++)
{
    // Binary search pass
    Vector3 middlePoint = (startPosition + endPosition) * 0.5f;
    if (middlePoint.Y < height) endPosition = middlePoint;
    else startPosition = middlePoint;
}

Vector3 collisionPoint = (startPosition + endPosition) * 0.5f;
```

You then create the Intersects method to check the intersection of a ray and the terrain. The Intersects method returns the distance between the ray's start point and the terrain's collision point, and if there is no collision with the terrain, the method will return null. Following is the code for the Intersects method of the Terrain class:

```
public float? Intersects(Ray ray)
{
    float? collisionDistance = null;
    Vector3 rayStep = ray.Direction * blockScale * 0.5f;
    Vector3 rayStartPosition = ray.Position;

    // Linear search - Loop until you find a point inside and outside the terrain
    Vector3 lastRayPosition = ray.Position;
    ray.Position += rayStep;
    float height = GetHeight(ray.Position);
    while (ray.Position.Y > height && height >= 0)
    {
        lastRayPosition = ray.Position;
        ray.Position += rayStep;
        height = GetHeight(ray.Position);
    }

    // If the ray collides with the terrain
    if (height >= 0)
    {
        Vector3 startPosition = lastRayPosition;
        Vector3 endPosition = ray.Position;

        // Binary search. Find the exact collision point
        for (int i = 0; i < 32; i++)
        {
            // Binary search pass
            Vector3 middlePoint = (startPosition + endPosition) * 0.5f;
            if (middlePoint.Y < height) endPosition = middlePoint;
```

```
                else startPosition = middlePoint;
        }
        Vector3 collisionPoint = (startPosition + endPosition) * 0.5f;
        collisionDistance = Vector3.Distance(rayStartPosition, collisionPoint);
    }
    return collisionDistance;
}
```

Summary

This chapter showed you how to create a terrain from a height map and render it to the screen. You first learned what height maps are and how to use them to represent the terrain. Then you learned how to create a vertex grid to represent the terrain's mesh, and how to use the height map values to change the height of the vertices of the grid. You also saw how to calculate the attributes needed for multitexturing, lighting, and normal mapping for each vertex in the vertex grid. You applied these concepts by creating an HLSL effect for the terrain rendering, which implements multitexturing and normal mapping. Additionally, you learned how to create some auxiliary methods to query the height of a position over the terrain and check the collision between a ray and the terrain.

CHAPTER 12

■ ■ ■

Skeletal Animation

Although the game scenery is mainly composed of static objects, you might want to use some animated models for animated characters—the player and the nonplayable characters (NPCs)—in your game. You can create animated models in different ways. For example, in a racing game, the car might be an animated model because its wheels rotate as the vehicle moves. You can easily reproduce this type of animation just by finding the part of the mesh that corresponds to a wheel and rotating this part over its axis. However, when you need to animate a character (running, jumping, falling, and so on), the animation process becomes more complex. This is because you'll need to modify the character's mesh, called *skinning*. This chapter focuses on techniques for animating characters. Let's begin by looking at the two main types of animation.

Types of Animations

Figure 12-1 shows the animation sequence of a character walking. The animation in Figure 12-1 is composed of five different frames, where each frame represents a different configuration of the character. Each animation frame also has a time, which defines when the model configuration needs to be changed. Finally, to be able to loop through the animation, the first and last animation frames must be identical.

There are two main types of animation: keyframed animation and skeletal animation. Each type of animation is used in different situations and has its advantages and disadvantages.

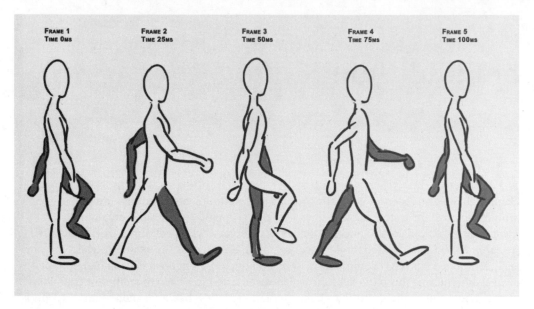

Figure 12-1. *In this animation of a character walking, the model's mesh must be modified over each frame. (Courtesy of Hugo Beyer, http://hugobeyer.carbonmade.com)*

Keyframed Animation

In *keyframed animation*, you store a static model mesh for each frame of the animation. If you were to animate the model in Figure 12-1, you would need to export four different static meshes (the fifth is identical to the first). This animation is called *keyframed* because only the frames with the main changes—the keyframes—are exported.

In the animation shown in Figure 12-1, you will need to add tweening between the first and second animation frames, to make the animation appear smooth. (*Tweening* refers to generating the intermediate frames between keyframes.) However, you don't necessarily need to create all of the frames beforehand, because you can obtain them by interpolating between the first and second frames. For example, using a linear interpolation, the position of each vertex in the mesh is calculated between the first and second frames. When you load the animated model, you create as many frames between the keyframes as you need to make the animation go smoothly, based on the few keyframes stored inside the model, and store them in memory. Then they are ready to be used for rendering the animation.

One of the advantages of keyframed animation is that it's fast, because all interpolation calculations have been done at startup. All the animation frames are stored in memory, and during the animation, you only need to change to the next mesh in the animation each frame. However, a disadvantage of this method is that it's necessary to store all the model meshes in memory. If a model needs 100 animation frames, it's necessary to store its mesh 100 times.

In a scene with hundreds of identical models, where all of them share the same animation, keyframed animation can be useful. In scenes with many different models with different animations, keyframed animation will take up too much memory.

The use of keyframed animated models with XNA is simple, because XNA already has the classes needed to handle static models. Therefore, you can treat a keyframed animation model in XNA as an array of static models using the Model class, where you store one Model object for each frame of the animation.

Skeletal Animation

Another way to animate the model is through skeletal animation. In this process, the entire model is structured on a skeleton, which is a combination of bones. The skeleton has one bone for each movable part of the model: one bone for a shoulder, one for an upper arm, one for a forearm, one for the hand plate, and then some more for the fingers.

Each bone needs to know to which parent bone it connects and how it is connected there, which is defined by the rotation about the connection point.

All vertices of the model must belong to a bone. Their positions are defined relative to bones. As a result, rotating one bone will rotate all vertices attached to the bone.

Skeletal animation also works with keyframes, where for each keyframe, the rotations of all bones are stored (in contrast to the keyframed animation method, where all positions of all vertices for each keyframe are stored). As a result, you need to interpolate only the rotation angles of the bones in order to obtain the frames between the keyframes.

To build the model's mesh, skeleton, and animations, you can use different modeling tools that support skeletal (or bone) animation, such as 3ds Max, Maya, Blender, and others. After you create the model, you also need to export it to a format that supports skeletal animation. Among the model formats that XNA supports natively, the X (DirectX) and FBX (Autodesk) formats support skeletal animation. Figure 12-2 illustrates a model with its mesh and skeleton.

Skeletal animation has several advantages over keyframed animation. It allows animations to be easily blended, so you can apply different animations over the model at the same time. For example, you could apply two different animations to the model in Figure 12-2, where one animation would make the model walk (rotating the leg bones), and another animation would make the model look around (rotating the neck bone). In keyframe animation, you could have one animation for walking and another animation for looking around, but since you wouldn't know which vertices belong to the legs and which to the head, you wouldn't be able to combine them.

Skeletal animation also allows a bone from one object to be linked to a bone in another object. For example, if you have a character that picks up a sword, you would connect the bone of the sword (since a sword is one movable piece, it has one bone) to the character's hand bone, which makes the sword move as the character's hand moves.

Nowadays, skeletal animation is more widely used than keyframed animation. Keeping that in mind, we'll focus on skeletal animations in this chapter.

XNA doesn't natively support skeletal animation. The default model processor in the XNA Content Pipeline is capable of extracting the model's vertices and bones, but discards the model's animation data.

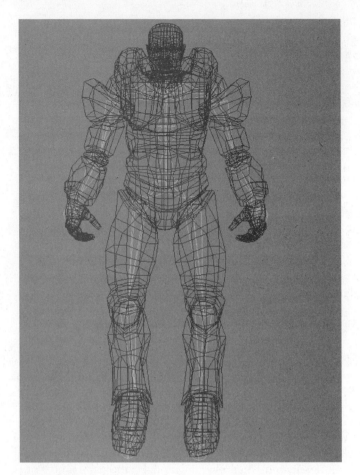

Figure 12-2. *Model with its mesh and skeleton*

Skeleton and Bone Representation

Before you start to work with skeletal animation in XNA, you should understand how the skeleton model is constructed and how its bones are represented and stored.

There are two different ways to store the model's skeleton: using bones or using joints. For example, 3ds Max represents a skeleton using its bones, while Maya represents a skeleton using its joints. However, when the model is exported to an XNA-compatible format (X or FBX format), there is no difference between them, and the skeleton is represented by its bones.

Therefore, you'll use bones to represent and store the skeleton. Each bone stores an initial position and rotation, defining where and how it is attached to its parent bone. It also stores its size, which is defined as the distance between its position and the position of a child bone. This bone representation creates the necessity of having an end bone (of zero size) to define the end of the skeleton.

Figure 12-3 illustrates a skeleton's arm representation using bones. Notice that it is necessary to have an end bone after the hand bone to define the hand bone's size and the end of the skeleton's arm. Furthermore, notice that the fingers are not separately movable, as they don't have their own bones. Finally, each model has a root bone, which is the main part of the model. As this also corresponds to a bone, it should be one solid, unmovable part. For a character, this should be the torso.

The position and orientation of each bone is related to its parent. For example, the hand's orientation and position are defined according to the orientation and position defined by the forearm, which has its orientation and position defined by the upper arm, repeating the same process until the root bone is reached. With this concept, you can see that modifying any particular bone affects all descendants of that bone. If the left shoulder bone were moved/rotated, all its descendants would also be moved/rotated.

To store the skeleton, you need to store the configuration (orientation and position) of every bone and the hierarchy of these bones inside the skeleton. The hierarchy is needed when you render the model, as then you need to find the absolute 3D position of each vertex, which we'll simply call the *absolute position*. For example, the absolute position of a vertex of the forearm is found by starting from the original position of the vertex, multiplied by the configuration of the forearm bone, the upper arm bone, the left shoulder bone, and the root bone. Luckily, as long as each bone stores its configuration, XNA will do these calculations for you.

The configuration of a bone is stored as a matrix. The skeleton hierarchy is stored as a list of bones, each with its matrix and a link to its parent bone.

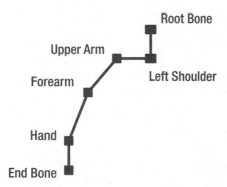

Figure 12-3. *Arm bones of a skeleton. The hierarchy begins in the root bone, and the end is defined by the end bone, where each bone is a descendant of the previous bone. All the bones begin at the position shown by a square, and they end at the next bone's starting point (the following square).*

A WORD ABOUT TRANSFORMATIONS

Each bone needs to store a position (where it attaches to its parent) as well as a rotation (how it is attached there). The "Object Transformation" section at the end of Chapter 10 explains that a matrix is perfectly suited for storing such a combination of position and rotation, which is why each bone will store a matrix (next to a number indicating its parent). There is, however, a very important second reason for storing this information as a matrix.

To explain this other reason for using a matrix, consider how you need to render the hand of a character. This requires you to know the absolute 3D position of each vertex of the hand. For each vertex of the hand, the position is defined relative to the origin of the hand bone (see Figure 12-3). To obtain the absolute 3D position of such a vertex, you would need to first transform it with the transformation of the hand matrix, then with the transformation of the forearm, and so on, until the transformation of the root bone. These operations would be quite computationally intensive if they needed to be done for each vertex.

Fortunately, an important property of matrix math is that by multiplying different matrices, you obtain the matrix that holds the combination of all transformations stored in all matrices. As a result, before you render the hand, you first calculate the total (or *absolute*) matrix of the hand by multiplying the matrices of all parent bones. This way, XNA only needs to transform all vertices of the hand with only this single matrix.

Extending the Content Pipeline for Model Animation

A you've learned, XNA has a well-defined Content Pipeline, which is responsible for loading your assets (images, models, sounds, and so on) from disk into an object that you can use in your XNA code. This Content Pipeline is separated into different layers, which should be divided into two steps:

- Read in the original asset file from disk, process its data, and store the processed data in a binary file on disk. This first step is performed only during compile time.

- Load the processed data from the binary file on disk, directly into objects you use in your game. This second step is done each time a user starts your program.

The benefit of this division is twofold. First, it makes sure the processing calculations, which can be very heavy, don't need to be redone each time the user loads the program. Second, the binary file is readable by the PC, Xbox 360, and Zune. Regular asset files are not cross-platform, while binary files are, so the benefit of this second step is that you can use one set of regular files across multiple platforms.

Figure 12-4 shows a simplified diagram of the Content Pipeline classes that are used to import, process, serialize (write to binary), and deserialize (read from binary) model files. During the first step, the models are imported by their corresponding content importer, where each content importer converts the input model's data to an XNA Document Object Model (DOM) format. The output of the model importers is a root NodeContent object, which describes a graphics type that has its own coordinate system and can have children. Two classes extend the NodeContent class: MeshContent and BoneContent. So, the root NodeContent object output from a model importer might have some NodeContent, MeshContent, and BoneContent children.

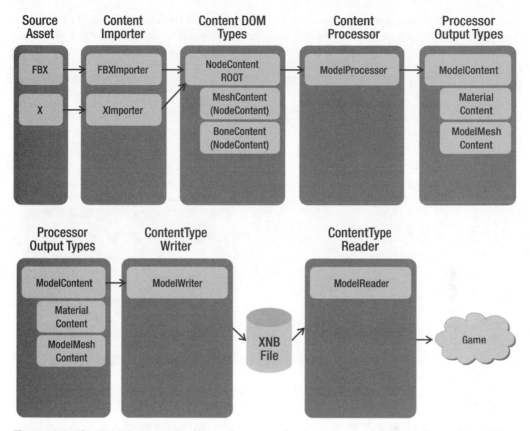

Figure 12-4. *The XNA Content Pipeline—classes used to import, process, compile, and read the game models*

After the models have been imported, they can be processed by their corresponding content processor, the ModelProcessor. This separation allows you to define two importers for importing X and FBX files, but use the same ModelProcessor to process their output.

The ModelProcessor receives as a parameter the root NodeContent object, generated by the model importer, and returns a ModelContent object. The default ModelContent object returned by the default ModelProcessor has the processed model data, containing vertex and bone data, but no animation data.

At the end of the first step, this processed data needs to be stored into an XNB binary file. To be able to store the ModelContent object into an XNB file, the ModelContent and each object inside it must have its own ContentTypeWriter. The ContentTypeWriter defines how the data of each object is written into the binary XNB file.

During the second step, at runtime, the ContentManager reads in the binary XNB file and uses the correct ContentTypeReader for each object it finds in the XNB file.

Because XNA's Content Pipeline does not have full support for models with skeletal animation, you need to extend the Content Pipeline, adding support for skeletal animation. Note that the Content Pipeline partially supports skeletal animation, because it can import the skeletal animation data from the X and FBX files, but it doesn't process the animation data contained in the files.

To add support for skeletal animation in XNA, you need to extend the default model processor, making it capable of processing and storing the model's skeleton and animations. To this end, you need to create some classes to store the skeletal animation data (each model's skeleton and animations). Since XNA does not know how to serialize and deserialize your custom classes, you will need to define a custom `ContentTypeWriter` and `ContentTypeReader` pair for each of them.

Figure 12-5 shows the classes that you need to create to extend the Content Pipeline, adding support to models with skeletal animation. The classes that you need to create are marked in Figure 12-5.

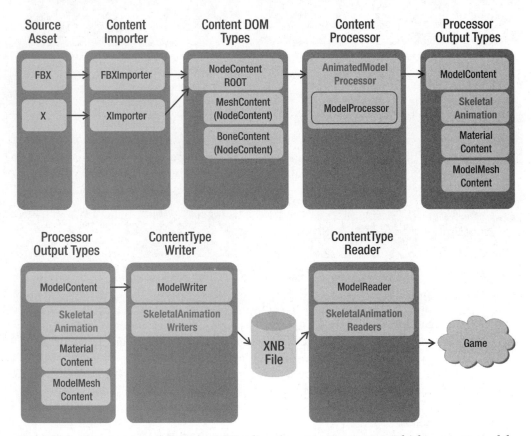

Figure 12-5. *An extension of the Content Pipeline shown in Figure 12-4, which supports models with skeletal animation*

Creating the Animation Data Classes

You'll create the classes used to store the skeletal animation data in a separate library, so that they can be used by the animated model processor to store the skeletal animation data and by the game application to load this data at runtime. Begin by creating a new Windows Game Library project named `AnimationModelContentWin`. The model processor will use the classes in this library on the Windows platform to store the skeletal animation data. If your game is targeted to the Windows platform, this library will also be used to load the skeletal animation data in runtime.

If you're targeting the Xbox 360, you need to create one more project: an Xbox 360 Game Library named AnimationModelContentXbox. This library contains the same files as the AnimationModelContentWin library, but Xbox 360 applications use it to load the skeletal animation at runtime. You need the AnimationModelContentWin project even if you're targeting the Xbox 360 platform, because the original model files are imported and processed on the Windows platform, and this project contains the class definitions.

You'll create the following three classes to store the skeletal animation data:

- The Keyframe class stores an animation frame of a skeletal animation, where each animation frame stores the configuration for a bone in the skeleton.

- The AnimationData class stores an array of keyframes, which compose a complete animation (such as running, jumping, and so on).

- The AnimatedModelData class stores the model skeleton (bones and hierarchy) and an array of type AnimationData, containing all the model animations.

Creating the Keyframe Class

The Keyframe class is responsible for storing an animation frame for a bone in the skeleton. An animation frame must have a reference for the animated bone, the new configuration (position and orientation) of the referenced bone, and the time in which this new configuration should be applied. Note that you use the keyframes to modify the original bone configuration, changing its current configuration to a new one. You store the bone configuration as a matrix using XNA's Matrix class, and you store the animation time (the time after which this keyframe should be applied) as a TimeSpan.

You store the reference for the bone that will be animated as an integer representing the index of the bone in the bones array of the AnimatedModelData class. The Keyframe class code follows:

```
public class Keyframe : IComparable
{
    int boneIndex;
    TimeSpan time;
    Matrix transform;

    // Properties...
    public TimeSpan Time
    {
        get { return time; }
        set { time = value; }
    }

    public int Bone
    {
        get { return boneIndex; }
        set { boneIndex = value; }
    }
```

```
    public Matrix Transform
    {
        get { return transform; }
        set { transform = value; }
    }

    public Keyframe(TimeSpan time, int boneIndex, Matrix transform)
    {
        this.time = time;
        this.boneIndex = boneIndex;
        this.transform = transform;
    }

    public int CompareTo(object obj)
    {
        Keyframe keyframe = obj as Keyframe;
        if (obj == null)
            throw new ArgumentException("Object is not a Keyframe.");

        return time.CompareTo(keyframe.Time);
    }
}
```

In the Keyframe class, you're implementing the interface IComparable to be able to compare Keyframe objects. You'll use this comparison further to use C# sorting functionality to easily sort the keyframes according to their time frame. In order to implement the IComparer interface, you need to define the CompareTo method. This method accepts an object that needs to be compared to the current object, and returns 1 if this object is larger than the object passed as argument, –1 if this object is smaller than it, or 0 if this object is equal to it. The Keyframe objects are compared based on their time attribute.

Creating the AnimationData Class

The AnimationData class is responsible for storing a complete model animation (such as running, jumping, and so on). You store each animation as a Keyframe array, and along with its keyframes, you store other useful data, such as the animation name and duration. The code for the AnimationData class follows:

```
public class AnimationData
{
    string name;
    TimeSpan duration;
    Keyframe[] keyframes;

    public string Name
    {
        get { return name; }
        set { name = value; }
    }
}
```

```
public TimeSpan Duration
{
    get { return duration; }
    set { duration = value; }
}

public Keyframe[] Keyframes
{
    get { return keyframes; }
    set { keyframes = value; }
}

public AnimationData(string name, TimeSpan duration,
    Keyframe[] keyframes)
{
    this.name = name;
    this.duration = duration;
    this.keyframes = keyframes;
}
}
```

Creating the AnimatedModelData Class

The AnimatedModelData class is responsible for storing the model's skeleton and animations. You store the model skeleton as an array of bones, where each bone is represented as a matrix. You construct the bone array through a depth traversal of the model's skeleton. The depth traversal starts in the root bone of the skeleton and goes to the deepest bone, backtracking until all bones have been visited. For example, a depth traversal of the hierarchy of Figure 12-6 returns the array root bone, neck, left shoulder, left forearm, left hand, left end bone, right shoulder, right forearm, right hand, and right end bone.

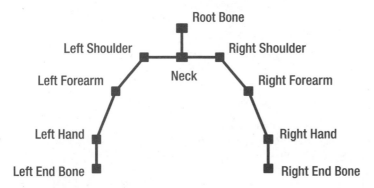

Figure 12-6. *An example of a skeleton hierarchy*

You store the skeleton's bones in its *bind pose* configuration. The bind pose is the pose in which the bones were linked to the model's mesh and is the starting pose of any animation. When the model is not being animated or when the animation starts, all the model's bones are in the bind pose.

In the AnimatedModelData class, you should create two attributes of type XNA Matrix array for storing the skeleton's bones, one attribute of type int array for storing the skeleton's bones hierarchy, and one attribute of type AnimationData array for storing the model's animation. The AnimatedModelData class code follows:

```
public class AnimatedModelData
{
    Matrix[] bonesBindPose;
    Matrix[] bonesInverseBindPose;
    int[] bonesParent;

    AnimationData[] animations;

    // Properties ...
    public int[] BonesParent
    {
        get { return bonesParent; }
        set { bonesParent = value; }
    }

    public Matrix[] BonesBindPose
    {
        get { return bonesBindPose; }
        set { bonesBindPose = value; }
    }

    public Matrix[] BonesInverseBindPose
    {
        get { return bonesInverseBindPose; }
        set { bonesInverseBindPose = value; }
    }

    public AnimationData[] Animations
    {
        get { return animations; }
        set { animations = value; }
    }

    public AnimatedModelData(Matrix[] bonesBindPose,
        Matrix[] bonesInverseBindPose, int[] bonesParent,
        AnimationData[] animations)
    {
        this.bonesParent = bonesParent;
        this.bonesBindPose = bonesBindPose;
        this.bonesInverseBindPose = bonesInverseBindPose;
        this.animations = animations;
    }
}
```

In the `AnimatedModelData` class, the `bonesBindPose` attribute stores an array containing the local configuration (related to its parent) of each skeleton's bone in its bind pose. The `bonesInverseBindPose` attribute stores an array containing the inverse absolute configuration (*absolute* meaning defined in world 3D space and not related to its ancestor) of each skeleton's bone in its bind pose, and the `bonesParent` attribute stores the index of the parent of each bone. Finally, the `animations` attribute stores the model's animations.

You use the inverse absolute configuration of a bone to transform the vertices that are linked to this bone from coordinate system of the model to the coordinate system of this bone, needed to animate (transform) the vertices. We'll explain this process in more detail in the "Skeletal Animation Equations" section later in this chapter.

Creating the Animated Model Processor

Now you are ready to create your animated model pipeline. You'll create a new model processor, by extending the default XNA model processor. You'll use this new processor to receive the output generated by an importer, extract the skeleton and animations, and store them as an `AnimatedModelData` object.

■Note You might think, if you've been reading carefully up until now, "Wait, don't I need to code a new importer too?" There's no need to create a new importer, as the default importers for X and FBX files also extract the animation data.

For the new model processor, create a new Content Pipeline Extension Library project named `AnimatedModelProcessorWin`. The Content Pipeline Extension Library project comes with a new content processor class, and automatically adds the Content Pipeline assembly (`Microsoft.Xna.Framework.Content.Pipeline`) to the project. Because you're going to use the `AnimatedModelContentWin` library (that you created in the previous section) to store the animation data, you need to add its assembly to the project, too. Following is the default code for the new content processor class that is created by the Content Pipeline Extension project:

```
[ContentProcessor]
public class ContentProcessor1 : ContentProcessor<TInput, TOutput>
{
    public override TOutput Process(TInput input,
        ContentProcessorContext context)
    {
        // TODO
        throw new NotImplementedException();
    }
}
```

The default content processor class extends the `ContentProcessor` class, which is the base class for any Content Pipeline processor, and it's used to process an object of the type `TInput`, outputting a new object of the type `TOutput`. But remember that you aren't interested in creating a new content processor, but rather in extending the features of an existing one. Thus, you must extend an existing content processor instead of the `ContentProcessor` class. In this case, you'll extend XNA's `ModelProcessor` class, which is the default model processor class. Also, you'll rename your new content processor class to `AnimatedModelProcessor`. Following is the base structure of your new model processor, the `AnimatedModelProcessor` class:

```
[ContentProcessor]
public class AnimatedModelProcessor : ModelProcessor
{
    public static string TEXTURES_PATH = "Textures/";
    public static string EFFECTS_PATH = "Effects/";
    public static string EFFECT_FILENAME = "AnimatedModel.fx";

    public override ModelContent Process(NodeContent input,
            ContentProcessorContext context)
    {
        ...
    }


    protected override MaterialContent ConvertMaterial(
        MaterialContent material, ContentProcessorContext context)
    {
        ...
    }
}
```

The `ModelProcessor` class has many methods that you can override, of which only the `Process` and `ConvertMaterial` methods need to be overridden for this example. The main method called to process a model is the `Process` method. This method needs to convert an input `NodeContent` object—which has the meshes, skeleton, and animations of the model—into a `ModelContent` object that stores the data for an XNA `Model` object. During this process, the `ConvertMaterial` method is called to process the model's materials.

Overriding the Default Process Method

In this section, you'll override the `Process` method of the `ModelProcessor` class, which is called to process the model. Also, you'll create two new methods to extract the model's skeleton and animations: the `ExtractSkeletonAndAnimations` method and the `ExtractAnimations` method, where the `ExtractAnimations` method is called from within the `ExtractSkeletonAndAnimations` method. Following is the code for the new `Process` method:

```
public override ModelContent Process(NodeContent input,
    ContentProcessorContext context)
{
    // Process the model with the default processor
    ModelContent model = base.Process(input, context);

    // Now extract the model skeleton and all its animations
    AnimatedModelData animatedModelData =
        ExtractSkeletonAndAnimations(input, context);
```

```
// Stores the skeletal animation data in the model
Dictionary<string, object> dictionary = new Dictionary<string, object>();
dictionary.Add("AnimatedModelData", animatedModelData);
model.Tag = dictionary;

return model;
}
```

At the beginning of the Process method, you call the Process method of the base class, the ModelProcessor. This processes the NodeContent object into a regular ModelContent object, which contains all of the vertex, effect, texture, and bone information.

Next, you call the ExtractSkeletonAndAnimations method, which performs a second round of processing on the input NodeContent object and returns an AnimatedModelData object containing the model's skeleton and animations. Finally, you create a dictionary that maps a string to an object, add the AnimatedModelData to this dictionary, and save it in the Tag property of the resulting ModelContent object. XNA's Model class has a Tag property that enables custom user data to be added to the model. Using a dictionary as the Tag property, you can add many different custom objects to XNA's Model class, and query for any of them at runtime using a string.

Note that the data you set in the Tag property of the ModelContent object is later stored together with the model data in a binary XNB file. This data is retrieved when the model is loaded using the content manager.

Extracting the Model's Skeleton

The ExtractSkeletonAndAnimations method receives the root NodeContent object as input, which might have MeshContent and BoneContent objects as its children, as described earlier in the chapter. To extract the model's skeleton, you first need to find the root bone of the skeleton inside the root NodeContent, and then you need to depth-traverse the skeleton, creating a list of bones. XNA's MeshHelper class provides some methods to help you in this process:

```
// Find the root bone node
BoneContent skeleton = MeshHelper.FindSkeleton(input);
// Transform the hierarchy in a list (depth traversal)
IList<BoneContent> boneList = MeshHelper.FlattenSkeleton(skeleton);
```

You can find the root bone of the skeleton using the FindSkeleton method of the MeshHelper class. Then you need to transform the skeleton tree into a list, using a deep search. You do this using the FlattenSkeleton method of the MeshHelper class. The result is a list of bones, where each bone is an object of the BoneContent class. Note that the bones in this list are in the same order as they are indexed by the mesh's vertices.

For each bone in the created list, you want to store its local configuration in the bind pose, its inverse absolute configuration in the bind pose, and the index of its parent bone. You can obtain the local and absolute configuration of a bone using the Transform and AbsoluteTransform properties of the BoneContent objects, and you can calculate the inverse absolute configuration of the bone using the Invert method of XNA's Matrix class:

```
bonesBindPose[i] = boneList[i].Transform;
bonesInverseBindPose[i] = Matrix.Invert(boneList[i].AbsoluteTransform);
```

Following is the complete code for the ExtractSkeletonAndAnimations method:

```
private AnimatedModelData ExtractSkeletonAndAnimations(NodeContent input,
    ContentProcessorContext context)
{
    // Find the root bone node
    BoneContent skeleton = MeshHelper.FindSkeleton(input);

    // Transform the hierarchy in a list (depth traversal)
    IList<BoneContent> boneList =
        MeshHelper.FlattenSkeleton(skeleton);
    context.Logger.LogImportantMessage("{0} bones found.",
        boneList.Count);

    // Create skeleton bind pose, inverse bind pose, and parent array
    Matrix[] bonesBindPose = new Matrix[boneList.Count];
    Matrix[] bonesInverseBindPose = new Matrix[boneList.Count];
    int[] bonesParentIndex = new int[boneList.Count];
    List<string> boneNameList = new List<string>(boneList.Count);

    // Extract and store the data needed from the bone list
    for (int i = 0; i < boneList.Count; i++)
    {
        bonesBindPose[i] = boneList[i].Transform;
        bonesInverseBindPose[i] =
            Matrix.Invert(boneList[i].AbsoluteTransform);
        int parentIndex =
            boneNameList.IndexOf(boneList[i].Parent.Name);
        bonesParentIndex[i] = parentIndex;
        boneNameList.Add(boneList[i].Name);
    }

    // Extract all animations
    AnimationData[] animations = ExtractAnimations(
        skeleton.Animations, boneNameList, context);

    return new AnimatedModelData(bonesBindPose, bonesInverseBindPose,
        bonesParentIndex, animations);
}
```

After extracting the model's skeleton, you call the ExtractAnimations method to extract the model's animations, as explained in the next section.

Extracting the Model's Animation

The importer has stored the model's animations as an animation dictionary that maps a string containing the animation name to an AnimationContent object containing the animation data. You can access the animation dictionary from the Animations property of the root node of type

BoneContent of the model's skeleton. Note that the Content Pipeline has its own classes to store the model's animation data: the AnimationContent, AnimationChannel, and AnimationKeyframe classes. The AnimationContent class stores a complete model animation as an array of AnimationChannel objects, where each AnimationChannel object stores the animation of a single bone as an array of AnimationKeyframe objects. Also, XNA's AnimationContent class stores the animation of each bone separately, while you are storing them together in a single array.

The following are the general steps necessary to extract the model's animations:

- Go through all the AnimationContent objects of the animation dictionary, containing full animations such as walking and jumping.

- For each full animation, go through all its bone channels, which can be accessed from the Channels property.

- For each bone, extract all its animation keyframes, which can be accessed from the Keyframes property.

This is exactly what the code for the ExtractAnimations method does:

```
private AnimationData[] ExtractAnimations(
    AnimationContentDictionary animationDictionary, List<string> boneNameList,
    ContentProcessorContext context)
{
    context.Logger.LogImportantMessage("{0} animations found.",
        animationDictionary.Count);

    AnimationData[] animations = new
        AnimationData[animationDictionary.Count];

    int count = 0;
    foreach (AnimationContent animationContent in animationDictionary.Values)
    {
        // Store all keyframes of the animation
        List<Keyframe> keyframes = new List<Keyframe>();

        // Go through all animation channels
        // Each bone has its own channel
        foreach (string animationKey in animationContent.Channels.Keys)
        {
            AnimationChannel animationChannel =
                animationContent.Channels[animationKey];
            int boneIndex = boneNameList.IndexOf(animationKey);

            foreach (AnimationKeyframe keyframe in animationChannel)
                keyframes.Add(new Keyframe(
                    keyframe.Time, boneIndex, keyframe.Transform));
        }
```

```
        // Sort all animation frames by time
        keyframes.Sort();
        animations[count++] = new AnimationData(animationContent.Name,
            animationContent.Duration, keyframes.ToArray());
    }

    return animations;
}
```

After all the keyframes of an animation have been stored, you should sort them by time, as this will allow you to easily move from one keyframe to the next, which is very important when it comes to playing the animation. As the keyframes are stored in a List and you implemented the IComparable interface for the KeyFrame class, you can use the Sort method to sort them. Remember that the IComparable interface you previously implemented in the Keyframe class sorts the KeyFrame objects by their time attribute.

At this point, you have the model's skeleton and animations extracted and stored in a friendly format, ready to be written to a binary XNB file.

Note You can find more information about the List generic class and IComparable interface in C# help files, since they are provided by the.NET Framework, not by XNA.

Reading and Writing Custom User Data

The AnimatedModelProcessor that you created stores the model's skeletal animation data using some custom user objects (AnimatedModelData, AnimationData, and Keyframe classes). As explained earlier in the chapter, the Content Pipeline needs to read and write these objects from a binary file, but the Content Pipeline doesn't know how to read or write your custom objects.

To define how the skeletal animation data should be read to and written from a binary file, you must create a content type reader and a content type writer for each custom class you created to store the skeletal animation data. In this case, you need to create a new content type reader and a new content type writer for the AnimatedModelData, AnimationData, and Keyframe classes. You can create content type readers and writers by extending XNA's ContentTypeReader and ContentTypeWriter classes.

Creating Content Type Writers

To begin creating the content type writers, add a new, empty file named AnimatedModelDataWriter to the AnimatedModelProcessorWin project. You'll add three new classes to the content type writer file: the KeyframeWriter, AnimationDataWriter, and AnimatedModelDataWriter classes, which are used to instruct XNA how to serialize the data for the Keyframe, AnimationData, and AnimatedModelData classes. Each of these classes needs to extend the ContentTypeWriter class and override its Write method.

The Write method of the ContentTypeWriter class receives two parameters. The first one is a ContentWriter object, used to write the object's data into the binary file, and the second is the object to be written. Inside the Write method, you must use the ContentWriter object to serialize all the attributes of the class. Note that the order in which you choose to write the objects in the binary file is important, as they must be in the same order as they are read. Following is the code for the KeyframeWriter, AnimationDataWriter, and AnimatedModelDataWriter classes:

```
[ContentTypeWriter]
public class KeyframeWriter : ContentTypeWriter<Keyframe>
{
    protected override void Write(ContentWriter output, Keyframe value)
    {
        output.WriteObject(value.Time);
        output.Write(value.Bone);
        output.Write(value.Transform);
    }

    public override string GetRuntimeReader(TargetPlatform targetPlatform)
    {
        return typeof(KeyframeReader).AssemblyQualifiedName;
    }
}


[ContentTypeWriter]
public class AnimationDataWriter : ContentTypeWriter<AnimationData>
{
    protected override void Write(ContentWriter output, AnimationData value)
    {
        output.Write(value.Name);
        output.WriteObject(value.Duration);
        output.WriteObject(value.Keyframes);
    }

    public override string GetRuntimeReader(TargetPlatform targetPlatform)
    {
        return typeof(AnimationDataReader).AssemblyQualifiedName;
    }
}


[ContentTypeWriter]
public class AnimatedModelDataWriter : ContentTypeWriter<AnimatedModelData>
{
    protected override void Write(ContentWriter output, AnimatedModelData value)
    {
        output.WriteObject(value.BonesBindPose);
        output.WriteObject(value.BonesInverseBindPose);
        output.WriteObject(value.BonesParent);
        output.WriteObject(value.Animations);
    }
```

```
    public override string GetRuntimeReader(TargetPlatform targetPlatform)
    {
        return typeof(AnimatedModelDataReader).AssemblyQualifiedName;
    }
}
```

Make sure you verify that the Write method of each writer defined in the preceding code serializes all necessary data. Furthermore, each writer should provide the GetRuntimeReader method, indicating the name of the type reader that is capable of deserializing the data back into an object. For each type writer, you specify the name of the corresponding type reader you'll define in the next section.

This string should uniquely define the TypeReader class, which includes its namespace, version number, culture, and more. As an example, the full string of this corresponding TypeReader class reads AnimatedModelContent.AnimatedModelDataReader, AnimatedModelContentWin, Version=1.0.0.0, Culture=neutral, PublicKeyToken=null, and is obtained through the AssemblyQualifiedName property of the TypeReader class.

Creating Content Type Readers

For the content type readers, add a new, empty file named AnimatedModelDataReader to the AnimatedModelContentWin project. Unlike the content type writer classes, which come into play at compile time, the game application needs the content type reader classes to load the animation data at runtime.

As defined in your type writers, you need to create three new classes: the KeyframeReader, AnimationDataReader, and AnimatedModelDataReader classes, which are used to deserialize the data of the Keyframe, AnimationData, and AnimatedModelData classes. Each of these classes needs to extend the ContentTypeReader class and override the Read method.

The Read method of the ContentTypeReader class receives two parameters. The first one is a ContentReader, used to read the object's data from the binary file, and the second parameter is a reference for an existing instance of the object. The second parameter will be always null because you're creating the object. Again, notice that inside the Read method the objects must be read in the exact same order as they were written by your type writer. Following is the code for the KeyframeReader, AnimationDataReader, and AnimatedModelDataReader classes:

```
public class KeyframeReader : ContentTypeReader<Keyframe>
{
    protected override Keyframe Read(ContentReader input,
        Keyframe existingInstance)
    {
        TimeSpan time = input.ReadObject<TimeSpan>();
        int boneIndex = input.ReadInt32();
        Matrix transform = input.ReadMatrix();

        return new Keyframe(time, boneIndex, transform);
    }
}
```

```
public class AnimationDataReader : ContentTypeReader<AnimationData>
{
    protected override AnimationData Read(ContentReader input,
        AnimationData existingInstance)
    {
        string name = input.ReadString();
        TimeSpan duration = input.ReadObject<TimeSpan>();
        Keyframe[] keyframes = input.ReadObject<Keyframe[]>();

        return new AnimationData(name, duration, keyframes);
    }
}

public class AnimatedModelDataReader :
    ContentTypeReader<AnimatedModelData>
{
    protected override AnimatedModelData Read(ContentReader input,
        AnimatedModelData existingInstance)
    {
        Matrix[] bonesBindPose = input.ReadObject<Matrix[]>();
        Matrix[] bonesInverseBindPose = input.ReadObject<Matrix[]>();
        int[] bonesParent = input.ReadObject<int[]>();
        AnimationData[] animations =
            input.ReadObject<AnimationData[]>();

        return new AnimatedModelData(bonesBindPose,
            bonesInverseBindPose, bonesParent, animations);
    }
}
```

Using the AnimatedModel Class in XNA

In this section, you'll create the class used to receive the skeletal animation model from the Content Pipeline at runtime. This class, named AnimatedModel, will have methods to load an animated model, play and update an animation, and draw the model. You'll begin constructing the AnimatedModel class by declaring its attributes.

The animated model is loaded as an XNA Model object, which has a dictionary containing an AnimatedModelData object stored in its Tag property. In this way, the Model class contains the model's mesh and effects, while the AnimatedModelData class contains the model's skeleton and animations. You declare the model attribute of type Model and the animatedModel attribute of type AnimatedModelData to store the model data, and you store the model's world transformation (containing its position, rotation, and scale in the absolute 3D world) separately in an attribute of type Transformation.

```
Model model;
AnimatedModelData animatedModelData;
Transformation transformation;
```

You still need to declare some attributes to handle how the animations are reproduced. You declare the activeAnimation attribute to store the current animation that is being played, and the activeAnimationKeyframeIndex and activeAnimationTime attributes to store the current animation frame and time, respectively:

```
AnimationData activeAnimation;
int activeAnimationKeyframe;
TimeSpan activeAnimationTime;
```

You need to declare two other attributes to be able to configure the animation speed and enable animation looping. These are the enableAnimationLoop attribute and the animationSpeed attribute:

```
bool enableAnimationLoop;
float animationSpeed;
```

During an animation of the model, you will need some temporary matrix arrays to store the current configuration of the skeleton's bones. You declare the bones attribute to store the current configuration of each bone, because the bones' configurations are modified as an animation is being played. You also declare the bonesAbsolute attribute to store the absolute configuration of each bone, calculated using the bones array and needed to animate the model at runtime. Finally, you declare the bonesAnimation attribute to store the final transformation of each bone, which combines the transformation needed to put the vertices in the coordinate system of the bone and animate them using the absolute configuration of each bone. (We'll explain the skeletal animation in more detail in the "Skeletal Animation Equations" section later in this chapter.)

```
Matrix[] bones;
Matrix[] bonesAbsolute;
Matrix[] bonesAnimation;
```

To be able to apply custom transformation over the bones, you declare another matrix array. You use these custom transformations to modify the skeleton's bones independently of the animation that is being played. This is very important, because it allows more flexibility (one of the main reasons we prefer skeletal animations over keyframed animation). For example, you could lower an arm while the walking animation is looping

```
Matrix[] bonesTransform;
```

Last, you need to declare two attributes to store the animated model effect, which you'll create later, and material:

```
AnimatedModelEffect animatedModelEffect;
LightMaterial lightMaterial;
```

You create the AnimatedModelEffect class to encapsulate the animated model effect, and use the LightMaterial class, which you created in Chapter 9, to configure it.

Loading an Animated Model

Before you attempt to load your model, make sure you've compiled your new Content Pipeline. Next, drop an animated model file into the Contents folder in the Solution Explorer window, and then select it. In the property box at the bottom-right side of your screen, select the AnimatedModel processor from the list of available processors. Next, load it using the content manager.

Now you need to check if the loaded model is a valid animated model—whether it contains a dictionary with an AnimatedModelData object as the model's Tag property:

```
model = Game.Content.Load<Model>(
    GameAssetsPath.MODELS_PATH + modelFileName);

// Get the dictionary
Dictionary<string, object> modelTag =
    (Dictionary<string, object>)model.Tag;
if (modelTag == null)
    throw new InvalidOperationException(
        "This is not a valid animated model.");

// Get the AnimatedModelData from the dictionary
if (modelTag.ContainsKey("AnimatedModelData"))
    animatedModelData = (AnimatedModelData)
        modelTag["AnimatedModelData"];
else
    throw new InvalidOperationException(
        "This is not a valid animated model.");
```

After loading the model, you should initialize some variables used to configure and reproduce the model's animations. The default model animation is set as the first animation in the Animations array of the AnimatedModelData object, and is stored in the activeAnimation attribute:

```
if (animatedModelData.Animations.Length > 0)
    activeAnimation = animatedModelData.Animations[0];
```

The initial animation keyframe and time are stored in the activeAnimationKeyframe and activeAnimationTime attributes, respectively. You configure the animation speed through the animationSpeed attribute:

```
// Default animation configuration
animationSpeed = 1.0f;
activeAnimationKeyframe = 0;
activeAnimationTime = TimeSpan.Zero;
```

While the model is being animated, it uses some temporary matrix arrays to calculate the final configuration of each bone. You create these matrix arrays here, because their size needs to be equal to the number of bones in the model's skeleton. You should initialize the bones array with the bones' configuration stored in the AnimatedModelData. Store the identity matrix in bonesTranform, as at this point, you're not interested in superposing other movements:

```
// Temporary matrices used to animate the bones
bones = new Matrix[animatedModelData.BonesBindPose.Length];
bonesAbsolute = new Matrix[animatedModelData.BonesBindPose.Length];
bonesAnimation = new Matrix[animatedModelData.BonesBindPose.Length];

// Used to apply custom transformation over the bones
bonesTransform = new Matrix[animatedModelData.BonesBindPose.Length];

for (int i = 0; i < bones.Length; i++)
{
    bones[i] = animatedModelData.BonesBindPose[i];
    bonesTransform[i] = Matrix.Identity;
}
```

Finally, you get the animated model effect of the model, and encapsulate it in an AnimatedModelEffect:

```
// Get the animated model effect - shared by all meshes
animatedModelEffect = new AnimatedModelEffect(model.Meshes[0].Effects[0]);
// Create a default material
lightMaterial = new LightMaterial();
```

Note that the effect used to render the model is shared by all the model's meshes. Following is the complete code for the Load method of the AnimatedModel class:

```
public void Load(string modelFileName)
{
    if (!isInitialized)
        Initialize();

    model = Game.Content.Load<Model>(
        GameAssetsPath.MODELS_PATH + modelFileName);

    // Get the dictionary
    Dictionary<string, object> modelTag =
        (Dictionary<string, object>)model.Tag;
    if (modelTag == null) throw new InvalidOperationException(
        "This is not a valid animated model.");

    // Get the AnimatedModelData from the dictionary
    if (modelTag.ContainsKey("AnimatedModelData"))
        animatedModelData = (AnimatedModelData)
            modelTag["AnimatedModelData"];
    else
        throw new InvalidOperationException(
            "This is not a valid animated model.");
```

```
// Default animation
animationSpeed = 1.0f;
activeAnimationKeyframe = 0;
activeAnimationTime = TimeSpan.Zero;
if (animatedModelData.Animations.Length > 0)
    activeAnimation = animatedModelData.Animations[0];

// Temporary matrices used to animate the bones
bones = new Matrix[animatedModelData.BonesBindPose.Length];
bonesAbsolute = new
    Matrix[animatedModelData.BonesBindPose.Length];
bonesAnimation = new
    Matrix[animatedModelData.BonesBindPose.Length];

// Used to apply custom transformation over the bones
bonesTransform = new
    Matrix[animatedModelData.BonesBindPose.Length];

for (int i = 0; i < bones.Length; i++)
{
    bones[i] = animatedModelData.BonesBindPose[i];
    bonesTransform[i] = Matrix.Identity;
}

// Get the animated model effect - shared by all meshes
animatedModelEffect = new AnimatedModelEffect(model.Meshes[0].Effects[0]);
// Create a default material
lightMaterial = new LightMaterial();
}
```

Skeletal Animation Equations

This section reviews some concepts and mathematical equations used in skeletal animation. A skeletal animation is made of many keyframes, where each keyframe stores the configuration of a bone (its orientation and position) and the time frame during which this bone needs to be animated. At every time interval, you use one or more keyframes to alter the configuration of the skeleton's bones. Figure 12-7 illustrates an animation in the skeleton shown in Figure 12-3, where the left shoulder bone has its orientation changed, affecting all the child bones.

To achieve the result in Figure 12-7, all you need is a keyframe animation for the left shoulder bone. Although the final configurations of all the left shoulder children have been changed, they still have the same relationship to the left shoulder. In other words, you don't need to store the new configuration of the left shoulder children, because you can calculate them based on the new left shoulder configuration. So, when you need to update the model, you should calculate the absolute configuration of every bone, and then transform the mesh's vertices using these bones.

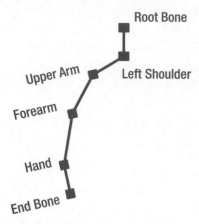

Figure 12-7. *Left shoulder bone animation of the original skeleton shown in Figure 12-3. Notice that the configuration of all the descendant bones is altered.*

In the following sections, we present some mathematical equations used to transform the model's mesh as the model is being animated. You'll use these mathematical equations to update and draw the model.

To take advantage of the calculation power of the GPU, you'll implement some of these equations in the animated model's HLSL effects. To allow smooth skeletal animations, the position of each vertex needs to be calculated for each frame, which makes this operation an excellent task to be handled by the vertex shader. You'll find the HLSL code for this in the "Creating the AnimatedModel Effect" section later in this chapter.

Transforming a Mesh's Vertex

For simple models, each vertex belongs to a single bone. This approach, however, can produce cracks in the mesh. For example, when a character bends its arm, a crack will appear at its elbow cap. To solve this problem, most vertices belong to multiple bones. Moreover, each vertex has an individual weighting describing how much it belongs to these bones. A vertex at the center of the upper arm, for example, will belong almost completely to the bone of the upper arm. A vertex closer to the elbow, however, will belong about 50 percent to the upper arm and about 50 percent to the forearm.

You can calculate the final position of a mesh's vertex, which is influenced by just one bone, with the following equation:

$$P_F = P'_0 \ [Bone \cdot W]$$

In this equation, P_F is the vertex's final position, P'_0 is the vertex's initial position, *Bone* is the matrix that contains the absolute configuration of the bone that influences the vertex, and W is the weight of the influence of this bone over the vertex. Because in this example the vertex is influenced by just one bone, the weight should be 1.0 (equivalent to 100 percent). This equation shows how you should calculate the vertex's final position: transform the vertex's initial position by the matrix that contains the bone's absolute configuration.

■Note The weights of a vertex need to be *normalized*; that is, the sum of all weights of a vertex needs to equal exactly 1. This is because 3D positions are vectors, and the operation shown here is nothing more than a linear interpolation between multiple vectors. As an example of another interpolation, in order to average two vectors, which is a simple interpolation, you need to add them together and divide the result by two. Using the first equation shown in this section, this would result in two weights of 0.5.

The vertex's initial position used in the preceding equation must be in the same coordinate system as its bone in its bind pose. Remember that when the vertices are linked to the skeleton's bones, all the bones are found in the bind pose position, and all bone animations are applied over the initial bind pose of the skeleton. You can transform the vertex's original position (the position stored inside the vertex) to the bone's bind pose coordinate system by multiplying the vertex's position by the inverse bone matrix, as shown in the following equation:

$$P'_0 = P_0 \, [Bone_{BindPose}^{-1}]$$

In this equation, P'_0 is the initial position of the vertex in the bone's bind pose coordinate system, P_0 is the vertex position in the object coordinates system (the position stored inside the vertex), and $Bone^{-1}{}_{BindPose}$ is the inverse matrix of the bone's absolute configuration in its bind pose. To place the vertex in the bone's coordinate system, you just need to multiply it by the inversed matrix of the bone in the bind pose. Using the two preceding equations, you can animate all the vertices of the mesh's model using its skeleton.

Combining Bone Transformations

The first equation in the preceding section doesn't allow more than one bone to affect a vertex. To calculate the final position of a vertex that is influenced by more than one bone, you need to calculate the final position of this vertex for each bone that influences it separately. Then you can calculate the vertex's final position as a sum of the vertices' final positions that you previously calculated, taking the influence (weight) of each bone on the vertex into account. The following equation shows the calculation of the final position of a vertex that is affected by many bones:

$$P_F = \sum_{i=0}^{n-1} P'_0 \, [Bone_i \cdot W_i]$$

$$\sum_{i=0}^{n-1} W_i = 1$$

Notice that the sum of the weights used to transform the vertices in the preceding figure must equal 1. Finally, the following equation shows the complete equation used to transform the mesh's vertices:

$$P_F = P_0 \sum_{i=0}^{n-1} [Bone_{BindPose}^{-1} \cdot Bone_i \cdot W_i]$$

$$\sum_{i=0}^{n-1} W_i = 1$$

Notice that in this equation, you'll first calculate the average sum of the matrices used to transform the vertex. As a result, the vertex is transformed only once.

Updating the AnimatedModel Class

During the model's animation, the code needs to constantly update the orientation of all bones according to the animation keyframes, where the keyframe contains the new configuration of the bones in its local coordinate system relative to its ancestor. You'll process the model animation using both the CPU and the GPU. You'll calculate the bone matrix (matrix $[Bone^{-1}_{BindPose} * Bone_i]$, shown in the last equation in the preceding section) on the CPU, because there are not that many bones. You'll use the GPU for each vertex to combine the bone matrices and transform the position of the vertex with the resulting matrix.

To handle the animation process done on the CPU, you'll create an Update method for the AnimatedModel, in this section. To handle the animation process done on the GPU, you'll create a new effect for the animated models, in the next section. In the CPU, you can divide the tasks to perform the model's animation into three main parts:

- First, you update the skeleton's bones according to the current animation that is being played and the elapsed time.

- Next, you calculate the absolute coordinate of each bone.

- Finally, you calculate the final bone matrix used to transform the vertices.

You start the first part of the animation process by calculating the current animation time. This is done by incrementing the animation time by the elapsed time in Ticks since the last update, where the elapsed time is scaled by the animation speed:

```
activeAnimationTime += new TimeSpan(
    (long)(time.ElapsedGameTime.Ticks * animationSpeed));
```

Then you check if the current animation has finished by comparing the activeAnimationTime with the duration of the current animation. If enableAnimationLoop is true, you can reset the animation time:

```
// Loop the animation
if (activeAnimationTime > activeAnimation.Duration && enableAnimationLoop)
{
    long elapsedTicks = activeAnimationTime.Ticks % activeAnimation.Duration.Ticks;
    activeAnimationTime = new TimeSpan(elapsedTicks);
    activeAnimationKeyframe = 0;
}
```

Next, you check if this is the first update of the animation. In this case, you need to restore the skeleton's bones to their bind pose:

```
// Put the bind pose in the bones in the beginning of the animation
if (activeAnimationKeyframe == 0)
{
    for (int i = 0; i < bones.Length; i++)
        bones[i] = animatedModelData.BonesBindPose[i];
}
```

To reproduce the animation, you loop through the keyframes of the current model animation, updating the model skeleton's bones when the `activeAnimationTime` is larger than the keyframe time:

```
// Browse all animation keyframes until the current time is reached
// That's possible because you have previously sorted the keyframes
int index = 0;
Keyframe[] keyframes = activeAnimation.Keyframes;
while (index < keyframes.Length && keyframes[index].Time <= activeAnimationTime)
{
    int boneIndex = keyframes[index].Bone;
    bones[boneIndex] = keyframes[index].Transform * bonesTransform[boneIndex];
    index++;
}
activeAnimationKeyframe = index - 1;
```

In the second part of the animation process, you need to loop through all the bones' matrices and calculate the absolute configuration for each of them. Because the skeleton's bone array was constructed by a depth traversal, the parent of a bone in this array cannot have an index bigger than its index. So, you can go through each element of the list in order, calculating each element's final position, without worrying about creating changes you'll need to reconcile later, because the final position of each element's parent will already have been calculated. Notice that the first bone of the array is already in its absolute coordinate system (because it doesn't have a parent), but you transform it with a custom user matrix.

```
// Fill the bones with their absolute coordinate
bonesAbsolute[0] = bones[0] * parent;
for (int i = 1; i < bonesAnimation.Length; i++)
{
    int boneParent = animatedModelData.BonesParent[i];

    // Here we are transforming a child bone by its parent
    bonesAbsolute[i] = bones[i] * bonesAbsolute[boneParent];
}
```

Finally, you calculate the final position of each bone by multiplying the inverse transformation of the bone in its bind pose and its current absolute position, corresponding to the last equation shown in the previous section:

```
// Before we can transform the mesh's vertices using the calculated
// bone matrix, we need to put the vertices in the coordinate system
// of the bone that is linked to it
for (int i = 0; i < bonesAnimation.Length; i++)
{
    bonesAnimation[i] = animatedModelData.BonesInverseBindPose[i] *
        bonesAbsolute[i];
}
```

Following is the complete code for the Update method of the AnimatedModel class:

```
private void UpdateAnimation(GameTime time, Matrix parent)
{
    activeAnimationTime += new TimeSpan(
        (long)(time.ElapsedGameTime.Ticks * animationSpeed));

    if (activeAnimation != null)
    {
        // Loop the animation
        if (activeAnimationTime >
            activeAnimation.Duration && enableAnimationLoop)
        {
            long elapsedTicks = activeAnimationTime.Ticks %
                activeAnimation.Duration.Ticks;
            activeAnimationTime = new TimeSpan(elapsedTicks);
            activeAnimationKeyframe = 0;
        }

        // Every time the animation starts put the local bind pose in
        // the bones array
        if (activeAnimationKeyframe == 0)
        {
            for (int i = 0; i < bones.Length; i++)
                bones[i] = animatedModelData.BonesBindPose[i];
        }

        // Browse all animation keyframes until the current time
        // is reached. This is possible because we have sorted the
        // keyframes by time during the model processing
        int index = 0;
        Keyframe[] keyframes = activeAnimation.Keyframes;
        while (index < keyframes.Length &&
            keyframes[index].Time <= activeAnimationTime)
        {
            int boneIndex = keyframes[index].Bone;
            bones[boneIndex] = keyframes[index].Transform *
                bonesTransform[boneIndex];
            index++;
        }
```

```
        activeAnimationKeyframe = index - 1;
    }


    // Calculate the bones absolute coordinate
    bonesAbsolute[0] = bones[0] * parent;
    for (int i = 1; i < bonesAnimation.Length; i++)
    {
        int boneParent = animatedModelData.BonesParent[i];
        // Transform the bone configuration by its
        // parent configuration
        bonesAbsolute[i] = bones[i] * bonesAbsolute[boneParent];
    }


    // Before we can transform the vertices we
    // need to put the vertices in the coordinate system of the
    // bone that is linked to it
    for (int i = 0; i < bonesAnimation.Length; i++)
    {
        bonesAnimation[i] = animatedModelData.BonesInverseBindPose[i]
            * bonesAbsolute[i];
    }
}
```

Creating the AnimatedModel Effect

At every time interval, you need to animate (transform) the model's mesh according to the current skeleton model. The advantage of transforming the model's mesh on the GPU is that it does this transformation much faster than the CPU can, as a GPU is optimized to run trivial operations such as multiplication and division in massive parallelism.

In this section, you'll create an effect for the animated model rendering that will transform the mesh's vertices in its vertex shader. This effect will also support two omnidirectional light sources and texturing.

Defining the Uniform Variables

As you've learned in previous chapters, it's a good practice to start by defining the uniform variables used by your effect. These are the variables set by your XNA program, and they remain constant for all vertices and pixels during the rendering of the entire frame.

Let's start with the general variables, which are not specific to this chapter and have been explained in previous chapters:

```
// Matrix
// -------------------------------------------------
float4x4 matW : World;
float4x4 matV : View;
float4x4 matVI : ViewInverse;
float4x4 matWV : WorldView;
float4x4 matWVP : WorldViewProjection;
```

```
// Material
// --------------------------------------------------
float3 diffuseColor;
float3 specularColor;
float specularPower;

// Light
// --------------------------------------------------
float3 ambientLightColor;
float3 light1Position;
float3 light1Color;
float3 light2Position;
float3 light2Color;
```

You need these for the usual 3D-to-2D transformations and lighting calculations. More important, and specific to this chapter's focus, is this uniform variable:

```
#define SHADER20_MAX_BONES 58
float4x4 matBones[SHADER20_MAX_BONES];
```

This means your XNA program should define an array of matrices. Needless to say, in this chapter, this will be the bone matrices of the current model. In shader model 2.0, a single array can contain a maximum of 58 matrices.

Finally, add the texture variables and samplers:

```
// Textures
// --------------------------------------------------
float2 uv0Tile;
texture diffuseTexture1 : Diffuse;

sampler2D diffuse1Sampler = sampler_state {
    texture = <diffuseTexture1>;
    MagFilter = Linear;
    MinFilter = Linear;
    MipFilter = Linear;
};
```

You'll need only a single texture in this effect: your model's texture.

Creating the Application to Vertex Shader Structure

Each vertex that your vertex shader receives is expected to carry the vertex position, normal, texture coordinate, and bone index and weight. Each vertex has four indices of bones that influence it, as well as the weight of these influences. If a vertex is attached to only a single bone, three of the four weights will be zero.

The vertex's indices and weight attributes are processed by the default XNA model processor, the ModelProcessor class.

```
struct a2v
{
    float4 position : POSITION;
    float3 normal : NORMAL;
    float2 uv0 : TEXCOORD0;
    float4 boneIndex : BLENDINDICES0;
    float4 boneWeight : BLENDWEIGHT0;
};
```

Creating the Vertex Shader to Pixel Shader Structure

The output of the vertex shader contains the vertex's final position, the topic of interest of this chapter. Besides the final position, it will contain the normal, the texture coordinates, view vector, and two lighting vectors.

```
struct v2f
{
    float4 hposition : POSITION;
    float2 uv0 : TEXCOORD0;
    float3 normal : TEXCOORD1;
    float3 lightVec1 : TEXCOORD2;
    float3 lightVec2 : TEXCOORD3;
    float3 eyeVec : TEXCOORD4;
};
```

The only mandatory action of the vertex shader is to produce the 2D screen coordinate of the vertex, which is done by transforming the absolute 3D position of the vertex by the combination of the view and projection matrices. However, this implies you *first* need to find the absolute 3D position, while the 3D position stored in the vertex and received by the vertex shader is defined relative to its bone. Therefore, the shader first needs to transform this position from bone space to object space or model space, by transforming it with the combined transformation of its bone. At this point, the position is defined relative to the model's origin. To obtain the absolute 3D position, or world position, you need to transform it to world space, which is done by transforming it by the world matrix, which contains the position and orientation of the object in the 3D world. After you know the 3D position in world space, you're ready to finally transform it into screen space by transforming it with the view and projection matrices.

AnimatedModel Vertex Processing

Inside the vertex shader, you should first calculate the final bone matrix used to transform the vertex position and normal. This corresponds to the final transformation equation presented in the "Skeletal Animation Equations" section earlier in this chapter. In this case, each vertex can depend on four bone matrices, where the four weights indicate the influence of each bone matrix. Remember that these bone matrices are updated at the beginning of each frame in the UpdateAnimation method, presented earlier.

```
// Calculate the final bone transformation matrix
float4x4 matTransform = matBones[IN.boneIndex.x] * IN.boneWeight.x;
matTransform += matBones[IN.boneIndex.y] * IN.boneWeight.y;
matTransform += matBones[IN.boneIndex.z] * IN.boneWeight.z;
float finalWeight = 1.0f - (IN.boneWeight.x + IN.boneWeight.y + IN.boneWeight.z);
matTransform += matBones[IN.boneIndex.w] * finalWeight;
```

Next, you transform the vertex position and normal by the final bone matrix, and store the result in the position variable. The position you calculate is the final 3D position of the vertex in the model, after taking the animation into account. After that, you transform it by a matrix that combines the world, view, and projection transformations, to move the model to its position in the absolute 3D world and transform this absolute 3D position to its 2D screen coordinates.

```
// Transform vertex and normal
float4 position = mul(IN.position, matTransform);
float3 normal = mul(IN.normal, matTransform);
OUT.hposition = mul(position, matWVP);
OUT.normal = mul(normal, matWV);
```

■**Note** Since the world, view, and projection matrices are the same for the entire model, they are often combined into what is called the WVP matrix, as in the previous example.

Last, you calculate the view vector and the two lighting vectors. These will be used in the pixel shader to calculate the lighting:

```
// Calculate light and eye vectors
float4 worldPosition = mul(position, matW);
OUT.eyeVec = mul(matVI[3].xyz - worldPosition, matV);
OUT.lightVec1 = mul(light1Position - worldPosition, matV);
OUT.lightVec2 = mul(light2Position - worldPosition, matV);
OUT.uv0 = IN.uv0;
```

Here is the completed vertex processing code:

```
v2f animatedModelVS(a2v IN)
{
    v2f OUT;

    // Calculate the final bone transformation matrix
    float4x4 matTransform = matBones[IN.boneIndex.x] *
        IN.boneWeight.x;
    matTransform += matBones[IN.boneIndex.y] * IN.boneWeight.y;
    matTransform += matBones[IN.boneIndex.z] * IN.boneWeight.z;
    float finalWeight = 1.0f - (IN.boneWeight.x + IN.boneWeight.y +
        IN.boneWeight.z);
    matTransform += matBones[IN.boneIndex.w] * finalWeight;
```

```
    // Transform vertex and normal
    float4 position = mul(IN.position, matTransform);
    float3 normal = mul(IN.normal, matTransform);
    OUT.hposition = mul(position, matWVP);
    OUT.normal = mul(normal, matWV);

    // Calculate light and eye vectors
    float4 worldPosition = mul(position, matW);
    OUT.eyeVec = mul(matVI[3].xyz - worldPosition, matV);
    OUT.lightVec1 = mul(light1Position - worldPosition, matV);
    OUT.lightVec2 = mul(light2Position - worldPosition, matV);
    OUT.uv0 = IN.uv0;

    return OUT;
}
```

AnimatedModel Pixel Processing

All the data for a pixel handled by the pixel shader is interpolated between the three vertices of the triangle to which the pixel belongs. Therefore, the first thing you do in the pixel shader is normalize all the vectors so that you can perform the lighting calculation correctly, making sure their length is exactly 1:

```
// Normalize all input vectors
float3 normal = normalize(IN.normal);
float3 eyeVec = normalize(IN.eyeVec);
float3 lightVec1 = normalize(IN.lightVec1);
float3 lightVec2 = normalize(IN.lightVec2);
float3 halfVec1 = normalize(lightVec1 + eyeVec);
float3 halfVec2 = normalize(lightVec2 + eyeVec);
```

At this point, you have all the necessary vectors for the lighting calculation. Now, you'll do the lighting calculation using the Phong equation, as discussed in the previous chapter:

```
// Calculate diffuse and specular color for each light
float3 diffuseColor1, diffuseColor2;
float3 specularColor1, specularColor2;
phongShading(normal, lightVec1, halfwayVec1, light1Color,
    diffuseColor1, specularColor1);
phongShading(normal, lightVec2, halfwayVec2, light2Color,
    diffuseColor2, specularColor2);
```

After this, the pixel color is read from its texture:

```
float4 materialColor = tex2D(diffuse1Sampler, IN.uv0);
```

Finally, you calculate the final color of each pixel, combining its color with the diffuse and specular components from the light sources:

```
float4 finalColor;
finalColor.a = 1.0f;
finalColor.rgb = materialColor *
    ( (diffuseColor1+diffuseColor2) * diffuseColor +
    ambientLightColor) + (specularColor1 + specularColor2) *
    specularColor ;
```

The code for the phongShading function is shown in Chapter 11. The final pixel shader code follows:

```
float4 animatedModelPS(v2f IN): COLOR0
{
    // Normalize all input vectors
    float3 normal = normalize(IN.normal);
    float3 eyeVec = normalize(IN.eyeVec);
    float3 lightVec1 = normalize(IN.lightVec1);
    float3 lightVec2 = normalize(IN.lightVec2);
    float3 halfwayVec1 = normalize(lightVec1 + eyeVec);
    float3 halfwayVec2 = normalize(lightVec2 + eyeVec);

    // Calculate diffuse and specular color for each light
    float3 diffuseColor1, diffuseColor2;
    float3 specularColor1, specularColor2;
    phongShading(normal, lightVec1, halfwayVec1,
        light1Color, diffuseColor1, specularColor1);
    phongShading(normal, lightVec2, halfwayVec2,
        light2Color, diffuseColor2, specularColor2);

    // Read texture diffuse color
    float4 materialColor = tex2D(diffuse1Sampler, IN.uv0);

    // Phong lighting result
    float4 finalColor;
    finalColor.a = 1.0f;
    finalColor.rgb = materialColor *
        ( (diffuseColor1+diffuseColor2) * diffuseColor +
        ambientLightColor) + (specularColor1+specularColor2) *
        specularColor ;
    return finalColor;
}
```

Now, all that remains to do is to define a technique that uses the vertex and pixel shaders created in the previous sections:

```
technique AnimatedModel
{
    pass p0
    {
        VertexShader = compile vs_2_0 animatedModelVS();
        PixelShader = compile ps_2_a animatedModelPS();
    }
}
```

Converting the Mesh Effect

You need to use the effect that you created in the preceding section to render the model. XNA's model processor has the `ConvertMaterial` method, which is called whenever the material of a model's mesh is found. You will override this method in the custom Content Pipeline project of your solution.

The `ConvertMaterial` method receives as a parameter a `MaterialContent` object that stores the material content used by the mesh. When a model is exported without an effect, it has only some basic material configuration, such as the color and texture. In this case, the generated `MaterialContent` is an instance of the `BasicMaterialContent` class. If the model has already been exported along with an effect, then the received material is an instance of the `EffectMaterialContent` class.

To change the materials used in the model, you need to override the `ConvertMaterial` method, and convert the `BasicMaterialContent` received to an `EffectMaterialContent`, integrating in the effect that you've created for the animated model. The following code shows the `ConvertMaterial` method, which you should add to the model processor class.

```
protected override MaterialContent ConvertMaterial(
    MaterialContent material, ContentProcessorContext context)
{
    BasicMaterialContent basicMaterial = material
        as BasicMaterialContent;
    if (basicMaterial == null)
        context.Logger.LogImportantMessage(
            "This mesh doesn't have a valid basic material.");

    // Only process meshes with basic material
    // Otherwise the mesh must use the correct effect (AnimatedModel.fx)
    if (basicMaterial != null)
    {
        EffectMaterialContent effectMaterial =
            new EffectMaterialContent();
        effectMaterial.Effect =
            new ExternalReference<EffectContent>(
            SHADERS_PATH + SHADER_FILENAME);
```

```
        // Correct the texture path
        if (basicMaterial.Texture != null)
        {
            string textureFileName = Path.GetFileName(
                basicMaterial.Texture.Filename);
            effectMaterial.Textures.Add("diffuseTexture1",
                new ExternalReference<TextureContent>(
                TEXTURES_PATH + textureFileName));
        }

        return base.ConvertMaterial(effectMaterial, context);
    }
    else
        return base.ConvertMaterial(material, context);
}
```

When the `BasicMaterialContent` is converted to an `EffectMaterialContent` with the correct texture path, the model texture used in the default material is passed again to the newly created effect.

Drawing the Model

Because the animated model is an XNA model that now contains your custom effect, it is simple to draw the model. First, you need to configure the animated model's effects as explained in Chapter 9, and then you just go through all its meshes, calling their respective `Draw` methods. Following is the code for the `Draw` method of the `AnimatedModel` class:

```
public override void Draw(GameTime gameTime)
{
    SetEffectMaterial();
    for (int i = 0; i < model.Meshes.Count; i++)
    {
        model.Meshes[i].Draw();
    }
}
```

Summary

In this chapter, you learned how to extend XNA's Content Pipeline by adding support for skeletal animation models, and how to create a class capable of handling the animated models at runtime. You also reviewed some concepts and mathematical equations behind the skeletal animation models.

In the next chapter, you will see how to put together all the concepts we've covered since Chapter 8 to create a real 3D game, a simple third-person shooter.

■■■

CHAPTER 13

Creating a Third-Person Shooter Game

In this chapter, you'll build a complete 3D game using most of the concepts covered in the previous chapters. You'll create a third-person shooter game. First, you'll create a basic engine for the game containing all the required objects, such as cameras, lights, terrains, and animated models. Then you'll create all the game play and logic for the game.

Designing the Game

Today's gaming market is full of first-person shooter (FPS) and third-person shooter (TPS) games, such as Crysis, Gears of War, and Resident Evil 4. These games all share certain common characteristics. They tend to either partially or totally lack a user interface (UI) on the main screen (unlike older games in this genre, such as Doom), they contain a good selection of indoor and outdoor scenery for realism, and they have higher-quality graphics than you would find in a strategy or an RPG game to promote immersive game play.

Bearing these features in mind, you're now going to create a basic design to guide you through the creation of your own game.

Game Definition

The game will be a TPS game, where the player will control a survivor of a human expedition that went to an unknown planet. The objective of the player is to avenge the death of his companions, fighting and destroying every living creature on this planet. The game environment will be a completely outdoor scene.

Game Play

The player will start the game equipped with a machine gun and ammunition. The player should be able to run (both forward and backward), jump, and attack (aiming and shooting). The player should not be able to move while aiming. A sprite with a circle will be used to show the target of the player's weapon.

The player will be controlled using the Xbox 360 controller or the keyboard. The game controls were created based on the principles of the game Resident Evil 4. Figure 13-1 shows the game controller.

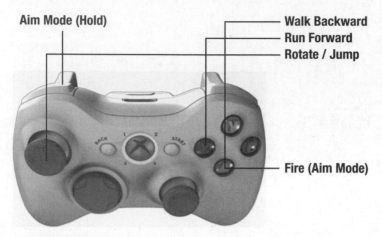

Figure 13-1. *The game controller*

Using the Xbox 360 controller, the left directional button is used to rotate the player and jump (when clicked). The X and A buttons move the player forward and backward. Button LB is used to enter into the aim mode. While in the aim mode, the player cannot move, and the A button is used to shoot.

The game map will have a few monsters (called NPCs for nonplayable characters, or less commonly *mobs*, for mobile objects) scattered in different positions. Each monster will be randomly walking around the map until it sees the player or is attacked by the player. When this happens, the monster will chase the player, and after approaching him, the monster will attack. Whenever the monster loses all its hit points, it will die. And if the player loses all his hit points, the game will be over.

Finally, the game UI will be as simple as possible. It will display the player's health points, ammunition, and the number of remaining creatures alive on the planet.

Technical Design

Now you'll define some technical design items. To ease the building of the game, you'll divide the game code into three different namespaces:

- GameBase: This namespace contains the entire game engine, with objects such as cameras, lights, terrain, models, and effects. Note that you created almost the entire game engine in Chapters 10, 11, and 12.

- GameLogic: This namespace contains the logic of the game, including player logic, the artificial intelligence (AI) for the NPCs, unit types, and others.

- Helpers: This namespace contains various helper objects, such as a controller helper and a random generator helper.

Using these namespaces makes it easier to keep the game logic separate from the game engine, which helps you to develop, reuse, and maintain the game code.

You'll start constructing the XNA TPS game by creating its game engine, and then you'll work on its game play.

Starting the Game Engine

Start the game development by creating a new Windows Game (3.0) project named XNA TPS. In this new game project, create the folders GameBase, GameLogic, and Helpers in the Solution Explorer. These folders will help you maintain the different parts of the game code, separated as described in the previous section. The game assets will be added to the Content project, which is inside the XNA TPS project.

As noted in the previous section, you made most of the XNA TPS game engine in Chapters 10, 11, and 12. Here, you'll add the classes that you created in the previous chapters to the GameBase namespace in the XNA TPS project.

Cameras, Lights, and Transformations

You made the Cameras, Lights, and Transformation classes in Chapter 10. To add these classes to the project in a clean way, you should first create the folders Cameras and Lights inside the GameBase folder. Then add all the camera and light classes created in Chapter 10 to the Cameras and Lights folders, respectively, and the Transformation class to the GameBase folder.

Terrain

You created the Terrain class and its effect and material classes in Chapter 11. To add these classes to the project, you first need to create the Shapes, Materials, and Effects folders. Then add the Terrain class to the Shapes folder, the TerrainEffect class to the Effects folder, and all the material classes to the Materials folder. You also need to add the VertexPositionNormalTangentBinormalTexture class used by the Terrain class to the Helpers folder in the XNA TPS project.

Finally, add the terrain assets (height map, textures, and effects) to the XNA TPS Content project. To add these assets to the Content project, create a few different folders: the Terrains folder, used to store the terrain's height map; the Textures folder, used to store the game textures; and the Effects folder, used to store the effects. After adding all the assets to their folders, remember to modify the properties of the terrain's height map, changing its Build Action property to None and its Copy to Output Directory property to Copy if Newer.

Animated Model

You created the animated model processor, content library, runtime class, and effects in Chapter 12. One way to import this would be to add the Content Pipeline project to your solution. Alternatively, assuming you have built the Content Pipeline and verified that it works, you can just add references to the compiled assemblies of these projects. To do that, in the Solution Explorer, on each References entry in your main project and in its Content folder, right-click and select Add Reference. In the dialog box that appears, select the Browse tab, and browse to the assemblies of your Content Pipeline project (at AnimatedModelContentWin/bin/x86/Release/AnimatedModelContentWin.dll).

After referencing the content library and processor, add the AnimatedModel and AnimatedModelEffect classes to the XNA TPS project. Add the AnimatedModel class to the Shapes folder and the AnimatedModelEffect class to the Effects folder.

Finally, you should add the animated model assets (model, textures, and effects) of the player and NPCs to the XNA TPS Content entry in the Solution Explorer. In the Content project, you just need to create a new folder named Models in which to put all the animated model files. You should add the animated model effect to the Effects folder and its textures to the Textures folder. After adding all the assets to the project, remember to select your custom content processor for the animated model files, as done at the end of Chapter 12.

Sky

In a game, the sky is used to create a background that covers all the scene objects, giving the sensation of infinite scenery around the player. Besides that, the sky also helps to place the player in the scene, allowing the player to have a notion of the environment around him.

When we refer to the game's sky, we are talking about all the landscape surrounding the player. One way to create a landscape around the player would be to draw a large amount of objects around the scene, positioned far away from the player. However, the cost of drawing these objects in real time would be far too high. Furthermore, these models would be positioned at such a great distance that they would not present a high level of detail.

A common way game designers use to create the landscape is to construct a solid volume that covers the entire scene. This volume can be a box, called a *skybox*; a hemisphere, called *skydome*; or any other type of solid. The landscape around the player is then stored into textures that are mapped to the skybox or skydome. To give the feeling of an infinite horizon, the camera is always positioned in the center of the sky. Whenever the camera moves, the skybox or skydome should move with the camera, so the camera always remains in the center of the volume. This will create the illusion that the horizon is infinitely far away from the camera.

The landscape creation techniques work as follows:

Skybox: In the skybox, the sky is created as a box, containing six faces, where each face has a different texture, as illustrated in Figure 13-2. Special care needs to be taken so that the textures transition seamlessly from one to another, or the edges of the box will be visible, and the illusion of a far horizon will be gone. The created box covers the entire scene, and all its faces are oriented to the inside of the cube—because you view the cube from its interior, not its exterior. One of the skybox's advantages is that it is simple to construct, as it has only 12 triangles. A disadvantage is that its textures are not so easy to create and must remain static.

Skydome: In the skydome, the sky is created as a hemisphere using only one texture, and is positioned above the scene. Figure 13-3 shows a wireframe model of a skydome. One of the advantages of the skydome is that it is easy to animate its textures. For example, you could use two textures for the sky: one for its background and the other to draw a second layer effect, such as moving clouds. One of the disadvantages of the skydome is that it has a much more detailed mesh than a skybox, as can be seen in Figure 13-3.

In your game, you'll use a skydome to draw the scene's horizon, as you'll want to animate it. The skydome you'll use is a conventional 3D model, previously made in a modeling tool and processed by the Content Pipeline. This allows the sky model to be loaded and handled through XNA's Model class. Note that it is also possible to generate a sky model dynamically, instead of loading it.

Now you'll create the class to load, update, and draw the sky model: the SkyDome class. You should create the SkyDome class inside the Shapes folder.

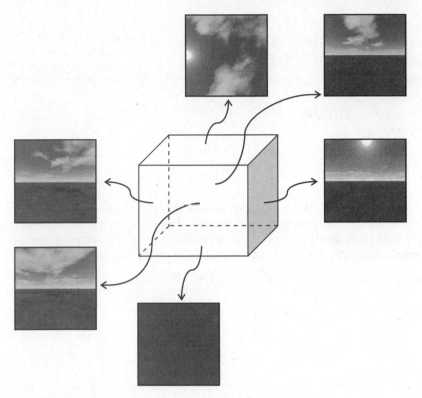

Figure 13-2. *A skybox*

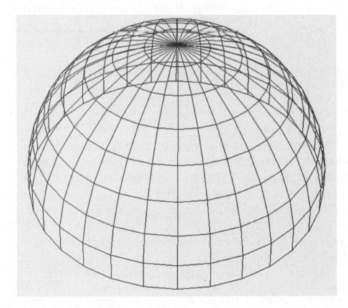

Figure 13-3. *A skydome wireframe model*

Loading the Sky

Because the skydome is an XNA Model, you simply use the content manager to load it. Following is the code for the Load method of the SkyDome class:

```
public void Load(string modelFileName)
{
    model = Content.Load<Model>(GameAssetsPath.MODELS_PATH
        + modelFileName);
}
```

Updating the Sky

Every time the Update method of the sky is called, you need to move its center position to the camera's position, ensuring that the camera remains positioned in the center of the sky. You can also rotate the sky model very slowly over the world's y axis, giving the impression of a moving horizon around the player. Following is the code for the Update method of the SkyDome class:

```
public override void Update(GameTime time)
{
    BaseCamera camera = cameraManager.ActiveCamera;

    // Center the camera in the SkyDome
    transformation.Translate = new Vector3(camera.Position.X,
        0.0f, camera.Position.Z);

    // Rotate the SkyDome slightly
    transformation.Rotate += new Vector3(0,
        (float)time.ElapsedGameTime.TotalSeconds * 0.5f, 0);

    base.Update(time);
}
```

Drawing the Sky

The skydome model has a BasicEffect linked to it, which you can use to draw it. As always, before rendering a model, you need to configure its effect. First, set the sky texture that you want to use in the model by means of basicEffect.Texture (this is necessary because no texture was imported with the sky model). Then, set the model's world and the camera's view and projection matrices to the basicEffect. Finally, draw the sky model.

Notice that it is important to disable the depth buffer before drawing the sky model; because the sky is the farthest drawing object, you don't need to store its depth. Also, if you draw the sky model with the depth buffer enabled, you would need to enlarge the far plane distance of your camera, which will cause precision problems when drawing other objects closer to the camera. Following is the code for the SetEffectMaterial and Draw methods used to draw the sky:

```
private void SetEffectMaterial(BasicEffect basicEffect)
{
    BaseCamera activeCamera = cameraManager.ActiveCamera;

    // Texture material
    basicEffect.Texture = textureMaterial.Texture;
    basicEffect.TextureEnabled = true;

    // Transformation
    basicEffect.World = transformation.Matrix;
    basicEffect.View = activeCamera.View;
    basicEffect.Projection = activeCamera.Projection;
}

public override void Draw(GameTime time)
{
    GraphicsDevice.RenderState.DepthBufferEnable = false;
    foreach (ModelMesh modelMesh in model.Meshes)
    {
        // We are only rendering models with BasicEffect
        foreach (BasicEffect basicEffect in modelMesh.Effects)
            SetEffectMaterial(basicEffect);

        modelMesh.Draw();
    }
    GraphicsDevice.RenderState.DepthBufferEnable = true;

    base.Draw(time);
}
```

Creating Helper Classes

In this section, you'll create some helper classes to manage the game input and settings, and to generate random values. You'll create all these classes inside the Helpers namespace.

Input Helper

Earlier, we noted that your game can be played using the keyboard or the Xbox 360 gamepad. The XNA Framework has all the classes that you need to manage the input through the keyboard, gamepad, or mouse (supported only in Windows). However, you will want to handle the keyboard and gamepad simultaneously in order to streamline the helper classes and create more robust code. In this regard, a helper class could be useful. Also, the XNA input classes lack some features, such as checking when a key is first pressed (pressed when it is released), which you can add to the input helper class. In this section, you'll create a helper class for the keyboard and gamepad input, named InputHelper.

Because you can play your game using the gamepad, you first map all the game actions to the gamepad, and then map the gamepad buttons to some keyboard keys. For example, you can define that the gamepad's A button is used to make the player jump. Then you can map the keyboard's spacebar to the gamepad's A button.

InputHelper Attributes and Constructor

The InputHelper class stores the state of the gamepad, the state of the keyboard, and the map of the gamepad buttons to the keyboard. The InputHelper class also stores the index of the current player, because each instance of the InputHelper class handles the input of only one player. So, if you have a two-player game, you need to have two InputHelper objects.

The current state and last state of the gamepad and keyboard are stored because you need them to check when a button or key is pressed for the first time. Following is the code for the attributes and constructor of the InputHelper class:

```
PlayerIndex playerIndex;

// Keyboard
KeyboardState keyboardState;
KeyboardState lastKeyboardState;
Dictionary<Buttons, Keys> keyboardMap;

// Gamepad
GamePadState gamePadState;
GamePadState lastGamePadState;

public InputHelper(PlayerIndex playerIndex)
    : this(playerIndex, null)
{
}

public InputHelper(PlayerIndex playerIndex,
    Dictionary<Buttons, Keys> keyboardMap)
{
    this.playerIndex = playerIndex;
    this.keyboardMap = keyboardMap;
}
```

The InputHelper constructor's parameters are the player index and the keyboard map. However, if you are not interested in using a keyboard, the class provides a version of the InputHelper method that takes only a PlayerIndex argument. This method calls the bottom InputHelper method by specifying null as second argument.

Updating the Input

To update the input, you need to save the last read state of the keyboard and gamepad and then read their new state. Note that in XNA 3.0, the GetState method of the Keyboard class receives the index of the current player. Following is the code for the Update method of the InputHelper class:

```
public void Update()
{
    lastKeyboardState = keyboardState;
    keyboardState = Keyboard.GetState(playerIndex);

    lastGamePadState = gamePadState;
    gamePadState = GamePad.GetState(playerIndex);
}
```

Checking Pressed Keys

In XNA 3.0, both the KeyboardState and the GamePadState have a method to check whether a button or a key was pressed. Because you're handling the input through the gamepad and keyboard, you need to check if the button or key was pressed on either of them, but you could avoid checking them both at the same time.

The InputHelper class allows checking if a gamepad button is pressed, but it internally checks whether the button was pressed on either the gamepad or on the keyboard. In this case, it first checks if the current player's gamepad is connected, and if so, it checks if a button was pressed on the gamepad. Otherwise, if the InputHelper class has a valid keyboard map, it will check if the keyboard key that is mapped to the gamepad button is pressed. This is done in the IsKeyPressed method of the InputHelper class:

```
public bool IsKeyPressed(Buttons button)
{
    bool pressed = false;

    if (gamePadState.IsConnected)
        pressed = gamePadState.IsButtonDown(button);
    else if (keyboardMap != null)
    {
        Keys key = keyboardMap[button];
        pressed = keyboardState.IsKeyDown(key);
    }
    return pressed;
}
```

Along with checking when a button is pressed, you also want to cover the possibility of a button being pressed for the first time. To do that, you can check if the desired button is pressed but was released in the previous update. Following is the code for the IsKeyJustPressed method of the InputHelper class:

```
public bool IsKeyJustPressed(Buttons button)
{
    bool pressed = false;

    if (gamePadState.IsConnected)
        pressed = (gamePadState.IsButtonDown(button) &&
            lastGamePadState.IsButtonUp(button));
```

```
        else if (keyboardMap != null)
        {
            Keys key = keyboardMap[button];
            pressed = (keyboardState.IsKeyDown(key) &&
                lastKeyboardState.IsKeyUp(key));
        }

        return pressed;
    }
```

Checking Analog Button State

You can use the IsKeyPressed and IsKeyJustPressed methods that you created for the InputHelper class to check whether a digital key is pressed or not. But if you try to use these methods to retrieve the state of the thumbsticks and triggers of the Xbox 360 gamepad, you'll just get a Boolean result, indicating whether the buttons are pressed or not. For thumbsticks, you need a more granular result in order to take full advantage of them and create the illusion of smooth motion.

In the XNA GamePadState class, the position of each thumbstick of the Xbox 360 controller is retrieved as a Vector2 object, and the triggers' state as a float value. In your InputHelper class, you'll create some methods to retrieve the state of the gamepad's thumbsticks in the same way it's done in the GamePadState class. Notice that you also need to properly handle the keyboard keys that are mapped to the thumbsticks. Following is the code for the GetLeftThumbStick method of the InputHelper class, used to retrieve the position of the gamepad's left thumbstick:

```
public Vector2 GetLeftThumbStick()
{
    Vector2 thumbPosition = Vector2.Zero;

    if (gamePadState.IsConnected)
        thumbPosition = gamePadState.ThumbSticks.Left;
    else if (keyboardMap != null)
    {
        if (keyboardState.IsKeyDown(
            keyboardMap[Buttons.LeftThumbstickUp]))
            thumbPosition.Y = 1;
        else if (keyboardState.IsKeyDown(
            keyboardMap[Buttons.LeftThumbstickDown]))
            thumbPosition.Y = -1;
        if (keyboardState.IsKeyDown(
            keyboardMap[Buttons.LeftThumbstickRight]))
            thumbPosition.X = 1;
        else if (keyboardState.IsKeyDown(
            keyboardMap[Buttons.LeftThumbstickLeft]))
            thumbPosition.X = -1;
    }
    return thumbPosition;
}
```

In the GetLeftThumbStick method, you take the same approach you did in the IsKeyPressed method: you first check if the gamepad is connected, and if so, you just return the desired value. Otherwise, you check the state of the keyboard keys that are mapped to the left thumbstick (up, down, left, and right) and return a Vector2 containing the resulting thumbstick position.

In addition to the GetLeftThumbStick method, you also need to create the GetRightThumbStick method to retrieve the position of the gamepad's right thumbstick. Following is the code for the GetRightThumbStick method:

```
public Vector2 GetRightThumbStick()
{
    Vector2 thumbPosition = Vector2.Zero;

    if (gamePadState.IsConnected)
        thumbPosition = gamePadState.ThumbSticks.Right;
    else if (keyboardMap != null)
    {
        if (keyboardState.IsKeyDown(
            keyboardMap[Buttons.RightThumbstickUp]))
            thumbPosition.Y = 1;
        else if (keyboardState.IsKeyDown(
            keyboardMap[Buttons.RightThumbstickDown]))
            thumbPosition.Y = -1;
        if (keyboardState.IsKeyDown(
            keyboardMap[Buttons.RightThumbstickRight]))
            thumbPosition.X = 1;
        else if (keyboardState.IsKeyDown(
            keyboardMap[Buttons.RightThumbstickLeft]))
            thumbPosition.X = -1;
    }

    return thumbPosition;
}
```

Settings Manager

You might want to configure different settings for your game for each computer on which the game is running, such as the screen resolution, the full screen mode, and the keyboard map. These settings can be stored and read from files, so you don't need to reconfigure your game every time you run it. To do that, you'll create some structures to store the game settings, and a helper class to help you store and read these settings from a file. The game settings will be read and saved from an XML file, for which the structures need to have the [Serializable] attribute. The XML format has the benefit of being human-readable and can be modified in any text editor.

Start the construction of the settings manager by creating a new class named SettingsManager in the Helpers namespace. Inside the file created for the SettingsManager class, create a struct named KeyboardSettings to store the keyboard map. Following is the definition of the KeyboardSettings struct:

```
[Serializable]
public struct KeyboardSettings
{
    public Keys A;
    public Keys B;
    public Keys X;
    public Keys Y;
    public Keys LeftShoulder;
    public Keys RightShoulder;
    public Keys LeftTrigger;
    public Keys RightTrigger;
    public Keys LeftStick;
    public Keys RightStick;
    public Keys Back;
    public Keys Start;

    public Keys DPadDown;
    public Keys DPadLeft;
    public Keys DPadRight;
    public Keys DPadUp;

    public Keys LeftThumbstickDown;
    public Keys LeftThumbstickLeft;
    public Keys LeftThumbstickRight;
    public Keys LeftThumbstickUp;
    public Keys RightThumbstickDown;
    public Keys RightThumbstickLeft;
    public Keys RightThumbstickRight;
    public Keys RightThumbstickUp;
}
```

In KeyboardSettings, you created an attribute of type Keys for each gamepad button that can be mapped to a keyboard key. Next, create the main game settings structure, named GameSettings. Following is the code for the GameSettings struct:

```
[Serializable]
public struct GameSettings
{
    public bool PreferredFullScreen;
    public int PreferredWindowWidth;
    public int PreferredWindowHeight;

    public KeyboardSettings[] KeyboardSettings;
}
```

The game settings structure stores the screen resolution, full-screen mode, and an array of keyboard settings, used to map the gamepad buttons to the keyboard.

Finally, you should create two methods inside the SettingsManager class to read and save the game settings. Because you don't need a specific instance of the SettingsManager class, you should make it and its methods static. Following is the code for the Read method of the SettingsManager class:

```
public static GameSettings Read(string settingsFilename)
{
    GameSettings gameSettings;
    Stream stream = File.OpenRead(settingsFilename);
    XmlSerializer serializer =
        new XmlSerializer(typeof(GameSettings));

    gameSettings = (GameSettings)serializer.Deserialize(stream);
    return gameSettings;
}
```

The Read method receives the name of the settings file to be read. It then uses the File class to open the file, and the XmlSerializer to transform the XML document into an object of the type GameSettings, and deserializes gameSettings into stream. You can save the GameSettings data into an XML file in a similar way that you used to read it. Following is the code for the Save method of the SettingsManager class:

```
public static void Save(string settingsFilename, GameSettings gameSettings)
{
    Stream stream = File.OpenWrite(settingsFilename);
    XmlSerializer serializer = new
        XmlSerializer(typeof(GameSettings));

    serializer.Serialize(stream, gameSettings);
}
```

Last, you'll create a method to transform the KeyboardSettings structure into a dictionary that maps a gamepad button to a key. The InputHelper class that you created needs this dictionary, instead of a KeyboardSettings, to map the gamepad buttons to the keyboard. Creating this dictionary is simple: add an entry to the dictionary for each gamepad button, mapping it to the key that is stored in the KeyboardSettings structure. Following is the code for the GetKeyboardDictionary, used to transform KeyboardSettings into a dictionary:

```
public static Dictionary<Buttons, Keys>
    GetKeyboardDictionary(KeyboardSettings keyboard)
{
    Dictionary<Buttons, Keys> dictionary =
        new Dictionary<Buttons, Keys>();

    dictionary.Add(Buttons.A, keyboard.A);
    dictionary.Add(Buttons.B, keyboard.B);
    dictionary.Add(Buttons.X, keyboard.X);
    dictionary.Add(Buttons.Y, keyboard.Y);
    dictionary.Add(Buttons.LeftShoulder, keyboard.LeftShoulder);
    dictionary.Add(Buttons.RightShoulder, keyboard.RightShoulder);
```

```
    dictionary.Add(Buttons.LeftTrigger, keyboard.LeftTrigger);
    dictionary.Add(Buttons.RightTrigger, keyboard.RightTrigger);
    dictionary.Add(Buttons.LeftStick, keyboard.LeftStick);
    dictionary.Add(Buttons.RightStick, keyboard.RightStick);
    dictionary.Add(Buttons.Back, keyboard.Back);
    dictionary.Add(Buttons.Start, keyboard.Start);
    dictionary.Add(Buttons.DPadDown, keyboard.DPadDown);
    dictionary.Add(Buttons.DPadLeft, keyboard.DPadLeft);
    dictionary.Add(Buttons.DPadRight, keyboard.DPadRight);
    dictionary.Add(Buttons.DPadUp, keyboard.DPadUp);
    dictionary.Add(Buttons.LeftThumbstickDown,
        keyboard.LeftThumbstickDown);
    dictionary.Add(Buttons.LeftThumbstickLeft,
        keyboard.LeftThumbstickLeft);
    dictionary.Add(Buttons.LeftThumbstickRight,
        keyboard.LeftThumbstickRight);
    dictionary.Add(Buttons.LeftThumbstickUp,
        keyboard.LeftThumbstickUp);
    dictionary.Add(Buttons.RightThumbstickDown,
        keyboard.RightThumbstickDown);
    dictionary.Add(Buttons.RightThumbstickLeft,
        keyboard.RightThumbstickLeft);
    dictionary.Add(Buttons.RightThumbstickRight,
        keyboard.RightThumbstickRight);
    dictionary.Add(Buttons.RightThumbstickUp,
        keyboard.RightThumbstickUp);

    return dictionary;
}
```

Random Helper

To help you generate random values and random positions over the game terrain—used to randomly position the enemies—you'll create a RandomHelper class inside the Helpers namespace. The RandomHelper class and all its attributes and methods will be static. To keep this example relatively simple, let's ignore obvious possibilities like NPCs spawning on top of each other, as this would require a more complex solution.

Inside the RandomHelper class, declare a public attribute of type Random, named RandomGenerator. The RandomGenerator will be used as the main random generator by all the game classes. Next, to generate a random position over the game terrain—constructed over the x and z axes—create a method named GeneratePositionXZ. Inside the GeneratePositionXZ method, you need to generate a random value for the x and z axes according to a distance parameter. To generate a random number, use the Random class's Next method. The Next method of the Random class generates a positive random value that is lower than the value passed as its parameter. Because the center of the game terrain is positioned at the scene origin in (0, 0, 0), your GeneratePositionXZ method must generate positive and negative values to cover the entire terrain. You can achieve this by subtracting the random values generated by half their maximum value. Following is the complete code for the RandomHelper class:

```
public static class RandomHelper
{
    public static Random RandomGenerator = new Random();

    public static Vector3 GeneratePositionXZ(int distance)
    {
        float posX = (RandomGenerator.Next(distance * 201)
            - distance * 100) * 0.01f;
        float posZ = (RandomGenerator.Next(distance * 201)
            - distance * 100) * 0.01f;

        return new Vector3(posX, 0, posZ);
    }
}
```

Creating the Game Logic

For each unit type in the game—player, player weapon, enemy (NPC)—you'll create a class in the GameLogic namespace. A game unit needs to store its attributes (for example: speed, hit points, damage, and so on) and its logic (states and actions). Besides the logic of the game units, you'll construct the main game logic, which defines the game controls and how the units are updated and drawn, outside the GameLogic namespace in the GameScreen class. You'll create the GameScreen class at the end of this chapter.

Before you start constructing the game logic classes, let's review some of the game play features described earlier in the chapter:

- The player will start the game equipped with a machine gun, ammunition, and the doable actions of running (forward and backward), jumping, and attacking (aiming and shooting).

- Each monster will be randomly walking around the map until it sees the player or is attacked by the player. When this happens, the monster will chase the player, and after approaching him, the monster will attack. Whenever the monster loses all its hit points, it will die. And if the player loses all hit points, the game will be over.

From the game play description, you can see that both the player and the enemies share some common attributes and actions, such as having hit points, moving over a terrain, being able to cause and receive damage, being drawn as animated models, and so on. Because of these common characteristics, you can create a generic base class for them, capable of storing the common attributes and methods they share. Then you create the player and enemy classes by extending this base class.

The Terrain Unit

In this section, you'll create the base class for the game units that are animated models. They should be able to move over the terrain, cause and receive damage. Create a new class in the GameLogic namespace and name it TerrainUnit. Begin constructing the TerrainUnit class by declaring some of the common attributes shared by the units, which are their hit points and speed:

```
// Basic attributes (life and speed)
int life;
int maxLife;
float speed;
```

You'll draw the TerrainUnit as an animated model using the AnimatedModel class defined in the previous chapter. Add an attribute of type AnimatedModel to your TerrainUnit class to store the TerrainUnit animated model. Next, declare an attribute of type int to store the current unit's animation reference, which you further need to properly control and change the unit's animation.

Each unit also needs a bounding box and bounding sphere volume used for collision detection, represented through the XNA's BoundingBox and BoundingSphere classes. The collision volumes of the unit are the collision volumes of its animated model, which are created by the animated model's content processor. Because the collision volumes of the animated model need to be moved as the unit moves around the map, you need an original copy of them inside the TerrainUnit class. To identify when the collision volumes need to be updated, create the needUpdateCollision flag:

```
// Animated model
AnimatedModel animatedModel;
int currentAnimationId;

// Collision volumes
BoundingBox boundingBox;
BoundingSphere boundingSphere;
bool needUpdateCollision;
```

Note that the animated model processor created in Chapter 12 doesn't create the collision volumes for the animated models, but in the "Unit Collision Volume" section you'll extend the animated model processor once again, creating a new one capable of generating the collision volumes for the models.

Each unit has two velocities: the linear velocity is used to update the unit's position (or translation), and the angular velocity is used to update the unit's orientation (or rotation). The angular and linear velocities are represented as a 3D vector. In the angular velocity, each component of this vector represents the angular velocity around the x, y, and z world axes. The last velocity that acts over the unit is caused by the gravity. The axis of gravity is globally defined as the world's y (up) axis (0, 1, 0). The velocity resulting from the gravity force may have a negative value (when the unit is falling) and a positive value (when the unit is jumping):

```
// Velocities and gravity
Vector3 linearVelocity;
Vector3 angularVelocity;
float gravityVelocity;
```

You store the unit's orientation similarly to the camera's orientation, using three orientation vectors: headingVec, strafeVec, and upVec. These vectors are oriented to the front, right side, and top of the unit, respectively:

```
// Unit coordinate system
Vector3 headingVec;
Vector3 strafeVec;
Vector3 upVec;
```

You use these vectors whenever you want to move a unit according to its axes. For example, if you wanted a unit to move backward, you would set its linear velocity by means of a negative headingVec value.

To identify when the unit is over the terrain or is alive, or if you need to adjust the unit's position to account for a jump, create some flags:

```
// Some flags
bool isOnTerrain;
bool isDead;
bool adjustJumpChanges;
```

Creating and Loading the Unit

The TerrainUnit class extends the DrawableGameComponent class, which needs a Game instance to be constructed. This means that the TerrainUnit constructor must receive a Game object as a parameter and use it in the constructor of its base class (the DrawableGameComponent). Its attributes are initialized inside the constructor of the TerrainUnit class. Following is the constructor code for the TerrainUnit class:

```
public TerrainUnit(Game game)
    : base(game)
{
    gravityVelocity = 0.0f;
    isOnTerrain = false;
    isDead = false;
    adjustJumpChanges = false;

    needUpdateCollision = true;
}
```

To load the unit's animated model, create a Load method. The Load method receives the animated model's file name, loads the model, positions the model above the terrain, and updates its orientation vectors. Following is the code for the Load method:

```
protected void Load(string unitModelFileName)
{
    animatedModel = new AnimatedModel(Game);
    animatedModel.Initialize();
    animatedModel.Load(unitModelFileName);

    // Put the player above the terrain
    UpdateHeight(0);
    isOnTerrain = true;

    NormalizeBaseVectors();
}
```

Making the Unit Jump

One of the unit's actions is jumping, which makes the unit move upward and then downward. The velocity that acts over the unit and makes it moves down is the gravity velocity. In the game, the gravity velocity is a negative scalar value that acts over the gravity axis, which points to the world's y (up) axis (0, 1, 0).

In order to make the unit jump, you could change the value of the gravity velocity that acts over it to a positive value, which makes the unit move upward. Then, while the unit is in the air, you slowly reduce the gravity velocity until it has a negative value again, which makes the unit move downward. Note that to make a smooth jump, you need to define a minimum and maximum value for the gravity velocity. So, when the unit is falling, its velocity decreases until it reaches its minimum value. For this example, you will skip the more complex inertial calculations that could provide a better illusion of real jumping, since the main aim here is to demonstrate the core principles at work and get you started coding in XNA.

While the unit is jumping, it moves faster than while it is walking. In this case, the camera's chase velocity is not enough to chase a unit while it jumps. To solve this problem, whenever a unit jumps, the camera's chase velocity is increased; when the unit reaches the ground, it is restored. You can also increase the unit's speed while it jumps, allowing it to jump bigger distances. Following is the code for the Jump method:

```
public void Jump(float jumpHeight)
{
    if (isOnTerrain)
    {
        // Update camera chase speed and unit speed
        ThirdPersonCamera camera = cameraManager.ActiveCamera
            as ThirdPersonCamera;
        camera.ChaseSpeed *= 4.0f;
        speed *= 1.5f;
        adjustJumpChanges = true;

        // Set the gravity velocity
        gravityVelocity = (float)GRAVITY_ACCELERATION *
            jumpHeight * 0.1f;
        isOnTerrain = false;
    }
}
```

Before the unit can jump, you need to check if it is positioned over the terrain, avoiding having the unit jump while it is in the air. The Jump method receives a parameter that is the height value that you want the unit to jump. Notice that after changing the camera's chase speed and unit speed, you set the adjustJumpChanges flag to true, reporting that these modifications need to be restored.

Updating the Unit's Height

The units created based on the TerrainUnit class are units that move only over the game terrain. These units need to have their height updated every time you update their position to ensure that they remain on the terrain. When a unit moves to a new position, the terrain's height in this new position could be equal to, higher, or lower than the unit's previous height, as shown in Figure 13-4.

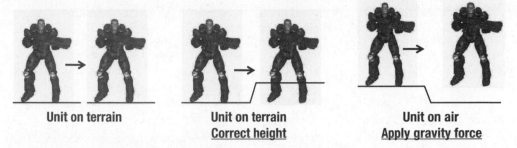

Figure 13-4. *Moving the unit over the terrain*

If the terrain's height at the new unit position is equal to or higher than the unit's current height, the unit is over the terrain. In this case, you need to set the unit's height as the terrain's height in that position. If the position is higher than the terrain's height, the unit is in the air, and you need to decrement the gravity velocity that acts over the unit. To update the unit's height according to its position over the terrain, you'll create the UpdateHeight method.

Note that to make sure that the unit is over the terrain, you need to verify that the gravity velocity is not positive. If the gravity velocity is positive, the unit is moving upward, and you cannot assume that it is over the terrain. Following is the code for the UpdateHeight method:

```
private void UpdateHeight(float elapsedTimeSeconds)
{
    // Get terrain height
    float terrainHeight = terrain.GetHeight(Transformation.Translate);
    Vector3 newPosition = Transformation.Translate;

    // Unit is on terrain
    if (Transformation.Translate.Y <= terrainHeight &&
        gravityVelocity <= 0)
    {
        // Put the unit over the terrain
        isOnTerrain = true;
        gravityVelocity = 0.0f;
        newPosition.Y = terrainHeight;

        // Restore the changes made when the unit jumped
        if (adjustJumpChanges)
        {
            ThirdPersonCamera camera = cameraManager.ActiveCamera
                as ThirdPersonCamera;
            camera.ChaseSpeed /= 4.0f;
            speed /= 1.5f;
            adjustJumpChanges = false;
        }
    }
```

```
    // Unit is in the air
    else
    {
        // Decrement the gravity velocity
        if (gravityVelocity > MIN_GRAVITY)
            gravityVelocity -= GRAVITY_ACCELERATION *
                elapsedTimeSeconds;
        // Apply the gravity velocity
        newPosition.Y = Math.Max(terrainHeight,
            Transformation.Translate.Y+gravityVelocity);
    }

    // Update the unit position
    Transformation.Translate = heightTranslate;
}
```

Whenever the unit is over the terrain, you check whether it is necessary to correct the changes that were made by the Jump method, through the adjustJumpChanges flag. Otherwise, if the gravityVelocity is bigger than the minimum gravity velocity, you decrement gravityVelocity and move the player. All transformations applied on the unit are made through the Transformation property, which actually modifies its animated model transformation. This way, whenever you draw the animated model, all the unit's transformations are already stored in it.

Updating the Unit

When updating the unit, you need to update its position and orientation (transformation), and its animated model. To update the unit's animated model, you just need to call the Update method of the AnimatedModel class. To update the unit's position, you calculate its displacement, based on its velocity and on the elapsed time since the last update, and add this displacement to its current position. The same is done to update its orientation, where the angular velocity is used to calculate the displacement on the unit's rotation. Following is the code for the Update and NormalizeBaseVectors methods:

```
public override void Update(GameTime time)
{
    // Update the animated model
    float elapsedTimeSeconds =
        (float)time.ElapsedGameTime.TotalSeconds;
    animatedModel.Update(time, Matrix.Identity);

    // Update the height and collision volumes if the unit moves
    if (linearVelocity != Vector3.Zero || gravityVelocity != 0.0f)
    {
        Transformation.Translate += linearVelocity *
            elapsedTimeSeconds * speed;
        UpdateHeight(elapsedTimeSeconds);
        needUpdateCollision = true;
    }
```

```
    // Update coordinate system when the unit rotates
    if (angularVelocity != Vector3.Zero)
    {
        Transformation.Rotate += angularVelocity *
            elapsedTimeSeconds * speed;
        NormalizeBaseVectors();
    }

    base.Update(time);
}

private void NormalizeBaseVectors()
{
    // Get the vectors from the animated model matrix
    headingVec = Transformation.Matrix.Forward;
    strafeVec = Transformation.Matrix.Right;
    upVec = Transformation.Matrix.Up;
}
```

In the Update method, you first update the unit's animated model, passing the elapsed time since the last update and a parent matrix used to transform the animated model. Because there is no need to transform the animated model, you can pass the identity matrix to update it. After that, you update the unit's linear and angular velocity. If the unit's linearVelocity or gravityVelocity is not zero, the unit is moving, and you need to call the UpdateHeight method to ensure that the unit is correctly positioned over the terrain. You also need to set the needUpdateCollision flag to true, to update the position of the unit's collision volumes.

Last, if the unit's angularVelocity is not zero, you call the NormalizeBaseVectors method to update its orientation vectors (heading, strafe, and up vectors) and make sure their lengths are exactly 1. You can extract these vectors from the transformation matrix of the unit's animated model.

Unit Collision Volume

You can check for collisions between the scene objects using some different approaches. One way is to check the intersection between all of their triangles. This method is the most accurate one, but it is also the most calculation-intensive. For example, to test the collision between two meshes having 2,000 triangles each, you would need to make 2000 × 2000 collision tests. This is more than you generally can afford.

Another method for checking for collisions between two models is to simply check whether their collision volumes collide. Collision volumes provide a faster, although more inaccurate, way of checking the intersection between objects. In your game, you'll use two different collision volumes for each unit—a box and a sphere—to check its collision against other objects. When the collision volume is a box, it's called a *bounding box*; when the volume is a sphere, it's called a *bounding sphere*. The bounding box of a model is the smallest box that fits around a model. The bounding sphere of a model is the smallest sphere that surrounds a model.

You can build the box you'll use for the collision aligned to the world axes. In this case, the box is called an *axis-aligned bounding box* (AABB). One of the advantages of the AABB is that the collision test with it is simple. However, the AABB can't be rotated, because it needs to keep its axes aligned with the world's axes. If the box used for collision is oriented with the unit's axes, it's then called an *object-oriented bounding box* (OOBB). A collision test using an OOBB is slower than one using an AABB, but the OOBB provides a box that always has the same orientation as the unit. Figure 13-5 illustrates the creation of an AABB and an OOBB for a unit with two different orientations.

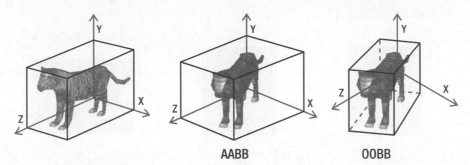

Figure 13-5. *Creating an AABB and an OOBB for a model. The AABB and the OOBB are the same when the model has the same orientation as the world (left). The AABB created for the new model orientation (middle). The OOBB created for the new model orientation (right).*

Because XNA already has a class to handle an AABB, you'll use it as the box volume for the unit. So, each unit will have an AABB and a bounding sphere volume, represented using XNA's BoundingBox and BoundingSphere classes.

The default model processor of the Content Pipeline generates a bounding sphere volume for each bone present in a model that is processed. In this way, you have a bounding sphere for each model's submesh. You can avoid testing the collision with each mesh of the model, by creating a global bounding sphere for the entire model. Also, because the default model processor doesn't generate a bounding box (AABB) volume, you need to generate one for the model.

You can create the bounding box and bounding sphere for the unit by extending its model processor, which is the AnimatedModelProcessor class created in Chapter 12. First, open the AnimatedModelProcessor class, which is inside the AnimatedModelProcessorWin project. Then create a method named GetModelVertices to extract all the vertices of the model's meshes. You'll use these vertices to create the collision volumes of the model, through the CreateFromPoints method of XNA's BoundingBox and BoundingSphere classes. The CreateFromPoints method creates a volume, making sure the volume contains all of the specified points. Following is the code for the GetModelVertices method:

```
private void GetModelVertices(NodeContent node,
    List<Vector3> vertexList)
{
    MeshContent meshContent = node as MeshContent;
    if (meshContent != null)
    {
        for (int i = 0; i < meshContent.Geometry.Count; i++)
        {
            GeometryContent geometryContent = meshContent.Geometry[i];
            for (int j = 0; j <
                geometryContent.Vertices.Positions.Count; j++)
```

```
                        vertexList.Add(geometryContent.Vertices.Positions[j]);
        }
    }

    foreach (NodeContent child in node.Children)
        GetModelVertices(child, vertexList);
}
```

In the `GetModelVertices` method, you travel through all the model nodes, starting at the root node, searching for the `MeshContent` nodes. The `MeshContent` nodes have the model's mesh data, from where you can extract the vertices of the mesh from its `Geometry` property. After processing a node, you need to call the `GetModelVertices` method for its children, ensuring that all nodes are processed. Note that all the vertices are stored in the `vertexList` variable of the type `List<Vector3>`.

You should call the `GetModelVertices` method at the end of the `Process` method of the `AnimatedModelProcessor` class, where you processed the model and extracted its skeletal animation data. You will use these vertices to generate the collision volumes for its model, after which you can store them in the model's `Tag` property. You can do that by adding the collision volumes to the dictionary you stored there, which already has the model's animation data. Following is the code that you can use to generate the collision volumes:

```
// Extract all model's vertices
List<Vector3> vertexList = new List<Vector3>();
GetModelVertices(input, vertexList);

// Generate the collision volumes
BoundingBox modelBoundBox = BoundingBox.CreateFromPoints(vertexList);
BoundingSphere modelBoundSphere =
    BoundingSphere.CreateFromPoints(vertexList);

// Store everything in a dictionary
Dictionary<string, object> tagDictionary =
    new Dictionary<string, object>();
tagDictionary.Add("AnimatedModelData", animatedModelData);
tagDictionary.Add("ModelBoudingBox", modelBoundBox);
tagDictionary.Add("ModelBoudingSphere", modelBoundSphere);

// Set the dictionary as the model tag property
model.Tag = tagDictionary;
return model;
```

Unit Collision Tests

Now, whenever you load a model using your custom-defined model processor, each model has a bounding box and a bounding sphere volume that you'll use to perform a few collision tests. To make things simple, you will perform only two different collision tests with the units in your game. The first verifies whether a ray collides with a unit, which is needed to check if a gunshot has hit the unit. The second verifies when the unit is inside the camera's visualization volume (the camera's frustum, as discussed in Chapter 10) and is used to avoid updating and drawing units that are not visible.

To check if a ray collides with a unit, you use the unit's bounding box, which is an AABB. The first thing you need to do is apply the same transformations made over the unit (translations and rotations) to the unit's AABB. This is necessary because you want to move the volume to the location of the model. Second, you need to make sure that the model is aligned with the world's axes to use its AABB, which prohibits you from rotating the unit.

To tackle this, instead of transforming the model's AABB, you can transform the ray that you are testing with the inverse transformation of the model. This guarantees that the AABB remains aligned with the world's axes. Following is the code for the BoxIntersects method of the TerrainUnit class, used to test the collision between a ray and the unit's AABB:

```
public float? BoxIntersects(Ray ray)
{
    Matrix inverseTransform = Matrix.Invert(Transformation.Matrix);
    ray.Position = Vector3.Transform(ray.Position,
        inverseTransform);
    ray.Direction = Vector3.TransformNormal(ray.Direction,
        inverseTransform);

    return animatedModel.BoundingBox.Intersects(ray);
}
```

In the BoxIntersects method, you first calculate the inverse transformation matrix of the unit and then transform the position and the direction of the ray by this matrix. You need to use the Transform method of the XNA's Vector3 class to transform the ray's start position because it is a 3D point, and the TransformNormal method to transform the ray's direction because it is a vector (which should not be affected by the translation contained in the transformation). After that, you can use the Intersects method of the bounding volume to do the collision test between the box and the ray.

Now, to verify if a unit is found inside the camera's frustum, you use the unit's bounding sphere. In this case, a collision test with the unit's bounding sphere is simpler, and the precision is not very important. To test the collision between the unit's bounding sphere and the camera's frustum, you need to use only the Intersects method of the XNA's BoundingSphere class:

```
boundingSphere.Intersects(activeCamera.Frustum);
```

Finally, whenever the unit moves, you must update its bounding sphere. To update the unit's bounding sphere, you just need to translate it, because a rotation has little effect on a sphere. Following is the code for the UpdateCollision method used to update the collision solids:

```
private void UpdateCollision()
{
    // Update bounding sphere
    boundingSphere = animatedModel.BoundingSphere;
    boundingSphere.Center += Transformation.Translate;

    needUpdateCollision = false;
}
```

Receiving Damage

To allow the unit to receive damage, you'll create the ReceiveDamage method, which receives the damage intensity as a parameter. The code for the ReceiveDamage method follows:

```
public virtual void ReceiveDamage(int damageValue)
{
    life = Math.Max(0, life - damageValue);
    if (life == 0)
        isDead = true;
}
```

When the unit's hit points reach zero, the isDead flag is marked as true. In this case, you can avoid updating this unit. The ReceiveDamage method should be virtual, allowing the units that extend the TerrainUnit class to override this method and, for example, play a death animation for the unit.

Changing Animations

During the game, every time a unit changes its current action (or state), you need to change its animation. For example, the animation used when the unit is idle is different from the animation used when the unit is running. The unit's animated model (AnimatedModel class) has an array that stores all the unit's animations. You can change the unit's animation manually, but to do that, you need to go over all its animations, searching for the desired animation. This is necessary because you don't know which animations the unit has, or in which order they were stored.

To ease the swap between animations, you can create an enumeration for the unit's animations inside each class that extends the TerrainUnit, where each enumeration lists the available animations of the unit's animated model in the order they were stored. For example, the Player class has an enumeration called PlayerAnimations and the Enemy class has an enumeration called EnemyAnimations, as shown in the following code:

```
public enum PlayerAnimations
{
    Idle = 0,
    Run,
    Aim,
    Shoot
}

public enum EnemyAnimations
{
    Idle = 0,
    Run,
    Bite,
    TakeDamage,
    Die
}
```

You use these enumerations to change the current animation of the model. To change the unit's animation, you create the SetAnimation method in the TerrainUnit class. In the SetAnimation method, you set the model's current animation using an integer value, which is the index of the animation inside the animation's array, stored inside the AnimatedModel class. However, because you don't know the index of the animations, this method is protected so only the classes that extend the TerrainUnit class (Player and Enemy) can use it. Then, in the Player and Enemy classes, you can change the model animation using the PlayerAnimations and EnemyAnimations enumerations. Following is the code for the SetAnimation method of the TerrainUnit class:

```
protected void SetAnimation(int animationId,
    bool reset, bool enableLoop, bool waitFinish)
{
    if (reset || currentAnimationId != animationId)
    {
        if (waitFinish && !AnimatedModel.IsAnimationFinished)
            return;

        AnimatedModel.ActiveAnimation =
            AnimatedModel.Animations[animationId];
        AnimatedModel.EnableAnimationLoop = enableLoop;
        currentAnimationId = animationId;
    }
}
```

The other parameters of the SetAnimation method allow the animation to be reset or looped, or prevent it from being changed before it has finished. Whenever an animation is set, its identifier is stored in the currentAnimationId variable and is used to prevent the current animation from being reset, unless you desire that, by setting the reset parameter to true. Following is the code for the SetAnimation method of the Player class:

```
// Player class
public class Player : TerrainUnit
{
    ...

    public void SetAnimation(PlayerAnimations animation,
        bool reset, bool enableLoop, bool waitFinish)
    {
        SetAnimation((int)animation, reset, enableLoop, waitFinish);
    }
}
```

And following is the code for the SetAnimation method of the Enemy class:

```
// Enemy class
public class Enemy : TerrainUnit
{
    ...
```

```
public void SetAnimation(EnemyAnimations animation,
    bool reset, bool enableLoop, bool waitFinish)
{
    SetAnimation((int)animation, reset, enableLoop, waitFinish);
}
}
```

The SetAnimation methods defined in the Player and Enemy classes allow the unit's animation to be easily switched and guarantee that a valid animation will always be set. The following code example illustrates how you would change the animation in the Player and Enemy classes:

```
player.SetAnimation(PlayerAnimations.Idle, false, true, false);
enemy.SetAnimation(EnemyAnimations.Run, false, true, false);
```

Drawing the Unit

To draw the unit, you just need to call the Draw method of the unit's animated model, which was defined in the previous chapter. Because all the unit transformations are stored directly in its animated model, you don't need to configure anything else. Following is the code for the Draw method of the TerrainUnit class:

```
public override void Draw(GameTime time)
{
    animatedModel.Draw(time);
}
```

Unit Types

The next classes you'll create are Player, Enemy, and PlayerWeapon. You'll use each of these classes to create (or instantiate) different types of units. For example, your game may have many types of enemies (created using the Enemy class), where each enemy may have specific attributes, such as velocity, hit points, and so on. To tackle this, you can create a class that stores the available types of units in the game and the attributes of each unit type.

To store the available types of a unit and its attributes, create a static class named UnitTypes. Although in this game you have only one type of each unit in your game—one type of player (a marine), one type of enemy (an alien spider), and one type of weapon—the UnitTypes class allows you to add new unit types to the game easily.

In the UnitTypes class, first create an enumeration with all the types of players. For each type of player, you need to store its animated model file name, hit points, and velocity, as shown in the following code:

```
// Player
// -----------------------------------------------------------------
public enum PlayerType
{
    Marine
}
```

```
public static string[] PlayerModelFileName = { "PlayerMarine" };
public static int[] PlayerLife = { 100 };
public static float[] PlayerSpeed = { 1.0f };
```

Next, create an enumeration with all the types of player weapons. For each player weapon, you need to store its animated model file name, its maximum amount of ammunition, and the amount of damage inflicted by its shot:

```
// Player Weapons
// -------------------------------------------------------------------
public enum PlayerWeaponType
{
    MachineGun
}

public static string[] PlayerWeaponModelFileName =
    {"WeaponMachineGun"};
public static int[] BulletDamage = { 12 };
public static int[] BulletsCount = { 250 };
```

Finally, you create an enumeration with all the types of enemies, where for each enemy you should store the name of its animated model, hit points, velocity, distance of perception, distance of attack, and damage. The distance of perception is the distance at which the enemy perceives the player and starts to chase him (sometimes referred to as *aggro range*), while the distance of attack is the distance within which the enemy is near enough to attack the player.

```
// Enemies
// -------------------------------------------------------------------
public enum EnemyType
{
    Beast
}

public static string[] EnemyModelFileName = { "EnemyBeast" };
public static int[] EnemyLife = { 300 };
public static float[] EnemySpeed = { 1.0f };
public static int[] EnemyPerceptionDistance = { 140 };
public static int[] EnemyAttackDistance = { 25 };
public static int[] EnemyAttackDamage = { 13 };
```

Player Weapon

Now you'll create the PlayerWeapon class, which is one of the simplest logic classes in your game. Just as in the TerrainUnit class, the player's weapon is drawn as an animated model. Although the weapon doesn't have any animation, it does have three bones:

- The first is the root bone, which doesn't have any transformation.

- The second bone is the weapon's butt bone, used to attach the weapon to the player's hand.

- The third bone is placed at the weapon's muzzle and is used as the starting point for the bullet shot.

Figure 13-6 illustrates the player's weapon and the weapon's bones.

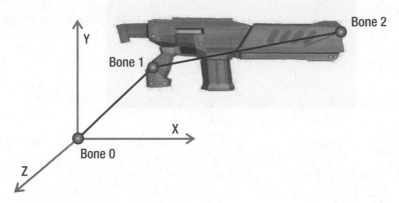

Figure 13-6. *Player's weapon and its bones*

You begin constructing the PlayerWeapon class by declaring its attributes. The PlayerWeapon class needs to store its weapon type, because you might have some different types of weapons in the game. You'll use the PlayerWeaponType enumeration of the UnitsType class to store the weapon type. The PlayerWeapon also stores other attributes, such as the current and maximum number of bullets, and the bullet damage:

```
UnitsType.PlayerWeaponType weaponType;
int maxBullets;
int bulletsCount;
int bulletDamage;
```

In the PlayerWeapon class, you need to store the position and direction in which a bullet exits the weapon (the fire position and direction). You'll use the fire position and direction to trace the shot ray, used to check whether the bullet hits an object. Finally, you need to declare an AnimatedModel for the weapon:

```
AnimatedModel weaponModel;
Vector3 firePosition;
Vector3 targetDirection;
```

Creating the Player Weapon

The PlayerWeapon class extends the DrawableGameComponent class. So, the PlayerWeapon constructor receives a Game (needed by its base class constructor) and a PlayerWeaponType as the constructor parameters. You use the PlayerWeaponType parameter to define which type of weapon you want to create. Inside the class constructor, the weapon's attributes are queried from the UnitTypes class, according to its weapon type. Following is the constructor code for the PlayerWeapon class:

```
public PlayerWeapon(Game game, UnitTypes.PlayerWeaponType weaponType)
    : base(game)
{
    this.weaponType = weaponType;
```

```
    // Weapon configuration
    bulletDamage = UnitTypes.BulletDamage[(int)weaponType];
    bulletsCount = UnitTypes.BulletsCount[(int)weaponType];
    maxBullets = bulletsCount;
}
```

Loading the Player Weapon

You can override the LoadContent method of the PlayerWeapon base class to load the weapon's animated model. You get the file name of the weapon's animated model from the UnitTypes class. Following is the code for the LoadContent method:

```
protected override void LoadContent()
{
    // Load weapon model
    weaponModel = new AnimatedModel(Game);
    weaponModel.Initialize();
    weaponModel.Load(PlayerWeaponModelFileName[(int)weaponType]);

    base.LoadContent();
}
```

Updating the Weapon

To update the weapon, you create a new Update method, which receives a GameTime and a Matrix. You use the GameTime to retrieve the elapsed time since the last update, and the Matrix class to update the weapon model according to a parent bone. The weapon's parent bone is the player's hand bone, as you saw in the previous chapter. In this case, the weapon is translated and rotated to the player's hand. You update the weapon by calling the Update method of its animated model and passing the received GameTime and parent Matrix.

After updating the weapon's animated model, the weapon's fire position—which is the position of its third bone, shown in Figure 13-6—is stored in the firePosition attribute. Following is the code for the Update method:

```
public void Update(GameTime time, Matrix parentBone)
{
    weaponModel.Update(time, parentBone);
    firePosition = BonesAbsolute[WEAPON_AIM_BONE].Translation;
}
```

Finally, to draw the weapon, you just need to call the Draw method of its AnimatedModel.

Player

In this section, you'll create the Player class, which has the player's attributes and logic. The Player class extends and adds some functionalities to the TerrainUnit class. Figure 13-7 shows the marine model used as the game player.

Figure 13-7. *The marine model used in this game (courtesy of Carlos Augusto, http://www.floatbox.com.br)*

In the `Player` class, you first store the type of player you're creating, because you might have some different types of players in the game. You also store the player's weapon, because it is updated according to the player. For example, the player's weapon is always positioned in the player's right hand.

```
// Player type
UnitTypes.PlayerType playerType;
// Player weapon
PlayerWeapon playerWeapon;
```

Next, declare two attributes to store and control the transformations made over the waist bone of the player's animated model. You can use this transformation to rotate the player's torso around his waist, in addition to the current animation of the character.

```
// Waist bone
float rotateWaistBone;
float rotateWaistBoneVelocity;
```

Updating the Camera's Chase Position

The camera's default chase position is the center of the player's bounding sphere. In this way, the camera is always focusing on the center of the player's model. You can make the camera focus on other parts of the player, such as his upper body, by changing the camera's chase position through an offset vector. Figure 13-8 illustrates the offset vectors used to modify the camera's chase position.

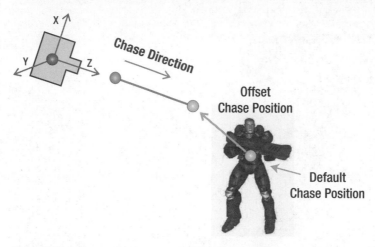

Figure 13-8. *Changing the camera's default chase position using the player's chase vector*

To change the camera's chase position, add a new attribute of type Vector3[] to the Player class, and name it chaseOffsetPosition. This attribute stores an offset vector for each camera in the scene:

```
// Camera chase position
Vector3[] chaseOffsetPosition;
```

Note that you need to manually set the camera offset vectors for the player character when he is created. When the player character is updated, you need to update the position and direction in which the camera chases him. To do that, create the UpdateChasePosition method inside the Player class. You can update the camera's chase position by setting it to the center of the player's bounding sphere summed with the camera's offset, which is stored in the player's chaseOffsetPosition attribute. And you can update the camera's chase direction by setting it as the player's heading vector. Note that the camera offset vector is oriented according to the player's orientation vectors (headingVec, strafeVec, and upVec vectors), and not according to the world axes. Following is the code for the UpdateChasePosition method:

```
private void UpdateChasePosition()
{
    ThirdPersonCamera camera = cameraManager.ActiveCamera
        as ThirdPersonCamera;
    if (camera != null)
    {
        // Get camera offset position for the active camera
        Vector3 cameraOffset =
            chaseOffsetPosition[cameraManager.ActiveCameraIndex];
        // Get the model center
        Vector3 center = BoundingSphere.Center;

        // Calculate chase position and direction
        camera.ChasePosition = center +
            cameraOffset.X * StrafeVector +
            cameraOffset.Y * UpVector +
            cameraOffset.Z * HeadingVector;
        camera.ChaseDirection = HeadingVector;
    }
}
```

Attaching a Weapon to the Player

To be able to attach a weapon to the player, create the AttachWeapon method. This method receives the type of weapon to be attached as a parameter. Inside the AttachWeapon method, create and initialize a new PlayerWeapon for the player. Following is the code for the AttachWeapon method:

```
public void AttachWeapon(EntityTypes.PlayerWeaponType weaponType)
{
    playerWeapon = new PlayerWeapon(Game, weaponType);
    playerWeapon.Initialize();
}
```

Aiming Objects

Since the player should be able to aim anywhere in the scenery, the player must be able to move his weapon's aim to the sides and also up and down. The player's weapon is connected to the player character through a bone in the weapon and a bone in the player character's right hand. You can make the player aim to the sides by rotating the player character around his y (up) axis, but you can't make the player aim up and down by rotating the player character around his x (right) axis, because that would visually detach the player model's feet from the floor. To solve this, instead of rotating the entire player model, you rotate only the player model's upper body around his waist bone. Figure 13-9 illustrates the rotation being applied over the waist bone of the player.

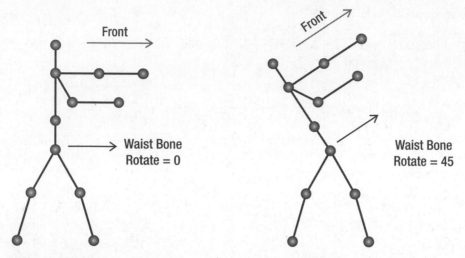

Figure 13-9. *Rotating the waist bone of the player's model*

You use the rotateWaistBone and rotateWaistBoneVelocity attributes of the Player class to apply a rotation over the player character's waist bone (see Chapter 12 for details on this technique). The rotateWaistBone attribute stores the current waist bone rotation, and the rotateWaistBoneVelocity attribute stores the velocity in which the waist bone is currently being rotated. You can modify the rotateWaistBoneVelocity through the player's RotateWaistVelocity property. To update the player's waist bone's rotation, you create the UpdateWaistBone method with the following code:

```
static float MAX_WAIST_BONE_ROTATE = 0.50f;
static int WAIST_BONE_ID = 2;

public float RotateWaistVelocity
{
    get { return rotateWaistBoneVelocity; }
    set { rotateWaistBoneVelocity = value; }
}

private void UpdateWaistBone(float elapsedTimeSeconds)
{
    if (rotateWaistBoneVelocity != 0.0f)
    {
        rotateWaistBone += rotateWaistBoneVelocity *
            elapsedTimeSeconds;
        rotateWaistBone = MathHelper.Clamp(rotateWaistBone,
            -MAX_WAIST_BONE_ROTATE, MAX_WAIST_BONE_ROTATE);
```

```
    // Rotate waist bone
    Matrix rotate = Matrix.CreateRotationZ(rotateWaistBone);
    AnimatedModel.BonesTransform[WAIST_BONE_ID] = rotate;
    }
}
```

Note that you're clamping the rotateWaistBone value to a range between -MAX_WAIST_ BONE_ROTATE and MAX_WAIST_BONE_ROTATE. The index of the player character's waist bone is stored in the WAIST_BONE_ID attribute, and the waist bone is rotated around its z axis.

Updating the Player

To update the player, you'll override the Update method of the player's base class (TerrainUnit). In the Update method, you first update the transformation of the player's waist bone. Then you can call the Update method of its base class, which updates the player's position and animated model. You must call the Update method of the player's base class after the player's waist bone has been transformed, to let the current animation take the new waist bone configuration into account. After that, you need to call the UpdateChasePosition method to update the camera's chase position and direction, and finally update the player's weapon.

You update the player's weapon by calling the weapon's Update method and passing the player's right hand bone as the weapon's parent bone. In this way, the weapon is updated according to the player's right hand. You also need to set the weapon's target direction as the player's front direction (as illustrated in Figure 13-9). Note that you need to transform the player's right hand bone by the player's transformation matrix before using it to update the player's weapon. Following is the code for the player's Update methods:

```
public override void Update(GameTime time)
{
    // Update the player's waist bone
    float elapsedTimeSeconds = (float)time.ElapsedGameTime.TotalSeconds;
    UpdateWaistBone(elapsedTimeSeconds);

    // Update player's base class
    // It's where the player's position and animated model are updated
    base.Update(time);
    // Update camera chase position
    UpdateChasePosition();

    // Update player weapon
    Matrix transformedHand = AnimatedModel.BonesAnimation[RIGHT_HAND_BONE_ID] *
        Transformation.Matrix;
    playerWeapon.Update(time, transformedHand);
    playerWeapon.TargetDirection = HeadingVector + UpVector * rotateWaistBone;
}
```

Enemy

The Enemy class is the one that has the enemy NPC's logic and attributes. Figure 13-10 shows the spider model used as an enemy in the game.

Figure 13-10. *An alien spider model (courtesy of Psionic, http://www.psionic3d.co.uk)*

Unlike the player, the enemy is computer-controlled, so you need to implement its AI. The enemy's AI is simple, with only four different states: Wandering, Chasing Player, Attacking Player, and Dead. Figure 13-11 shows the diagram of the AI built for the enemies.

In the AI diagram shown in Figure 13-11, each circle represents a different enemy state, and the arrows represent the actions that make an enemy change its state. The enemy's AI starts in the Wandering state. In this state, the enemy keeps moving around the map randomly looking for the player. Whenever the enemy sees the player or gets shot by the player, it changes its state to Chasing Player. In the Chasing Player state, the enemy moves closer to the player until it is near enough to attack the player. When that happens, the enemy state is altered to Attacking Player. In this state, the enemy attacks the player successively until the player dies or the player runs. If the player tries to run away from the enemy, the enemy's state is changed back to Chasing Player. Notice that once the enemy starts to chase the player, the enemy stays in a cycle between the states Chasing Player and Attacking Player, not returning to the Wandering state.

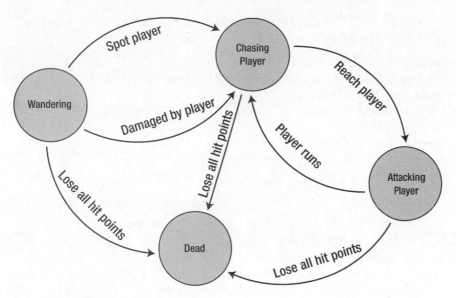

Figure 13-11. *Enemy AI diagram*

Each enemy has an attribute to store its current state, among an enumeration of possible states.

```
// Possible enemy states
public enum EnemyState
{
    Wander = 0,
    ChasePlayer,
    AttackPlayer,
    Dead
}

// Current enemy state (default = Wander)
EnemyState state;
```

For each one of the possible enemy states, you'll declare some attributes and create a method to execute this state. To control the transitions between the enemy states, you'll override the Update method of its base class.

Updating the Enemy

The enemy's Update method manages the transition between the enemy states. For every arrow in the AI state diagram shown in Figure 13-11, there must be a condition in the Update method.

In the beginning of the Update method, you calculate the enemy's chaseVector, which contains the direction from the enemy's position to the player's position. You use the length of this vector to check the distance between the enemy and the player. Then, for each player's state, you check if you can execute this state or need to change it to a new state. Note that all enemies have a reference to the Player class, which is used to obtain the player's current position. Following is the Update method's code:

```
public override void Update(GameTime time)
{
    // Calculate chase vector every time
    chaseVector = player.Transformation.Translate -
        Transformation.Translate;
    float distanceToPlayer = chaseVector.Length();

    switch (state)
    {
        case EnemyState.Wander:
            // Enemy perceives or is hit by the player - Change state
            if (isHit || distanceToPlayer < perceptionDistance)
                state = EnemyState.ChasePlayer;
            else
                Wander(time);
            break;

        case EnemyState.ChasePlayer:
            // Enemy is near enough to attack - Change state
            if (distanceToPlayer <= attackDistance)
            {
                state = EnemyState.AttackPlayer;
                nextActionTime = 0;
            }
            else
                ChasePlayer(time);
            break;

        case EnemyState.AttackPlayer:
            // Player flees - Change state
            if (distanceToPlayer > attackDistance * 2.0f)
                state = EnemyState.ChasePlayer;
            else
                AttackPlayer(time);
            break;

        default:
            break;
    }

    base.Update(time);
}
```

Wandering

In the Wandering state, the enemy walks randomly through the map, without a specific goal. To execute this action, you need to generate random positions over the map within a radius from the enemy's actual position and make the enemy move to these positions. Following are the attributes of the Enemy class used by the Wandering state:

```
static int WANDER_MAX_MOVES = 3;
static int WANDER_DISTANCE = 70;
static float WANDER_DELAY_SECONDS = 4.0f;

static float MOVE_CONSTANT = 35.0f;
static float ROTATE_CONSTANT = 100.0f;

// Wander
int wanderMovesCount;
Vector3 wanderStartPosition;
Vector3 wanderPosition;
```

The WANDER_MAX_MOVES variable defines the number of random movements that the enemy makes until it returns to its initial position, and the wanderMovesCount variable stores the number of movements that the unit has already made. You can use these variables to restrict the distance that the enemy could reach from its initial position, forcing it to return to its start position after a fixed number of random movements. Besides that, the WANDER_DELAY_SECONDS variable stores the delay time between each movement of the unit. The WANDER_DISTANCE variable stores the minimum distance that the unit walks in each movement, and the variables wanderStartPosition and wanderPosition store the enemy's initial position and destination while in the Wandering state, respectively. Finally, MOVE_CONSTANT and ROTATE_CONSTANT store a constant value used to move and rotate the enemy, respectively.

To execute the enemy's Wandering state, you'll create the Wander method. In the Wander method, you first check if the enemy has already reached its destination position, which is stored in the wanderPosition attribute. To do that, you create a vector from the enemy's position to its destination and use the length of this vector to check the distance between them. If the distance is below a defined epsilon value (for example, 10.0), the enemy has reached its destination, and a new destination must be generated:

```
// Calculate wander vector on X, Z axis
Vector3 wanderVector = wanderPosition - Transformation.Translate;
wanderVector.Y = 0.0f;
float wanderLength = wanderVector.Length();

// Reached the destination position
if (wanderVector.Length() < DISTANCE_EPSILON)
{
    // Generate a new wander position
}
```

In the preceding code, when an enemy is created, its first destination position is equal to its start position.

If the number of random movements the enemy makes is lower than the maximum number of consecutive random movements that it could make, its new destination position will be a randomly generated position. Otherwise, the next enemy destination will be its starting position.

```
// Generate a new random position
if (wanderMovesCount < WANDER_MAX_MOVES)
{
    wanderPosition = Transformation.Translate +
        RandomHelper.GeneratePositionXZ(WANDER_DISTANCE);
    wanderMovesCount++;
}
// Go back to the start position
else
{
    wanderPosition = wanderStartPosition;
    wanderMovesCount = 0;
}

// Next time wander
nextActionTime = (float)time.TotalGameTime.TotalSeconds +
    WANDER_DELAY_SECONDS + WANDER_DELAY_SECONDS *
    (float)RandomHelper.RandomGenerator.NextDouble();
```

The enemy's random destination position is generated through the GeneratePositionXZ method of your RandomHelper class. After generating the enemy's new destination, you also generate a random time when the enemy should start moving to its new destination so that it does not appear that all the enemies are moving in unison, which would ruin the game's realism. Following is the complete code for the Wander method of the Enemy class:

```
private void Wander(GameTime time)
{
    // Calculate wander vector on X, Z axis
    Vector3 wanderVector = wanderPosition - Transformation.Translate;
    wanderVector.Y = 0.0f;
    float wanderLength = wanderVector.Length();

    // Reached the destination position
    if (wanderLength < DISTANCE_EPSILON)
    {
        SetAnimation(EnemyAnimations.Idle, false, true, false);

        // Generate a new random position
        if (wanderMovesCount < WANDER_MAX_MOVES)
        {
            wanderPosition =  Transformation.Translate +
                RandomHelper.GeneratePositionXZ(WANDER_DISTANCE);
            wanderMovesCount++;
        }
```

```
    // Go back to the start position
    else
    {
        wanderPosition = wanderStartPosition;
        wanderMovesCount = 0;
    }

    // Next time wander
    nextActionTime = (float)time.TotalGameTime.TotalSeconds +
        WANDER_DELAY_SECONDS + WANDER_DELAY_SECONDS *
        (float)RandomHelper.RandomGenerator.NextDouble();
}

// Wait for the next action time
if ((float)time.TotalGameTime.TotalSeconds > nextActionTime)
{
    wanderVector *= (1.0f / wanderLength);
    Move(wanderVector);
}
}
```

At the end of the Wander method, you check if the time for the next wander action has arrived. In this case, you normalize the wanderVector, which contains the direction from the enemy to its destination, and makes the enemy move in this direction through the Move method.

You'll create the Move method to move the enemy from its original position using an arbitrary direction vector. You can move the enemy by setting its linear velocity as the desired direction vector, inside the Move method. Remember that the enemy's position is updated according to its linear velocity by the Update method's base class (TerrainUnit). While moving the unit, you also need to set its angular velocity, heading the unit in the same direction it is moving. Following is the code for the Move method:

```
private void Move(Vector3 direction)
{
    // Change enemy's animation
    SetAnimation(EnemyAnimations.Run, false, true,
        (CurrentAnimation == EnemyAnimations.TakeDamage));
    // Set the new linear velocity
    LinearVelocity = direction * MOVE_CONSTANT;

    // Angle between heading and move direction
    float radianAngle = (float)Math.Acos(
        Vector3.Dot(HeadingVector, direction));
    if (radianAngle >= 0.1f)
    {
        // Find short side to rotate
        // Clockwise or counterclockwise
        float sideToRotate = Vector3.Dot(StrafeVector, direction);
```

```
            Vector3 rotationVector = new Vector3(0, ROTATE_CONSTANT *
                radianAngle, 0);

            if (sideToRotate > 0)
                AngularVelocity = -rotationVector;
            else
                AngularVelocity = rotationVector;
        }
    }
```

In the Move method, you first activate the running animation and set the linear velocity of the enemy as its direction parameter multiplied by the MOVE_CONSTANT variable. Next, you calculate the angle between the enemy's heading vector and its direction vector. You need this angle to rotate the unit and head it in the same direction it is moving. You can use the Dot method of XNA's Vector3 class to get the cosine of the angle between the enemy's heading vector and its direction vector, and the Acos method of the Math class to get the angle between these vectors from its cosine. After calculating the angle between the enemy's heading and direction, you still need to know from which side to rotate the unit: clockwise or counterclockwise. For example, you can find that the angle between the enemy's heading and direction is 90 degrees, but you still don't know whether it should be rotated clockwise or counterclockwise.

You can find the correct side to rotate the enemy by calculating the cosine osf the angle between the enemy's strafe vector—which is perpendicular to the heading vector—and its direction vector. If the cosine is positive, you need to apply a negative rotation on the enemy (to its right), making it rotate clockwise; otherwise, you need to apply a positive rotation, making it rotate counterclockwise (to its left). The rotation is set as the enemy's AngularVelocity and is multiplied by the ROTATE_CONSTANT variable.

Chasing Player

In the Chasing Player state, the enemy needs to move to the player's current position. You can do this by making the enemy move through the chaseVector vector, which is the direction from the enemy to the player, and is calculated in the enemy's Update method. Following is the code for the ChasePlayer method:

```
private void ChasePlayer(GameTime time)
{
    Vector3 direction = chaseVector;
    direction.Normalize();
    Move(direction);
}
```

Attacking Player

In the Attacking Player state, the enemy keeps attacking the player character successively, causing damage to him. To make the enemy do that, you can simply execute the ReceiveDamage method of the Player instance and wait for the next time to attack. The attributes that you need to create to handle the Attacking Player state are the delay time in seconds between each attack and the time at which the enemy can execute a new attack action:

```
float nextActionTime;
```

Following is the code for the `AttackPlayer` method:

```
private void AttackPlayer(GameTime time)
{
    float elapsedTimeSeconds = (float)time.TotalGameTime.TotalSeconds;
    if (elapsedTimeSeconds > nextActionTime)
    {
        // Set attacking animation
        SetAnimation(EnemyAnimations.Bite, false, true, false);

        // Next attack time
        player.ReceiveDamage(attackDamage);
        nextActionTime = elapsedTimeSeconds + ATTACK_DELAY_SECONDS;
    }
}
```

Finishing the Game Engine

At this point, you have created all the game engine classes, helper classes, and almost all the game logic classes. Now you need to create a class to control the main game logic, and some classes to store and create the game levels. You also need to create the main game class that extends the XNA `Game` class. You'll create all these classes in the following sections.

Game Level

Each game level is composed of a fixed set of objects: cameras, lights, a terrain, a skydome, a player, and enemies. For the game levels, create a structure named `GameLevel` inside the `GameLogic` namespace. Following is the code for the `GameLevel` struct:

```
public struct GameLevel
{
    // Cameras, lights, terrain, and sky
    public CameraManager CameraManager;
    public LightManager LightManager;
    public Terrain Terrain;
    public SkyDome SkyDome;

    // Player and enemies
    public Player Player;
    public List<Enemy> EnemyList;
}
```

In the XNA TPS game, you create the game levels inside the game code, instead of loading them from a file. To do that, create a static class named `LevelCreator` in the `GameLogic` namespace. The `LevelCreator` class is responsible for constructing the game levels and returning a `GameLevel` structure with the constructed level.

First, create an enumeration inside the LevelCreator class enumerating all the available game levels. You'll use this enumeration further to select the game level to be constructed. Initially, this enumeration has only one entry, as follows:

```
public enum Levels
{
    AlienPlanet
}
```

Next, create a static method named CreateLevel to create the game levels. This method needs to receive an instance of the Game class, because it uses the Game's ContentManager to load the game assets and the Game's ServicesContainer. When the level is created, you add the CameraManager, LightManager, and Terrain to this Game class ServiceContainer, allowing these objects to be shared with all the scene objects. The CreateLevel method also receives a Levels enumeration containing the desired level to be created. Following is the code for the CreateLevel method:

```
public static GameLevel CreateLevel(Game game, Levels level)
{
    // Remove all services from the last level
    game.Services.RemoveService(typeof(CameraManager));
    game.Services.RemoveService(typeof(LightManager));
    game.Services.RemoveService(typeof(Terrain));

    switch (level)
    {
        case Levels.AlienPlanet:
            return CreateAlienPlanetLevel(game);
            break;

        default:
            throw new ArgumentException("Invalid game level");
            break;
    }
}
```

In the beginning of the CreateLevel method, you must try to remove any CameraManager, LightManager, or Terrain objects from the game services container, avoiding adding two instances of these objects to the service container. Then you use a switch to select the desired level to be created.

The first level of the XNA TPS game is called AlienPlanet. Create the CreateAlienPlanetLevel method to construct this level. Inside the CreateAlienPlanetLevel method, first create the game cameras:

```
float aspectRate = (float)game.GraphicsDevice.Viewport.Width /
    game.GraphicsDevice.Viewport.Height;
```

```
// Create the game cameras
ThirdPersonCamera followCamera = new ThirdPersonCamera();
followCamera.SetPerspectiveFov(60.0f, aspectRate, 0.1f, 2000);
followCamera.SetChaseParameters(3.0f, 9.0f, 7.0f, 14.0f);
ThirdPersonCamera fpsCamera = new ThirdPersonCamera();
fpsCamera.SetPerspectiveFov(45.0f, aspectRate, 0.1f, 2000);
fpsCamera.SetChaseParameters(5.0f, 6.0f, 6.0f, 6.0f);

// Create the camera manager and add the game cameras
gameLevel.CameraManager = new CameraManager();
gameLevel.CameraManager.Add("FollowCamera", followCamera);
gameLevel.CameraManager.Add("FPSCamera", fpsCamera);

// Add the camera manager to the service container
game.Services.AddService(typeof(CameraManager),
    gameLevel.CameraManager);
```

You need to create two different game cameras, where each camera is of the type ThirdPersonCamera. The first camera, named followPlayer, is used to follow the player from behind, and the second camera, named fpsCamera, is used while the player is in the "aim mode." You need to add both cameras to the CameraManager of the GameLevel structure, and the CameraManager needs to be added to the Game's ServiceContainer. Next, create the game lights:

```
// Create the light manager
gameLevel.LightManager = new LightManager();
gameLevel.LightManager.AmbientLightColor = new Vector3(0.1f);

// Create the game lights and add them to the light manager
gameLevel.LightManager.Add("MainLight",
    new PointLight(new Vector3(10000, 10000, 10000),
    new Vector3(0.2f)));
gameLevel.LightManager.Add("CameraLight",
    new PointLight(Vector3.Zero, Vector3.One));

// Add the light manager to the service container
game.Services.AddService(typeof(LightManager),
    gameLevel.LightManager);
```

The game level has two lights: a main light positioned at (10000, 10000, 10000), which barely illuminates the scene, and a camera light positioned at the camera position, which highly illuminates the scene. You add these lights to the LightManager, which is also added to the game services container. After creating the camera and lights, create the game's terrain and its material:

```
// Create the terrain
gameLevel.Terrain = new Terrain(game);
gameLevel.Terrain.Initialize();
gameLevel.Terrain.Load("Terrain1", 128, 128, 12.0f, 1.0f);
```

```
// Create the terrain material and add it to the terrain
TerrainMaterial terrainMaterial = new TerrainMaterial();
terrainMaterial.LightMaterial = new LightMaterial(
    new Vector3(0.8f), new Vector3(0.3f), 32.0f);
terrainMaterial.DiffuseTexture1 = GetTextureMaterial(
    game, "Terrain1", new Vector2(40, 40));
terrainMaterial.DiffuseTexture2 = GetTextureMaterial(
    game, "Terrain2", new Vector2(25, 25));
terrainMaterial.DiffuseTexture3 = GetTextureMaterial(
    game, "Terrain3", new Vector2(15, 15));
terrainMaterial.DiffuseTexture4 = GetTextureMaterial(
    game, "Terrain4", Vector2.One);
terrainMaterial.AlphaMapTexture = GetTextureMaterial(
    game, "AlphaMap", Vector2.One);
terrainMaterial.NormalMapTexture = GetTextureMaterial(
    game, "Rockbump", new Vector2(128, 128));
gameLevel.Terrain.Material = terrainMaterial;

// Add the terrain to the service container
game.Services.AddService(typeof(Terrain), gameLevel.Terrain);
```

The terrain material is composed of a LightMaterial and some TextureMaterial. After creating the terrain material, you need to set it into the terrain's effect, and you also need to add the terrain to the game services container. In the preceding code, you're using the GetTextureMaterial method to ease the creation of the TextureMaterial. The code for the GetTextureMaterial follows:

```
private static TextureMaterial GetTextureMaterial(Game game,
    string textureFilename, Vector2 tile)
{
    Texture2D texture = game.Content.Load<Texture2D>(
        GameAssetsPath.TEXTURES_PATH + textureFilename);
    return new TextureMaterial(texture, tile);
}
```

Next, create the game's sky:

```
// Create the sky
gameLevel.SkyDome = new SkyDome(game);
gameLevel.SkyDome.Initialize();
gameLevel.SkyDome.Load("SkyDome");
gameLevel.SkyDome.TextureMaterial = GetTextureMaterial(
    game, "SkyDome", Vector2.One);
```

The game's sky also has a TextureMaterial that you can create through the GetTextureMaterial method.

Last, you need to create the game's logic objects, which are the player and the enemies. The code used to create the player follows:

```
// Create the player
gameLevel.Player = new Player(game, UnitTypes.PlayerType.Marine);
gameLevel.Player.Initialize();
gameLevel.Player.Transformation = new Transformation(
    new Vector3(-210, 0, 10), new Vector3(0, 70, 0), Vector3.One);
gameLevel.Player.AttachWeapon(UnitTypes.PlayerWeaponType.MachineGun);

// Player chase camera offsets
gameLevel.Player.ChaseOffsetPosition = new Vector3[2];
gameLevel.Player.ChaseOffsetPosition[0] =
    new Vector3(3.0f, 5.0f, 0.0f);
gameLevel.Player.ChaseOffsetPosition[1] =
    new Vector3(3.0f, 4.0f, 0.0f);
```

After creating the player character, you can set his initial position and rotation, modifying his transformation. To add a weapon to the player character, you use the AttachWeapon method. You can also change the default camera's chase position, creating an offset vector in the player for each game camera.

Now it's time to create the game's enemies. Because the game level usually has many enemies, create a method named ScatterEnemies, to create the enemies and randomly position them on the map:

```
private static List<Enemy> ScatterEnemies(Game game, int numEnemies,
    float minDistance, int distance, Player player)
{
    List<Enemy> enemyList = new List<Enemy>();
    for (int i = 0; i < numEnemies; i++)
    {
        Enemy enemy = new Enemy(game, UnitTypes.EnemyType.Beast);
        enemy.Initialize();

        // Generate a random position with a minimum distance
        Vector3 offset = RandomHelper.GeneratePositionXZ(distance);
        while (Math.Abs(offset.X) < minDistance &&
            Math.Abs(offset.Z) < minDistance)
            offset = RandomHelper.GeneratePositionXZ(distance);

        // Position the enemies around the player
        enemy.Transformation = new Transformation(
            player.Transformation.Translate + offset,
            Vector3.Zero, Vector3.One);

        enemy.Player = player;
        enemyList.Add(enemy);
    }

    return enemyList;
}
```

The ScatterEnemies method receives as its parameter the number of enemies to be created, the minimum distance from the player that an enemy can be created, the distance used to randomly position the enemies, and an instance of the Player. Inside the ScatterEnemies method, you generate all the enemies in a loop. For each enemy, you first generate a random offset vector using the distance parameter, and then check if each component of this offset vector is larger than the minDistance parameter. In this case, you set the enemy's position as the player's position summed to the generated offset vector. You also need to set a reference to the player in each enemy created. At the end, the ScatterEnemies method returns a list containing all the enemies created.

You should call the ScatterEnemies method at the end of the CreateAlienPlanet method, as follows:

```
// Enemies
gameLevel.EnemyList = ScatterEnemies(game, 20, 150, 800,
    gameLevel.Player);
```

Now that you've created all the game level objects, your level is ready to be played.

GameScreen Class

Now it's time to put all the game objects and logic together in a new class named GameScreen. GameScreen is the main game class, where you define which game map should be loaded, how the player is controlled, and how the scene objects are updated and drawn. In summary, the GameScreen class contains the main update and drawing logic.

You should create the GameScreen class in the main namespace of your game project, the XNA_TPS namespace. The GameScreen class extends the DrawableGameComponent class, allowing it to be added to the GameComponents collection of the Game class. Start the GameScreen class by declaring its attributes:

```
// Game level
LevelCreator.Levels currentLevel;
GameLevel gameLevel;

// Necessary services
InputHelper inputHelper;

// Text
SpriteBatch spriteBatch;
SpriteFont spriteFont;

// Weapon target sprite
Texture2D weaponTargetTexture;
Vector3 weaponTargetPosition;

// Aimed enemy
Enemy aimEnemy;
int numEnemiesAlive;
```

The gameLevel stores the game level that is currently being played, while the currentLevel stores an identifier for the current game level. The inputHelper attribute, of type InputHelper, handles the game inputs. Next, the spriteBatch handles the drawing of the game's UI components, which are sprites; the spriteFont stores a font used to write on the game screen; the weaponTargetTexture stores the sprite of the weapon target; and the weaponTargetPosition stores the position, in world coordinates, that the weapon is aiming at. Finally, aimEnemy stores a reference for the enemy, if any, that the weapon is targeting, and numEnemiesAlive stores the number of enemies alive. After declaring the attributes of the GameScreen class, create its constructor:

```
public GameScreen(Game game, LevelCreator.Levels currentLevel)
    : base(game)
{
    this.currentLevel = currentLevel;
}
```

The constructor for the GameScreen class is simple: it receives an instance of the Game class and an enumeration with the name of the level to be played, which is stored in the class's currentLevel attribute.

Initializing and Loading Content

You can override the Initialize method of the DrawableGameObject class to initialize the game objects and get all the necessary game services:

```
public override void Initialize()
{
    // Get services
    inputHelper = Game.Services.GetService(typeof(InputHelper)) as InputHelper;
    if (inputHelper == null)
        throw new InvalidOperationException("Cannot find an input service");

    base.Initialize();
}
```

In the preceding Initialize method, you're getting a service of type InputHelper from the service container of the Game class, and if the InputHelper service is not present in the service container, you throw an exception. Next, override the LoadContent method to load all the necessary game assets:

```
protected override void LoadContent()
{
    // Create SpriteBatch and add services
    spriteBatch = new SpriteBatch(GraphicsDevice);

    // Font 2D
    spriteFont = Game.Content.Load<SpriteFont>(
        GameAssetsPath.FONTS_PATH + "BerlinSans");
```

```
    // Weapon reticule
    weaponTargetTexture = Game.Content.Load<Texture2D>(
        GameAssetsPath.TEXTURES_PATH + "weaponTarget");

    // Load game level
    gameLevel = LevelCreator.CreateLevel(Game, currentLevel);

    base.LoadContent();
}
```

In the `LoadContent` method, you first create the `SpriteBatch` used to draw the game UI. Then, you load the `SpriteFont` used to write on the screen and the texture for the weapon's reticule sprite. Finally, you call the `CreateLevel` method of the `LevelCreator` class to generate the game level, which you store in the class's `gameLevel` attribute.

Game Update

The game update logic is divided into three methods: `Update`, `UpdateInput`, and `UpdateWeaponTarget`, where the main method called to update the game is the `Update` method. You use the `UpdateInput` method to handle the user input, and the `UpdateWeaponTarget` method to check which enemy the player's weapon is targeting.

You create the main `Update` method by overriding the `Update` method of the `DrawableGameComponent` class. In the `Update` method, you first need to call the `UpdateInput` method to handle the user input. Then you call the `Update` method of all the scene objects that need to be updated. Following is the code for the `Update` method:

```
public override void Update(GameTime gameTime)
{
    // Restart game if the player dies or kills all enemies
    if (gameLevel.Player.IsDead || numEnemiesAlive == 0)
        gameLevel = LevelCreator.CreateLevel(Game, currentLevel);

    UpdateInput();

    // Update player
    gameLevel.Player.Update(gameTime);
    UpdateWeaponTarget();

    // Update camera
    BaseCamera activeCamera = gameLevel.CameraManager.ActiveCamera;
    activeCamera.Update(gameTime);

    // Update light position
    PointLight cameraLight = gameLevel.LightManager["CameraLight"]
        as PointLight;
    cameraLight.Position = activeCamera.Position;
```

```
// Update scene objects
gameLevel.SkyDome.Update(gameTime);
gameLevel.Terrain.Update(gameTime);

// Update enemies
foreach (Enemy enemy in gameLevel.EnemyList)
{
    if (enemy.BoundingSphere.Intersects(activeCamera.Frustum) ||
        enemy.State == Enemy.EnemyState.ChasePlayer ||
        enemy.State == Enemy.EnemyState.AttackPlayer)

        enemy.Update(gameTime);


}

base.Update(gameTime);
}
```

Note that the order in which you update the objects is important. After reading the user input, you need to update the game's player. The player updates his position, the position that the camera uses to chase him, and the position of his weapon. Only after the player has been updated can you call the UpdateWeaponTarget method to update the enemy that the player's weapon is targeting, and you can also update the camera. After updating the camera, you can update the position of the point light that is placed in the same position as the camera. To do that, you just need to set the light position as the new camera position. Last, you should update the game terrain, sky, and enemies. Note that you don't need to update all the enemies in the scene; you can update only the visible enemies or the ones that are chasing or attacking the player.

Controlling the Player

To handle the user input and the player controls, you create a separate method named UpdateInput. Inside the UpdateInput method, you handle each player action as described in the section "Game Play" in the beginning of this chapter. The player has two different types of controls: the normal player controls and the "aim mode" controls.

While the user holds the left shoulder button of the gamepad, the player is in the aim mode and cannot move. In the aim mode, the left thumbstick of the gamepad is used to move the player's weapon target and the A button is used to fire. The following code handles the player controls while in the aim mode:

```
ThirdPersonCamera fpsCamera = gameLevel.CameraManager[
    "FPSCamera"] as ThirdPersonCamera;
ThirdPersonCamera followCamera = gameLevel.CameraManager[
    "FollowCamera"] as ThirdPersonCamera;

Player player = gameLevel.Player;
Vector2 leftThumb = inputHelper.GetLeftThumbStick();
```

```
// Aim mode
if (inputHelper.IsKeyPressed(Buttons.LeftShoulder)&&
    player.IsOnTerrain)
{
    // Change active camera if needed
    if (gameLevel.CameraManager.ActiveCamera != fpsCamera)
    {
        gameLevel.CameraManager.SetActiveCamera("FPSCamera");
        fpsCamera.IsFirstTimeChase = true;
        player.SetAnimation(Player.PlayerAnimations.Aim,
            false, false, false);
    }

    // Rotate the camera and move the player's weapon target
    fpsCamera.EyeRotateVelocity = new Vector3(leftThumb.Y * 50, 0, 0);
    player.LinearVelocity = Vector3.Zero;
    player.AngularVelocity = new Vector3(0, -leftThumb.X * 70, 0);
    player.RotateWaistVelocity = leftThumb.Y * 0.8f;

    // Fire
    if (inputHelper.IsKeyJustPressed(Buttons.A) &&
        player.Weapon.BulletsCount > 0)
    {
        // Wait for the last shoot animation to finish
        if (player.AnimatedModel.IsAnimationFinished)
        {
            player.SetAnimation(Player.PlayerAnimations.Shoot,
                true, false, false);

            // Damage the enemy
            player.Weapon.BulletsCount--;
            if (aimEnemy != null)
                aimEnemy.ReceiveDamage(
                player.Weapon.BulletDamage);
        }
    }
}
```

Every time the player mode is changed, you change the camera used to view him, and when the camera is changed, you need to set its IsFirstTimeChase property as true. Next, you use the left thumbstick to control the player's angular velocity, the player's waist bone rotation velocity, and the camera's rotation velocity. When the player aims up and down, you rotate the camera and the player's waist bone; when the player aims to the sides (left and right), you rotate the camera and the player. Finally, when the fire button is pressed, you first check if the player's weapon has any bullets. In this case, he fires a bullet at the aimed object. Here, you're using the duration time of the fire animation as a delay for the fire action. So, the player can fire again only after the last fire animation has finished.

If the player is not in the aim mode, he is in the normal mode. In the normal mode, the left thumbstick of the gamepad is used to rotate the player character to his left and right, and rotate the camera up and down, while the A and B buttons move the player character forward and backward. Also, clicking the left thumbstick makes the player jump, as defined by the following code:

```
// Normal mode
else
{
    bool isPlayerIdle = true;

    // Change active camera if needed
    if (gameLevel.CameraManager.ActiveCamera != followCamera)
    {
        // Reset fps camera
        gameLevel.CameraManager.SetActiveCamera("FollowCamera");
        followCamera.IsFirstTimeChase = true;
        player.RotateWaist = 0.0f;
        player.RotateWaistVelocity = 0.0f;
    }

    followCamera.EyeRotateVelocity = new Vector3(leftThumb.Y * 50, 0, 0);
    player.AngularVelocity = new Vector3(0, -leftThumb.X * 70, 0);

    // Run forward
    if (inputHelper.IsKeyPressed(Buttons.X))
    {
        player.SetAnimation(Player.PlayerAnimations.Run, false, true, false);
        player.LinearVelocity = player.HeadingVector * 30;
        isPlayerIdle = false;
    }
    // Run backward
    else if (inputHelper.IsKeyPressed(Buttons.A))
    {
        player.SetAnimation(Player.PlayerAnimations.Run,
            false, true, false);
        player.LinearVelocity = -player.HeadingVector * 20;
        isPlayerIdle = false;
    }
    else
        player.LinearVelocity = Vector3.Zero;

    // Jump
    if (inputHelper.IsKeyJustPressed(Buttons.LeftStick))
    {
        player.Jump(2.5f);
        isPlayerIdle = false;
    }
```

```
    if (isPlayerIdle)
        player.SetAnimation(Player.PlayerAnimations.Idle,
            false, true, false);
}
```

Updating the Weapon Target

The last method used to update the game is the UpdateWeaponTarget method. In this method, you need to check the nearest enemy that the player's weapon is targeting. To do that, you trace a ray starting at the muzzle of the player's weapon, with the same direction as the heading vector of the player's weapon. Then you check for possible collisions between this ray and the bounding box of each enemy. In case the ray collides with the bounding volume of multiple enemies, you store the enemy that is closest to the player's weapon. Finally, you calculate the position, in world coordinates, that is used to draw the sprite of the weapon's target and store it in the weaponTargetPosition variable. Following is the code for the UpdateWeaponTarget method:

```
private void UpdateWeaponTarget()
{
    aimEnemy = null;
    numEnemiesAlive = 0;

    // Fire ray
    Ray ray = new Ray(gameLevel.Player.Weapon.FirePosition,
        gameLevel.Player.Weapon.TargetDirection);

    // Distance from the ray start position to the terrain
    float? distance = gameLevel.Terrain.Intersects(ray);

    // Test intersection with enemies
    foreach (Enemy enemy in gameLevel.EnemyList)
    {
        if (!enemy.IsDead)
        {
            numEnemiesAlive++;

            float? enemyDistance = enemy.BoxIntersects(ray);
            if (enemyDistance != null &&
                (distance == null || enemyDistance < distance))
            {
                distance = enemyDistance;
                aimEnemy = enemy;
            }
        }
    }

    // Weapon target position
    weaponTargetPosition = gameLevel.Player.Weapon.FirePosition +
        gameLevel.Player.Weapon.TargetDirection * 300;
}
```

Drawing the Scene

You override the Draw method of the GameScreen base class to add your drawing code. You can separate the drawing code in two parts, where you first draw the 3D scene objects, and then draw the 2D objects (such as text and sprites) on top of those. Following is the code to draw the 3D scene objects:

```
GraphicsDevice.Clear(Color.Black);
BaseCamera activeCamera = gameLevel.CameraManager.ActiveCamera;

gameLevel.SkyDome.Draw(gameTime);
gameLevel.Terrain.Draw(gameTime);
gameLevel.Player.Draw(gameTime);

// Draw enemies
foreach (Enemy enemy in gameLevel.EnemyList)
{
    if (enemy.BoundingSphere.Intersects(activeCamera.Frustum))
        enemy.Draw(gameTime);
}
```

First, you clear the screen before drawing anything on it, and then you call the Draw method of all the scene objects to render them to the screen. Note that the order in which you draw the scene objects here is not important.

Next, you need to draw the 2D UI objects. You draw all these objects using the XNA's SpriteBatch class. Following is the code to draw the game's UI:

```
spriteBatch.Begin(SpriteBlendMode.AlphaBlend,
    SpriteSortMode.Deferred, SaveStateMode.SaveState);

// Project weapon target position
weaponTargetPosition = GraphicsDevice.Viewport.Project(weaponTargetPosition,
    activeCamera.Projection, activeCamera.View, Matrix.Identity);

// Draw weapon reticule
int weaponRectangleSize = GraphicsDevice.Viewport.Width / 40;
if (activeCamera == gameLevel.CameraManager["FPSCamera"])
    spriteBatch.Draw(weaponTargetTexture, new Rectangle(
        (int)(weaponTargetPosition.X - weaponRectangleSize * 0.5f),
        (int)(weaponTargetPosition.Y - weaponRectangleSize * 0.5f),
        weaponRectangleSize, weaponRectangleSize),
        (aimEnemy == null)? Color.White : Color.Red);

// Draw text
Player player = gameLevel.Player;
spriteBatch.DrawString(spriteFont, "Health: " + player.Life + "/" +
    player.MaxLife, new Vector2(10, 5), Color.Green);
spriteBatch.DrawString(spriteFont, "Weapon bullets: " +
    player.Weapon.BulletsCount + "/" + player.Weapon.MaxBullets,
    new Vector2(10, 25), Color.Green);
```

```
spriteBatch.DrawString(spriteFont, "Enemies Alive: " +
    numEnemiesAlive + "/" + gameLevel.EnemyList.Count,
    new Vector2(10, 45), Color.Green);

spriteBatch.End();

base.Draw(gameTime);
```

You should place all the code used to draw the 2D objects between the Begin and End methods of the SpriteBatch class. The SpriteBatch usually changes some render states before drawing the 2D objects. Because you don't want the hassle of restoring them after you finished using the SpriteBatch, you can make the SpriteBatch restore them for you automatically after the objects have been drawn. To do that, you need to call the Begin method of the SpriteBatch, passing its third parameter as the SaveStateMode.SaveState. The first and second parameters passed to the SpriteBatch's Begin method are the default parameters.

Next, you need to draw the weapon reticule sprite. However, before you can draw it, you need to transform its position from 3D world coordinates to 2D screen coordinates. To do that, you can project the weapon's target position on the screen using the Project method of the Viewport class. In this case, you need to call this method from the Viewport property of the current GraphicsDevice, which takes the screen resolution and aspect ratio into account. After that, you just need to scale the sprite, making it independent of the screen resolution. Finally, you use the DrawString method of the SpriteBatch class and the SpriteFont that you have loaded to draw the player's health, number of weapon bullets, and number of remaining enemies in the map.

TPSGame Class

The last class you create is the TPSGame class, which extends the Game class and is the main game class. Start the TPSGame class, declaring its attributes:

```
GraphicsDeviceManager graphics;
InputHelper inputHelper;
```

The GraphicsDeviceManager attribute is responsible for creating and managing the GraphicsDevice for the game. Also, you use the InputHelper attribute to handle the user input. Now, create the constructor for the TPSGame class:

```
public TPSGame()
{
    Window.Title = "XNA TPS v1.0";
    Content.RootDirectory = "Content";

    // Creating and configuring graphics device
    GameSettings gameSettings = SettingsManager.Read(
        Content.RootDirectory + "/" + GameAssetsPath.SETTINGS_PATH +
        "GameSettings.xml");
    graphics = new GraphicsDeviceManager(this);
    ConfigureGraphicsManager(gameSettings);
```

```
    // Input helper
    inputHelper = new InputHelper(PlayerIndex.One,
        SettingsManager.GetKeyboardDictionary(
        gameSettings.KeyboardSettings[0]));
    Services.AddService(typeof(InputHelper), inputHelper);

    // Game screen
    Components.Add(new GameScreen(this,
        LevelCreator.Levels.AlienPlanet));
}
```

In the class constructor, you first set the game screen title and the root directory of the content manager. Next, you read the game settings from an XML file, using the SettingsManager class, and use the game settings to configure the GraphicsDeviceManager and the InputHelper. After reading the game settings, you create the GraphicsDeviceManager and call the ConfigureGraphicsManager method, configuring it with the struct containing the GameSettings that have been read in and deserialized earlier in this chapter. After that, you create the InputHelper, and use the KeyboardSettings of the GameSettings to configure it. Last, you create a GameScreen and add it to the Components of the Game class. After you've added the GameScreen to the Components of the Game class, it will be updated and drawn automatically when needed by the XNA Framework, since it inherits from the GameComponent class. Following is the code for the ConfigureGraphicsManager method used to configure the GraphicsDeviceManager:

```
private void ConfigureGraphicsManager(GameSettings gameSettings)
{
#if XBOX360
    graphics.PreferredBackBufferWidth =
        GraphicsAdapter.DefaultAdapter.CurrentDisplayMode.Width;
    graphics.PreferredBackBufferHeight =
        GraphicsAdapter.DefaultAdapter.CurrentDisplayMode.Height;
    graphics.IsFullScreen = true;
#else
    graphics.PreferredBackBufferWidth =
        gameSettings.PreferredWindowWidth;
    graphics.PreferredBackBufferHeight =
        gameSettings.PreferredWindowHeight;
    graphics.IsFullScreen = gameSettings.PreferredFullScreen;
#endif

    // Minimum shader profile required
    graphics.MinimumVertexShaderProfile = ShaderProfile.VS_2_0;
    graphics.MinimumPixelShaderProfile = ShaderProfile.PS_2_A;
}
```

In the ConfigureGraphicsManager method, if the current platform is the Xbox 360, you set the width and height of the screen's buffer as the width and height of the current display adapter. Otherwise, you set the width and height of the screen's buffer according to the GameSettings parameter. Last, you check if the current video card supports shader 2.0.

Summary

In this chapter, you created a simple but complete TPS game. There's a lot of room for you to add more features to this game. For example, you could add more sophisticated enemy movement, more realistic movement animations, and enemy AI. However, the game is functionally complete. We've shown you an underlying structure on which you can build.

You began by creating a basic design for your game, divided into the game definition, game play, and technical design parts. After that, you started to develop the game code, which was divided into three main namespaces: GameBase, GameLogic, and Helpers. In the GameBase namespace, you added all the classes for the game engine, some of which you created in the previous chapters. Then you created all the helper classes in the Helpers namespace and all the game logic classes in the GameLogic namespace. After that, you created a LevelCreator class to create your game levels, and finally, you put it all together by creating a GameScreen class that handles the main game update and drawing logic.

CHAPTER 14

Closing Words

If you've reached this page, you've probably read the entire book, and may be wondering what the next steps are. What should you do to sharpen your XNA knowledge further to create the next generation of games? That's the purpose of this final chapter: to give you some insights and tips on where to go from here.

Before we do so, we would like to thank you for your confidence in buying our book, and we hope that you had as much fun playing around with the samples and games as we did writing them.

If you didn't have fun, please let us know what we can do better, so our next books can meet suit your expectations and needs. (You can find our latest contact information at `http://www.apress.com`.)

Where You Are Now

At this point, you should have created a few games: Rock Rain, a simple 2D game running on the Windows and Xbox 360 platforms; Rock Rain Live, a network-enabled version; Rock Rain Zune, a Zune version; and XNA TPS, a simple 3D third-person shooter game. If you've followed along, you should be familiar with game programming terms and have a basic knowledge of the XNA Framework.

By following our instructions, you have experienced the real effort that goes into planning and coding complete 2D and 3D games. Along the way, we have stressed some important points regarding game development:

Creating a game is more than just a good idea: Creating a game is a team effort, or, if you will, a multidisciplinary effort. In addition to a good idea and clean code, you need neat graphics, cool sound effects, effective testing, and more. You'll need to wear a few different hats if you want to do it all yourself.

Use the framework; don't re-create the wheel: XNA is not a game engine, but it does provides basic classes for calculating collisions (such as `Rectangle`, `BoundingBox`, and `BoundingSphere`), for doing vector and matrix operations, and much more.

Know where you stand: Are you just interested in creating casual games, or do you want to enter the game industry as a creator of sophisticated pieces of software? You'll need to study and practice different things for each case.

Consider extending the Content Pipeline: Animating 3D models is far easier to do with modeling tools than in XNA. Don't let the Content Pipeline's lack of native support for animations hold you back! Also consider creating helper tools to position 3D objects in your scenes. You can save those configurations to a file, and then write Content Pipeline extensions to read them.

Keep on coding: The bad news is that your first few games will probably be crap—everyone starts out with some bad games. The fact is that creating games is something that you learn, exclusively, by creating games. The good news is that with XNA, you can create a new game every week. So what you are waiting for?

Write games, not engines: The best way to stay motivated is to see the actual results of your work. Create a simple game, and then improve and polish it until it's ready to be the new LIVE Community Game blockbuster!

We recommend that you go back and have a quick look at each chapter's summary, so you can refresh your memory about the material presented, and note topics that you didn't understand well or want to revisit.

And remember that you can find the most recent code for this book's examples, as well as any text and code errata at the Apress web site (http://www.apress.com). Just go to this book's details page, and click the appropriate link.

When you're sure that you've gotten everything you can from this book, you can proceed further.

Where Do You Go from Here?

If you search for "XNA" in any common Internet search engine, you'll get (as of February 2009) around four million hits. When you narrow down the search to "XNA Tutorial," you'll get about half a million results, without quotation marks, and about thirty thousand results with them. So, forget about searching the Internet for your next steps, unless you know exactly what you need!

Riemer Grootjans presents a variety of XNA tutorials that may help you go a step further in exploring new XNA horizons at his site (http://www.riemers.net). We also recommend Riemer's excellent *XNA 3.0 Game Programming Recipes* book (Apress, 2009).

■**Note** If you are interested in creating casual games, and read Portuguese, you'll find some tutorials, news, and samples at the Sharp Games community site (http://www.sharpgames.net), coordinated by José Leal de Farias, and dozens of presentations and simple XNA examples at Alexandre Lobão's site (http://www.AlexandreLobao.com). Note that while the sites are in Portuguese, the code samples comments are mostly in English.

At Bruno Evangelista's site (http://www.brunoevangelista.com/), you'll find more elaborate 3D code, sophisticated shader examples, an improved version of the 3D shooter game we created in this book, and much more. Another excellent way to learn more about shaders is by following the thread at the XNA Creators Club site (http://forums.xna.com/thread/24109.aspx), where many people have posted links to basic to advanced shaders tutorials.

In fact, for good examples of any XNA techniques, the XNA Creators Club (`http://creators.XNA.com`) should always be your starting point. This site has samples for almost anything you'll need for your 2D and 3D games. Explore the samples, and don't forget to download and study all the starter kits, which are complete games that will give you very good starting points for more sophisticated games.

Additionally, CodePlex (`http://www.codeplex.com`) is another good source for XNA projects, including some open source game engines and components. Just order your view by latest release date and rating, which will present you with the most up-to-date and interesting projects.

Create Your Own Game

As we've said, if you really want to learn XNA, create a game on your own. Of course you can—and are encouraged to—write original games, but as a start, we recommend a simple but fairly interesting game: Tetris.

If you start from the ground up and create your own version of Tetris, you'll exercise many concepts you'll use in every one of your future games. For example, the game calls for a set of classes with different behaviors (each block turns in a different way), but share a common ground (every block falls), so you'll create a hierarchy with a base and derived classes. You'll also need to detect collisions and control the game state, checking for full lines when the blocks fall; deal with user input; code for game end and game scoring; and so on.

An XNA Tetris clone is also a good place to start because you can create it within a couple weeks, so you can stay motivated for your next challenge. This project will give you more insight about the difficulty of creating a game from the ground up. You will understand the complexity of building a game and how each of the game components fits together. And don't forget the roles of a game team we talked about in Chapter 1—even in a simple project like this, you should not limit yourself to just one role!

After creating your Tetris clone, as your next step, consider a game that uses the same concepts, but includes some extra challenges. A good exercise is creating a Breakout clone or a pinball game. For this type of game, you use the concepts from Tetris, plus sound, some advanced collision-detection algorithms, and some animated sprites.

■**Tip** You can find a simple Breakout clone at Alexandre Lobão's site (`http://www.alexandrelobao.com/Jogos/Alexandre_Lobao-Palestras_Jogos.asp`), coded with less than 100 lines, which surely is a good starting point to create something new. For example, you might include bonus bricks or extra levels, to better understand and explore XNA's basic features. And if you think that 100 lines are too few for a game, think again: The Brazilian version of the Xbox 360 magazine published a simpler version for this game, with around 40 lines! That's what XNA is about!

If you are interested in 3D games, consider creating a 3D version of Tetris, Breakout, or a pinball game. Such games are good learning tools because, although they use 3D objects, you can still use simplified, 2D-like versions of the collision-detection algorithm. After you "break the ice" with such simple 3D games, it will be time to try something harder. Consider creating a simple flight simulator, where you control the plane flying around buildings and maybe shooting at some of them!

After that, we suggest you create a network-enabled version of the Pong game. The game logic and graphics are simple, so you can concentrate on the networking details.

The next step is to create a game that involves some artificial intelligence concepts, such as a Pac Man clone. Search for "A-Star path finding algorithm" on the Internet. You'll find many implementations of this algorithm, which guides the ghosts through the labyrinth right to the player character.

When you finish this . . . well, you get the idea. Start by defining your goal—a simple but complete game—and stick with it until you're finished. Don't choose too bold an objective, or you might get tired of programming before you complete the game. Again, you don't need to create an original game at this point. Just work on a clone for a well-known game. After your first game, choose another simple game, so you explore new concepts with each project.

We can't stress enough the importance of creating your own real games as a way to learn XNA. Don't start by analyzing samples or by trying to collect code on the Internet to create your own game engine, including everything you might need for a game. Too many people out there are creating samples, components, and game engines with XNA, and too few are creating real games, even simple ones.

Keep on creating new games, looking for bright new ideas, and exploring new concepts in game creation. But never forget the golden rule for any game: a game, no matter how simple or how sophisticated it is, must be fun. So keep on playing, keep on coding, and you'll be on the right track!

Happy XNA coding!

Index

■S

You Need the Companion eBook

Your purchase of this book entitles you to buy the companion PDF-version eBook for only $10. Take the weightless companion with you anywhere.

We believe this Apress title will prove so indispensable that you'll want to carry it with you everywhere, which is why we are offering the companion eBook (in PDF format) for $10 to customers who purchase this book now. Convenient and fully searchable, the PDF version of any content-rich, page-heavy Apress book makes a valuable addition to your programming library. You can easily find and copy code—or perform examples by quickly toggling between instructions and the application. Even simultaneously tackling a donut, diet soda, and complex code becomes simplified with hands-free eBooks!

Once you purchase your book, getting the $10 companion eBook is simple:

❶ Visit **www.apress.com/promo/tendollars/**.

❷ Complete a basic registration form to receive a randomly generated question about this title.

❸ Answer the question correctly in 60 seconds, and you will receive a promotional code to redeem for the $10.00 eBook.

THE EXPERT'S VOICE™

2855 TELEGRAPH AVENUE | SUITE 600 | BERKELEY, CA 94705

Offer valid through 10/09.